Goethe and
Judaism

Goethe and Judaism

The Troubled Inheritance of Modern Literature

✦

Karin Schutjer

NORTHWESTERN UNIVERSITY PRESS
EVANSTON, ILLINOIS

Northwestern University Press
www.nupress.northwestern.edu

Printed in the United States of America

10 9 8 7 6 5 4 3 2 1

Library of Congress Cataloging-in-Publication Data

Schutjer, Karin Lynn, 1966– author.
Goethe and Judaism : the troubled inheritance of modern literature / Karin Schutjer.
pages cm
Includes bibliographical references and index.
ISBN 978-0-8101-3133-0 (cloth : alk. paper) — ISBN 978-0-8101-3173-6 (pbk. : alk. paper) — ISBN 978-0-8101-3166-8 (ebook)
1. Goethe, Johann Wolfgang von, 1749–1832—Criticism and interpretation. 2. Jews in literature. 3. Judaism in literature. I. Title.
PT2200.J4S38 2015
832.6—dc23

2015025325

For Ben, Noah, and Mira

CONTENTS

Acknowledgments *ix*

List of Abbreviations *xi*

Translations *xiii*

Introduction *3*

Chapter 1
Itinerancy, Suffering, and Providence: Goethe's Encounters with Judaism in *Poetry and Truth* *29*

Chapter 2
Moses and the Modern Nation: Goethe on Exodus *67*

Chapter 3
The People of the Book: Goethe's *Volksbuch* Project and the *Journeyman Years* *97*

Chapter 4
Faust as Keeper of the Covenant: *Part One of the Tragedy* *125*

Chapter 5
Faust and the Promised Land: *Part Two of the Tragedy* *151*

Conclusion *187*

Notes *191*

Works Cited *225*

Index *239*

ACKNOWLEDGMENTS

This project has benefited from tremendous institutional support as well as from the generosity of countless colleagues, friends, and family members, of whom I can here only name a few.

My interest in this topic dates back two decades to Eric Santner's Princeton graduate seminar on "Judaism and Modernity" and the lively conversations with classmates, including Talia Bloch, James Goldwasser, and Leora Batnitzky, that emerged out of it. When, some years later, I began exploring the subject anew, I looked especially to Jonathan Hess's work as a model and valued greatly his encouragement. Clint Stevens, an undergraduate research assistant sponsored by the University of Oklahoma Honors College, helped lay the initial groundwork through his resourceful collection of secondary literature.

A year at the National Humanities Center (funded by an NEH Fellowship) in 2004–5 provided me with the time, resources, and intellectual camaraderie to get started in earnest. My great fortune was to have a distinguished biblical scholar as my office neighbor: Joel Marcus entertained my steady stream of questions with patience, interest, and unfailing good humor. Other fellows who contributed their expertise to the project at that stage were Matt Giancarlo, Michael Gillespie, Tom Kaiser, and Cara Robertson. I am also in debt to the excellent NHC staff librarians Eliza Robertson, Jean Houston, and Betsy Dain.

This project profited further from a year in Leipzig, Germany (2007–8) funded by a Research Fellowship from the Alexander von Humboldt Foundation, for which I am especially indebted to my gracious host at the University of Leipzig, Professor Ludwig Stockinger. I also found a helpful conversation partner in Bernard Levinson, in residence that year at the Wissenschaftskolleg in Berlin. While in Germany, I took advantage of the special collections at the University of Leipzig, the Library of the Francke Foundations in Halle, and the Duchess Anna Amalia Library in Weimar. The Research Board of the University of Oklahoma supported research trips on other occasions to the Herzog August Library in Wolfenbüttel and to the Yale Beinecke Collection in New Haven.

Parts of this manuscript have appeared elsewhere and I thank those journals and their editors for the permission to reprint. A section of chapter 2 appeared as "German Epic / Jewish Epic: Goethe's Exodus Narrative in *Hermann und Dorothea* and 'Israel in der Wüste,'" *German Quarterly* 80, no. 2 (Spring 2007): 165–84. Chapter 1 includes a lightly revised version of "Goethe's Kabbalistic Cosmology," *Colloquia Germanica* 39, no. 1 (2006): 21–30. Finally, for inclusion in chapter 3, I have revised the article, "Beyond the Wandering Jew: Anti-Semitism and the Myth of Supersession in *Wilhelm Meisters Wanderjahre*," *German Quarterly* 77, no. 4 (Fall 2004): 60–78.

A note of thanks is also due to Henry Carrigan and the staff of Northwestern University Press, as well as to two anonymous readers for the care and attention given my manuscript.

I suspect I would have never finished this book had it not been for the supportive, spirited, scholarly community I found through the Goethe Society of North America (GSNA). Among the *many* mentors, colleagues, and friends in the GSNA who have provided encouragement and orientation along the way, I owe special thanks to Simon Richter, Astrida Tantillo, Clark Muenzer, Daniel Purdy, Horst Lange, Heather Sullivan, Jane Brown, Claire Baldwin, and Johannes Anderegg. This project has also been tremendously enriched through the Duke German-Jewish Studies Workshops organized by Martha Helfer and Bill Donahue. In both scholarly and professional respects, Martha has served as a model to me. Stanley Corngold's unwavering support and kindness over more than two decades have also helped shape this book. At the University of Oklahoma, I have profited from exchange with my Judaic Studies colleagues, especially Alan Levenson and Carsten Schapkow. Rienk Vermij provided valuable Latin translation help. Meanwhile my smart, patient, generous, resilient, and, above all, fun German colleagues have created a happy work environment that has made everything easier, including this book. The many students over the years who have shared—or graciously humored—my passion for Goethe have been more important than they realize.

Finally, I thank the members of my own family, who, in blending religious as well as secular traditions, are the true inspirations for this book. This book tries to honor the spirit of religious openness and searching inquiry embodied especially by my own father, a Protestant minister, but also by my mother, siblings, late grandmother, and others. This book also owes something to the wide intellectual universe of my in-laws. My late father-in-law Paul Alpers read my work with warmth and encouragement. My mother-in-law Svetlana Alpers has been actively supportive of the project from its inception and even made a photographic excursion to help with a detail of my analysis. But at its core, this book is the product of ongoing conversation with my husband, Ben Alpers. It is dedicated with love and profound appreciation to Ben and our children, Noah and Mira.

ABBREVIATIONS

The following works will be cited parenthetically using the abbreviations noted:

FA	Goethe, Johann Wolfgang von. *Sämtliche Werke, Briefe, Tagebücher und Gespräche*, ed. Dieter Borkmeyer et al. 40 vols. Frankfurt am Main: Deutscher Klassiker Verlag, 1985–99. My citations refer to the two sections within this edition, (1) works and (2) letters; followed by volume numbers; followed by part number (occasionally volumes are published in two parts).
HW	Herder, Johann Gottfried. *Werke in zehn Bänden*. Edited by Günter Arnold et al. 10 vols. Frankfurt: Deutscher Klassiker Verlag, 1993.
Schöne	Albrecht Schöne, ed. *Kommentare: "Faust,"* by Johann Wolfgang von Goethe. Frankfurt: Deutscher Klassiker Verlag, 2005. (6th revised edition of FA 1.7.2).
SW	Herder, Johann Gottfried. *Sämtliche Werke*. Edited by Bernhard Suphan et al. 33 vols. Berlin: Weidmann, 1877–1913.
WA	Goethe, Johann Wolfgang von. *Goethes Werke: Herausgegeben im Auftrage der Großherzogin Sophie von Sachsen*. 133 vols. Weimar: H. Böhlau, Weimar, 1887–1919.

Following convention, references to *Faust* will be provided parenthetically as line numbers.

TRANSLATIONS

I have provided the German original for all quotations by Goethe, but for other German authors, I have given English translations only, with key German words occasionally supplied parenthetically. When not otherwise indicated, translations of Goethe or other authors are my own.

Whenever possible, I have used the standard translation cited parenthetically with the following abbreviation:

CW Goethe, Johann Wolfgang von. *Collected Works*. Ed. Victor Lange, Eric Blackall, and Cyrus Hamlin. 12 vols. New York: Suhrkamp, 1983–89.

With *Faust*, I worked with the following translations and made the selection for each passage based on precision, connotations, and syntax. Translators are indicated parenthetically.

Arndt, Walter, trans. *Faust: A Tragedy,* by Johann Wolfgang von Goethe. Ed. Cyrus Hamlin. New York: Norton, 2000.

Atkins, Stuart, trans. and ed. *Faust I & II* by Johann Wolfgang von Goethe. Vol. 2, *Collected Works*. New York: Suhrkamp, 1984.

Kaufman, Walter, trans. *Goethe's Faust: Part One and Sections from Part Two,* by Johann Wolfgang von Goethe. New York: Anchor, 1990.

Luke, David, trans. *Faust Part One,* by Johann Wolfgang von Goethe. Oxford: Oxford University Press, 2008.

Luke, David, trans. *Faust Part Two,* by Johann Wolfgang von Goethe. Oxford: Oxford University Press, 2008.

Where not otherwise indicated, I have used the New Jewish Publication Society (NJPS) translation of the Hebrew Bible and the New Revised Standard Version (NRSV) of the New Testament and Apocrypha. Citations of Luther's German translation refer to the Wittenberg edition of 1545.

Goethe and Judaism

Introduction

Goethe's relationship to Judaism has been a subject of debate for nearly two centuries. Goethe's view of Judaism has mattered because Goethe has mattered, on his own terms certainly, but also as the iconic representative of a German national culture in its many historical variations. The latter half of the nineteenth century witnessed the transformation of Goethe into a national-pedagogical institution: civic organizations arose to tend his legacy, Goethe's works became required reading in the schools, while Goethe philology emerged in the universities as a nearly distinct academic field. With the unveiling of the Goethe-Schiller statue on the theater square in 1857 and the opening of Goethe's home as the Goethe National Museum in 1885, the city of Weimar evolved into a living monument to the poet.[1] Throughout the tumultuous twentieth century, Goethe was cast and recast to fit political exigencies. In 1919 the founders of the Weimar Republic held their constitutional convention in the German National Theater in Weimar, on the site of the court theater Goethe had once directed. They thus simultaneously borrowed his symbolic authority and effectively recast the conservative patrician as a republican. In the Nazi period Goethe served as a versatile ideal for nearly every occasion: he was held up alternately as consummate sportsman, worker and warrior, champion of the German agricultural sector, forerunner of Nazi biologism, and, predictably, as piercing judge of Jewish character.[2] After the war Goethe became the paradigmatic "good German," embodying a cosmopolitan anti-nationalist orientation. His status in a postwar West Germany was probably best exemplified by the founding in 1951 of the "Goethe Institute," the Federal Republic's official purveyor of German language and culture worldwide. Goethe was no less important in East Germany, which saw its own brand of socialism as heir to Faust's dying vision of a free people on a free land.[3] The Goethe for our new millennium tends in turn to embody ideals of the Berlin Republic such as environmentalism and multiculturalism.

Parallel to the history of Goethe's appropriation in the name of a German state or nation runs his significant if controversial role within an evolving German-Jewish culture. Even within Goethe's lifetime, Jewish readers such as the celebrated Jewish saloniere Rahel von Varnhagen advanced his reputation within intellectual circles.[4] Goethe's secretary F. W. Riemer reports that educated Jews were often "more obliging" (*zuvorkommender*) and "more reliable" (*nachhaltiger*) in their admiration for Goethe and his works than his own co-religionists.[5] Ludwig Geiger, the son of Rabbi Abraham Geiger, was a founding father of Goethe studies and initiated the *Goethe-Jahrbuch* in 1866. But other Jewish readers viewed Goethe in his conservatism and obdurate elitism critically, including the authors Heinrich Heine, who perceived Goethe's works as "sterile," and Ludwig Börne, who saw Goethe as "the smallest of men," "the slave of circumstance," and a "cowardly philistine."[6] Schiller, with his stronger endorsement of Enlightenment ideals, was received far more enthusiastically among Jewish audiences in the nineteenth century.[7] Toward that century's end, however, Goethe's impact on German-Jewish culture began to deepen.[8] He was an important intellectual influence for a number of leading twentieth-century Jewish thinkers including Walter Benjamin, Gustav Landauer, and Franz Rosenzweig.[9] After the Nazis came to power and in the postwar period, Jewish exiles were key in preserving and extending Goethe's positive legacy.[10] Certainly, the German-Jewish reception of Goethe is no mere footnote within German cultural history. According to Giuseppe Veltri, the conflicting responses to Goethe "comprise the core of a German-Jewish conflict with consequences reaching into the present."[11]

But the object of this book is in fact not to trace the twists and turns in this history of reception but to reconsider its starting point—the representation of Judaism within Goethe's works. Critics over the years have been thorough in cataloging and categorizing Goethe's disparate statements and representations concerning Jews, and in evaluating the evidence in biographical, political, or historical terms. But still lacking is any real appreciation of a deeper structural role for Judaism in Goethe's worldview and creative production.[12] This book aims to provide a broad, though by no means exhaustive, literary study that is neither apologetic nor reductive, that attends to the complexity and irony of Goethe's literary work but takes his representations of Judaism seriously as an integral part of his thought and writing.[13] I am therefore concerned not simply with accusing or acquitting Goethe of prejudice but rather with discerning the function and logic of his relationship to Judaism, as seen within his work.

My premise is that Goethe's conception of modernity—his anxieties as well as his most affirmative vision concerning the trajectory of his age—are deeply entwined with his conception of Judaism. I argue that behind his very mixed representations of Jews and Judaism stand crucial tensions within his own thinking and a distinct anxiety of influence.[14] Indeed, I contend that Goethe paradoxically wrestles against precisely those impulses in Judaism for which he feels the greatest affinity, which most approach his own vision of modernity. As I will explain, the discourse of wandering in Goethe's work serves as a key site where Judaism and modernity meet.

My exploration of the role of Judaism in Goethe's conception of modernity takes a cue from Jonathan Hess's important book *Germans, Jews and the Claims of Modernity*. Hess traces how late eighteenth-century Christian and Jewish thinkers competed in a bid to articulate religious and cultural identities compatible with the modern world and especially with the Enlightenment ideal of secular universalism. Goethe's own vision of modernity is idiosyncratic, less concerned with Enlightenment rationality or universalism per se. Central for Goethe is what Hardt and Negri have called the "primary event of modernity," that is "the affirmation of the powers of *this* world, the discovery of the plane of immanence."[15] I will lay out the many respects in which Judaism seems to Goethe to embody this dynamic, modern posture and thus, in turn, becomes an object of competition.

Anti-Semitism or Philo-Semitism?

Was Goethe an anti-Semite? This was the question posed by the Swiss author Adolf Muschg in a 2004 speech before the august New Wednesday Society (Neue Mittwochsgesellschaft). Muschg's answer can serve as a starting point rather than as the destination of this book: he conceded, "There are statements in Goethe's letters, journals and conversations that have to be forthrightly called anti-Semitic."[16] So much Goethe scholarship over the years has been apologetic if not hagiographic that this basic acknowledgment opens the way from the first for a more honest and complex analysis.[17]

Of course, some would challenge the term anti-Semitism, with its suggestion of racial rather than strictly religious prejudice, as anachronistic in the Age of Goethe. But even the narrow definition of anti-Semitism as an overtly racial conception seems satisfied by the following offensive joke, recorded (uncritically) by Eckermann. In a lively table conversation in the autumn of 1828, Goethe and several guests considered the nature of the various human races and whether they all shared descent from common ancestors, in short the question of human polygenesis or monogenesis. Goethe takes the polygenetic position that nature, instead of producing humanity from one source, did so by the dozen or by hundreds. When his guest Herr von Martius playfully points out that this claim does not accord with the Bible, Goethe asserts, in highly sarcastic tones, that he gladly grants the Jews exclusive claim to a descent from Adam and Eve.

> "The holy scriptures," Goethe replied, "admittedly speak of only one human couple, which God created on the sixth day, but then again the talented men who recorded the word of God, which the Bible hands down to us, were concerned in the first instance with their chosen people, and so we don't want to dispute the honor of their lineage from Adam. We others however, as well as the Negroes and Laplanders, and slender human beings, who are more beautiful than all of us, certainly had other ancestors; so our esteemed company will assuredly concede that we differ from the authentic descendants of Adam in quite diverse ways and that they, particularly in matters of money, outdo us all." We laughed.

> "Die Heilige Schrift," erwiederte Goethe, "redet allerdings nur von Einem Menschenpaare, das Gott am sechsten Tage erschaffen, allein die begabten Männer, welche das Wort Gottes aufzeichneten, das uns die Bibel überliefert, hatten es zunächst mit ihrem auserwählten Volke zu thun, und so wollen wir auch diesem die Ehre seiner Abstammung von Adam keineswegs streitig machen. Wir andern aber, sowie auch die Neger und Lappländer, und schlanke Menschen, die schöner sind als wir alle, hatten gewiß auch andere Urväter; wie denn die werthe Gesellschaft gewiß zugeben wird, daß wir uns von den echten Abkömmlingen Adams auf eine gar mannigfaltige Weise unterscheiden und daß sie, besonders was das Geld betrifft, es uns allen zuvorthun." Wir lachten. (FA 2.12: 279–80)

Here Goethe combines an increasingly fashionable racial polygenism with an age-old slur concerning a Jewish relationship to money. This economic stereotype is a recurring one, especially in his letters, conversations, and notes, where he often casts Jews as petty swindlers, debt collectors, ruthless businessmen, and usurers.[18] Should one insist upon terminological distinctions, Goethe's record offers ample evidence of traditional religious and social anti-Judaism, with hints of a biologically essentialist anti-Semitism. For my purposes this distinction in terms is however neither precise nor useful.[19] If, in my discussion, I more frequently opt for the less historically charged term "anti-Judaism," I do so merely for the sake of a milder rhetoric, one that summons less quickly the crushing specter of the Holocaust.

But beyond the question, "was Goethe an anti-Semite?" one could pose the question, "was Goethe a philo-Semite?" For Goethe's anti-Jewish attitudes coexisted with marked fascination with, and admiration for, Jews and Judaism, as well as, certainly, friendly acquaintances with Jewish contemporaries.[20] Extensive and poignant testimony to this strikingly mixed record is offered in a book published in 1934 by an American professor named Mark Waldman: *Goethe and the Jews: A Challenge to Hitlerism*. Waldman was eager to put Goethe to polemical use against the Nazis, who were claiming Goethe as their own. But in good scholarly fashion, he attempts to give the whole picture, documenting Goethe's "dualism" concerning Judaism and Jews. In his final chapter he devotes twenty-two pages to cataloging all of Goethe's unfavorable comments about Jews and then another thirteen listing his favorable comments. Despite the mixed evidence, Waldman argues that Goethe's ideals of humanity outweigh his human failings and prejudice, and therefore still make him a powerful ally against the hatred and inhumanity of Hitler's regime.[21]

But Waldman's term "dualism" could suggest that Goethe's anti- and pro-Jewish sentiments were somehow distinct, dissociated phenomena whereas in fact they are almost inextricably bound up with each other. Alan Levenson's characterization of philo-Semitism in Imperial and Weimar Germany could apply as well to Goethe's intermittently positive portrayal of Judaism: "[It] was ambivalent, defensive, compromised by residual anti-Semitic prejudices, the byproduct of conflicting agendas, and based on certain misunderstandings about the nature of Jews and Judaism."[22] But as Levenson further suggests, if one cannot fully separate philo- and anti-Semitism, nor should one simply resolve the former into the latter.[23] Goethe's complex and ambiguous relationship to Judaism calls for a nuanced description that can have some explanatory value when it comes to his later reception, his significance for Jewish readers as well as for Nazi ideologues. One of the foremost challenges in writing this book has been to try to link yet not collapse Goethe's pro- and anti-Jewish tendencies.

Thus I refocus the question of Goethe's pro- or anti-Jewish attitudes around an analysis of his conflicting agendas and the varied functions Judaism served in his thinking. In his autobiography, Goethe acknowledges that as a young man struggling against religious orthodoxy, he worked to construct a Christianity to suit his own leanings, "for my own private use" (*zu meinem Privatgebrauch*), which he then sought to ground and develop through careful study of history and sources (*CW* 4: 466; FA 1.14: 692). Similarly, Goethe's conception of Judaism, while constructed from the materials at hand (including biblical, historical, and philosophical sources as well as the great store of European stereotypes and slander), was ultimately also shaped for his own ends. What intellectual, cultural, and political purposes did his conception of Jews and Judaism serve?

Certainly his prejudices against Jews, his representation of them as not trustworthy or like other Germans, supported his authoritarian social and political commitments, as W. Daniel Wilson has prominently argued.[24] Goethe's consistent opposition to Jewish emancipation is well documented. In 1797, after a French assault the previous year had destroyed the Frankfurt ghetto and led to a period of integration, Goethe suggested his desire for a reconstruction of the ghetto, that is, for re-segregation (FA 1.16: 120).[25] On the same trip in 1797 while stopping in Heilbronn he wrote approvingly in his diary of the "good, natural, calm, civic mindset" (*gute natürliche stille bürgerliche Denkart*) of its inhabitants, adding "no Jews are tolerated here" (*Es werden keine Juden hier gelitten*) (FA 2.4.1: 405). In 1808 in a letter to Bettina von Arnim, he sided with the prince primate against those who argued for greater civil rights for Frankfurt Jews (FA 2.6: 286); in 1816, in a letter to Boiserée, he praised an old law prohibiting Jews from spending the night in Jena (FA 2.8: 19); in 1823, in a conversation with Müller, Goethe reportedly expressed his "impassioned rage" (*leidenschaftlichen Zorn*) concerning a law extending Jewish civil rights in Sachsen-Weimar (FA 2.10: 112).[26] According to Wilson, Goethe's hostility toward Jewish emancipation is to be understood first and foremost within the context of his broader conservative principles, "his opposition to democratic encroachments on princely authority and sovereignty."[27]

Yet at the same time that Goethe opposed emancipation for actual Jews, he found in Judaism a space of freedom and heterodoxy, an alternative to all that seemed constraining or distasteful in his Christian environment. Goethe, who at one point described himself as "definitely a non-Christian" (*ein dezidierter Nichtchrist*),[28] objected to the tendency toward passivity, sentimentality, and inwardness he found in his own Protestant culture: "In Protestantism sentimentality took the place of good works" (*In dem Protestantismus trat an die Stelle der guten Werke Sentimentalität*).[29] He represents the excessive ethereality of Christian Pietism, for example, in the devout Beautiful Soul in *Wilhelm Meister's Apprenticeship* (*Wilhelm Meisters Lehrjahre*) who fantasizes her own spirit mystically free of its body and focuses on her invisible friend Jesus (FA 1.9: 747, 788). In contrast to this Christian otherworldliness, he viewed Judaism as active and existential in its orientation. In a maxim on "Jewish nature" (*Jüdisches Wesen*) he writes,"Energy the basis of everything. Immediate ends. No Jew, not even the most lowly, unimportant one, who would not betray a decisive striving and indeed of an earthly, temporal and present-oriented sort" (*Energie der Grund von allem. Unmittelbare Zwecke. Keiner, auch nur der kleinste geringste Jude, der nicht entschiedenes Bestreben verriethe, und zwar ein irdisches, zeitliches, Augenblickliches*) (FA 1.13: 273). While this maxim certainly plays into well-worn stereotypes of relentless Jewish stratagems, when understood in the context of Goethe's broader intellectual commitments, it suggests more admiration than disapproval. Indeed, an earth-bound striving (*Streben*) is Faust's distinct form of heroism.

Goethe also rejects Christianity's tendency towards a dogmatic metaphysics, its orientation toward realms beyond the limits of human understanding. His devout Christian friend Lavater is the poster child for the epistemological category error of confusing things accessible to experience with things unknown and principally unknowable. Both Lavater's four-volume *Views into Eternity* and his physiognomic writings, which read character from face, conflate the sensory with the moral or spiritual, according to Goethe:

> His *Views into Eternity* really presents nothing more than a continuation of our present existence under pleasanter circumstances than those endured here. His physiognomy is based on the conviction that the physical being fully coincides with the spiritual one and bears witness to it, indeed even represents it. (*CW* 5: 582)

> Seine Aussichten in die Ewigkeit sind eigentlich nur Fortsetzungen des gegenwärtigen Daseins, unter leichteren Bedingungen als die sind welche wir hier zu erdulden haben. Seine Physiognomik ruht auf der Überzeugung dass die sinnliche Gegenwart mit der geistigen durchaus zusammen falle, ein Zeugnis von ihr ablege, ja sie selbst vorstelle. (FA 1.14: 818)

Goethe exposes the dangers of this dogmatic fallacy, for example, in Werther's delusional and ultimately suicidal fantasy of finally getting his girl in the next life. Presumably related to Goethe's dislike of Christianity's morbid, metaphysical bent, is his discomfort with the doctrine of Christ's divinity (in contrast to his respect for Jesus's life and teachings). As Horst Lange has lain bare, Goethe rejected the atonement theology surrounding Christ's death and resurrection.[30] He famously calls the doctrine of Christ's divinity "a piece of crap" (*ein Scheisding*) and the symbol of the cross "the wretched martyr-wood, the most repulsive thing under the sun" (*das leidige Marterholz, das Widerwärtigste unter der Sonne*) (FA 2.1: 451; FA 2.11: 409).[31] In his poem, "Sweet child, the string of pearls" ("Süsses Kind, die Perlenreihen"), Goethe treats devotion to the Catholic crucifix as a form of idol worship (FA 1.38.1: 509).[32]

The theme of idolatry in Judaism and the Hebrew Bible offered Goethe in turn a means of exploring the dangers of falsifying or static representations of what he viewed as a dynamic reality. The Jewish ban on images came to take on a very modern meaning for Goethe and his contemporaries—precisely as a ban on dogmatic metaphysics, as the refusal to fix the absolute or the whole in a temporal sign.[33] Kant writes in his *Third Critique*, "Perhaps there is no more sublime passage in the Jewish Law than the commandment: Thou shalt not make unto thee any graven image, or any likeness of any thing that is in heaven or on earth, or under the earth, etc."[34] Taking off from cycles of sin and idolatry in the Hebrew Bible, Goethe analyzes basic patterns of human cognition and experience—the longing for fixed representations and the imperative to let them go. The challenge of conceptualizing the flux of nature is a fundamental theme in his scientific investigations as well as in his literary works.

Judaism also serves as an example for Goethe in a very different matter—the question of nationhood. An analogy between Germany and the Jewish people—both the ancient Israelites and Modern Jews—recurs throughout his career and cuts in both positive and negative ways. As expressed in his famous *Xenia*, composed together with Schiller, Goethe had no interest in a unified German state (or the more egalitarian political structure typically associated with it): "Germany? But where is it? I cannot find the country, Where the land of letters begins, the political one ends" (*Deutschland? aber wo liegt es? Ich weiß das Land nicht zu finden, / Wo das gelehrte beginnt, hört das politische auf*) (FA 1.1: 507). As an alternative he seems struck by the notion of Jews as a people constituted in relationship to a book rather than to a state, as a kind of *Kulturnation*.[35] As a German author working within an underdeveloped national culture, he looks to "the bible-producing nation" (*das bibelschöpferische Volk*), a people that has persisted through millennia, mostly without benefit of a state.[36] In 1808 he went so far as to suggest that the Germans would be better off if, like the Jews, they were dispersed throughout the world (FA 2.6: 428). As will be discussed, a more troubled analogy extends between Germany and the Israelites in the Exodus story, where he sees a volatile people inclined towards revolution and violence.

Goethe thus finds in Judaism existential activism (as opposed to otherworldy sentimentality), semiotic fluidity (as opposed to an idolatrous metaphysics), and a diasporic *Kulturnation* rooted in a text rather than a state (albeit, Goethe suggests, with a lurking revolutionary potential). Further, Judaism, as Goethe conceives it, converges in important ways with his own literary and cultural project—above all in its focus on the immanent, historical world. But because Goethe embraces these aspects of Judaism as his own while rejecting the civic claims of his Jewish contemporaries, a deep instability lies at the heart of his reception. The topos of wandering is a focal point of this tension in Goethe's work.

Wandering

Both Judaism and modernity are linked in Goethe's thought to the nearly ubiquitous topos of wandering. The discourse of wandering is itself intrinsically ambiguous—it can suggest productive exploration or aimless error, or both. As Andrew Cusack has recently shown, the wanderer emerged as one of the foremost cultural symbols in nineteenth-century German literature, accumulating a vast array of meanings centering upon the status of the modern individual.[37] While the potency of this metaphor throughout the nineteenth century had much to do with increasing social mobility, technologies of transit, and even recreational habits, Cusack also attributes its prominence early in the century to Goethe's influence, in whose work "the motif attains a unique functional range."[38] For Goethe, indeed, wandering takes on aesthetic, semiotic, philosophical, and political dimensions that suggest nothing less than an all-encompassing existential project.

Meanwhile, the discourse of the wanderer in Goethe's work intersected unavoidably with popular perceptions and representations of Jews. Exile is a nearly constant theme in Jewish history. The five hundred years preceding Goethe's era witnessed, in addition to other forms of persecution, a relentless series of expulsions from England, France, Spain, Portugal, Italy, and most of the German-speaking cities and regions. In the eighteenth century, many Jews continued to suffer from social and political homelessness in the German territories. While a privileged few were officially tolerated by local authorities, others were denied any form of citizenship, residency permission or protection. Indeed, an estimated 10 percent of the Jewish population was simply condemned to a life of poverty and itinerancy on the open road.[39] Goethe describes the peculiar apparition of one such wandering "beggar Jew" (*Betteljude*) in his autobiography (FA 1.14: 745–46).

The miserable spectacle of Jewish homelessness and poverty created by Christian policies conveniently fit a Christian notion that Jews were a "witness-people" doomed to suffer as punishment for and testament to the suffering of Christ.[40] Augustine, for example, compares the Jewish people to the biblical Cain, who is forced to wander the earth after killing his brother but, because he bears the Lord's mark, will not be put to death.[41] This ideology took on popular form in the early modern Christian legend of Ahasverus, the wandering Jew (*der ewige Jude*). The legend appeared in a chapbook, the pulp fiction of its day, in 1602 under the title, *Short Description and Tale of a Jew with the Name Ahasverus* . . . In the story, Ahasverus embodies the putative collective guilt of the Jewish people, as implied by certain New Testament passages (esp. Matt. 27:25). He is a follower of the scribes and Pharisees and supports Christ's arrest and execution. When led past Ahasverus's house on the way to his crucifixion, Christ pronounces Ahasverus's sentence upon him—that when he (Christ) rests, Ahasverus will walk. Henceforth Ahasverus travels restlessly through the ages, doomed perhaps to wander until judgment day, "a living witness of the Passion of Christ."[42]

Certainly Ahasverus was one of Goethe's early archetypes of the restless wanderer. He encountered the legend as a child among the chapbooks offered for pennies by a neighborhood book peddler (FA 1.14: 42). As a young man, he conceived of his own satirical epic of the Wandering Jew, of which a fragment and a synopsis in his autobiography survive. Meanwhile the plot of *Wilhelm Meister's Journeyman Years*, his mature work that explores an individual and communal ideal of wandering, is framed with reference to the Wandering Jew: Wilhelm sets out to overcome his status as a wandering Jew, to be relieved of the conditions of the requirements of constant mobility, "that stamped him as a wandering Jew" (*ihn zum ewigen Juden stempelte*) (*CW* 10: 194; FA 1.10: 408). Faust, who characterizes himself as the fugitive" (*der Flüchtling*) and "the aimless, restless reprobate" (*Der Unmensch ohne Zweck und Ruh*), has also been associated by critics with the Wandering Jew (Luke, *Faust Part One,* 3348; 3349).[43]

Goethe seems to have conceived his philosophical hero Spinoza too as a kind of wanderer, as a modern voice in the wilderness. Spinoza was himself descended from Portuguese Jewish exiles and, while banned as an apostate from the Jewish community, was nevertheless recognized by Goethe as Jewish, as a product of "rabbinical culture" (*CW* 5: 524; FA 1.14: 731).[44] Goethe's own notes and descriptions of Spinoza describe the expansive breadth of his thought as if it were the emergence of a new landscape. He opens up for the young Goethe "a broad, free view over the physical and moral world" (*eine große und freie Aussicht über die sinnliche und sittliche Welt*) (*CW* 4: 459; FA 1.14: 681). At the same time, in its bold flouting of orthodoxy, Spinoza's thought seems to render him into an almost supernatural figure: "such persons are generally considered monsters, without respect for God or the world, and they are imagined as having all manner of horns and claws" (*so werden solche Personen gewöhnlich für Unmenschen gehalten, für Gott- und Weltlose; ja man weiß nicht was man ihnen alle für Hörner und Klauen andichten soll*) (*CW* 5: 523; FA 1.14: 730). Goethe claims to have elaborately planned out in his mind a visit that the Wandering Jew would pay Spinoza in his epic poem (FA 1.14: 731). While these plans do not survive, the association in Goethe's thinking between Spinoza and the Wandering Jew is itself suggestive.

But the most obvious source for the topos of Jewish wandering was the Hebrew Bible itself—the nomadism in Genesis, the wilderness journey in Exodus, the pervasive imagery of Israel's error and exile in the Psalms and the Prophets. I argue then that Goethe's encounter from his youth with the Hebrew Bible is of primary significance, not only for the topos of wandering in his work and for his understanding of Judaism, but indeed, for his entire literary program. Goethe's modern wanderers lead paradoxically back to this very ancient set of texts, which became for Goethe a surprising source and model for modern literature.

Goethe and the Hebrew Bible

Harold Bloom has identified the Old Testament as "that captive work" produced by "the Christian triumph over the *Hebrew Bible*" (emphasis mine).[45] I will use both terms in this book: "Old Testament" acknowledges the Christian context from which Goethe comes, and "Hebrew Bible" reflects the dawning recognition in his age that Christianity does not own this canon. From our current critical vantage point, it can require some imagination to reconstruct the initial shock and sense of discovery Christian authors experienced as they began to perceive the Hebrew scriptures in an independent light. One nineteenth-century Lutheran pastor's son registers nothing short of outrage at the deception perpetrated by the Christian exegetical tradition, calling it "that unheard-of philological farce." Friedrich Nietzsche continues,

> I mean the attempt to pull the Old Testament under the feet of the Jews with the assertion that it contained nothing but Christian teaching and *belonged* to the Christians as the *true* people of Israel, the Jews being only usurpers.[46]

The Christian prophetic framework linking the two canons long defined not only Christianity's relationship to Judaism, but also its own religious self-concept. The Gospels draw their narrative authority and persuasiveness to a great extent from their explicit or implicit appeal to scriptural precedents. To be sure, the Hebrew Bible also creates patterns of meaning through repetition and variation, but as Erich Auerbach's classic essay "Figura" points out, what is distinctive about the New Testament is not just the sense of pattern and fulfillment it creates, but its simultaneous denigration of its antecedent. To take an easy example: Joshua's miraculous crossing of the Jordan into the Land of Canaan (Josh. 3) recalls Moses's miraculous crossing of the Sea of

Reeds (Exod. 14) and thereby lends Joshua authority in the role of Moses's successor. In the New Testament by contrast, Jesus is frequently compared to Moses but also supersedes him. In the words of John the Baptist, "The law indeed was given through Moses; grace and truth came through Jesus Christ" (John 1:17) or in the Epistle to the Hebrews, "Yet Jesus is worthy of more glory than Moses, just as the builder of a house has more honor than the house itself" (Heb. 3:3).[47]

According to Auerbach, Paul in particular uses figural interpretation "to strip the Old Testament of its normative character and show that it is merely a shadow of things to come."[48] Auerbach summarizes the basic Pauline dichotomies that serve to both relate and divide Christianity and Judaism:

> Grace versus law, faith versus works: the old law is annulled; it is shadow and *typos*; observance of it has become useless and even harmful since Christ made his sacrifice; a Christian is justified not by works in observance of the law, but by faith; and in its Jewish and Judaistic legal sense the Old Testament is the letter that kills, while the new Christians are servants of the new covenant, of the spirit that gives life.[49]

These typologies were then further developed by the church fathers into an all-encompassing prophetic, Christological framework for understanding the Old Testament, which, according to Auerbach, became in turn the basis for the medieval European conception of history in general and remained largely in force up to the eighteenth century.[50] These biblical patterns of typology and fulfillment arguably also serve as a core paradigm for the way meaning has been constructed in secular European literature.[51]

In the wake of Luther, German culture became, of course, deeply oriented around the biblical text. And readers of the Lutheran Bible were well trained to understand the Old Testament prophetically: Luther rendered passages of presumed prophetic significance in capital letters and included marginal annotations indicating when Christ's coming reign was supposedly being referenced. German authors of the late eighteenth century, regardless of their actual theological commitments, remained rooted in this scriptural tradition. Goethe was extraordinarily *bibelfest* (solid in his biblical knowledge), as his own essays of biblical criticism as well as the ubiquitous, sophisticated biblical allusions in his work attest.

For Goethe as a young child, it was not only the biblical text, but the accompanying pictures that transmitted biblical knowledge. In his autobiography, Goethe mentions that, with children's books uncommon, he pored through, among other books, the family's Folio Bible (1630) with engravings by Matthäus Merian. It is worth briefly looking at a couple of these markedly complex and ambivalent images that captivated Goethe as a child, for they surely provided a foundation for his understanding of Judaism.

Figure 1. Engraving by Matthäus Merian of Genesis 37: "Joseph thrown in a pit by his brothers, then sold." From the 1630 Folio Bible, a copy of which was owned by the Goethe family. Herzog August Bibliothek Wolfenbüttel: H: A 153.2 Helmst, 25 verso. Used by permission.

Consider first Merian's illustration of Genesis 37, from the life of Joseph (fig. 1). In the scene, Joseph's older brothers, having cast him into a pit, now draw him forth again in order to sell him as a slave to Midianite merchants. Despite the act of familial violence being perpetrated, the spacious pastoral landscape lures the imagination with calmly grazing sheep, a lounging shepherd in a classical drape of fabric, undulating foliage, sloping hills, a castle ruin, birds in patterned flight, and a passing camel train (presumably the Midianites). At closer look, the young Joseph, as he is pulled from the pit, recalls, in his poignant curvature and tensed chest muscles, Michelangelo's bound slave (fig. 2).[52] He thereby easily attracts the viewer's attention and sympathy. Merian's image is meanwhile pregnant with a great narrative: an adolescent with remarkable gifts but wronged by his family finds himself on the verge of an epic adventure, like a biblical Harry Potter.

Evidence suggests this Joseph image had a particularly strong impact on Goethe's imagination. In his early adolescence he wrote a prose epic based on the life of Joseph, which unfortunately he later burned (FA 1.14: 156–57; 1110n). Remarkably, as a boy of approximately ten, he developed his own proposal for a cycle of paintings on the Joseph theme, of which a few were

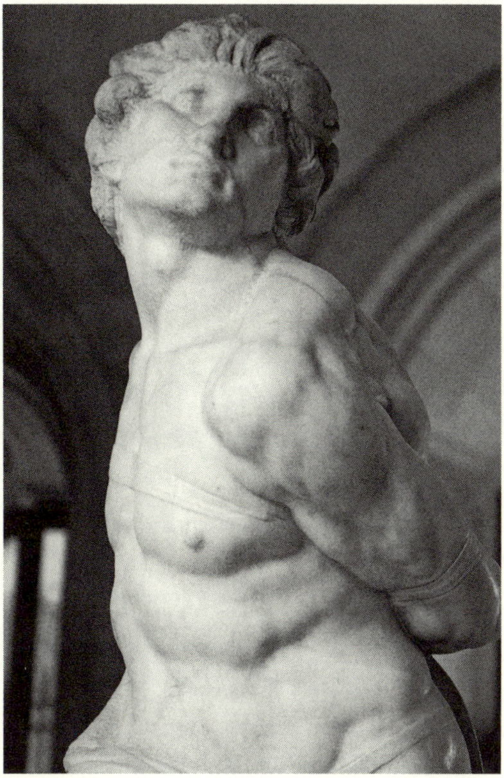

Figure 2. Michelangelo's *Rebellious Slave*, 1513. Musée du Louvre, Paris. Archive Timothy McCarthy / Art Resource, N.Y. Used by permission.

produced by the artist Johann Georg Trautmann for Count Thoranc, a French lieutenant who was quartered in the Goethe family home during the Seven Years' War (FA 1.14: 100). One canvas renders the transaction as Joseph is handed over to his Midianite enslavers, presumably just moments after the scene depicted by Merian (fig. 3). According to tradition, the boy Goethe was himself the model for Trautmann's rendering of the boy Joseph in this painting.[53] One can also discern in Joseph's angled head, parted lips, and fearfully raised eyes, echoes of Merian's Joseph.[54] In a very concrete sense, then, the boy Goethe was able to project himself into Merian's engraving of Genesis 37.

But to identify with Merian's boy Joseph is to become entangled in layers of Christian anti-Judaism. On the same page in the Folio Bible with Merian's engraving, a marginal note directs the reader to a verse in the New Testament book of Acts, where the apostle Stephen declares, "The patriarchs, jealous of Joseph, sold him into Egypt; but God was with him, and rescued him from all his afflictions" (Acts 7:9–10). The context is Stephen's inflammatory speech before the Jewish Council, in which the soon-to-be martyr suggests that

Figure 3. Painting by Johann Georg Trautmann: "Joseph is sold to the Midianites." Oil on canvas; from a cycle of paintings on Joseph (1759–63) commissioned by the French officer quartered in the Goethe family home. Freies Deutsches Hochstift: Inv. Nr. IV-00499. Photo credit: David Hall. Used by permission.

Israel is a "stiff-necked people" that has repeatedly persecuted its own prophets, including those who "foretold the coming of the Righteous One" (Acts 7:51–52). In his brief reference to Joseph, Stephen impeaches the Jews generally by identifying Joseph's persecutors not as his *brothers* specifically, but as the *patriarchs* generally. While Joseph is naturally also a patriarch, Stephen presumably counts him among those who anticipated Christ, who "foretold the coming of the Righteous One." Merian's engraving enacts this prophetic meaning by subtly offering the suffering Joseph as a prefiguration of Christ. Indeed, an epigram accompanying this engraving in an earlier publication leaves no question about Merian's Christological meaning: "Christ in prefiguration [*im Fürbild*] sold and delivered to the pagans."[55] In the image, Joseph emerges from the earth, as if from a tomb. Furthermore, he rises directly in front of the trunk of the tree that in its canopy divides into two boughs. His upward directionality could suggest his ultimate positioning on the cross of this tree. More to the point, while most of his brothers are depicted in a neutral way, the most active brother, who pulls on the rope to Joseph's right, has the hooked nose and beard that signifies in Merian's visual vocabulary, as we will see shortly, a Jew. And so while this scene from Genesis remains pastoral, even idyllic, it contains seeds of the problematic bifurcation that runs deep in the Christian interpretation: the Hebrew scriptures are made to prefigure both Christ and the "bad Jews" who reject him.

The darker cast becomes more prominent in Merian's engraving of the first Passover on the verge of the Israelite departure from Egypt in Exodus 12 (fig. 4). Here the open, pastoral landscape in the earlier image has been

Figure 4. Engraving by Matthäus Merian, Exodus 12: "Passover." From the 1630 Folio Bible, a copy of which was owned by the Goethe family. Herzog August Bibliothek Wolfenbüttel: H: A 153.2 Helmst, 41 recto. Used by permission.

replaced by the architecture of a town. Most of the action falls in a narrow shadowy space between an imposing wall in the background and a drawn-up curtain in the foreground. Now, on the face of it, this biblical episode should be less ambiguous than the Joseph one, for it involves no Israelite villains, only Egyptian ones. But the marginal annotations pointing to New Testament verses John 19: 36 and 1 Corinthians 5–7 tell another story. In both passages, Jesus is represented as the paschal lamb. This Christological message is also explicit in Merian's earlier publication venue for these engravings, where the epigram for this scene reads, "Our Easter lamb is Christ, sacrificed for us."[56] Consequently, the focus of this image is as much the lamb as the Israelites themselves.

Indeed, this scene bears disturbing similarity to an engraving also by Merian in Gottfried's *Chronicle*, another book that Goethe, by his own account, pored through as a young child (FA 1.14: 41) (fig. 5). The image of Jews torturing a Christian child to death is based on the so-called blood libel, according to which Jews collect Christian blood for their Passover matzos. The text explains that the young boy Simon was murdered in 1475 on Maundy Thursday. Maundy Thursday is of course the day Christians

Figure 5. Engraving by Matthäus Merian: "Jews torture Christian children to death." From Gottfried's *Chronicle*, owned by the Goethe family. Herzog August Bibliothek Wolfenbüttel: M: Gb 2 8:3. p. 689. Used by permission.

commemorate the Last Supper, which according to the three synoptic Gospels coincided with Jesus's celebration of the first night of Passover.[57] Goethe presumably had this very image in mind in a later passage in his autobiography, where he notes how Merian's dark depiction of reputed Jewish atrocities against children in Gottfried's *Chronicle* shaped his own early view of Jews. The pierced prostrate body of little Simon also appeared in the "painting of mockery and shame" depicting Jewish outrages, which Goethe reports having viewed under the bridge tower in Frankfurt as a child (FA 1.14: 165).

The torture image from Gottfried's *Chronicle* echoes and intensifies elements present in the Exodus image. From the partial shadows in the imposing space in the biblical image, we have now receded into the darkness of a low vaulted chamber. In both engravings men surround a small, doleful-looking creature—the dead lamb with its little hooves extended and the tormented Christian child on the cross. In the Exodus image, one man grabs a piece of flesh from the lamb's abdomen; another chews or sucks crudely on a leg. In the torture image two figures plunge knives into the boy to drain his blood. In both images, the headwear of the men recall the pointed or bent Phrygian caps required of Jews as ordained by the Fourth Lateran Council (1215). Several of the Jews in the torture scene combine long beards with the stereotypical hooked noses; one of the Israelites in the Exodus scene also has a clearly discernible hooked nose. In short, Merian teaches his viewer to see, in this celebration of the first Passover, ominous shadows of future Passovers: the sacrifice of Jesus the Paschal Lamb (for which Jews are held guilty) at Passover time, and the alleged sacrifice of Christian children for Passover matzos in medieval and early modern times.

For the boy Goethe, then, the Old Testament must have seemed a loaded, nearly explosive text, with sinister future villains lurking ambiguously within biblical heroes. But in the very ambiguity of these images, his imagination may have found a certain stimulus, for, in any case, he soon developed an intense fascination with the Old Testament. According to his account in his autobiography, he was deeply attracted to it from his youth because of its peculiarity (*Eigentümlichkeit*) (FA 1.14: 138). The New Testament, by contrast, seemed "all too easy" (*allzu leicht*), "even trivial" (*sogar trivial*) as the result of sermons and religious instruction (FA 1.14: 40). He describes at length his intensive engagement with the book of Genesis as an adolescent and devotes a remarkable amount of space to the recapitulation of its content in order to indicate, he explains, the powerful impact it had on his developing imagination (FA 1.14: 155).[58]

As formative as Merian's images may have been, Goethe's reading of the Hebrew scriptures quickly took him beyond the Christian prophetic paradigm. As he grew older, Goethe did not find what he was supposed to in the Old Testament—a mere prologue to the New Testament harmonizing neatly with Christian theological doctrine—but discovered instead a vastly heterogeneous text, full of fissures, fault lines, and challenging, unresolved questions. He found meanings, in short, that were divergent rather than convergent in nature. He not only read of wanderers, but at the deepest level, his experience of reading became itself an exploratory, heterodox wandering.

Fault Lines and Heterodoxy

The first and most obvious biblical fault line emerged, as I have already suggested, between the New and Old Testaments. Christian writers and scholars began to see the Old Testament as a product of a certain culture in a certain time and place, long before such things were thinkable, or at least sayable, concerning the New Testament. And this loosening of the old interpretive constraints freed the Hebrew Bible from its forced conformity to church doctrine. Herder points out, for instance, that the serpent in the Garden of Eden has nothing to do with the Christian devil; and the plural Hebrew name for God, Elohim, does not refer to the Christian Trinity (HW 5: 167–75).[59] With the concomitant explosion in interpretive possibilities, the Old Testament became in this period, as Jonathan Sheehan puts it, "the focus of increasingly vibrant inquiry" and "the gravitational center of the poetic Bible." Sheehan argues further that while truth and morality remained associated with the New Testament, the Old Testament now became associated with sublimity, beauty, and emotional power. This divide between morality and aesthetics was the "story of the Enlightenment Bible *in nuce*."[60]

In many ways, the new view of the Hebrew Bible anticipated what we think of as the "Bible as Literature." A brief look ahead to later readers of the Bible in this vein can help us characterize the secular literary contours and textures that first began to emerge for Goethe's contemporaries as Christian hermeneutics receded. To many twentieth- and twenty-first-century critics and authors, the ancient Hebrew scriptures have appeared as paradoxically modern in their indeterminacy, open-endedness, and emphasis on the dilemmas of *this* life.[61] Erich Auerbach, in his classic essay "Odysseus' Scar," finds in Genesis a resonantly modern experience of history (which in his own case included the First World War and the rise of the Nazis) because it embraces "the confused, contradictory multiplicity of events, the psychological and factual cross-purposes, which true history reveals."[62] The author and critic Gabriel Josipovici notes too a certain opacity in the Hebrew Bible narratives, observing that while history is viewed as meaningful in both Old and New Testaments, "the New Testament claims to know *what* that meaning is, whereas for the most part the Old Testament merely claims that there *is* meaning."[63] Robert Alter points out that the Hebrew Bible stories tend to foreground a very complex human drama—full of failings, ironic twists, and strange ambiguities—set against a puzzling cosmic background, whereas the New Testament tends to place transcendent meanings in the foreground.[64]

Thus modern readers have found the human predicament writ large in these ancient Hebrew texts. John Updike declares the heroes of Genesis "the patriarchs and matriarchs of modern fiction," as they "pursue difficulties oddly similar (compared with those of Greek gods and aristocrats) to those in our own problematical, mostly domestic lives" within "a universe often beautiful and gracious but also implacable and unfathomable."[65] In a diary entry, Kafka compares the conclusion of the Pentateuch—where Moses views Canaan from a distance before dying—to the final scene of Flaubert's *Sentimental Education*. Moses's unfulfilled journey portrays "what an incomplete moment human life is, incomplete because this sort of life can last endlessly and still it would produce nothing more than a moment."[66]

For Goethe, then, standing at the advent of this new era in biblical interpretation, the Hebrew Bible opened up as a new, challenging terrain for literary exploration. His reading of the Hebrew Bible as an adolescent, in the company of his droll and eccentric tutor Rector Albrecht, comes across as a kind of liberal intellectual inquiry. In the Pentateuch he finds provocative moral complexity and ambiguity, as flawed, all-too-human characters contend with a vast and overwhelming universe. Goethe's literary sensibilities were also deeply shaped by the wisdom books, especially Job, Ecclesiastes, and the Song of Songs, the content of which was challenging and eccentric, so divergent from a Christian theological program. The Song of Songs offers an unbridled sensuality that is certainly unmatched in the Christian canon. Koheleth, the voice of Ecclesiastes, seems to verge on blasphemy, "Consider God's doing! Who can straighten what He has twisted?" (Eccl. 7:13). Job is anything but patient in his questioning of divine justice: "I insist on arguing with God," he declares (Job 13:3). Indeed, according to Clark Muenzer, Goethe discovered in the book of Job a Spinozistic God-as-nature, which, in its dynamic, ever-creating and destroying activity, was consonant with his own scientific conceptions.[67] Thus the Hebrew Bible served as a rich alternative source for Goethe's thinking about fundamental questions of nature and the moral order, providence, and the problem of evil.

The new historical-critical approach to the Bible brought not only a testamental divide, but also drew attention to a set of fissures within the Hebrew scriptures themselves, which were likewise of great consequence for Goethe's conception of literature. Indeed, the observation of internal contradictions within Genesis—specifically between the two creation stories with their different names for God (Gen. 1:1–2:4; Gen. 2:4–25)—was a cornerstone of the new hermeneutics. Source criticism, which reached its clearest formulation only in the late nineteenth century in the work of Julius Wellhausen, emerged gradually through much of Goethe's lifetime. Pioneered by Jean Astruc in 1753, its assumptions enter into a manuscript by Herder in the late 1760s, which points to "many repetitions, interpolations and recapitulations" as evidence that the first chapters of Genesis do not amount to a unified account by a single author (HW 5: 22–3). Johann Gottfried Eichhorn's monumental *Introduction to the Old Testament* (*Einleitung in das Alte Testament*) (published 1780–83), which Goethe reported reading in 1797 (FA 2.4: 319), includes a chart breaking down the verses of Genesis according to three different sources—Jehovah, Elohim, and the editor of the two.[68]

In his autobiography, Goethe identifies himself as an early adherent of this emerging view of the Bible "as a collective work that had come into existence little by little, with revisions at various times" (*als ein zusammengetragenes, nach und nach entstandenes, zu verschiedenen Zeiten überarbeitetes Werk*) (CW 4: 377; FA 1.14: 554). His essays of biblical criticism, "Two Important Hitherto Unexamined Biblical Questions" ("Zwo wichtige bisher unerörterte biblische Fragen") and "Israel in the Desert" ("Israel in der Wüste"), testify to his extraordinary attention to textual detail and variation in the Pentateuch. Further examples of his style of critical reading can be found in notes from his renewed study of Genesis in 1797. Alluding to the fact that, while in Genesis 6:19 Noah is ordered to take two of each kind of animal onto the ark, in Genesis 7:2, he is told to take seven pairs of every clean animal and one pair of every unclean animal, Goethe attributes the second passage to a later source: "The mention of clean and unclean animals points to a late period" (*Die Erwähnung des reinen und unreinen Viehes deutet auf späte Zeit*) (FA 1.3.1: 629). At the same time, textual criticism of this sort was a much more delicate affair when it concerned the New Testament. By 1804, according to Eichhorn, the "higher criticism" had hardly been attempted on the New Testament.[69] While Goethe claims in book 12 of his autobiography not to have spared the New Testament in this sort of analysis, it is with a crucial caveat concerning the inviolability of its religious revelation: "The Gospel writers may contradict each other, so long as the Gospel does not contradict itself!" (*Die Evangelisten mögen sich widersprechen, wenn sich nur das Evangelium nicht widerspricht*) (*CW* 4: 379; FA 1.14: 557). Indeed, his more or less ancillary mention of the New Testament in this discussion of the "Bible" reinforces the point that the Hebrew Bible was the more essential focus of his attention.

The peculiar way in which ancient source texts are woven together in the Pentateuch—with glosses, variants, gaps, and repetitions—does indeed produce a distinctive, intriguing texture. To use Robert Alter's terms, it is a narrative characterized by "bumpiness" and "quirkiness."[70] Marc Zvi Brettler explains, "in contrast to modern editing, which works toward articulating a single viewpoint, the redaction of the Torah, like the editing of other ancient works, did not create a purely consistent, singular perspective but incorporated a variety of voices and perspectives."[71] I show in the course of this book that the peculiar form and texture of the Hebrew Bible in general and Genesis in particular are an essential source for Goethe's own literary experimentations with fictional editors, ironic discrepancies, and disparate compound structures. The Bible thus becomes a model for some of Goethe's most formally innovative work.

Finally, Goethe experienced a further fundamental divide in the Hebrew Bible between the books of Genesis and Exodus, which I contend helped structure his assessment of his own age, including its productive and destructive potentialities. In his autobiography, as I have already indicated, Goethe confesses his inability to express fully the powerful impact of Genesis on his young imagination. But when, as a young man, he undertakes the study of Exodus, he finds a chasm (*Kluft*) separating the first and second books of Moses: "But what a difference! In the same way that the abundance of childhood had vanished from my life, I also found there was an enormous chasm between the first and second books" (*Allein welch ein Unterschied! Gerade wie die kindliche Fülle aus meinem Leben verschwunden war, so fand ich auch das zweite Buch von dem ersten durch eine ungeheure Kluft getrennt*) (*CW* 4: 378; FA 1.14: 556).

There is certainly some basis in the biblical texts themselves for Goethe's perceived divide. The story of Exodus begins with a forgetting. After the death of Joseph "a new king arose over Egypt who did not know Joseph" (Exod. 1:8). Goethe reportedly often quoted this line to describe a generational divide in Weimar.[72] With this break in memory comes as well a dramatic shift in focus between the two books from individual to collective. In Exodus, God's personal, close exchanges with the human protagonists disappear. The God who walks through the Garden of Eden in the cool of the day becomes a God heralded by fire who threatens to consume any who approach too closely on Sinai.[73] Israel, which names an individual patriarch (Jacob) in Genesis, designates in Exodus a massive population of descendants. Martin Buber speaks here of the movement from a "clan god in non-historical situations" to a "national god in historical situations."[74]

Goethe strongly registers a break between the individual and interpersonal, "patriarchal" focus of Genesis and the national-collective focus of Exodus (as well as Leviticus, Numbers, and Deuteronomy). We already saw the ominous contrast in Merian's engravings between the pastoral Genesis scene and the more sinister town-dwellers in the Passover scene. In his essay "Israel in the Desert," Goethe describes the transition from a story of Abraham beneath the golden tent of the night sky in Genesis to the Exodus account of "an innumerable people, moving sullenly in a sad wilderness" (*ein unzählbares Volk, mißmuthig in einer traurigen Wüste*) (FA 1.3.1: 235).

To be sure, the Genesis-Exodus shift presents itself here as an easy analogy for the modern European transition from an agrarian to a more administratively centralized, urbanized society. Yet I argue that in Goethe's work the Genesis-Exodus divide does not simpy signal an anti-modern nostalgia for a lost "patriarchal" past; rather it corresponds to a complex reckoning of the productive versus negative possibilities within his own age. The patriarchal world of Genesis also figures as *modern* for Goethe perhaps above all because it offers him an ethical, intellectual, aesthetic, even erotic liberty that stands in opposition to the constraints of a tired Christian pedantry and formulaic morality. And in this broadened sense, he finds a "patriarchal" sensibility not just in Genesis, but in other Hebrew Bible books and other cultures and periods as well. At the same time, the peculiar brand of liberalism and individualism that Goethe associates with the patriarchal world is, as the term strongly suggests today, of a resolutely aristocratic, anti-egalitarian, anti-democratic variety. In Goethe's vision of intellectual and aesthetic freedom, there is no hint of universal political liberation.

Goethe's political conservatism and reflexive elitism also help explain his negative reaction to Exodus. There he perceives the forces of uniformity, legalism, collectivism, and revolution that he fears in his own era. And yet ultimately the history of Goethe's reception of Exodus may be more complex and dialectical even than his admiration for Genesis. Despite his instincts, Goethe struggles to come to terms with the figure of Moses and the kind of future that Moses, in Goethe's view, heralds.

Thus the Hebrew Bible serves as a paradigmatic text for Goethe in multiple ways. Once freed from Christian hermeneutics, it reveals narratives that diverge radically from Christian morality tales of ultimate conversion and sacrifice, instead offering heroes who are almost anti-heroes in their capacity for repeated sin and error. The wisdom books invite the exploration of existential themes and questions not countenanced by Christian doctrine. As seen through the lens of the emerging source criticism, the Hebrew Bible also suggests to Goethe a model for an internally complex, even contradictory, polyvocal text. Finally, the transition between Genesis and Exodus provides Goethe with a paradigm shift that he recapitulates throughout his work as he struggles to characterize the direction of his own age.

Goethe also draws on the Hebrew Bible as a source for his own ethos of wandering. He finds in Israel a model of *Kulturnation*—of dispersal and diaspora combined with a faithfulness to the "book," to literature and culture and the work of interpretation. Further, in the recurring theme of idolatry, he finds inspiration for an intellectual and artistic ideal that resists absolute and fixed meanings. Rather, he sees in the lives of the biblical patriarchs a pattern of contraction and expansion that mirrors his own scientific conception of the fundamental processes that structure life. Ultimately Goethe's positive ideal of wandering matches what he finds in his Hebrew Bible figures—the capacity to sustain divergence, loss, anomy and yet to retain a commitment to meaning.

Yet throughout Goethe's avid reception of the Old Testament lingers the problem of inheritance, for Goethe is keenly aware that these are *Jewish* scriptures.[75] Ironically then, despite his sophisticated historicism and rejection of the Christian interpretive agenda, Goethe reproduces, in form if not in content, the act of appropriation so basic to Christian biblical hermeneutics. For if the heir to the Old Testament was previously the New Testament, now it is a secular German literature. Of Goethe's friend and contemporary Herder, Jonathan Sheehan writes, "the Jews were irrelevant to the ultimate goal of recasting Hebrew literature as a form of German national literature."[76] The dynamic with Goethe can be cast more malevolently: in his bid to appropriate the Hebrew Bible for a secular, modern literature, Goethe repeatedly, pointedly strives to distinguish himself from modern Jews, to denigrate and disinherit them of their own tradition. Goethe's love of the Hebrew Bible is a double-edged sword.

Chapter Organization

In the preceding I have laid out the key issues that run throughout the book; the individual chapters focus closely on a specific work or cluster of works in their development of these philosophical-existential, political-cultural, and formal-aesthetic themes. The book does not aim to resolve the dissonances in Goethe's relationship to Judaism, but offers variations on Goethe's debt to Judaism and his denigration of it in his work.

Chapter 1 considers how Goethe uses Jewish sources and traditions to construct alternative intellectual itineraries in his autobiography *Poetry and Truth* (*Dichtung und Wahrheit*). Taking off from Gusdorf's insight that autobiography traditionally constructs a kind of theodicy out of the individual life. I read Goethe's confessions as a reply to the Christian providential design of Augustine's *Confessions*. Goethe, like Augustine, makes prominent use of a metaphor of wandering but radicalizes it and rejects a redemptive Christian destination. He finds resources for his conception of an existential wandering in the Hebrew Bible, the Kabbalah, the legend of the Wandering Jew, and Spinoza.

Chapter 2 begins with the idea that the young Goethe absorbed from his friend Herder that the Old Testament should be read as Hebrew national poetry, and explores how Goethe's own evolving view of German national culture becomes thoroughly enmeshed with his reflections on this supposed Hebrew national model. He attends, in particular, to the biblical Exodus, for Goethe as for Herder the original national epic, and boldly reinterprets and reconfigures it according to his literary and cultural agenda. I consider first three early essays from the 1770s, his brief period of German national enthusiasm. I then look at a pair of texts penned a quarter of a century later when, in the wake of the French Revolution, he had grown suspicious of popular nationalisms: his verse epic *Hermann and Dorothea* (*Herrmann und Dorothea*) and his biblical critical essay "Israel in the Desert." Ultimately he develops his conception of a non-statist German *Kulturnation* along the lines of the uprooted ancient Hebrew "people of the book," yet simultaneously distances his German model from the radical revolutionary impulses he reads into biblical Israelites and supposes in modern Jews.

Chapter 3 considers Goethe's further experimentations with the Hebrew Bible as a literary model. His little known national *Volksbuch* project of 1808 reveals perhaps most clearly the competition with the Hebrew Bible at the core of his literary and cultural program. In particular he focuses on the heterogeneous form of the Hebrew Bible uncovered by the new biblical criticism: he wants to create for the Germans a historically and rhetorically disparate, composite, edited collection that he hopes will rival the Bible. I suggest that his unfinished *Volksbuch* plan came to fruition in one of his most formally innovative works, *Wilhelm Meister's Journeyman Years* (*Wilhelm Meisters Wanderjahre*), which I read as an attempt at literary and cultural supersession. Wilhelm strives, in his own words, to overcome his status as a wandering Jew and becomes instead a wanderer in a Goethean-Christian mode. The *Journeyman Years* represents Goethe's attempt to refashion Christianity into a more active, wordly religion of deeds rather than creeds, that is, a Christianity that comes closer to the ethos he believes he finds in Judaism. Meanwhile the explicit exclusion of Jews from the new Society of Emigrants in this novel stands as an anti-Semitic low point within Goethe's oeuvre.

And yet, if the *Journeyman Years* is organized around a rejection of Judaism, Goethe's *Faust*, which in its two parts occupied him for nearly his entire adult life, suggests the more productive side of his sustained engagement with Judaism and especially the Hebrew Bible.

In chapter 4 on *Faust, Part One*, I argue that the Faust legend converges in important ways with early modern representations of Jews, and that Goethe draws on and underscores these convergences. Indeed, Goethe positions Faust typologically as *like* a Jewish figure, as a member of what the New Testament calls the Old Covenant. I read the pact in the drama as a version of a Hebrew Bible covenant framed from the first by the analogy between Faust and Job in the play's "Prologue in Heaven." But the chapter explores not only the analogy with Job, but also a related, recurring comparison between Faust and King Solomon, who, according to various canonical and non-canonical sources, was an author, philosopher, natural scientist, magician, tamer of demons, and famous lover. Solomon is at once one of the great heroes of the Bible—builder of the Temple—and a great sinner, because, at the end of his life, his lovers lure him to break the covenant and commit the sin of idolatry. Like Solomon, Faust struggles to resist the seductions of stasis, certitude, and dogmatic metaphysics, to hold fast to his anti-idolatrous pact.

In chapter 5, I read *Faust, Part Two*, through a further sustained biblical analogy, this time between Faust and the figure of Moses. Goethe uses the same word *Kluft* (chasm) to describe the radical divides between Genesis and Exodus and between *Part One* and *Part Two* of the drama. *Part Two* and Exodus both offer accounts of absolutisms and mass movements, including revolt, migration, war, and the establishment of a new state. Through the figure of Moses Goethe thematizes Faust's forgetting of the flux and dynamism of creation in a bid to reinstate paradise by force. But in this, his final literary testament, Goethe, himself by now a reluctant protagonist within a German national narrative, struggles to come to terms with the figure of Moses, as the compromised agent of historical forces beyond his control. This chapter ends with two possible, divergent interpretations of the final scene of Faust's redemption: the first reads a typology of Christian supersession from the speeches of the penitential female figures; the second reads in the scene's multiple ironies an affirmation of the existential commitment that Goethe has drawn throughout his life from Judaism.

Note: The Trouble with Goethe

Any broad study of Goethe's work requires some account of the unique challenges presented by this author. Goethe's body of work—144 volumes in the Weimar edition—can feel like its own vast and complex galaxy. To isolate one theme or question seems arbitrary and distorting. A serious reader of Goethe will certainly ask what Goethe's treatment of Judaism has to do with his representations of, say, Islam or classical antiquity, which also serve for him as alternatives to the felt impoverishments of German culture. Indeed Goethe's conception of Judaism is inevitably linked, by affinity or contrast in his thinking, to a vast network of other cultures, periods, and religious or philosophical movements. But this study cannot even claim to offer an exhaustive survey of the representation of Jews and Judaism in Goethe's oeuvre. For example, for the sake of economy, I do not discuss several short or fragmentary early works that offer testimony to Goethe's almost ethnographic interest in modern Jewry as a young man: his version of a Purim play in *The Plundersweil Fair* (*Jahrmarktsfest zu Plundersweilen*), his "Jewish Sermon" ("Judenpredigt"), and his review "Poems by a Polish Jew" ("Gedichte von einem polnischen Juden").[77] Moreover, Goethe scholars will certainly be able to think of passages from Goethe's oeuvre that could contradict almost any generalization made in this book. For instance, a key contention here is that Goethe simply found himself less engaged by the New Testament than by the Hebrew Bible. Others will inevitably be able to point to passages and works that unfold a rich and meaningful relationship to the Christian scriptures. The only reply to all these objections is that Goethe's work is indeed larger, more internally complex, contradictory, and ironic than can be accounted for here. I venture a thesis that tries to explain as much data as possible but cannot and does not explain it all. I hope that my readings will seem compelling and well supported, but invite others to expand or amend. This will not be, and does not aim to be, the last word on Goethe and Judaism.

Chapter 1

✦

Itinerancy, Suffering, and Providence

Goethe's Encounters with Judaism in *Poetry and Truth*

Wandering is a constitutive metaphor in Goethe's autobiography, *Poetry and Truth*. Goethe refers to himself in the opening sentence of book 12 with a nickname he has acquired from his friends: "the Wanderer" (*der Wanderer*) (FA 1.14: 548, 567). He employs metaphors of wandering throughout the work and, in a letter to Rochlitz, makes wandering a meta-designation for the whole project, referring to it as "my own wanderings" (*meine eigenen Wanderungen*) (WA 4.22: 164). But the rhetoric of wandering encapsulates an uncertainty at the heart of the work: while wandering (*wandern*) can serve as a salutary exercise with a predictable course, it can also suggest that one is lost, literally or figuratively. Goethe reports that many of his gifted contemporaries went off course in their pursuits: "When anyone ran about the world on foot, without clearly knowing why or whither, that was called a 'genius journey,' . . . Energetic, often genuinely gifted younger men went astray in their lack of restraint" (*Wenn einer zu Fuße, ohne recht zu wissen warum und wohin, in die Welt lief, so hieß dies eine Geniereise. . . . Jüngere lebhafte, oft wahrhaft begabte Menschen verloren sich ins Grenzenlose*) (CW 5: 585; FA 1.14: 823). The final lines of part 4, where he left the project in the last months of his life, suggest a continuing sense of uncertainty concerning his own life-itinerary. He takes from *Egmont* the image of a charioteer barely in control of the wagon of fate: "Who knows what the destination is? The driver scarcely remembers from whence he came" (*Wohin es geht, wer weiß es? Erinnert er sich doch kaum, woher er kam*) (CW 5: 605; FA 1.14: 852).

This chapter argues that the pervasive metaphor of wandering is linked to representations of Judaism. We begin by considering the theological deep structure of European autobiography as inherited from Augustine. Judaism provides resources for Goethe's deviation from a Christian-Augustinian theodicy of sin and redemption toward a process-oriented mythos in which human action plays a central role.

Autobiography and Evil

The pervasive metaphor of wandering is of course not new in the autobiographical tradition, but rather links Goethe squarely back to the founding text of Western autobiography, Augustine's *Confessions*. Augustine describes his early life as a wandering away from God: "But I deserted you, my God. In my youth I wandered away, too far from your sustaining hand, and created of myself a barren waste."[1] Augustine's use of wandering as a correlative or consequence of sin clearly has its origins in the Hebrew Bible, for example in the punishment of Cain in Genesis, in the fate of the Israelites in Numbers, or in the many exhortations of the prophets concerning Israel's disobedience. But Augustine makes clear there is a solution to the wandering, fallen state; and that solution of course is to be found in the New Testament. Helpless to free himself from evil, he has to rely solely on "the grace of God, through Jesus Christ our Lord."[2] Only through the grace of God and Jesus can Augustine find relief from his condition of error. For Augustine, then, the trope of wandering is but prelude to the assertion of eternal providence.

Indeed Augustine's life story amounts to a narrative elaboration of his doctrine of sin and redemption, embodying his own take on the problem of evil. The problem of evil in its classic formulation, dating back at least to Epicurus, questions how a God presumed to be omnipotent and all good can be reconciled with the existence of horrendous evils in the world. As Hume phrases it, "Is God willing to prevent evil but not able? then is he impotent. Is he able, but not willing? then is he malevolent. Is he both able and willing? Whence then is evil?"[3] Augustine holds fast to the all-goodness of God and by extension God's creation. Addressing God, Augustine writes, "you made man, but you did not make sin in him."[4] Evil is attributed then entirely to human sinfulness—a sinfulness inherited from Adam's first transgression. In his autobiography, Augustine tries to locate his own intrinsic sinfulness even in his infancy. While he lacks the memory, he concludes that, "if babies are innocent, it is not for lack of will to do harm, but for lack of strength."[5] He recounts his own version of Adam's disobedience in his theft of pears at age sixteen, done, not out of hunger, but for the pleasure "in doing something that was forbidden."[6] As we will discuss later in the chapter, Goethe explicitly rejects the Augustinian doctrine of original sin and dependence on grace but does not dispense with Augustine's fundamental narrative task of coming to terms with evil. Evil, in Goethe's account, is neither monolithic nor capable of clear delimitation but appears in an ambiguous, deliberately modern guise, like the devil in *Faust*. There Mephistopheles notes that, while Satan's name has been "consigned to storybooks for youngsters" (*schon lang ins Fabelbuch geschrieben*), the issue of evil has not gone away, "the Fiend is gone, the fiends are still amongst us" (*Den Bösen sind sie los, die Bösen sind geblieben*) (Arndt, *Faust: A Tragedy*, 2507, 2509).

Indeed, while the "problem of evil" is usually defined as the familiar paradox concerning divine power and goodness, it can also be formulated in a non-theistic way. According to Peter Berger, the construction and legitimation of any meaningful order or "nomos" demand an account of the forces of chaos or "anomy" that are inimical to that construct. He writes, "Every nomos is established over and over again, against the threat of its destruction by the anomic forces endemic to the human condition."[7] These anomic phenomena, including suffering, evil, and death, "must not only be lived through, they must also be explained—to wit, explained in terms of the nomos established in the society in question."[8] Susan Neiman describes "evil" in similarly non-metaphysical terms, as that which "threatens our ability to act in the world and to understand it."[9] She writes, "The problem of evil can be expressed in theological or secular terms, but it is fundamentally a problem about the intelligibility of the world as a whole."[10] The problem of evil can therefore be broadened into a fundamental hermeneutic question: how to assimilate—or otherwise account for—that which destroys meaning, which menaces and defies one's very framework for understanding the world. The suffering and lamentation at the heart of the problem, according to Paul Ricoeur, typically lends itself to a narrative or mythic account of origins, rather than rational analysis. He writes: "If there is one human experience ruled by myth, it is certainly that of evil."[11] Goethe's friend Herder recognized this as well, identifying the creation of a "cosmogony, an anthropogenesis, and philosophy of good and evil" as a fundamental human impulse across cultures (HW 5: 12).

Autobiography is thus a particularly rich genre for this narrative or mythic task of making sense out of suffering and contingency. In a classic essay, Georges Gusdorf reads autobiography as a modern variant of theodicy organized around an individual life: the "deepest intentions" of autobiography, he writes, are "directed toward a kind of apologetics or theodicy of the individual being."[12] Gusdorf identifies Augustine, in contrast to classical antique authors, as a point of origin for the modern autobiographical turn where "every destiny, however humble it be, assumes a kind of supernatural stake."[13] He sees in Goethe's era, with its conception of creative genius, a renewed investment in the genre.[14]

Indeed this era, later dubbed by Heine the "epoch of art," offers many variants of aesthetic theodicy, where the world in all its multiplicity is justified through the education of an artist or genius who, in turn, redeems the world. Works in the prophetic mode such as Novalis's *Heinrich von Ofterdingen*, or the anonymous fragment (in Hegel's hand) "The Oldest Systematic Program of German Idealism" ("Das älteste Systemprogramm des deutschen Idealismus"), or even Schiller's more tempered treatise, *On the Aesthetic Education of Man* (*Über die ästhetische Erziehung des Menschen*) all suggest this justification of the world through the artist it forges. Goethe's autobiography too serves as an interpretation and justification of his creative endeavors.

But Goethe has a self-confessed "realistic Tic" (*realistischer Tic*) (FA 2.4: 208) that makes him skeptical of any definitive, unified conception, including that of his own aesthetic *Bildung*. One sees this centrifugal urge clearly in his "Foreword" to his autobiography. In an apocryphal letter, a "friend"—perhaps recalling the voice of the long-departed Schiller—puzzles over the disparateness of the author's recently published, twelve-volume collected works. Goethe's invented correspondent confesses that the whole oeuvre appears to him "disjointed" (*unzusammenhängend*) and urges Goethe to provide the biographical "context" (*Zusammenhang*) for his readers (FA 1.14: 11–12). Hence Goethe strikes forth with an assignment—to create a unified self-representation that can serve an explanatory role. But as he tries to take account of the many facets of his own development, he verges ever further from his goal: "but my exertions and reflections kept leading me farther" (*allein diese Bemühungen und Betrachtungen führten mich immer weiter*) (CW 4: 16; FA 1.14: 13). Consideration of the many external influences on his life soon forces him from a merely personal path: "lo! I found myself transported out of my narrow private life into the wide world" (*so ward ich aus meinem engen Privatleben in die weite Welt gerückt*) (CW 4: 16; FA 1.14: 13). Indeed, he has to consider the great impact on his life of seismic political changes, "the immense motions of the general political course of the world" (*die ungeheueren Bewegungen des allgemeinen politischen Welt*) (FA 1.14: 13). He thus endeavors to take account of his entire interaction with the world and how it has supported or hindered his artistic development.

In short, Goethe's self-portrait as artist strives to grasp the role of contingency and indeed, to return to Berger's term, anomy in his own development. He asserts that one must grasp oneself as an identity over time, amidst various circumstances and know one's century as an ineluctable force that both shapes and sweeps one away (FA 1.14: 13). And yet, he admits that this level of transparency concerning the relationship of self and world is a "virtual impossibility" (*kaum Erreichbares*) (FA 1.14: 13). He therefore regards with a certain irony constructs such as selfhood, genius, or destiny that might organize the material of his life, constantly pressing their limits, contradicting, and revising them. They constitute the necessary but tenuous realm of *Poetry* imposed upon an anomic *Truth*.

And this brings us back to the ambiguity inherent in wandering. Wandering suggests the unmediated reality of the wilderness. It retains the sense of an encounter with the unknown, of sin, suffering, loss, and estrangement, but also of discovery and creation. The journey through the wilderness can be an existential rite of passage—but only if it is ultimately a passage into *something*. That is, the journey must at some point, if only provisionally, or if only in retrospect, acquire a direction. In his study of the wandering motif in Goethe's era, Andrew Cusack writes, "To narrate a life as if it were a journey means to impose a symbolic order on contingency, to ratify the past (and rob it of its power to accuse and hence to paralyze) by interpreting it with regard to a moral goal."[15] Along the periphery of his autobiographical wanderings, Goethe encounters fellow wanderers who help him explore the border between meaning and its anomic opposite. This, I will argue, is the marginal, yet crucial role of Jews and Judaism in Goethe's autobiography.

Jewish Wanderers

In the fourth part of *Poetry and Truth*, Goethe recounts the sufferings of Jung-Stilling, his devout Christian friend, who has botched an eye operation on a worthy and wealthy man. Jung-Stilling, who believes in God's direct and personal intervention in his life, is tormented by the possible meaning of this sudden change in fortune. As a further foil to Jung-Stilling's faith in a divine economy of rewards and punishments, Goethe introduces the figure of a Jewish beggar (*Betteljude*) for whom the eye operation *was* successful. While Goethe finds the Jewish beggar amusing, the case can hardly be mentioned in the presence of the tormented Jung-Stilling.

> An individual case that made us laugh was that of an old, blind Jewish beggar from the Isenburg estates, who had been led to Frankfurt in extreme misery, and could barely find shelter or wretched nourishment and care. But his tenacious Oriental nature stood him in such good stead that he soon, with rapture, found himself fully cured, and without the slightest difficulty. When he was asked whether the operation had been painful, he answered hyperbolically, "If I had a million eyes, I would have them all operated on in turn, for a penny apiece." As he went on his way [*abwandern*] he behaved with equal eccentricity in Passage Lane, thanking God in good Old Testament terms, and praising the Lord and his envoy, the miracle man. So going toward the bridge, he slowly walked through this long commercial street. Salesmen and their customers stepped out of their stores, startled by such rare pious enthusiasm being emotionally displayed in public. Everyone's sympathy was aroused, so much so that he, without any demanding or begging was abundantly showered with gifts of food for his journey. (*CW* 5: 534)
>
> Denn so machte uns im Einzelnen ein alter blinder Betteljude aus dem Isenburgischen zu lachen, der, in dem höchsten Elend nach Frankfurt geführt, kaum ein Obdach, kaum eine kümmerliche Nahrung und Wartung finden konnte, dem aber die zähe orientalische Natur so gut nachhalf, daß er vollkommen und ohne die mindeste Beschwerde sich mit Entzücken geheilt sah. Als man ihn fragte: ob die Operation ihn geschmerzt habe? So sagte er nach der hyperbolischen Weise: wenn ich eine Million Augen hätte, so wollte ich sie jedesmal für ein halb Kopfstück, sämtlich nach und nach operieren lassen. Bei seinem

> Abwandern betrug er sich in der Fahrgasse eben so exzentrisch, er dankte Gott auf gut alttestamentlich, pries den Herren und den Wundermann seinen Gesandten. So schritt er, in dieser langen, gewerbreichen Straße, langsam der Brücke zu. Verkäufer und Käufer traten aus den Läden heraus, überrascht durch einen so seltenen frommen, leidenschaftlich vor aller Welt ausgesprochenen Enthusiasmus; alle waren angeregt zur Teilnahme, dergestalt daß er, ohne irgend zu fordern oder zu heischen, mit reichlichen Gaben zur Wegezehrung beglückt wurde. (FA 1.14: 745–46)

Despite notes of sympathy, the Jewish beggar does not emerge as an altogether attractive figure in Goethe's description: the anecdote subtly trades on an anti-Jewish juxtaposition of Christian generosity with Jewish soliciting. While Jung-Stilling has presumably done the operation for free—we learn earlier that he has operated on many indigent people—the Jewish beggar expresses his gratitude by imagining a scheme where he would have a million eyes operated upon for a penny apiece. When he leaves town, the gifts and money showered upon him by sympathetic customers and shopkeepers preempt the demands he would implicitly otherwise make ("he, without any demanding or begging was abundantly showered with gifts").

And yet destiny seems to have chosen the pitiful Jewish beggar over the deserving Christian patient. Goethe juxtaposes the happiness of the impoverished Jewish beggar, described as if an exotic nomad "in his sandy homeland" (*in seiner sandigen Heimat*) on the other side of the river Main, with the "wealthy, worthy" (*wohlhabend, würdig*) Christian man on this side of the river, deprived of the comfort he had so desired (FA 1.14: 746; *CW* 5: 534). The Jewish beggar, with his nomadism, his "tenacious Oriental nature," his eccentric expressions of piety "in good Old Testament terms" seems, like the Wandering Jew of legend, an uncanny phantom from another time and place. His inexplicable *chosenness* in this episode points to a broader way in which, within Goethe's autobiography, modern Judaism stands as a mysterious challenge to a Christian narrative teleology.

Indeed, the riddle presented by the Jewish beggar recalls another, earlier section in *Poetry and Truth* where Goethe describes his response to the Jewish ghetto as a boy. He is overwhelmed by the unpleasantness of the ghetto and frightened by the grisly legends surrounding their torture of Christian children. And yet he affirms that in some sense these modern Jews remain "chosen." He writes, "Nevertheless, they were God's chosen people and, however this may have come about, walking reminders of the most ancient times" (*Indessen blieben sie doch das auserwählte Volk Gottes, und gingen, wie es nun mochte gekommen sein, zum Andenken der ältesten Zeiten umher*) (*CW* 4: 120; FA 1.14: 165). Despite the extreme ghettoization of modern Jews within German society, they haunt, in their very survival, Christian conceptions of providence, the expectation of religious supersession.

The figure of the Wandering Jew is thus a recurring one in Goethe's autobiography. He mentions the easy availability in his childhood of chapbooks concerning the Wandering Jew (FA 1.14: 42) and also devotes several paragraphs to recounting his own plans for an epic on the "History of the Wandering Jew" ("Die Geschichte des ewigen Juden") (FA 1.14: 692–94). The Wandering Jew of legend is a witness of Christ's crucifixion condemned to roam through the centuries until the Second Coming brings at last the decisive triumph of Christianity. But as much as he is supposed to serve as a witness to Christ's suffering, his modern presence also points to the continued deferral of that promise of Christian providential resolution. For his own Wandering Jew, Goethe had planned an encounter with another Jew, the apostate philosopher Spinoza, who, for his uncompromising philosophical rigor and audacity, is cast as a godless monster by posterity (FA 1.14: 731, 730). While Goethe never penned the episode, he sets up a clear parallel in book 16 between what the fictional Wandering Jew would have gleaned from Spinoza and what he himself took from this controversial philosopher in his own intellectual peregrinations.

It is as a foil for all kinds of orthodox logic and preordained plots, then, that Judaism fits into Goethe's account of his own life. In this massive work, Jewish sources and figures can seem to play a merely peripheral role, but that is precisely the point. Goethe's off-road encounters with what appears contradictory, divergent, recalcitrant, even amoral or evil from the perspective of his Christian upbringing provide him in his own narrative with a wedge of freedom and taste of modernity. In short, there are repeated, crucial links in the narrative between Judaism and the emergence of Goethe's creative freedom as an artist. Of course, Judaism is in no way the only alternative tradition that Goethe explores: his influences are almost infinitely extensive and diverse, and frequently heterodox and provocative. But Judaism strikes especially close to home—it is a tradition at once foreign and exotic and yet deeply familiar, woven, as it is, into Christianity. It must be stressed again that Goethe's reception of Jewish traditions is idiosyncratic and serves in no way as a true or fair representations of Jewish tradition or religion. This chapter does not depict what Judaism has to say about the problem of evil so much as what Goethe seems to think Judaism has to say—or what it says to *him*. Further, Goethe's conception is itself not unified or consistent. We will consider his fascination with what he calls the Old Testament God, his study of the book of Genesis, his adoption of key elements of Lurianic Kabbalah in his own creation myth, his experimentation with the legend of the Wandering Jew, and his devotion to Spinoza.

A paradox will become apparent here. Judaism is important because it falls out of the traditional providential narrative, but to the extent that it contributes to Goethe's artistic development, it is recuperated into his own secular providential logic. And yet as suggested in the preface, that process of integration or recuperation is far from definitive or complete within the autobiography.

A Shaken Universe

If Augustine's *Confessions* is the orthodoxy against which Goethe constructs his own autobiography, the contrast is especially rich in the opening books of *Poetry and Truth*. As mentioned, Augustine seeks the keys to understanding the nature of God or the cosmos in his early years and provides his own allegorical fall from grace. Rousseau's *Confessions*, another autobiographical model at hand for Goethe, also prominently employs this biblical myth of a fall, representing it, however, by contrast, as a guiltless expulsion from paradise in the wake of a false accusation of vandalism.[16] Goethe's account of his early years follows in this mythic-cosmological mode, but deviates further from the Christian model. In a perhaps satirical nod to a cosmological combat myth, Goethe begins his account of his life with the positive influence of the stars and the competing and delaying "counterglow" (*Gegenschein*) of the moon at the hour of his birth (FA 1.14: 15)

After surviving his difficult birth, the child Goethe experiences the family home as his universe. From the very first, the house architecture shapes his character and defines his experience, while the adults who govern his home life seem like divine agents. But whereas Goethe's grandparents and mother serve at best as lower or alternative deities, his father emerges as the all-controlling architect and director of his son's world and life. After some career disappointments, Johann Caspar Goethe was an at-home father who planned out in meticulous detail not only his son's daily lessons, but effectively his whole life. The implicit analogy in book 1 between father and God cuts negatively in both directions, indicting both God and father, but is nevertheless far-reaching and extremely productive for Goethe's development as a writer and thinker. For in the end, it is this controlling, arbitrary paternal principle—embodied by both father and God—with which Goethe grapples in staking his own creative place in the world. I maintain that because of the resonances with his own experiences, Goethe ultimately finds greater descriptive power as well as greater space for his own individuality in what he takes to be the God of the Old Testament rather than in the Christian God of the New Testament.

Certainly the dominant feature in Goethe's portrait of his father in book 1 is the "strong didactic bent" (*lehrhafte Natur*) (*CW* 4: 24; FA 1.14: 20) that Johann Caspar Goethe relentlessly brings to bear upon his family. The elder Goethe takes over the instruction of his son and daughter himself and plans out in detail his son's entire future educational itinerary on the model of his own life course (*Lebensgang*): "I was to pursue the same path, only farther and more comfortably" (*ich sollte denselben Weg gehen, aber bequemer und weiter*) (*CW* 4: 36; FA 1.14: 38). Nothing is allowed to distract from, or interfere with, this rigorous pedagogical program. In a particularly bitter passage, Goethe describes how his father viewed the ravaging childhood diseases that plagued him and killed several siblings as mere aggravating distractions and imposed a redoubled instructional pace so as not to fall behind his intended schedule (FA 1.14: 44). Goethe makes clear that this pressing pedagogical agenda stifles his own developmental impulses: "[the lessons] retarded and to some extent repressed my inner development, which had now taken a definite direction" (*es [hielt] meine innere Entwickung [auf], die eine entschiedene Richtung genommen hatte, und [drängte sie] gewissermaßen [zurück]*) (*CW* 4: 40; FA 1.14: 45).

If one pursues the parallelism between father and deity, overbearing didacticism is something that in fact Goethe clearly identifies with Christianity. He describes the "dry moralism" (*trockne Moral*) of the Lutheran religious instruction he received (*CW* 4: 44; FA 1.14: 50) and, as noted earlier, confesses that he found the New Testament "all too easy," "even trivial" (FA 1.14: 40). His encounters with the church seem largely occasions to hone his proficiency at memorization: he quickly memorizes both the questions and answers of the Lutheran catechism (FA 1.14: 161), and to impress his elders he mechanically reconstructs and recites in detail the dull didactic sermons of a new pastor (FA 1.14: 159–60). Thus his early exposure to the church, like his early relationship to his father, seems to consist mostly of arid lessons. Yet at the same time, darker elements in the young Goethe's experience begin to belie the wholesomeness and moral consistency of the God of his Christian religious instruction.

And in its very strangeness, the Old Testament will begin to accord better with the young Goethe's experience of the world. As Sheehan argues, eighteenth-century Enlightenment reformers held the New Testament up as a pedagogical text: the Old Testament was thought to offer little in the way of moral edification. It is not difficult to see why the Hebrew Bible does not smoothly fit this agenda. The God of the Hebrew Bible, with his sweeping acts of destruction (his flood consumes the whole earth), his terrible demands (Abraham must offer his only son for sacrifice), and his unexplained preferences (the second-born Jacob will prevail over the first-born Esau), does not always seem to conform to Christian Sunday school lessons.

What is distinctive in the Hebrew Bible is that its heroes challenge the necessity of human suffering. When as a young adult, Goethe develops a more emotional relationship to the New Testament, it is a passive relationship born of illness and focused on the next life: "To a sufferer, to someone with tender, even effete sensibilities, the Gospel was something very welcome" (*Einem Duldenden, zart, ja schwächlich Fühlenden war daher das Evangelium willkommen*) (*CW* 4: 251; FA 1.14: 366). The heroes of the Hebrew Bible are by contrast hardly acquiescent in the face of suffering and injustice: they cry out and even dispute with God, calling him to account for evil in the world. When God is prepared to destroy Sodom, Abraham eloquently pleads with him not to "sweep away the innocent along with the guilty" but to forgive the whole city for the sake of its few righteous ones (Gen. 18:23). The very name Israel is won through a struggle with the divine. After Jacob wrestles with an angel, and forces from him a blessing, the being proclaims: "Your name shall no longer be Jacob but Israel for you have striven with beings divine and human, and have prevailed" (Gen. 32:28). The Psalmist laments God's inaction while Israel is disgraced: "Rouse Yourself; why do You sleep, O Lord? / Awaken do not reject us forever! / Why do You hide Your face, / ignoring our affliction and distress?" (Ps. 44:24–26). In Isaiah, God openly acknowledges his double-edged impact on human life, "I form light and create darkness, I make weal and create woe—" (Isa. 45:7). Paul Ricoeur suggests that uncertainties about the nature of God lurk deep within the very myth of Adam's fall: "the essentially ethical affirmation of God's saintliness can never entirely rid us of the suspicion that God is somehow beyond good and evil and that for this very reason he sends evil as well as good."[17]

Goethe's father also creates his share of woe. As the agent of "didactic and pedagogical afflictions" (*didaktische pädagogische Bedrängnisse*) he seems a parodic version of this more ambiguous divinity (*CW* 4: 40–41; FA 1.14: 45). His first appearance in the autobiography is telling. The old family house with its dark and gloomy corners frightens the children and at night sometimes drives them to sneak out of their beds to find the company of the servants. The elder Goethe is guided by the enlightened educational principle that "the young [were] to be weaned without delay from all fear of the invisible and ominous and to be inured to horror" (*den Kindern frühzeitig alle Furcht vor dem Ahndungsvollen und Unsichtbaren zu benehmen, und sie an das Schauderhafte zu gewöhnen*) (*CW* 4: 23; FA 1.14: 18–19). In a perverse twist of logic, he thus undertakes to cure his children of their irrational fears by ambushing them on their nocturnal flight, and, with his dressing gown turned inside out, frightening them back to bed (FA 1.14: 19). Not surprisingly, this approach does not achieve its therapeutic aim. But this disturbing initial image of Goethe's father terrorizing children in an inside-out dressing gown suggests quite effectively the dark flip side of his pedagogical nature.

The ambivalent impact appears perhaps most clearly in Johann Caspar Goethe's renovations of the family house, where he acts quite literally as architect of the child's world. While the outcome of the father's "well-conceived plan" (*wohlausgedachter Plan*) is ultimately satisfactory, providing a light, spacious interior with good views of the garden (*CW* 4: 33; FA 1.14: 33), that process is utterly unnerving for the child. In order to circumvent building ordinances limiting the overhang of upper stories in any new construction, Goethe's father treats the renovation as a mere repair. Relying on support beams for the upper stories, he tears down and then reconstructs the bottom stories one by one. The young boy undergoes the trauma not only of witnessing familiar spaces hacked apart, but also of sensing the ground pulled out beneath his feet. And yet in the midst of this insecurity and instability he remains subject to his father's unrelenting didactic agenda:

> These were the very rooms in which we had often been closely confined and plagued with disagreeable lessons and studies; these were the very corridors in which we had played; these were the very walls

> we had been so constantly admonished to keep clean and unblemished! To see all of this fall beneath the mason's ax and the carpenter's hatchet, and what is more, in reverse order, from bottom up! And meanwhile to hover, as it were, up there in the air on supported rafters, and yet to be held to a particular lesson, a definite piece of work! It put more confusion into our young heads than could easily be straightened out again. (*CW* 4: 25)

> Die Zimmer, in denen man sie oft enge genug gehalten und mit wenig erfreulichem Lernen und Arbeiten geängstigt, die Gänge auf denen sie gespielt, die Wände, für deren Reinlichkeit und Erhaltung man sonst so sehr gesorgt, alles das vor der Hacke des Maurers, vor dem Beile des Zimmermanns fallen zu sehen, und zwar von unten herauf, und indessen oben auf unterstützten Balken, gleichsam in der Luft zu schweben, und dabei immer noch zu einer gewissen Lektion, zu einer bestimmten Arbeit angehalten zu werden—dieses alles brachte eine Verwirrung in den jungen Köpfen hervor, die sich so leicht nicht wieder ins Gleiche setzen ließ. (FA 1.14: 21)

Furthermore when the roof too is torn down, rain reaches the children in their beds (FA 1.14: 22). Finally the father relents and sends the children out of the house to stay with friends and to attend a public school, where they find themselves the defenseless victims of other, rougher children (FA 1.14: 22).

The child's experience of exposure and vulnerability as the walls and floors of his house give way has its parallel in his "shaken" (*erschüttert*) reaction when, as a six-year-old, he hears reports of the Lisbon earthquake: "The earth quivers and rocks, the sea rages, ships collide, houses collapse. . . . The unfortunate survivors are exposed to robbery, murder, and every possible mistreatment" (*Die Erde bebt und schwankt, das Meer braust auf, die Schiffe schlagen zusammen, die Häuser stürzen ein. . . . Die unglücklichen Übriggebliebenen sind dem Raube, dem Morde, allen Mißhandlungen bloßgestellt*) (CW 4: 35; FA 1.14: 36). And yet now the agent of this destruction is not Goethe's father, but God the creator. Here for the six-year-old, the problem of evil already appears in stark relief. Again, the question in its traditional formulation is how an omnipotent, benevolent creator could be compatible with the horrendous sufferings in the world. The boy's solution to this antinomy is to question the goodness of God.[18]

> God, the Creator and Preserver of heaven and earth, who had been presented to me as so very wise and merciful in the explanation of the first article of the Creed, had shown Himself by no means fatherly when He abandoned both the just and the unjust to the same destruction. (*CW* 4: 35)

> Gott, der Schöpfer und Erhalter Himmels und der Erden, den ihm die Erklärung des ersten Glauben-Artikels so weise und gnädig vorstellte, hatte sich, indem er die Gerechten mit den Ungerechten gleichem Verderben preis gab, keineswegs väterlich bewiesen. (FA 1.14: 37)

This God's failure to prove himself "fatherly" serves paradoxically as a point of comparison with Goethe's own father. Neither God nor father appears wholly benevolent. Like the father in the inverted robe, who, with some perverse pedagogical pretense, terrifies his children at night and produces the opposite of his ostensible aim, this God too seems to bring about the inverse of goodness and justice. The innocent perish with the guilty; criminals are freed from their prisons to rob, murder, and victimize anew (FA 1.14: 36). Indeed, within this passage the relationship is ambiguous between God and another agent, the "demon of terror" (*Dämon des Schreckens*) who disseminates a chilling sense of dread throughout the world (FA 1.14: 37; CW 4: 35).

Goethe describes the God who brings not only earthquakes to Portugal but ravaging storms closer to home as the wrathful God of the Old Testament (FA 1.14: 37). But in his lament that God has abandoned the just with the unjust, he echoes Abraham's appeal on behalf of Sodom: "Far be it from You to do such a thing, to bring death upon the innocent as well as the guilty so that innocent and guilty fare alike" (Gen. 18: 25). That is, what might seem like a wholesale rejection of religion actually places him directly in a Hebrew Bible tradition of lamenting suffering and demanding justice. This passage can serve as an affirmation as much as a criticism of a Hebrew Bible sensibility.

Goethe describes how, in order to escape the dry moralism of his Christian upbringing, he begins to look toward various separatist movements that attract him through their "originality, warmth, resoluteness, and independence" (*Originalität, Herzlichkeit, Beharren und Selbständigkeit*) (CW 4: 44; FA 1.14: 50). He refers here to various Christian Pietist sects, but gives their initial attractions a Hebrew Bible cast. For instance, he tells the story of a pious man who, when asked who his father-confessor was, replied that it was the same as that of King David (i.e., God) (FA 1.14: 50). This exemplary man thereby insists upon a relationship to God that elides not only the mediation of the clergy but also implicitly the mediation of Christ. Thus Goethe represents his boyhood drift away from orthodox Lutheranism into Christian separatism quite peculiarly as a move away from Christian theology into the Hebrew Bible.

Book 1 ends with another glimpse of the young Goethe's preference for the so-called God of the Old Testament over the Christian God. He expresses his primary devotion to the first article of the creed—to God as creator of heaven and earth (FA 1.14: 51) and in doing so, implicitly disregards the rest, that is, the Christian doctrines of Son and Holy Ghost. Although in this passage he claims New Testament support for his conception of a God "in direct contact with nature" (*in unmittelbarer Verbindung mit der Natur*) (*CW* 4: 44; FA 1.14: 51), Genesis is of course the primary source for a conception of God the creator. In a further jab at a Christian theology of incarnation, he remarks that he could not conceive of this God in any distinct form and chooses an Old Testament manner of worship: "The boy could not ascribe any form to this Being, and so he sought Him in His works, and in good Old Testament fashion set about erecting an altar to Him" (*Eine Gestalt konnte der Knabe diesem Wesen nicht verleihen; er suchte ihn also in seinen Werken auf, und wollte ihm auf gut alttestamentliche Weise einen Altar errichten*) (*CW* 4: 44; FA 1.14: 51).

The outcome of his homemade worship service emphasizes again the moral ambiguity of the divine. The boy constructs his homemade altar in such a way that as the sun rises though the windows at daybreak, it ignites incense candles set within a porcelain bowl. On a repeat attempt however, the porcelain bowl is missing and the candles destroy the flowered design of a music stand, leaving behind "black, indelible marks" (*schwarze unauslösliche Fußstapfen*), "as if an evil spirit had vanished" (*gleich als wäre ein böser Geist verschwunden*) (*CW* 4: 45; FA 1.14: 52). God the creator has a destructive flip side and in a sense remains beyond good and evil.[19]

Goethe's Patriarchs

While book 1 alludes to the Old Testament in broad, mythic terms, it is only in book 4 that Goethe describes his direct and extensive encounter with the biblical text, specifically Genesis.[20] Goethe's discussion of Genesis falls into two parts: a description of his study of the Bible with a tutor and his imaginative and analytic summary of the book of Genesis told to a great extent in the present tense. Presumably this resumé offers something like an outcome of his study, although clearly telescoped through the later perspective of the adult memoirist.

Goethe's insertion of an extensive commentary on Genesis into his autobiography once again sets up a comparison with Augustine, who devotes the final book of his *Confessions* to a wide-ranging reflection on the first chapter of Genesis. But Goethe intends a contrast with Augustine as well, for, as Linder points out, while Augustine experiences full Christian conversion through a crucial encounter with the biblical text, Goethe begins to develop a critical, skeptical position toward religion.[21]

Initially the young Goethe undertakes study of the Hebrew Bible as something of a detour. He develops the notion of writing an epistolary novel in which six or seven siblings correspond, each in a different language. In this scheme, the smart-alecky youngest brother chooses—obviously as a spoof—Jewish German (*Judendeutsch*), described by Goethe as a "corrupt" (*verdorben*) and "distorted" (*verzerrt*) derivative of Hebrew (*CW* 4: 102; FA

1.14: 138). While Goethe initially takes up Hebrew in order to carry out this scheme, he also acknowledges a higher motivation: to be able to read the Old Testament in the original. He could already read the New Testament with facility, but the Old Testament held particular attraction for him because of its "peculiarity" (*Eigentümlichkeit*) (FA 1.14: 138). Goethe's study of Hebrew soon stalled over the challenging system of vowel points, but his relationship with the Hebrew Bible—aided by translations and commentaries—took off.

Intellectually and creatively, the Hebrew Bible seems to have granted young Goethe an extraordinary breath of fresh air. Much of his description conveys a sense of wide-open spaces, as he imagines the valleys, rivers, deserts, and mountains through which Abraham and his descendants wandered as shepherds. "The life they lived on the sea of deserts and pastures lent breadth and freedom to their ideas, while the vaulted sky under which they dwelt, with all its stars at night, gave sublimity to their feelings" (*Ihre Lebensweise auf dem Meere der Wüsten und Weiden gab ihren Gesinnungen Breite und Freiheit, das Gewölbe des Himmels unter dem sie wohnten, mit allen seinen nächtlichen Sternen, ihren Gefühlen Erhabenheit*) (CW 4: 110; FA 1.14: 150).

The sense of breadth in Goethe's description of the patriarchs stands in pointed contrast to his depiction of Frankfurt's Jewish ghetto later in book 4, which is pervaded by a sense of utter claustrophobia. He describes the "most unpleasant impression" (*unangenehmsten Eindruck*) made on him by the "narrowness, filth, the swarms of people, the disagreeable sound of their accent" (*die Enge, der Schmutz, das Gewimmel, der Akzent einer unerfreulichen Sprache*) as, in passing, he glanced through the gate. (CW 4: 119; FA 1.14: 165). Goethe leaves no question, then, about the disjunction between his Jewish contemporaries confined in the ghetto and the wandering patriarchs of Genesis. This juxtaposition within a few pages serves Goethe's broader logic of appropriation: the degraded circumstances of contemporary Jews in contrast to their ancestors, in combination with the weakening of Christianity's grip on the Old Testament, leaves the Hebrew Bible like an unclaimed inheritance available to Goethe and his generation.

Meanwhile the young Goethe's discovery of the Old Testament is mediated by his (Christian) Hebrew tutor, the sardonic and relatively broad-minded Doctor Albrecht, rector of the gymnasium. This older man, whom he describes as "one of the oddest-looking people imaginable" (*eine der originalsten Figuren der Welt*) as "strange" (*seltsam*) and an "eccentric" (*Sonderling*) (CW 4: 102, 103; FA 1.14: 138, 140, 139), seems a fitting guide to the felt "peculiarity" of the text they share between them. In his account of the lessons, Goethe does not reveal the precise content of his inquiry with Rector Albrecht, and thereby mirrors as memoirist the discreet, amused bearing he attributes to his teacher. While the pupil Goethe boldly pushes the limits of acceptable inquiry, the Rector dodges any direct affirmation, but nevertheless seems to egg the boy on with his receptive attitude, his amused exclamations, and his signature laugh: "and since his behavior seemed to encourage me in this, I grew ever more eager and bold. However, I got nothing more out of him than one belly laugh after the other, as he shouted: 'You silly fellow! You silly fellow!' " (*so wurde ich immer lebhafter und kühner, wozu er mich durch sein Betragen zu berechtigen schien. Übrigens konnte ich nichts aus ihm bringen, als daß er ein über das andre Mal mit seinem bauchschütternden Lachen ausrief: Er närrischer Kerl! Er närrischer Junge!*) (*CW* 4: 105; FA 1.14: 142). The lack of concrete response from the rector does not discourage the boy Goethe, whose chief interest is in the freedom to bring forth doubts rather than in receiving answers (FA 1.14: 142).

The clearest clue Goethe gives concerning the direction of their discussions is his remark that even before his lessons with the rector he noted "discrepancies between tradition and what is real and possible" (*die Widersprüche der Überlieferung mit dem Wirklichen und Möglichen*) (*CW* 4: 40; FA 1.14: 141). The only example he offers of such an implausible biblical claim is the episode in Joshua where the movements of sun and moon miraculously halt in order to prolong a day of battle (Josh. 10:12–13; FA 1.14: 141). Perhaps not coincidentally this example has an important heretical history, figuring in Galileo's "Letter to the Grand Duchess Christina," and Spinoza's *Theological-Political Treatise*.[22] If Goethe's youthful investigation taps into a tradition of heterodox and suppressed thought, it is not surprising that the rector takes care with what he says and does not say. Yet the clandestine intellectual pleasure and palpable sympathy shared between student and teacher clearly afford a taste of something quite new and very tempting for the boy.

Another aspect of the Bible perhaps adds to its allure for the young Goethe, who, at approximately age thirteen, would have been on the cusp of adolescence.[23] The laughter, the discretion concerning content, the rector's ever-present volume of Lucian, the ancient author of bawdy tales, all could allude to another possible attraction of the Old Testament for the boy: that which he later refers to as its "rugged naturalness" (*die derbe Natürlichkeit*) (*CW* 4: 378; FA 1.14: 556). Goethe's contemporary readers would presumably not have needed to be reminded of the rather direct sexual content in Genesis. Examples of episodes that might make a particular impression on a budding adolescent include Onan's divinely ordained death sentence for letting his seed go to waste (Gen. 38: 9) or Rachel's clever concealment of her father's stolen household idols by sitting upon them and claiming to have "the period of women" (Gen. 31: 35). In Genesis there are also unambiguous episodes of heterosexual and (attempted) homosexual rape, incest, and prostitution to rival in sexual drama Lucian or any other literature to which the boy might have been allowed access. Furthermore, the unconventional sexual behavior—for example, Tamar disguises herself as a prostitute in order to become impregnated by her father-in-law (Gen. 38)—does not necessary receive strong censure within the biblical narrative. These lively stories set the Hebrew canon very much apart from the more delicate sexual mores, what Goethe calls the "tender naiveté" (*naïve Zärtlichkeit*) of the New Testament (FA 1.14: 556).

Whatever the precise fruits of Goethe's biblical investigations, his interaction with the rector makes clear that these discoveries have a tempting forbidden quality. He also suggests his encounter with the Hebrew Bible is of the greatest consequence for his own development, amounting to a kind of destiny or providence. He writes, "A person may turn in any direction he pleases and undertake anything whatever, yet he will always return to the path that nature has once and for all laid out for him. That was the case for me too in the present instance" (*Der Mensch mag sich wenden wohin er will, er mag unternehmen was es auch sei, stets wird er auf jenen Weg wieder zurückkehren, den ihm die Natur einmal vorgezeichnet hat. So erging es auch mir im gegenwärtigen Falle*) (CW 4: 105; FA 1.14: 143). And thus he transitions into his own lengthy recapitulation of Genesis. The point of view here is complex, suggesting at once both the boy and the adult, both critical distance and a deep attraction and personal implication in the world he represents.

The issue of a personal providence carries over from Goethe's prefatory remarks to his biblical analysis. He observes among the patriarchs a lack of conventional moral virtue: the scriptures present them "by no means . . . as models of virtue" (*keineswegs als Tugendbilder*), but rather as people "of the most varied character, with many defects and frailties" (*von den verscheidensten Charaktern, mit mancherlei Mängeln und Gebrechen*) (CW 4: 111–12; FA 1.14: 153). And yet, as Goethe simultaneously notes, these same figures are "favorites of God" (*von Gott begünstigte Männer*) (CW 4: 111; FA 1.14: 153). This of course raises the question, *why* God should favor these figures, despite their flaws. As Gabriel Josipovici sees it, this "why?" is one of the fundamental unanswered questions in the Bible: "Why was Abel chosen and Cain rejected? Why was Abraham chosen? In neither case can election be explained, either theologically or morally, by the text as we have it."[24] In addition, the biblical text is full of striking intimations of sympathy for those secondary figures who have not been chosen—whether the exiled surrogate mother Hagar or the unloved first wife Leah or the deceived, disinherited brother Esau or even the fratricidal Cain. On the matter of providence, Genesis offers Goethe a richly puzzling source.

In pursuing this question of providence, Goethe decisively removes his account from any recognizably Christian framework. Perhaps most strikingly, he repeatedly refers to the divine in the plural as "the gods" (*die Götter*). While he implicitly justifies this usage as a translation of the plural Hebrew name for God, Elohim (FA 1.14: 144), his concern is not just linguistic precision. At the time of composition, Goethe was highly aware of the thesis that the appearance of two names for God—Jehovah and Elohim—corresponds to two separate biblical sources in the Pentateuch. Goethe could have known, either through his own consultation of the Hebrew text or through the handy chart of sources provided in Eichhorn's book, that the divine protagonist of the Tower of Babel episode is "Jehovah" and not "Elohim." But in his own retelling he tendentiously opts for Elohim.[25] Moreover, by translating the Elohim as "the gods" Goethe also pointedly rejects—as Herder for example also did (HW 5: 167)—the Christian notion that the plural form of the noun alludes to the Trinity. Goethe emphasizes not only the plurality but also the variability of the divine and thereby edges Genesis away from any Christian doctrine of divine sovereignty and transcendence. For example, the Elohim seem not fully prepared for human behavior and bring the flood out of frustration: "the Elohim, not yet inured to the wickedness of the race, lost patience and annihilated it root and branch" (*die an die Unarten dieses Geschlechts noch nicht gewohnten Elohim wurden ungeduldig und vernichteten es von Grund aus*) (CW 4: 106; FA 1.14: 144). In general Goethe's description leans toward a pagan cosmology governed by an arbitrary fate rather than a beneficent plan. In this way it trains the spotlight on a human response to this existential uncertainty.

Indeed, Goethe suggests that any characterization of the divine is radically filtered through human needs and desires. In a stunningly circular formulation, he reflects upon the episode in which God commands Abraham to sacrifice his son Isaac: "So barbaric a form of worship could not rise up in Abraham's gentle, truly patriarchal character. But the gods, to test us, sometimes seem to assume the very attitudes that men are inclined to impute to them, and now they order him to do a monstrous thing." (*In den sanften, wahrhaft urväterlichen Charakter Abrahams konnte eine so barbarisch Anbetungsweise nicht enstpringen; aber die Götter, welche manchmal, um uns zu versuchen, jene Eigenschaften hervorzukehren scheinen, die der Mensch ihnen anzudichten geneigt ist, befehlen ihm das Ungeheure.*) (CW 4: 110; FA 1.14: 151).[26] The horrific filicidal idea could not have come from Abraham but only from the gods, who in turn are only conforming—as a temptation or trick—to the manner in which humans tend to imagine them. While Goethe falls short—at least grammatically—of reducing the divine to a mere human construction, the character of the divine here certainly mirrors human conceptions. Human acts of interpretation are thus crucial in a way that recalls, in more optimistic guise, Goethe's famous poem "The Divine" ("Das Göttliche"; 1783).[27]

Similarly, in two key passages Goethe suggests that personal providence—the special divine promises and blessings bestowed upon the patriarchs—is also but a human construction. Drawing upon a common distinction between natural and revealed religion, he argues that while natural religion recognizes a universal providence operating in the very order of things, revealed or particular religion insists upon a particular providence revealed to a particular people: "[it] is associated with belief in a particular Providence promised by the Divine Being to certain favored men, families, tribes and nations" (*[sie] führt den Glauben an eine besondre Vorsehung mit sich, die das göttliche Wesen gewissen begünstigten Menschen, Familien, Stämmen und Völkern zusagt*) (CW 4: 109; FA 1.14: 149). While natural religion requires no faith, particular religion, with its insistence on the special status of certain individuals, groups, or territories, depends on it: "This kind of religion is based on faith, which must be unshakable if it is not to be destroyed immediately and totally" (*Diese Religion ist auf den Glauben gegründet, der unerschütterlich sein muß, wenn er nicht sogleich von Grund aus zerstört werden soll*) (*CW* 4: 112; FA 1.14: 153).

What then is this unshakable faith of the patriarchs in their own special providence? Faith (*Glaube*) is already a surprising term for Goethe to stress in a discussion of the Old Testament. Luther's catechism is clear on this point: the Old Testament is associated with the law and external discipline; faith, on the other hand, is an internal matter, having to do with Christianity and the New Testament. Goethe would also presumably have known Moses Mendelssohn's essay "Jerusalem," in which Mendelssohn claims that Judaism requires no assent to specific points of doctrine or salvational truths. According to Mendelssohn, among all the ordinances of Mosaic Law not one demands, "*Thou shalt believe! Or not believe*; rather all command: *thou shalt do, or not do*!"[28]

Presumably Goethe has in mind, then, a faith very different from that embodied by the Apostolic Creed in his Lutheran catechism. Indeed, Hezel's *Biblisches Real-Lexikon*, which Goethe consulted at the time he wrote this section (FA 1.14: 1109), paraphrases the term *glauben* (believe) in the famous verse concerning the aged Abraham's reaction to the Lord's promise of offspring (Gen. 15:6) as "trusted [*trauete*] him, was convinced, that he would fulfill his promise."[29] Mendelssohn also translates Abraham's "faith" as "trust" (*Vertrauen*) as well as "confidence" (*Zuversicht*);[30] Herder too uses the word "trust" (*Vertrauen*) (*SW* 11: 413). In his book *Two Types of Faith*, Martin Buber illuminates this distinction. Buber explores the difference between Christian faith as an *assent* to the truth of something, through a conversion event, and Jewish faith as *trust* in a covenantal relationship in which one already stands, describing this latter form of faith as "the state of persevering" and "trust in the existential sense."[31]

Goethe perceived in his own mother a model of Old Testament trust or confidence. In a letter to Zelter after her death, he describes her as a woman "who, in Old Testament reverence, spent a brave life full of confidence in the unwavering national- and family-God" (*die in alttestamentlicher Gottesfurcht, ein tüchtiges Leben voll Zuversicht auf den unwandelbaren Volks- und Familiengott zubrachte*) (FA 2.10: 138). In 1794, even in the midst of great turmoil, she persists in this existential faith, refusing to leave war-torn Frankfurt. Goethe writes in his annals, "she fortified herself in her Old Testament faith" (*sie bestärkte sich in ihrem alttestamentlichen Glauben*) (FA 1.17: 29). Goethe too, then, conceives Old Testament faith not as doctrinal belief but rather as a more practical capacity for steadiness within an unsteady world.

Indeed, in Goethe's discussion in book 4 of patriarchal faith, he employs metaphors that recall the great historical trauma of his early years—the Lisbon earthquake, those tremors that left his own composure and faith so "shaken" (*erschüttert*) (FA 1.14: 36). The patriarchs too find themselves in a precarious position in relationship to the ground beneath them. Their religion is "*grounded* on a faith" (*auf den Glauben gegründet*) that must in turn be unshakable if it is not to be destroyed "from the *ground* up" (*von Grund aus*) (FA 1. 14: 153). Yet these "heroes of faith" (*Glaubenshelden*) remain unshaken (FA 1.14: 149). Three times in the book 4 passage he pairs the term "faith" (*Glauben*) with the adjective "unshakable" (*unerschütterlich*) (FA 1.14: 150, 153).

In fact, Goethe explains the patriarchs' belief in a special providence as an almost inevitable reaction to the wide-open uncertainty of their lives. The faith of the patriarchs in a particular providence could only have emerged, according to Goethe, through a certain isolation of their circumstances that came with the division of human beings into different occupations. As others hunted or farmed, the patriarchs roamed the countryside as shepherds. While this nomadic occupation cultivated in them a sense of freedom and sublimity, the sheer vastness of their liberty made necessary the unshakable faith "that a god walked beside them, that he visited them, took an interest in them, and led and saved them" (*daß ein Gott ihnen zur Seite ziehe, daß er sie besuche, an ihnen Anteil nehme, sie führe und rette*) (CW 4: 110; FA 1.14: 150). Within this claim is a crucial idea for Goethe the self-identified wanderer: that the reflexive reaction to a wide-open freedom is the urge to believe there is still somehow a special meaning in one's fate.

The complementary relationship here between the experience of wide-open space and the belief in a special destiny is echoed throughout Goethe's Genesis narrative. An alternation between focus and dispersal forms the basic contrapuntal rhythm structuring the narrative. From the first, he characterizes the geographical setting of the events as "simple and intelligible" (*einfach und faßlich*) on the one hand and "diverse" (*mannigfaltig*) on the other, as suitable for both "migrations" (*Wanderungen*) and "settlements" (*Ansiedlungen*) (CW 4: 105; FA 1.14: 143). The first people are allotted a circumscribed little territory "a small, extremely pleasant space" (*ein kleiner höchst anmutiger Raum*)—presumably paradise (CW 4: 105; FA 1.14: 143). But just as man begins to develop his capacities in this ideal setting, he comes to face banishment as his destiny: "losing his peace in the pursuit of knowledge" (*seine Ruhe zu verlieren, indem er nach Erkenntnis strebte*) (CW 4: 106; FA 1.14: 143).[32]

One can recognize this alternating experience between disorientation and orientation most clearly where Goethe deviates from the biblical account. Having left paradise behind, humanity proliferates and deteriorates, leading the Elohim to bring a flood. But as the waters recede, the passengers on the ark seem to have returned to a familiar place—they glimpse "the familiar native soil" (*der bekannte vaterländische Boden*) (CW 4: 106; FA 1.14: 144). The original text lacks this sense of return and familiarity: the ark lands on a previously unmentioned location, "the mountains of Ararat" (Gen. 8:4).

Goethe also elaborates in pointed ways the Tower of Babel story. In the biblical text, the builders overreach themselves in a hubristic bid for glory "to make a name for ourselves" (Gen. 11:4); their punishment is linguistic confusion. But in Goethe's account, human beings build the tower to serve as a geographical point of orientation "that would point the way back home from a long distance" (*der ihnen aus weiter Ferne den Weg wieder zurück weisen sollte*) (*CW* 4: 106; FA 1.14: 144). In his version, the punishment has no linguistic dimension: it is simply confusion and dispersal: "The Elohim sowed confusion among them, construction halted, the people dispersed, and while the world became populated, it was no longer unified" (*Die Elohim verwirrten sie, der Bau unterblieb, die Menschen zerstreuten sich; die Welt war bevölkert aber entzweit*) (*CW* 4: 106; FA 1.14: 144).

Goethe also brings out a pattern of loss and recovery, wandering and rest in the ironic turn of events he recounts. In particular, he shows how, in the constitution of families that is so central to the narrative, just where one expects fulfillment and peace, things lean toward chaos. For example, after Sara has arranged for her maidservant Hagar to bear Abraham a son, she becomes pregnant herself and great conflict ensues. Abraham had so long awaited a child in fulfillment of God's promise and now, as an old man, he suddenly has two: "in his hundredth year [Abraham] finds himself the spouse of two women and the father of two sons; and simultaneously the peace of his house is shattered" (*[er] findet sich in seinem hundertsten als Gatte zweier Frauen, als Vater zweier Söhne, und in diesem Augenblick ist sein Hausfriede gestört*) (*CW* 4: 108; FA 1.14: 148). Hagar and Ishmael's exile also brings no peace, for now comes God's instruction to Abraham to sacrifice his son: "in such circumstances, domestic peace and earthly bliss might finally be expected! By no means. The powers above are still preparing the patriarch's hardest test of all" (*hier sollte man doch endlich eine häusliche Ruhe, ein irdisches Glück erwarten! Keineswegs. Die Himmlischen bereiten dem Erzvater noch die schwerste Prüfung*) (*CW* 4: 109; FA 1.14: 148). The same confounding forces seem to be at work in Jacob's family. He ends up unintentionally with two wives: the one whom he does not love produces children; the one whom he does love produces none; both draft their maidservants to bear Jacob further offspring: "and now the good patriarch is the most harassed man in the world: four wives, children from three of them, but none from the one he loves!" (*und nun ist der gute Erzvater der geplagteste Mann von der Welt. Vier Frauen, Kinder von dreien, und keins von der geliebten*) (*CW* 4: 112; FA 1.14: 154). And yet this entropy is always followed in turn by new and surprising forms of fulfillment: Ishmael becomes father of a great people; Isaac grows up to continue the line; Jacob's beloved wife Rachel at last conceives and gives birth to the great patriarch Joseph. What distinguishes these patriarchs in Goethe's account is their confidence in the promise that things will make sense: "they never doubt, or tire of waiting for, the fulfillment of His promises, however tardy" (*ohne zu zweifeln [ermüden sie nicht,] die späten Erfüllungen seiner Verheißungen abzuwarten*) (CW 4: 109; FA 1.14: 149).

The fundamental rhythm in Goethe's version of Genesis emerges at last perhaps as a hermeneutic dynamic, alternating between open-ended receptivity and the supposition of meaning. Goethe's notion of Old Testament faith then might be characterized as a kind of working interpretive assumption that sense can be made out of the confusion and dispersal. The conception of special providence, the faith that God is taking one's part, amounts to a reassertion of narrative order.

Goethe does not hesitate to suggest a danger inherent in this assertion. Indeed, a critical tone is unmistakable in parts of the discussion. The first passage in which he discusses the patriarch's conception of special providence serves as an introduction to the episode in which Abraham nearly sacrifices his beloved son. He returns to the same conceptual ground concerning natural and revealed religion, universal and special providence, just half a dozen paragraphs later in a discussion of Jacob. Jacob's brand of faith seems to justify any means to the fulfillment of the special destiny, including "tricks and cunning" (*Klugheit und List*) (CW 4: 111; FA 1.14: 152–53). What might have been an existential confidence in Abraham (or, in other contexts, Goethe's mother) becomes in Jacob, Goethe suggests, a reckless arrogance. In discussing Jacob, Goethe even hurls a gratuitous slur against modern Jews. Pointing out—in a manner that distorts the biblical text—Jacob's manipulations in appropriating the best of his father-in-law's flock,[33] Goethe declares him to be "truly worthy of becoming the progenitor of the people of Israel and a model for his descendants" (*der wahrhaft würdige Stammvater des Volkes Israel und ein Musterbild für seine Nachkommen*) (CW 4: 113; FA 1.14: 154).

Yet, as so often is the case with Goethe, an anti-Jewish comment, far from ruling out identification, points to a troubled form of it: throughout the autobiography, beginning with the favorable constellations he reports at the hour of his birth, Goethe suggests his own inclination to believe in a special providence. In his interpolated fairy tale, "Der neue Paris," the first-person narrator—whom Goethe's credulous playmates take to be a true depiction of their friend—identifies himself as "a favorite of the gods" (*ein Liebling der Götter*) (CW 4: 58; FA 1.14: 72). This phrase is echoed in book 4 where Abraham is "a man beloved by the gods" (*ein . . . [von] den Göttern geliebte[r] . . . Mann*) (CW 4: 107; FA 1.14: 145). As explored in the introduction, Goethe clearly identified with the patriarch Joseph, the gifted but misunderstood youth favored by destiny.

But of much further-reaching significance is the way that Goethe's experience of interpretation, as a reader of Genesis, reenacts the experience of the wandering patriarchs. Just as the wandering begins in Genesis with the loss of peace through the striving for knowledge, so are Goethe's investigations propelled by "questions and doubts" (*Fragen und Zweifel*) (FA 1.14: 143). And in book 8, he applies this biblical fate quite explicitly to himself: "the truth of that old saying, 'Increase of knowledge is increase of disquiet' had hit me with full force" (*die Wahrheit jenes alten Worts, Zuwachs an Kenntnis ist Zuwachs an Unruhe, hatte mich mit ganzer Gewalt getroffen*) (*CW* 4: 243–44; FA 1.14: 354). Just as this ancient swath of land provides a space for Abraham to move "to and fro," "back and forth" (*hin und her; hin und wider*) (*CW* 4: 106, 107; FA 1.14: 145), the biblical text offers a space in which Goethe can roam freely, indulging in "digressions" (*Abschweifungen*), and following his inclinations "to crisscross the Bible in all directions" (*die Bibel nach allen Seiten durchkreuzend*) (*CW* 4: 105; FA 1.14: 142).

Yet his rhetoric suggests that this text offered him not only a space for wandering but also a source of orientation. As already noted, he prefaces his recapitulation of Genesis with reference to providence at work in his own life: despite his scattered approach, nature had guided him along its own preordained path, from his efforts with Hebrew to his study of the Bible with its highly productive impact on his imagination (FA 1.14: 143). Near the end of his discussion, Goethe offers a justification for spending so many pages recounting Genesis. In describing here the impact of the Bible on his youthful imagination, he employs images of focus and calm to contrast with the confusion and distraction he otherwise experienced. In his distracted (*zerstreut*) life and fragmentary (*zerstückelt*) education, Genesis provided him with a calm focal point (*Punkt*) for his mind and feelings. When the world around him was wild and strange (*wild und wunderlich*), when his busy imagination threatened to become confused (*verwirren*), he could immerse himself (*versenken*) in the first books of the Pentateuch. In that great breadth, among the spread-out herding tribes (*unter den ausgebreiteten Hirtenstämmen*) he found at once both the greatest solitude (*Einsamkeit*) and the greatest companionship (*Gesellschaft*) (FA 1.14: 155). Thus in Goethe's description of the Hebrew Bible's impact on him as a reader, one can observe the same juxtaposition of wandering and rest, dispersal and focus that one finds in his description of the patriarchs.

In summary: as described in book 4, the text of Genesis offers Goethe a broadened descriptive universe. The patriarchs stand exposed in a wide-open world upon which the virtues and mores of the eighteenth century seem to have little bearing. Yet in his Genesis narrative, Goethe also stresses the counter-reflex that has great consequence for his thinking generally. In the face of too much unfiltered reality, one inevitably reasserts meaning. While this insistence can clearly tend to violent extremes, the undeterred, *unshaken* confidence of the patriarchs that there *is* some kind of sense to be made of their wandering lives makes them—like Goethe's own mother—into existential models for him. Ultimately he finds in Genesis a primal scene of interpretation that in turn lends focus and structure to his own ongoing task of self-interpretation. The "providence" in *Poetry and Truth* appears then, not as a truth inhering in events, a *Thing in itself*, but as a providence-effect, the outcome of an irrepressible human drive for meaning in the wilderness.

Goethe's Kabbalistic Myth of Creation

The fundamental hermeneutic pattern of focus and dispersal just identified in Goethe's reading of Genesis in book 4 has its correlate in the core rhythm of concentration and expansion in Goethe's creation myth in book 8. The myth represents another surfacing of the undercurrent of heterodoxy that runs through the book: he explains it as a youthful attempt to construct his own religion born from his own "spirit of contradiction" (*Geist des Widerspruchs*) and "taste for paradox" (*Lust zum Paradoxen*) (CW 4: 261; FA 1.14: 382). His intellectual sources he identifies as Neoplatonic, hermetic, mystical and, significantly, *kabbalistic*. Below I will argue for the distinct influence of Lurianic Kabbalah in Goethe's conception of contraction and expansion as the basic pulse of life—a conception that becomes critical to his literary semiotics as well to his scientific thinking. Other aspects of the myth that align with Lurianic Kabbalah and have great consequence for Goethe's self-conception as artist include the notions that the divine unfolds itself immanently in the world, that creation is an ongoing process in which human beings have a key role to play, and that evil is a necessary by-product of creation that precedes any human sin.[34]

Goethe's myth commences with a divinity that eternally produces, differentiates, and multiplies itself, that is, that emanates according to a Neoplatonic model. In an obvious allusion to the Christian trinity, he has his divinity produce at first two coequal entities, one of which is identified as the son. While this threefold godhead is set apart within a "closed circle of divinity," it is not omnipotent, for "even they themselves could not have produced another entity altogether equal to themselves" (*Hiermit war jedoch der Kreis der Gottheit geschlossen, und es wäre ihnen selbst nicht möglich gewesen, abermals ein ihnen völlig Gleiches hervorzubringen*) (CW 4: 262; FA 1.14: 382–83). As their drive to create continues, they produce a fourth entity, Lucifer, who contains an internal contradiction, for he is at once unconditioned through his divine origin and conditioned by the higher godhead. All creative power is now invested in Lucifer and all further being proceeds from him. Yet surrounded by his own glorious self-productions (the angels) Lucifer forgets his divine origin and in his ingratitude becomes ever more concentrated within himself. Goethe associates this concentration with the legendary fall of the angels as well as with the origin of matter. When this ever-darkening, thickening tendency of creation comes to threaten its very continuance, the godhead, which Goethe now calls the Elohim, intervenes to allow creation again to expand toward the divine. Goethe associates this moment with the emergence of light and the biblical moment of creation, where "God said, 'Let there be light'; and there was light" (Gen. 1:3). Now, at last, the human being appears as the creature that, like Lucifer, contains an internal contradiction and is given to contraction and ingratitude, but is also uniquely capable of restoring the original connection to the divine. Towards the end, Goethe inserts another Christian allusion: the deity appears in human form to provide joy and comfort. But this intervention carries little narrative or salvific weight in Goethe's account, for both redemption and evil are built into the very process of creation: "the whole creation is nothing and was nothing but a rebelling against and returning to the original source" (*die ganze Schöpfung [ist] nichts und [war] nichts, als ein Abfallen und Zurückkehren zum Ursprünglichen*) (*CW* 4: 261; FA 1.14: 384).

How can a distinctly Jewish kabbalistic component be distilled out of this brew of Christian, pagan, and various other eclectic ingredients? There are at least two challenges here: first, Goethe offers little direct information about his knowledge of Kabbalah; second, the sources he does mention elsewhere in his autobiography are Christian assimilations of Kabbalah. For example, earlier in book 8 he mentions having read Georg Welling's *Opus-Magus Cabbalisticum*, a heavily Christianized mishmash of kabbalistic and alchemical concepts. Finding the work "obscure and incomprehensible" (*dunkel und unverständlich*), he set out to investigate its sources and found his way to authors such as Paracelsus and Basilius Valentinus (*CW* 4: 256; FA 1.14: 373), still both Christian authors. Certainly much of the Kabbalah that filtered down to Goethe and his contemporaries was already mixed through with Christian mysticism as well as other intellectual currents, including hermeticism and alchemy. Thus commentators on the myth in book 8 have tended to view Goethe's influences as largely indistinguishable currents within the esoteric tradition in which the young Goethe immersed himself.[35]

Yet despite the Christian mystical reception of Kabbalah, important distinctions remained into the eighteenth century. A Latin defense of Kabbalah by the Christian author Johann Franciscus Buddeus, published in 1702, contrasted the "old" and "true" Kabbalah, based on the Zohar and appropriated by Christian gnostic thought, with the "new" and "false" Kabbalah of the sixteenth-century rabbi Isaac Luria (transmitted into European letters via the author Abraham Herrera).[36] As I will show below, Lurianic Kabbalah had become of interest to theosophic and heterodox eighteenth-century Christian authors, but was still much more closely identified with its Jewish roots and was certainly less filtered through Christian conceptions.[37] Therefore I will challenge the reigning assumption that the term "kabbalistic" in Goethe's lexicon has no meaningful and specifically Jewish content. I will consider how Goethe likely came into contact with Lurianic Kabbalah, what he might have known about it, and how it might have contributed to the vision of divine and human creation he articulates in book 8.

Excursus: The Reception of Lurianic Kabbalah

Isaac Luria lived from 1534 to 1572, mostly in Palestine. His thought was largely disseminated by his student Hayyim Vital (1543–1620) and later disciples, including Abraham Cohen Herrera (c. 1570–1635). Lurianic, as well as other kabbalistic treatises, were introduced to a Christian readership in Latin translation in the work *Kabbala Denudata* by Christian Knorr von Rosenroth (published in two volumes in 1677 and 1684). As the scholarship of Alison Coudert has explored, Lurianic ideas culled from the *Kabbala Denudata* were highly influential for an important group of intellectuals associated with Knorr at the Court of Sulzbach including Francis Mercury van Helmont, Anne Conway, Henry More, and even Gottfried Wilhelm Leibniz. Among the Lurianic treatises included in the *Kabbala Denudata*, the most far-reaching impact was had by Herrera's work *Porta Coelorum* (*Gates of Heaven*). (Knorr's version of this treatise was his own condensed Latin translation of a Hebrew translation of Herrera's Spanish original.) There is no direct evidence that Goethe read the *Kabbala Denudata*, but given how widely the work was cited in discussions of Kabbalah in Goethe's era—Herder writes about it, for example (*SW* 6: 486)—and given Goethe's exploration of esoteric source texts in his youth, it seems fair to imagine he would have known something of it.

Lurianic ideas also entered the Pietist circles with which Goethe was associated in Frankfurt, via the Swabian theologian Friedrich Christoph Oetinger (1702–1782). Oetinger became familiar with Kabbalah not only through Knorr's Latin translation, but also through Hebrew sources and through direct contact with rabbis, especially Rabbi Hecht in Frankfurt.[38] Both Goethe's father and Goethe's spiritual mentor Susanne von Klettenberg owned books by Oetinger.[39] While Oetinger transformed Lurianic Kabbalah for Christian purposes, he took seriously its Jewish provenance.

Goethe's knowledge of Lurianic Kabbalah was also informed by more deliberately scholarly accounts. The most important of these for Goethe would have been the vast histories of philosophy by the early eighteenth-century writer Johannes Jacob Brucker. Goethe claims to have read Brucker diligently in his youth (FA 1.24: 442). Later his own library contained a condensed version of Brucker's magnum opus in Latin called the *Historia Critica Philosophiae* (FA 1.24: 1072). In *Poetry and Truth*, Goethe also mentions discussions of a German version of Brucker's work in question-and-answer format nicknamed "Little Brucker" ("Der kleine Brucker") (FA 1.14: 243). This work devotes most of a volume to "Jewish philosophy," including Kabbalah. Another source on Kabbalah for Goethe would have been Johann Gottlieb Buhle's *History of Modern Philosophy* (*Geschichte der neuern Philosophie*).[40] Published in 1800 and checked out from the ducal library by Goethe in 1809, this work obviously could not have influenced him in his youth but certainly could have influenced his *representation* of his youth in his autobiography.[41] One can perhaps also assume that Goethe shared in a general received wisdom concerning Kabbalah among the educated elite. That Lurianic Kabbalah was by no means unknown within educated circles is indicated by a focus on Luria in a 1780 encyclopedia article on "Kabbalists" ("Cabbalisten").[42]

Goethe's interest in Kabbalah might also have been sparked by a prominent argument concerning its philosophical reception: the claim that kabbalistic ideas underlie Spinoza's philosophy. This thesis was advanced in the late seventeenth century in a book by Johann Georg Wachter: *Spinozism in Judaism*.[43] Wachter notes similarities specifically between the first part of Spinoza's *Ethics* and the opening chapters of Herrera's Lurianic treatise "Porta Coelorum." According to Wachter, both Spinoza and Kabbalah share a pantheistic vision of God as identical with nature, and individual things as but modifications of God.[44] References to this thesis are nearly ubiquitous in Goethe's period: the question of Spinoza's relationship to Kabbalah comes up in Mendelssohn's *Morning Hours*, Friedrich Heinrich Jacobi's *Letters Concerning the Doctrine of Spinoza in Letters to Herr Moses Mendelssohn*, in Solomon Maimon's *Life History*, in the eighteenth-century histories of philosophy by Brucker and Tiedemann, and even in the 1780 encyclopedia article.[45] In short, one can conclude that Goethe would have been highly aware of an alleged genealogy between Kabbalah and Spinoza, and one can assume that this association would also have provided strong impetus for him to attain some grasp of Kabbalah.

A further question arises whether Goethe, like Oetinger, the Pietist theologian, would have had direct exposure to Lurianic Kabbalah through Jewish acquaintances in Frankfurt. In *Poetry and Truth*, Goethe represents himself as having had substantial contact with the Frankfurt ghetto in his youth. He claims to have repeatedly attended the synagogue, observed a circumcision, a wedding, and a celebration of Sukkot, and writes, "I was well received everywhere, well entertained and invited to return, for influential persons either took me there or recommended me" (*Überall war ich wohl aufgenommen, gut bewirtet, und zur Wiederkehr eingeladen: denn es waren Personen von Einfluß, die mich entweder hinführten oder empfahlen*) (CW 4: 120; FA 1.14: 166). Of course one never knows whether to take Goethe at his word in his autobiography; and at least one historian has suggested that Goethe's description of the ghetto may have been gleaned more from published accounts than his own experiences.[46] But assuming Goethe did have substantial, repeated contacts with the ghetto in his adolescence, perhaps he might have heard about or encountered the charismatic young ghetto prodigy Nathan Adler, a teacher and practitioner of Lurianic Kabbalah, just eight years older than himself. Adler, regarded as a deeply learned and holy man, founded his own yeshiva as a young man. Later on in the early 1770s, his heterodox teachings and practices excited great controversy and, by the end of that decade, they were officially banned by the Jewish authorities.[47] While it may be impossible to know whether Goethe was aware of the religious foment surrounding Lurianic Kabbalah in the Frankfurt Jewish community, such knowledge, it seems, cannot be strictly ruled out.

What would Goethe have gathered about Lurianic cosmology through these various sources? Certainly Goethe would have known—through

Brucker, Buhle, and their source text Herrera—that the kabbalistic conception of creation is a variation on the Neoplatonic notion of emanation, the idea that God creates eternally out of his own divine substance. Brucker refers to this immanent unfolding of the divine in creation as "effusion" (*Ausfluß*). In his translation of Herrera, Knorr employs the verb *extendo*.[48] That this process produces ten emanations or attributes of God called the Sephiroth is also well-rehearsed material within the Christian reception of Kabbalah. But while emanation is a theory of creation that conforms to the classical principle that "nothing comes from nothing," Lurianic Kabbalah nonetheless attempts to square this account with the diametrically opposed biblical account of a discrete creation event that indeed occurs "out of nothing."

Lurianic Kabbalah combines Neoplatonic emanation with "ex nihilo" creation through a dynamic called "Zimzum," which Gershom Scholem pronounces "one of the most amazing and far-reaching conceptions ever put forward in the whole history of Kabbalism."[49] Zimzum is the act of divine self-limitation that serves as the precondition for the Genesis creation moment. In the beginning, so the account goes, divine light was infinite and all pervading, but because there was no void, there could be no space for creation. Thus the light contracted away from a middle point in order to form a sphere in which creation could occur. According to Herrera's treatise, Luria wrote

> that that infinite divinity extends to all imaginable and possible places and fills them with the light of its countenance: since however it wanted to reveal itself and to bring forth essences, it withdrew itself from itself into itself, as if it contracted and pressed together, and it left behind a certain place within those infinite spaces.[50]

In this passage we see the juxtaposition of the contrary but complementary motions of contraction (*contrahere*) and expansion or extension (*extendere*): the divine originally *extends* everywhere but chooses to *contract* in order to allow a domain of creation. At last, the divine expands again: a ray of divine light reenters the void and so begins the process of divine self-revelation through creation. Herein lies the "cabbalistic doctrine of the expanded and contracted God" (*Cabbalistische Lehre de Deo expanso & contracto*), a phrase Goethe could have come across in "Little Brucker."[51] The notion of the contracting God in Kabbalah was indeed common enough currency by the late eighteenth century that in Jacobi's famous account of his conversations with Lessing on Spinoza, Lessing makes a joke about it.[52]

The larger significance of this doctrine would not have been lost on Goethe. Buhle discusses it specifically within the context of the traditional problem of evil. According to Buhle, emanation theory in general grapples with the familiar paradox that God represents absolute goodness and perfection and yet is the author of the material world from which evil springs.[53] While earlier (Neoplatonic) emanation theory poses the expanding light of creation against a realm of darkness at the outer limit of divine power, kabbalistic thought begins with unconditioned, omnipresent light. Instead of being limited by something outside of itself, the divine limits itself. As Buhle describes it, "God, the infinite, most perfect being, decided to reveal itself in finitude and imperfection"[54] Thus the kabbalistic account asserts the original omnipotence of the divine and in this regard, comes closer to the Christian view.

But only to a point, for the explanation of the root of evil still stands in marked contrast to the traditional Christian doctrine. Again, Augustine's conception of original sin attributes evil entirely to the human sinfulness inherited from Adam's first disobedience. The corollary to God's perfect goodness and power is, in this view, the perfect goodness of creation. By comparison, the Lurianic conception of creation is more ambivalent, predicated on divine absence and self-limitation. While there is actually a secondary event in Lurianic Kabbalah called the breaking of the vessels (Shevirat Ha-Kelim) that more explicitly marks the catastrophic origin of evil, Scholem argues, "In the final resort . . . the root of all evil is already latent in the act of *Tsimtsum*."[55] While creation is affirmed for its ultimate revelation of the glory and majesty of the divine, that revelation occurs through a process rather than as a complete state of perfection from the start. Goethe rejects the doctrine of original sin explicitly in his autobiography (FA 14: 691): his creation myth in book 8 suggests an alternative view of the nature of evil that bears important affinities with the Lurianic account.

Goethe's Kabbalistic Myth (Reprise)

Thus we return to Goethe's myth of creation in book 8 to seek traces of these conceptions. As noted, he clearly works with an emanative model of creation that Kabbalah shares with Neoplatonism where the world emerges as successive self-productions from an eternal divine source. On a superficial level, the progress of these emanations in Goethe's narrative seems to play with number symbolism that he would have found in Brucker's discussion of Kabbalah. His obvious allusion to the first three emanations as the Christian Trinity in fact echoes the tradition in Christian Kabbalah, as Brucker dismissively reports, that interprets the first three sephiroth in this manner.[56] The identification of Lucifer with the fourth stage of emanation appears to play with another level of Lurianic cosmology—not with the sephiroth or divine attributes—but with the "worlds" or planes of reality. From Brucker, Goethe would have learned that the fourth world or Asiah is the "region of evil spirits."[57] There the light becomes dense and concentrated. Brucker writes, "Because the Asiahtic world lies furthest from the original light of the Godhead, it is also the darkest and the light is most pressed together and therefore it is solid [*cörperlich*]."[58] Similarly, in Goethe's account, Lucifer concentrates into himself and then produces the material world, all that is "heavy, firm and opaque" (*schwer, fest und finster*) (*CW* 4: 262; FA 1.14: 383).

But by far the most significant conception traceable to Luria is the notion of contraction and expansion as the fundamental dynamic of creation. Just as creation occurs in the Lurianic narrative when expansion follows upon the original contraction, so creation occurs in Goethe's myth when Lucifer's concentration within himself is overcome to allow for extension again. In Goethe's account, expansion and contraction stand quite explicitly in complementary relation to each other. Lucifer's actions are "unilateral" (*einseitig*); once the Elohim introduce the possibility of countermotion, "the real pulse of life was restored again" (*der eigentliche Puls des Lebens war wiederhergestellt*) (*CW* 4: 262; FA 1.14: 383, 384). Admittedly Goethe treats the Lurianic paradigm in a flexible way: while with Luria, the emanative creation process occurs only *after* the original contraction, with Goethe, a whole cosmic drama of emanation unfolds *before* Lucifer's contraction and the subsequent biblical creation moment.

In any event, by associating contraction with Lucifer in his narrative, Goethe underscores the complex view of evil latent in Zimzum. Lucifer's evil, such as it is—"all the mischief, if we may call it that" (*das ganze Unheil, wenn wir es so nennen dürfen*) (*CW* 4: 262; FA 1.14: 383)—emerges as part and parcel of the creation process. Indeed, the whole creative power for the continuing process of creation becomes transferred to Lucifer (FA 1.14: 383). Human beings, once they enter the story, reproduce Lucifer's one-sidedness: "Before long, he was also playing Lucifer's role entirely" (*Es währte nicht lange, so spielte [der Mensch] auch völlig die Rolle des Lucifer*) (*CW* 4: 263; FA 1.14: 384). In stark contrast to Augustine's conception of original sin, human beings, while certainly implicated in evil, are not its origin in the universe.

Moreover, humanity implicitly shares Lucifer's creative powers and has thereby a decidedly non-Augustinian role to play in Goethe's narrative. In a later passage where he rejects the doctrine of original sin, Goethe's chief complaint is the passive stance attributed to humanity in relationship to the divine: "the human being must absolutely renounce his own powers and rely completely on the workings of grace" (*der Mensch [habe] auf seine eignen Kräfte durchaus Verzicht zu tun, und alles von der Gnade und ihrer Einwirkung zu erwarten*) (*CW* 4: 466; FA 1.14: 690–91). Instead, Goethe identifies with Pelagianism, the resurgent heretical belief "in the ability of man to determine his own destiny as well as that of the world's."[59] His own myth, then, assigns an active, restorative role to humankind, as the "being qualified to restore the original connection with the deity" (*Wesen, welches die ursprüngliche Verbindung mit der Gottheit wiederherzustellen geschickt wäre*) (*CW* 4: 263; FA 1.14: 384).

Restoration or Tikkun is also a core idea of Lurianic Kabbalah.[60] Scholem defines it as "striving for the perfection of the world."[61] In "Little Brucker"

Goethe would have read: "Finally the soul raises itself up fully to the unified Being from which it comes and on which it depends and becomes in this way similar to its first cause, uniting itself with it, as the universal beginning and end of all things."[62] In this description, the soul brings *itself* into a restorative relationship with the first cause of creation. The idea is essentially Pelagian that human beings help redeem the world and indeed complete the work of creation.

What then does Lurianic Kabbalah contribute to Goethe's vision of creation in book 8? Certainly it suggests a much more active role for humanity in remaking the world than did the Lutheran orthodoxy of Goethe's age. Furthermore, Zimzum seems to offer Goethe, by analogy with divine creation, a sophisticated model for understanding his own artistic creation. He links himself both to Lucifer, the seat of creative power, and humanity in general through the word "contradiction." After acknowledging the origin of the myth in his own "spirit of contradiction" (*Geist des Widerspruchs*), he identifies "contradiction" as the defining characteristic of both Lucifer and human beings (*CW* 4: 261–63; FA 1.14: 382–84). The creative process, he suggests, is morally ambivalent and contradictory. It contains in its very structure the necessity of evil, isolation, and reification, and yet it is progressive, directed toward an ultimate restoration of the good. In its peculiar mix of pessimism and optimism, Lurianic Kabbalah presents Goethe with a complex, modern view of human destiny and artistic vocation.

Lurianic Kabbalah also seems a possible source for the recurring motif of contraction and expansion elsewhere in Goethe's thinking. Certainly this defining figure in Goethe's youthful cosmic myth plays a role in his scientific apprehension of the world.[63] Expansion and contraction (*Ausdehnen und Zusammenziehen*) is famously the pattern he discovers in his "Metamorphosis of Plants" ("Versuch die Metamorphose der Pflanzen zu erklären") from seed to the stem leaf, calyx to flower, and on back to seed again (FA 1.24: 132–33). Goethe writes in a similar vein in his *Farbenlehre*, "Inhalation assumes exhalation and vice versa; likewise every systole, its diastole. It is the eternal formula of life that expresses itself here" (*So setzt das Einatmen schon das Ausatmen voraus und umgekehrt; so jede Systole ihre Diastole. Es ist die ewige Formel des Lebens, die sich auch hier äußert*) (FA 1.23.1: 41). For Goethe, as this book will continue to explore, contraction and expansion also constitute the rhythm of basic forms of human cognition like interpretation and signification.

Ahasverus

After Kabbalah, the next key Jewish source in Goethe's autobiographical itinerary is the philosophy of Spinoza: but his epic of the Wandering Jew serves as a curious link between these two intellectual stations. Goethe sketches out his *plan* for an epic in book 15 (while the epic itself survives only as an inchoate fragment with little obvious connection to the sketch). Goethe's presentation of the project both reveals his identification with the heterodox wanderer, and at the same time employs negative Jewish typologies to be overcome. His brief treatment of the legend thus encapsulates his broader pattern of appropriation and transfiguration of all things Jewish.

The immediate context in book 15 for Goethe's presentation of his plans for the Wandering Jew is his own heretical inclinations. He portrays himself as "a foreigner, a stranger, even a heathen" (*einen Auswärtigen, Fremden, sogar als einen Heiden*) (CW 4: 464; FA 1.14: 689) in his exchanges with his deeply Christian friend Susanne von Klettenberg and gradually distances himself ever more from the tenets of the faith. Eventually he realizes that neither von Klettenberg nor other members of her Pietist community perceive him as a Christian because of his emergent Pelagianism. As we have just seen, Goethe's Pelagianism sets him apart from his forbearer in the autobiographical genre, Augustine, and meanwhile brings him closer to Jewish Kabbalah. Brucker, his important source on the history of philosophy, characterizes Jewish teachings on free will as essentially Pelagian.[64] The young Goethe undertakes his own study of church history to observe the ebb and flow of Pelagian ideas through the centuries. The Wandering Jew epic is in some sense the (unfinished) product of this exploration, his attempt to lend his Pelagian religious investigations a "poetic form" (*dichterische Form*) (CW 4: 466; FA 1.14: 692).

In his description, the parallels are indeed clear between his own rebellion and the religious recalcitrance of his character Ahasverus. Both he and Ahasverus reject Christianity and yet feel a fondness for Christ: Goethe attributes this affection (*Neigung*) once to himself and twice to his fictional character (FA 1.14: 692, 694). He intended the epic as a vehicle for depicting "the principle events of religious and church history" (*die hervorstehenden Punkte der Religions- und Kirchengeschichte*) (CW 4: 466–67; FA 1.14: 692). In this way, his own historical explorations were to be reflected in Ahasverus's pilgrimage through the centuries.

But Goethe trades in negative Jewish typologies in his portrayal of Ahasverus, which simultaneously work to establish his narrative distance from the figure. Ahasverus is described as dwelling only in concrete meanings, incapable of grasping Christ's higher import (FA 1.14: 692). In characterizing Ahasverus's obtuseness, Goethe employs a prominent New Testament metaphor: the failure to bear spiritual fruit. Christ's efforts "never bore fruit in the coarse man" (*[wollte] bei dem derben Manne nicht fruchten*) (FA 1.14: 693). This sentence clearly plays on the Parable of the Sower in the three synoptic Gospels where Jesus describes the word, including his own parables, as seeds sown on different kinds of soil, some of which never bear fruit (Matt. 13:3–23; Mark 4:3–20; Luke 8:4–15). As we will see in the next chapter, Goethe elsewhere employs this biblical metaphor to characterize Judaism as a fruitless trunk. The characterization of Ahasverus as incapable of grasping symbolic meaning partakes generally of the New Testament opposition between a Jewish focus on the flesh and on the letter of the law on the one hand, and the Christian fruits of the spirit such as love and kindness on the other (see for example Gal. 5:22). In Goethe's portrayal, then, Ahasverus feels no sympathy for Christ's suffering. Rather, his inappropriate sense of justice (*unzeitige Gerechtigkeit*) leads him to pile on reproach as Christ makes his way to his crucifixion (FA 1.14: 693).

Goethe's account thus opens a gap between his clear identification with Ahasverus on the one hand, and his equally clear criticism of him through traditional Christian-Jewish typologies on the other. The actual fragment Goethe produced, "First Scrap of the Wandering Jew" ("Des ewigen Juden erster Fetzen"), far from mediating this gap, seems another species altogether. Its object appears to be more Christianity than Judaism—Ahasverus is described as a member of an ancient Jewish sect, "half Essene" (*halb Essener*) but also as a Christian sectarian, "half Methodist, / Herrnhuter, more Separatist" (*halb Methodist, / Herrnhuter mehr Separatist*) (FA 1.8: 637). Most of the extant lines are devoted to a satirical depiction of Jesus's return to earth, leaving the reader to wonder whether the label Wandering Jew in the title might as well apply to Christ. But regardless of what Goethe actually wrote or intended in the 1770s, we are concerned with the internal logic of his memoir written almost forty years later.[65] The gap in this brief sketch between identification and critical distance encapsulates a pattern: Goethe's largely sympathetic reception of Judaism in his autobiography almost invariably includes an impulse to transform and overcome his source. The original Christian legend of the Wandering Jew is the narrative of Christian supersession par excellence and therefore provides a provocative narrative vehicle for Goethe's secularized concerns. I argue in chapter 3 that Goethe's *Wilhelm Meisters Wanderjahre* can be read as a working out of this complex dynamic of identification with, and rejection of, the figure of the Wandering Jew.

Encounters with Spinoza

In *Poetry and Truth*, Goethe reveals little about the further adventures of the Wandering Jew in his peregrinations through history, except that Ahasverus would encounter the philosopher Spinoza (FA 1.14: 731). What would have been the point of this meeting? Some critics speculate that Spinoza's role would have been to represent a freethinker capable of releasing the Wandering Jew from his bondage to religion generally.[66] And yet as with the figure of the Wandering Jew, critics tend to overlook or understate the significance of a specifically Jewish connection in Goethe's thinking.[67] Although Spinoza was of course an apostate, Goethe nevertheless acknowledges the importance of his Jewish background, characterizing him as a product of both mathematic and rabbinic culture (FA 1.14: 731). My brief discussion here will focus on the thematic threads linking Goethe's Spinoza discussion with other representations of Judaism in the work. I will show the continuities between Spinoza's philosophy, Kabbalah, and the Hebrew Bible as sources for Goethe on the question of providence and evil as well as for a process conception of God, nature, and human activity.[68]

Goethe's description of his response to Spinoza's *Ethics* in book 14 recalls quite strikingly his subjective experience of the Hebrew Bible in book 4. In both cases, he describes in emphatic terms the decisive impact the source had on the further course of his development after he had previously cast about vainly and haphazardly (FA 1.14: 143,155, 681). Both Spinoza and the Genesis patriarchs are associated in his accounts with an open, free perspective: Goethe finds "breadth and freedom" (*Breite und Freiheit*) in the attitude of the patriarchs (*CW* 4: 110; FA 1.14: 150) and in Spinoza "a broad, free view over the physical and moral world" (*eine große und freie Aussicht über die sinnliche und sittliche Welt*) (*CW* 4: 459; FA 1.14: 681).[69] But in both he experiences not just a sense of expanse but also a counteracting focus or delimitation: his distracted life finds a point of focus in Genesis; the agitated striving of his poetic mind finds its counterpart in the soothing calmness of Spinoza's mathematical method (FA 1.14: 155, 681). Indeed, in his response to these two sources, imagery of limitation (or contraction) and breadth (or expansion) seem to converge: in Genesis he experiences simultaneously the greatest solitude and greatest companionship (FA 1.14: 155); in Spinoza he finds himself "bound" (*fesseln*) by the "boundless" (*grenzenlos*) selflessness of the philosophy (FA 1.14: 681). A kinship emerges between Genesis and Spinoza, then, through the terms of Goethe's subjective response to them.

In book 16, Goethe explores the substance of Spinoza's impact, considering first the issue of resignation or renunciation, which bears, in turn, on the broader question of providence in the autobiography. Resignation, as Goethe uses the term, is an individual attitude one adopts in the face of disappointment and suffering, presumably while retaining some broader sense of purpose or necessity. It thus can entail a conception of providential design, in recognition of which individual goals or plans are relinquished. Goethe lays out three forms of renunciation—one associated with his own Christian culture, one apparently associated with the Jewish scriptures, and one associated with Spinoza.

Goethe begins with an indictment of the overwhelming societal and cultural pressure to renounce (*entsagen*) (FA 1.14: 729). Renunciation, he says, involves the relinquishing of opportunities for personal development, of external needs and hard-won gains until, bit by bit, one abandons one's personality altogether (FA 1.14: 729). Goethe characterizes this spirit of submission with a New Testament allusion: "the bitterer the cup, the sweeter the expression one is supposed to assume, so that the tranquil spectator may not be offended by any grimace" (*vielmehr soll man, je bittrer der Kelch ist, eine desto süßere Miene machen, damit ja der gelassene Zuschauer nicht durch irgend eine Grimasse beleidigt werde*) (*CW* 5: 523; FA 1.14: 729–30). Clearly this line refers to Christ's characterization—in all four Gospels—of his self-sacrifice on the cross as a cup (*Kelch*), which he wishes he could avoid but will drink in accordance with his Father's will (see Matt. 26:39; Mark 14:36; Luke 22:42; John 18:11).[70] Who then is Goethe's "tranquil spectator," whom one dare not offend by any grimace, other than the Christian God? Thus buried in this single line is a nearly sarcastic rejection of eternal providence guaranteed by a personal God.

But Goethe continues with a further possibility—a merely partial renunciation followed by an ever-renewed pursuit. Human beings, he argues, are invested by nature with the resilience and energy to renounce one desired object, only to replace it in the next moment with another desire (FA 1. 14: 730). This resilience can recall Goethe's portrayal of the Genesis nomads in book 4 as persisting through adversity, confident in the covenantal promise, as they await new forms of fulfillment. Yet Goethe points out that this sequence of ever new pursuits can lead us at last to the conclusion that "all is vanity" (*alles [sei] eitel*) (*CW* 5: 523; FA 1.14: 730). This claim too has a strong biblical resonance. For the book Ecclesiastes, attributed to King Solomon, begins with the proclamation "All is futile" (Eccl. 1.2) and then offers a long catalog of passions and pursuits that have led the speaker to this conclusion (Eccl. 2). Ecclesiastes also appears to deny eternal providence—"The only future is nothingness!" (Eccl. 11:8). I argue in chapter 4 that Goethe constructs the figure Faust very much by analogy with King Solomon, and indeed this passage seems an apt description of Faust's sequence of partial renunciations and assumption of futility. Yet in this passage, Goethe indicts the Solomonic declaration of the vanity of all things as "false" (*falsch*) and "blasphemous" (*gotteslästerlich*) (*CW* 5: 523; FA 1.14: 730) and turns to a more radical form of renunciation he finds in Spinoza.

Total resignation is achieved, according to Goethe, by determining eternal, necessary laws and by forming incontrovertible concepts (FA 1.14: 730). Goethe has in mind Spinoza's conception of an impersonal God identical with nature, to whom neither intellect, nor will, nor moral categories, can be attributed. Spinoza's system obviously has no place for any traditional understanding of providence as a dispensation attending to the fate, moral good, or salvation of individuals.[71] Personal providence is also ruled out by the non-reciprocity of the divine in Spinoza's vision, which Goethe sums up in his book 14 discussion: "He who loves God rightly must not require God to love him in return" (*Wer Gott recht liebt, muß nicht verlangen, daß Gott ihn wieder liebe*) (*CW* 4: 459; FA 1.14: 681). In his eschewal of all personal, moral providence, Spinoza is the most radical of Goethe's existential journeyers. In Goethe's view of the patriarchs we identified a hermeneutic "providence effect," a working assumption that there is a meaning or purpose to one's sojourn in the wilderness. Spinoza renounces all illusions about the special meaning of his own, or any individual, existence. This extreme intellectual move, which few can sustain, makes Spinoza into a kind of devil in the mind of others, according to Goethe: "But because there is really something superhuman about this, such persons are generally considered monsters, without respect for God or the world, and they are imagined as having all manners of horns and claws" (*Weil aber hierin wirklich etwas Übermenschliches liegt, so werden solche Personen gewöhnlich für Unmenschen gehalten, für Gott- und Weltlose; ja man weiß nicht was man ihnen alles für Hörner und Klauen andichten soll*) (CW 5: 523; FA 1.14: 730). Ultimately Spinoza seems to inhabit the outer intellectual boundary of Goethe's autobiography, representing a courageous intellectual position to which Goethe himself does not consistently adhere.[72]

As Goethe continues, he promises to reveal the most important ideas he took from Spinoza, which would have come through in the planned episode in the Wandering Jew epic, had he written it. For Goethe the crux of Spinoza's philosophy was its assertion of the continuity of all nature, extending even to the human realm. Goethe applies this insight to his own artistic talent, concluding that his poetic talent is, like all things, an involuntary activity of nature, subject to natural laws: "I had gotten to the point of viewing my indwelling poetic talent altogether as nature, especially since I had been directed to look upon external nature as its subject matter" (*Ich war dazu gelangt das mir inwohnende dichterische Talent ganz als Natur zu betrachten, um so mehr als ich darauf gewiesen war, die äußere Natur als den Gegenstand desselben anzusehen*) (CW 5: 525; FA 1.14: 732). Spinoza's key contribution to Goethe's conception of the artist resides, then, in this reflexive structure: through the artist, nature takes nature as its subject matter, that is, nature comes to know itself. Perhaps Goethe takes inspiration here from the reflexive structure found in Spinoza's "intellectual love of God":

> The mind's intellectual love toward God is the love of God wherewith God loves himself not insofar as he is infinite, but insofar as he can be explicated through the essence of the human mind considered under a form of eternity. That is, the mind's intellectual love toward God is part of the infinite love wherewith God loves himself.[73]

Since in this conception human beings are forms of God-or-nature, God-or-nature encounters itself through either the highest forms of rational human understanding (Spinoza) or through poetry (Goethe).

It is not hard to see in this reflexive relationship an echo of kabbalistic elements in Goethe's creation myth in book 8. There creation emanates eternally from a divine source and essentially amounts to one substance. The human being comes onto the scene uniquely "qualified to restore the original connection with the deity" (CW 4: 263). Lurianic Kabbalah grants this special role to humanity in completing the work of creation, a task called "tikkun" or restoration. As also already noted, Goethe would have been highly aware of the charge that Spinoza got his ideas from Kabbalah because of the broad influence of the 1699 polemic by Johann Georg Wachter, *Spinozism in Judaism*.[74] Thus Kabbalah and Spinoza seem to constitute part of a genealogy in Goethe's thinking, both contributing to his view of his artistic enterprise as part of an unfolding natural (or divine) process. Meanwhile, his encounter with Genesis serves as an earlier precedent for the impact of Spinoza; and his plan for the Wandering Jew provides a curious, oblique link in the chain of Jewish-identified inspirations.

The Primal Fall

But Goethe does not offer Spinoza—nor any other intellectual or personal encounter—as a decisive destination in his autobiography. Lacking an end point, we conclude this chapter by returning to the work's mythically resonant opening. We have discussed the cosmological import of the family home, its controlling patriarch, and its unsettling renovations. We turn now to consider the paradigmatic "fall" in the life of the young Goethe, a wanton, primal act of destruction, which corresponds to the gratuitous theft of pears in Augustine and the unjust accusation of destruction in Rousseau. I argue that Goethe constructs a lighthearted version of the "fall" according to the Lurianic kabbalistic narrative—the breaking of the vessels. Although clearly intended playfully, this episode illuminates again the unavoidability of destruction and deviation in the ongoing process of creation.

The breaking of the vessels (Shevirat Ha-Kelim) figures less prominently in the Christian reception of Kabbalah than does the divine contraction and expansion (Zimzum); still Goethe could have known about it through a variety of sources.[75] The event occurs when the divine light, after its original withdrawal to form a space of creation in the Zimzum, now reenters that space of creation into vessels formed by the Sephiroth or divine emanations. The lower Sephiroth are too weak to hold the light so they are shattered. According to Herrera's Lurianic treatise, in the breaking of the vessels lies not only the secret of the fall but also a revelation of divine glory and majesty.[76] According to Gershom Scholem, the breaking of the bowls is at once "the decisive turning point in the cosmological process" and "the cause of that inner deficiency which is inherent in everything that exists and which persists as long as the damage is not mended."[77] For through the shattering, sparks are sent out into the world that set in motion the process of Tikkun, the restitution and reintegration that is the very purpose of creation. This cosmic process, inaugurated by the introduction of evil, eventually results in greater actuality and evolution of the original divine forms.[78]

We see a possible allusion to this event in Goethe's first account of any childhood deed.[79] Just as Augustine detects an inherited capacity for sinfulness even in his infancy, Goethe locates in his earliest childhood a joyful penchant for destruction and transgression. He sets the scene by describing the "Geräms," the wooden latticework frame or bird cage that jutted out into the street from the family house. From this vantage point, little Wolfgang could have direct contact with life outside, including with the von Ochsenstein brothers who live across the street. While sitting there one fine afternoon playing with his miniature toy pots and bowls, he discovers a new use for the ceramics:

> Tiring of this I threw one out into the street and was pleased that it broke so merrily into pieces. The von Ochsensteins, who saw I was so delighted by this that I clapped my hands for joy, shouted "More!" Without hesitation I immediately hurled a pot, and then, to their continued shouts of "More!" eventually *all* my little bowls, saucepans, and mugs, onto the pavement. My neighbors kept on showing their approval, and I was more than happy to please them. But my supply was exhausted, and yet they went on shouting, "Still more!" So I ran straight into the kitchen and fetched some earthenware dishes, which of course made an even merrier spectacle as they broke; and I ran back and forth taking one dish after the other from the crockery shelf, where I could reach them in succession. And because those men would not be satisfied, all the tableware I could drag out was smashed to pieces in the same way. It was only later that someone came to hinder and restrain me. The damage was done, but in exchange for all that broken crockery there was at least a funny story, especially for the mischievous instigators, who delighted in it to the end of their days. (*CW* 4: 24)

> Da weiter nichts dabei herauskommen wollte, warf ich ein Geschirr auf die Straße und freute mich, daß es so lustig zerbrach. Die von Ochsenstein, welche sahen, wie ich mich daran ergetzte, daß ich so gar fröhlich in die Händchen patschte, riefen: Noch mehr! Ich säumte nicht, sogleich einen Topf und auf immer fortwährendes Rufen: Noch mehr! nach und nach sämtliche Schüsselchen, Tiegelchen, Kännchen gegen das Pflaster zu schleudern. Meine Nachbarn fuhren fort, ihren Beifall zu bezeigen und ich war höchlich froh ihnen Vergnügen zu machen. Mein Vorrat aber war aufgezehrt, und sie riefen immer: Noch mehr! Ich eilte daher stracks in die Küche und holte die irdenen Teller, welche nun freilich im Zerbrechen noch ein lustigeres Schauspiel gaben; und so lief ich hin und wieder, brachte einen Teller nach dem anderen, wie ich sie auf dem Topfbrett der Reihe nach erreichen konnte, und weil sich jene gar nicht zufrieden gaben, so stürzte ich alles, was ich von Geschirr erschleppen konnte, in gleiches Verderben. Nur später erschien Jemand zu hindern und zu

> wehren. Das Unglück war geschehen, und man hatte für so viel zerbrochene Töpferware wenigstens eine lustige Geschichte, an der sich besonders die schalkischen Urheber bis an ihr Lebensende ergetzten. (FA 1.14: 16–17)

The original German plays with a language of fall or perdition (*so stürzte ich . . . alles . . . in gleiches Verderben*) (FA 1.14: 17) that mimics the actions of God in the Lisbon earthquake, who abandons all to the same perdition (*gleichem Verderben preisgab*) (FA 1.14: 37). But the story is startlingly free of any sense of guilt or grave consequences in this defining encounter with the outside world. This primal act of destruction is arguably also Goethe's first act of artistic creation—a little piece of theater (*Schauspiel*) performed from his window stage purely for his own pleasure and the pleasure of an enthusiastic audience and producing ultimately, in exchange for the destruction, a story (*Geschichte*) that would last a lifetime. Positioned at the beginning of Goethe's autobiography, it also sets a lifelong creative process in motion. Later he characterizes his entire poetic oeuvre as "fragments of one great confession, which this little book is a bold attempt to complete" (*Brüchstücke einer großen Konfession, welche vollständig zu machen dieses Büchlein ein gewagter Versuch ist*) (*CW* 4: 214; FA 1.14: 310). Perhaps here too Goethe borrows his metaphor from the kabbalistic conception of Tikkun as the restoration of connection.

Goethe's debt to Jewish sources and texts is a marginal theme in his autobiography, but that is precisely the point. Along the heterodox margins of his wanderings he finds support for an active, open-ended conception of human destiny in which creativity, even with its divergent routes and attendant evils, could play a redemptive role. And yet, it must be remembered, his rich appropriation stands in sharp contrast to the passing glance, equal parts curiosity and pity, with which he eyes his actual Jewish contemporaries. In a meager defense of those fellow Frankfurt dwellers, forced into the cramped, squalid ghetto, he concedes: "they were also human beings" (*[sie] waren ja auch Menschen*), and "besides, the girls were pretty" (*Überdies waren die Mädchen hübsch*) (*CW* 4: 120; FA 1.14: 165). But, as his description makes clear, he was the one in motion (*vorbeigehend*), while they were very much trapped in place (FA 1.14: 165).

Chapter 2

Moses and the Modern Nation

Goethe on Exodus

While chapter 1 focused on the existential resources Judaism offered Goethe in his representation of his own individual life journey, this chapter considers his thinking about Judaism in connection with nations and nationalism. Goethe reads the latter books of Moses—comprising the exodus narratives and Sinaitic covenant—as accounts of an emerging nation, with implications for understanding Germany as a national culture. This chapter divides into two epochs: Goethe's early career in the early 1770s, the so-called Storm and Stress period in German letters, and the post-Revolutionary period in the 1790s. In both eras the comparison between Germans and Israelites is triangulated through a contemporary political foe. The French, whether in pre- or post-Revolutionary guise, are discursively aligned with Jews.

Part One: Moses in the 1770s

From the earlier period we consider three essays: "On German Architecture" ("Von Deutscher Baukunst"; 1772), "Letter of the Pastor at *** to the New Pastor at * * *" (Brief des Pastors zu *** an den neuen Pastor zu ***), and "Two Important, Hitherto Undiscussed Biblical Questions" ("Zwo wichtige bisher unerörterte biblische Fragen") (both 1773). While the first essay concerns national culture explicitly and religion only implicitly, and the other two concern religion explicitly and national culture only implicitly, taken together, they chart the position of Judaism in Goethe's early thinking about German identity. Most importantly, all three explorations of identity share common discourses concerning wholeness and the mediation between individual and collective.

Herderian Visions

The terms in which Goethe frames his discussions show the marked influence of Johann Gottfried Herder. Herder and Goethe developed an intense intellectual relationship in Strasburg in late 1770 and early 1771 while Herder was convalescing from an eye operation. As Goethe reports in *Poetry and Truth*, it was through both "Hebraic poetry" (*[d]ie hebräische Dichtkunst*) and local traditions of "folk poetry" (*Volkspoesie*) that Herder taught him to see poetry in collective cultural terms: "that poetry is truly a gift given to the world and all nations, and is not the private heritage of a few distinguished, cultivated men" (*daß die Dichtkunst überhaupt eine Welt- und Völkergabe sei, nicht ein Privaterbteil einiger feinen, gebildeten Männer*) (*CW* 4: 303; FA 1.14: 445). The parallel established in this passage between Hebrew national poetry and German folk poetry is essential to Goethe's thinking about nation.

What could Herder have conveyed to the young Goethe in these conversations? In manuscripts from this period, Herder represents the Bible as "fundamentally human" in character (HW 5: 29). The Bible does not represent a direct transmission, according to Herder, for God does not think in human words or conceptions. Rather, it must be understood as an expression of author, place, time, nation, and language (HW 5: 29). Yet despite their thoroughly human character, the Hebrew scriptures remain "sacred," precisely because they are the expressions of a people, as the "ancient, poetic, national documents of the Orient" (HW 5: 30). Their age and their sensuous, poetic language suggest their connection to some remote, holy origin. Herder uses a favorite metaphor to describe this connection: "the roots of the rise of every nation lie buried in the sequence of events just like the roots of a tree" (HW 5: 18). Cultures are like plants for Herder, rooted deeply in their own proper soil, raised in their own distinctive climate, and bearing their own unique fruit. In this plant metaphor, human culture converges with both nature and the sacred.

While Herder observes the disparate, composite character of the Genesis text, he sees it as further evidence of its representative status for a whole people. Instead of endorsing the orthodox view that Moses authored (or transmitted from God) the whole Pentateuch, Herder casts Moses as the collector and editor of older traditions (HW 5: 22–24).[1] The idea of the editor as the creative archivist of a diverse cultural transmission—as indeed a kind of poet—plays a significant role in Goethe's later literary production.

Thus Goethe takes from Herder a vitalistic, plant-like conception of a nation, as well as an understanding of the Hebrew Bible as an exemplary *Urpoesie*, an age-old collective expression of a national culture, and therefore a reference point for German art. But in these essays, Goethe complicates the analogy between the German and Hebrew national traditions: here the Hebrew scriptures represent alternately an original, patriarchal culture that Germany must recover in itself, and a legalistic collectivism that it must overcome. Goethe identifies the post-Exodus Israelites specifically (and, by implication, modern Jews) not with Herder's vibrant, organic vision of national community, but with a perceived modern malaise of dessicated rationalism, uniformity, and absolutism. The Israel constituted by Moses serves

Goethe as a historical analogue for a contemporary German society that he and other writers of the Storm and Stress period experience as fragmented, highly regimented, and cut off from its cultural inheritance.

Erwin and Moses

The essay "On German Architecture" holds up a medieval architectural monument, the Strassburg cathedral, as the embodiment of German culture, and its most celebrated architect, Erwin von Steinbach, as an exemplary artist. The essay locates itself squarely within a Herderian framework, appearing anonymously in Herder's edited collection of essays *Of German Character and Art* (1773), which served as an informal manifesto of the Storm and Stress movement. Indeed, Herder's mentor Hamann assumed that Herder must be its author (FA 1.18: 1107).

In Herderian fashion, the essay tries to define an intrinsically German art form, free of foreign, classicizing influence and inspired by genius rather than determined by abstract principles (FA 1.18: 111–12). Goethe describes this authentic art in vitalistic terms: it must be a "living whole" (*ganz und lebendig*), springing from "a sincere, unified, original autonomous feeling" (*inniger, einiger, selbstständiger Empfindung*) (CW 3: 8; FA 1.18: 117). As in a work of nature, no part is extraneous: "down to the smallest fiber, all is form, all serves the whole" (*Wie in Werken der ewigen Natur, bis aufs geringste Zäserchen, alles Gestalt, und alles zweckend zum Ganzen*) (CW 3: 6; FA 1.18: 115). Thus he compares the cathedral to a plant—simultaneously natural and divine, "like a towering, wide-spreading tree of God" (*gleich einem hocherhabenen, weitverbreiteten Baume Gottes*) (CW 3: 5; FA 1.18: 113).

Moses serves as an implicit point of comparision. The cathedral, this definitively German monument, seems parallel, in Goethe's essay, to the revelation on Sinai, which served as a foundation for ancient Israel. Erwin receives architectural instruction as a kind of revelation by his (godlike) Genius: "diversify the immense wall, raise it to heaven" (*Vermannigfaltige die ungeheure Mauer, die du gen Himmel führen sollst*) so that it can proclaim "the glory of the Lord, its master" (*die Herrlichkeit des Herrn, seines Meisters*) (FA 1.18: 113; CW 3: 5). Similarly Moses receives, along with the Law, precise building directions for the Tabernacle, the dwelling place for the Lord (Exod. 25). Of course Moses's broader bequest to his nation is traditionally the five books of Moses. Here too Erwin and Moses are parallel as artists and assemblers of a national culture. Even though the Gothic portion of the Strassburg cathedral took more than 250 years to construct, Goethe attributes the architectural achievement to Meister Erwin. He acknowledges of course that there were other builders besides Erwin, but it was Erwin, he contends, "who first created a living whole out of scattered elements" (*der zuerst die zerstreuten Elemente, in Ein lebendiges Ganze zusammen schuf*) (CW 3: 8; FA 1.18: 116). In the same immediate context, Goethe makes oblique reference to the theory that Homer was but the collector of earlier traditions, that "there was a Homer before Homer" (*ein Homer sei schon vor dem Homer gewesen*) (*CW* 3: 8; FA 1.18: 115–16). As we will explore further in the second half of this chapter, the scholarship surrounding Homeric poetry and the books of Moses evolved simultaneously to see both as analogous national compilations rather than single-authored works. Thus Erwin, like Homer and Moses, fits a developing conception of a national artist as one who is able to shape and coalesce preexisting ideas and materials.

Goethe sprinkles the essay with a number of references to the Hebrew scriptures that reinforce a positive analogy between the two national cultures. The narrator imagines Erwin's creation as like the biblical creation, with Erwin as a hovering spirit like the Lord in Genesis 1: "who can look down on such a creation and say, as did God, 'it is good!'" (*der auf solch eine Schöpfung herabschauen und gottgleich sprechen kann: es ist gut!*) (*CW* 3: 6; FA 1.18: 115). Further, the cathedral is compared—in a positive, quite unorthodox sense—to the tower of Babel in Genesis (FA 1.18: 110). Elsewhere the narrator speaks in the language of the Psalms (FA 1.18: 118), which, like Genesis, represent a Hebrew *Urpoesie* to Herder and others.[2]

Moreover, the Germans and biblical patriarchs are linked rhetorically through an imperializing cultural menace—the French/Babylonians. The narrator opposes the genius of his German architect to the reliance on artistic principles and doctrines of a "philosophizing expert of the new French school" (*neufranzösischer philosophierender Kenner*) (*CW* 3: 4; FA 1.18: 112). These French authorities argue from a supposed original form of construction (four posts and a roof) to the universal validity of an architecture based on columns. The narrator protests: "From this you derive the appropriateness of our own buildings, as if you wanted to rule your new Babylon with a simplistically patriarchal attitude" (*Daraus entscheidest du das gehörige unsrer heurigen Bedürfnisse, eben als wenn du dein neues Babylon, mit einfältigem Patriarchalischem Hausvatersinn regieren wolltest*) (*CW* 3: 4; FA 1.18: 112). In this analogy, the philosophizing French represent the decadent Babylonians who may have taken the Jews captive but have not thereby gained access to the authentic culture of the patriarchs.

But Hebrew and German culture also diverge within the essay, for elsewhere Goethe allies Jews with the French in opposition to his paradigmatic German architect. In the branches of a beech tree the narrator ties a handkerchief containing a mixed array of items gathered on a walk: "flowers, blossoms, leaves, but also dry grass and moss and toadstools sprung up over night" (*Blumen, Blüten, Blätter, auch wohl dürres Gras und Moos und über Nacht geschoßne Schwämme*) (*CW* 3: 3–4; FA 1.18: 111). He compares this offering of diverse botanical materials left for Erwin to a sheet full of diverse animals that descended from heaven to the Apostle Peter according to the book of Acts: "It resembles the sheet that was let down from the clouds to the holy apostle, full of clean and unclean beasts" (*Nicht ungleich jenem Tuche, das dem heiligen Apostel aus den Wolken herab gelassen ward, voll reiner und unreiner Tiere*) (CW 3: 3; FA 1.18: 111). In the episode in Acts referred to here, a voice commands Peter to slaughter and eat of the animals. When he resists the command, for fear of consuming meat considered impure by Jewish law, the voice insists, "What God has made clean, you must not call profane" (Acts 10:15). Later when he is called to the home of the Roman Cornelius, who wants to hear his message, Peter reveals the moral of the earlier episode: "You yourselves know that it is unlawful for a Jew to associate with or to visit a Gentile; but God has shown me that I should not call anyone profane or unclean" (Acts 10:28). This is a critical story for Christianity's self-definition. Peter's rejection of Jewish definitions of purity marks an important step in Christianity's expansion from a Jewish sect to a Gentile religion.[3] What does this story mean in the context of Goethe's essay? Clearly Erwin, the recipient of blossoms and toadstools, has trespassed French rules of propriety in his architecture, just as Peter, recipient of clean and unclean beasts, trespasses Jewish law and distinctions.

Thus, Erwin, the exemplary German artist, is both aligned with the ancient Hebrew patriarchs (*against* the French) and opposed to Jewish rabbinical culture (which is in turn identified *with* the French). This scheme depends of course on Goethe's sense of the Genesis-Exodus divide, separating a "good" authentic originary culture of the patriarchs and a "bad" narrow, legalistic Judaism. In short, the architecture essay makes German art the inheritor of the patriarchal and poetic (including psalmic) culture so admired by Herder; at the same time it dispossesses not only the rule-bound classicizing French, but also—paradoxically—the post-Exodus Jews of that same patriarchal tradition. In the next two essays Goethe moves further to position Judaism outside of the Herderian holistic ideal.

Anti-Jewish Tolerance

The essays, "Letter of the Pastor . . ." and "Two . . . Biblical Questions" are more closely related on the face of it: both concern religious topics and both take the form of a fictional letter written by a pastor. But "Letter" seems to stand apart in its strong defense of tolerance. And yet even its conception of tolerance relies on a distinction from Judaism.

Goethe assumes here the voice of a country pastor of Pietist leanings, who professes his own Christian faith but refuses to condemn beliefs at variance with his own. Tolerance stands within the essay as a middle ground between a perspective embedded within one's own culture or religion and a strict relativism. This essay thus still operates very much within a Herderian framework, celebrating the particular within a vision of the whole, where the whole now is not a certain culture but all of humanity.

At the core of the pastor's ideal of tolerance is his refusal to draw distinctions among religions on a metaphysical or salvational plane. He rejects the doctrine of eternal damnation for non-believers, and finds himself attracted instead to the heretical notion of a universal redemption, known as *apocatastasis* or "Wiederbringung." By removing the question of ultimate salvation from the table, the pastor turns religious difference into something closer to cultural difference in Herder's sense. Echoes of Herder can be heard in the pastor's use of a plant metaphor to celebrate the wonderful variety of religious manifestations: "If we always kept in mind and felt in our hearts what religion really is . . . how it would give us pleasure to see divine seed yield fruit in so many different ways" (*Wenn wir das immer bedächten, und recht im Herzen fühlten was das sei Religion . . . wie würde es uns freuen, den göttlichen Saamen auf so vielerlei Weise Frucht bringen zu sehen*) (FA 1.18: 125).

Yet while maintaining his tolerance for all peoples, the pastor makes clear that not all peoples are themselves capable of tolerance: once again the French and the Jews are the target. But here Jewish particularism and French Enlightenment rationalism (a kind of strict universalism) inhabit opposite poles of intolerance that nevertheless converge in their contrast with the true tolerance of Christian love. The pastor illustrates false tolerance through an anecdote concerning Voltaire, the paragon of Enlightenment, and Isaac de Pinto, a Portuguese Jew who responded to Voltaire's relentless attacks on Judaism in his philosophical dictionary (FA 1.18: 122). In that response, De Pinto seizes upon the false gesture of tolerance that Voltaire appends to his venomous description of Jews as ignorant, barbarous, and hateful toward those very nations that tolerate them. De Pinto quotes Voltaire, inserting his own parenthetical comment: "we must not however (he says in his tender mercy) we must not burn them!"[4] In his reply to de Pinto, Voltaire acknowledges that he was wrong "in attributing to a whole nation the vices of some individuals."[5] He advises de Pinto: "As you are a Jew, remain so," then adds, "But be a philosopher. This is my best wish to you in this short life."[6]

But Goethe's pastor in turn exposes Voltaire's conciliatory-sounding response to De Pinto as but another instance of false tolerance. The pastor turns Voltaire's phrase "as you are a Jew remain one" on the French philosopher, rhetorically equating the philosopher and the Jew: "Remain a philosopher then because you already are one and may God have sympathy with you" (*Bleibt denn Philosoph weil ihrs einmal seid, und Gott habe Mitleiden mit Euch!*) (FA 1.18: 122). That the pastor indeed attributes no greater tolerance to Jews than to philosophers becomes clear a couple paragraphs later (FA 1.18: 122): "What bliss is it to think that the Turk who considers me a dog and the Jew who considers me a pig, will some day rejoice to be my brother" (*Welche Wonne ist es zu denken, daß der Türke der mich für einen Hund, und der Jude der mich für ein Schwein hält, sich einst freuen werden meine Brüder zu sein*) (FA 1.18: 123). Here the pastor essentially repeats Voltaire's contention that Jews are full of hatred for non-Jews.

Thus this essay sheds light on the nature and limits of Goethe's anti-Judaism at this stage. Jews and Christians are not distinguished in their eternal prospects but only in their cultural character as fruits on a Herderian tree. While embracing Herder's relativistic anthropology, Goethe nevertheless creates a hierarchy prizing those individuals and cultures deemed best able to harmonize their own particularity with a universal order. The ideal of art in the architecture essay was to bring all disparate parts together into a whole that mirrors the operations of nature. German art, embodied by the Strassburg cathedral, achieves this ideal. Meanwhile, the Pietist pastor aims for a tolerance bridging his own particular religious experiences and his vision of God as all-embracing love. In these two essays, mediation between individual and whole is the ideal. German art and heterodox Christian Pietism approach this ideal, while both Judaism and the French Enlightenment, imputed respectively with an intolerant insistence on particularity and an intolerant drive towards uniformity, stand outside of it.

The Middle Road

The third essay, "Two . . . Biblical Questions," employs a similar conceptual framework of religious extremes—such as particularity and uniformity—and their mediation. The explicit issue at hand is interpretive method: how does one approach the peculiarities of the Bible in a productive rather than reductive way? The pastor has rejected what he was taught as a student: that all biblical passages are universal in import, that "the *whole* world should share in *every* passage" (*die* ganze *Welt sollte an* jedem *Spruche Teil haben*) (emphasis in original, FA 1.18: 132). This maxim, he finds, simply meets with too much resistance in the biblical text. The pastor's freshly educated son has learned a new approach, which the father takes to be a diametrically opposed form of foolishness: to treat all difficult, opaque passages as merely local in import (FA 1.18: 133). In short, one approach is too generalizing, while the other is too particularizing.

Yet the pastor's search for a "middle road (*Mittelstraße*) (FA 1.18: 133) between these two extremes has implications beyond hermeneutical technique: it bears on the nature and form of religious community. The pastor writes from a position of solitude and out of a great longing for company. His concerns are not primarily academic: he wants to serve his congregation by providing them with a *usable* message from the Bible: "the sole usable religion has to be simple and warm" (*die einzige brauchbare Religion muß einfach und warm sein*) (FA 1.18: 132). Employing a plant analogy that runs throughout the essay, he describes the ideal teacher as a skilled gardener who understands the proper care for each stage of each plant. Through his interpretation of the Bible, he thus hopes simultaneously to nurture individual souls and religious community.

It makes sense then that the two passages on which the pastor focuses in order to show his own interpretive approach represent constitutive moments for religious community: the gift of the law on Mount Sinai and the gift of tongues to the apostles after Christ's ascension. This pairing is no accident: the Christian event occurs on Pentecost or Shavuot, the Jewish harvest festival, which by the second century C.E., also came to mark the bestowal of the Law on Sinai.[7] From Augustine, to Luther, to Herder, these two passages have been conjoined as a typological pair.[8] While the gift of the law on Mount Sinai is an essential episode in God's special covenant with the nation of Israel, the gift of tongues through the Holy Spirit explicitly inaugurates Christianity's evangelical mission to the whole world. The pastor's juxtaposition of these two episodes therefore highlights essential themes in Christianity's hermeneutic of supersession toward Judaism: spirit replaces law; universalism replaces particularism.

The Jewish Trunk

As a preface to his analysis, the pastor characterizes the relative status of Judaism and Christianity with a metaphor both biblical and Herderian: Judaism is a tree trunk onto which Christianity has been grafted:

> I see the Jewish people as a wild, unproductive trunk, which stood in a circle of wild unproductive trees, upon which the eternal gardener planted the noble shoot Jesus Christ, that, in prospering there, it might ennoble the nature of the trunk, and whence might be gathered grafting shoots for the fructification of all remaining trees.
>
> Das jüdische Volk seh ich für einen wilden unfruchtbaren Stamm an, der in einem Kreis von wilden unfruchtbaren Bäumen stund, auf den pflanzte der ewige Gärtner das edle Reis Jesum Christum, daß es darauf bekleibend, des Stammes Natur veredelte, und von dannen Pfropfreiser zur Befruchtung aller übrigen Bäume geholt würden. (FA 1.18: 133)

Obviously this analogy transforms the tolerant Herderian vision of diverse religious fruits springing from a sacred origin.[9] Judaism does not bear fruit here except through an artificial graft.

The image of Israel as a tree damaged by God for its sins has precedents within the Hebrew Bible (Jer. 11:16). In identifying the new branch on the trunk as Christ, the pastor plays typologically on a passage from Isaiah heralding the Jewish messiah: "But a shoot shall grow out of the stump of Jesse, A twig shall sprout from his stock" (Isa. 11:1). In Isaiah however, the messiah is not grafted, but emerges organically from the root. This image of a grafted branch derives from Paul's Epistle to the Romans. Addressing the Gentiles about their relationship to Judaism, he writes:

> If some of the branches have been broken off, and you, though a wild olive shoot, have been grafted in among the others and now share

in the nourishing sap from the olive root, do not boast over those branches. If you do, consider this: You do not support the root, but the root supports you. (Rom. 11:17–18)

As Bernard Levinson has observed, Goethe inverts Paul's terms.[10] In Paul's account, the "wild" Gentile branch is reminded that it takes nourishment from the Jewish root; in the pastor's account, it is now the Jewish root that is "wild" and dependent on the ennobling and fructifying Christian graft.

The pastor thus transforms the tree metaphor in a manner that largely disconnects the Jewish people from any fruitful meaning. Indeed, he insists on the radical particularity of Judaism.

> The history and teachings of this people, from its first germination to its grafting is indeed *particular*, and the small component of universality, which, with regards to the future great act, might have proceeded along with it, is difficult and perhaps unnecessary to seek out.
>
> Die Geschichte und Lehre dieses Volks, von seinem ersten Keime bis zur Pfropfung ist allerdings *particular*, und das wenige universelle, das etwa in Rücksicht der zukünftigen großen Handlung mit ihm möchte vorgegangen sein, ist schwer und vielleicht unnöttig aufzusuchen. (FA 1.18: 133)

Christianity, according to his account, is just the opposite. After the Christian graft, biblical doctrine and history become universal:

> And although every tree ennobled accordingly has its special history and, according to the character of its circumstances, its special teaching, nevertheless it is my opinion that here there is to be assumed and construed as little particularism as there universalism.
>
> Und obgleich jeder von daher veredelte Baum seine Spezialgeschichte, und nach Beschaffenheit der Umstände seine Speziallehre hat, so ist doch meine Meinung: hier sei so wenig particulares als dort universelles zu vermuten und zu deuten. (FA 1.18: 133)

This then is the hermeneutic framework the pastor offers as his "middle road" between biblical approaches that cast everything as universal and those that cast far too much as merely local. The pastor's alternative appears to be the treatment of Judaism (or the Hebrew Bible) as entirely particular, and Christianity (or the New Testament) as entirely universal.

Now in all three essays under discussion we have repeatedly seen Goethe's rejection of both particularity and universality in favor of an organic equilibrium, an individual in harmony with the whole. Thus our question becomes:

are Jewish particularity and Christian universality in this essay two bad poles, two extremes that touch (like Jews and French Enlightenment philosophers in the previous essay), or is there a qualitative difference between them? Does the essay direct its critique toward both Christianity and Judaism or just Judaism? To consider this issue, we turn now to the two biblical questions to which the pastor applies his interpretive approach: "What was written on the tablets of the Covenant?" (*Was stund auf den Tafeln des Bunds*) concerning Exodus, and "What does it mean to speak in tongues?" (*Was heißt mit Zungen reden?*) concerning Acts (FA 1.18: 133, 137).

The pastor's short answer to the first question—what was written on Moses's stone tablets?—is that it was *not* the Ten Commandments, as is usually assumed. Rather, the pastor argues that a list of laws governing worship practices, which appears later in the text (Exod. 34:17–26) was the basis of the covenant. This list for example establishes festivals, sabbath practices, and rituals of sacrifice. Thus the pastor sees the nation of Israel as founded on particular, ceremonial laws rather than on fundamental imperatives valid for all human beings: "How gladly one dispenses with the burdensome old error that the most particularistic covenant could have been founded on universal obligations (for such are indeed most of the so-called Ten Commandments)" (*Wie gerne wirft man den beschwerlichen alten Irrtum weg: es habe der particularste Bund auf Universalverbindlichkeiten [denn das sind doch die meisten der sogenannten zehen Gebote] gegründet werden können*) (FA 1.18: 136).

It is worth taking a closer look at the pastor's justification for his claims. His argument relies on a somewhat confusing sequence of events in the Book of Exodus. After Moses receives both the Ten Commandments and an additional set of obligations, criminal penalties, and ritual practices, he writes it all down in the "record of the covenant" and reads it aloud to the people (Exod. 24:7). God then calls Moses to Sinai again, promising, "I will give you the stone tablets with the teachings and commandments which I have inscribed to instruct them" (Exod. 24:12). The Lord provides detailed specifications for the tabernacle, priestly vestments, and sacrifice, and then gives Moses "the two tablets of the Pact, stone tablets inscribed with the finger of God" (Exod. 31:18). What precisely is written on the two tablets is not revealed. Soon thereafter, when Moses discovers his people down below have been busy building a golden calf, he shatters these first tablets. After the people have been punished for their idolatry, the Lord bids Moses, "Carve two tablets of stone like the first, and I will inscribe upon the tablets the words that were on the first tablets, which you shattered" (Exod. 34:1). Once Moses has carved the tablets and returned to Sinai, God proclaims, "I hereby make a covenant" (Exod. 34:10), promises Israel success in invading Canaan, and then enumerates the ritual laws. Thus the pastor identifies these laws as the true content of the tablets and the covenant that constitute the nation of Israel.

This entire encounter with God on Sinai, according to Jeffrey Tigray, "is extraordinarily difficult to follow" because of the weaving together of divergent accounts from different sources that stand in clear tension with each other.[11] But what speaks directly against the pastor's claim is a passage in Deuteronomy that, after listing the Ten Commandments, makes clear that these were the laws God inscribed on the stone tablets (Deut. 5:22). The pastor nevertheless dismisses the testimony of Deuteronomy as unreliable because "it is probable that this book was cobbled together in the Babylonian Captivity. Its disarray makes it almost certain" (*Es ist wahrscheinlich, daß dieses Buch in der Babylonischen Gefangenschaft zusammengestoppelt worden sei. Die Unordnung desselben macht es fast gewiß*) (FA 1.18: 137). Given obvious discrepancies in the Exodus account, it seems tendentious that the pastor would apply this modern view of the Bible as a redacted text *only* to Deuteronomy. We recall that in his account of this period of his life in *Poetry and Truth*, Goethe describes his view of the Bible in general "as a collective work that had come into existence little by little, with revisions at various times" (*CW* 4: 377; FA 1.14: 554). Clearly the pastor's uneven application of this understanding of the Pentateuch serves a broader polemical purpose.[12]

If the pastor does not allow that the Ten Commandments belong to Israel's covenant as a nation, how then does he understand their role? He concludes that they serve as a preface to the other laws, as doctrines applicable to all people, "teachings that God presupposed in his people as human beings and as Israelites" (*Lehren, die Gott bei seinem Volke als Menschen und als Israeliten voraussetzte*) (FA 1.18: 136). The effect of this claim, however, is more to disinherit Jews than to find broader significance in their legacy. As quoted earlier, the pastor contends that Jewish history and doctrine are entirely particular and doubts that anything universal could be located there. If the Ten Commandments are universal and Jewish history is almost entirely particular, then it would seem that the Ten Commandments do not belong to Jewish history. That is, Jews have no original or proprietary relationship to this collection of laws. This view of course suppresses—as most Christian iterations of the Ten Commandments tend to do—the very historically specific first line: "I the LORD am your God *who brought you out of the land of Egypt, the house of bondage*: You shall have no other gods besides Me" (italics mine, Exod. 20:2–3).

But Jewish *particularism*, in the pastor's polemic, should not be confused with *individualism*. Moses figures here as a founder of a state, concerned with a collective fate rather than individual salvation. To contextualize this political reading of Moses, commentators often refer to Spinoza's *Theological-Political Treatise*.[13] (While there is no proof that Goethe knew this work at this time, perhaps he benefited from indirect transmission of the ideas.)[14] According to Spinoza, the Decalogue contains eternal, universally accessible truths, which the Israelites understood as decreed law rather than necessary moral truth simply because of their lack of knowledge.[15] The ceremonial and criminal laws promulgated by Moses were, by contrast, particular in nature and purpose. Their aim was to render the specific state of Israel strong, secure, and prosperous. According to Spinoza, while universal moral laws contribute to the virtue and blessedness of individuals, ceremonial laws are practiced in a collective context, and cultivate subservience rather than individual volition. The ceremonial observances and the whole Mosaic law, he says, "were relevant only to the Hebrew state, and consequently to no more than temporal prosperity."[16] In Spinoza's view then, Moses instituted a "state religion" for pragmatic reasons, for a particular people, and for a particular time.

According to this reasoning, Goethe could conceive of Moses's legislation as both *general* (in its collectivism and uniformity) and *particularistic* (directed towards a particular people) without conceding either its *universal* significance or its import for *individual* development or salvation. *Particular* then is not synonymous with *individual* within this essay.[17] Further, while Goethe does not make a terminological distinction, his argument relies on an underlying conceptual distinction between what I will call the merely *general* and the fully *universal*.[18] Thus two sets of dichotomies operate in Goethe's essay: *particular* versus *universal* and *general* versus *individual*.

Goethe's account of his dissertation *De Legislatoribus* (1771) eludicates the second conflict—general versus individual—for, according to his friend Lersé, his dissertation provided the groundwork for the Exodus portion of "Two . . . Biblical Questions" (FA 1.18: 1116). The dissertation, which was rejected by the faculty and is not extant, concerned the fundamental conflict between the individual and the state: "The goals of the state are always public and general, those of the individual are domestic, heartfelt and personal" (*Der Staat will alles zu öffentlichen, allgemeinen Zwecken, der Einzelne zu häuslichen, herzlichen, gemütlichen*) (FA 1.14: 516; *CW* 4: 351). Goethe views the church as poised between these colliding principles.

This description of the problem provides a clue to the structure of Goethe's biblical essay. If religion (here: the "church") must decide between the state and the individual, clearly in the first question, Goethe associates Mosaic law with the state, and its general goals. If Goethe follows his dissertation scheme, the gift of tongues to the Christian apostles might suggest the opposite: a religion inclined towards individuality. But we can anticipate a further twist on this dichotomy. If, in Goethe's portrayal of Exodus, Judaism amounts to a general (collectivist) particularism, might Christianity by contrast be deemed capable of that organic Herderian ideal—an individuality that reaches out and shares in the universal?

The Christian Fruit

Hence we turn to the pastor's Christian topic: what does it mean to speak in tongues? The pastor immediately supplies a definition of speaking in tongues (quoting the author Diodorus) that with its repetition of the keyword "spirit" heralds the switch to a New Testament typology: "filled with the spirit, in the language of the spirit, declaring the secrets of the spirit" (*Vom Geist erfüllt, in der Sprache des Geists, des Geists Geheimnisse verkündigen*) (FA 1.18: 137). The pastor also adopts a more individualized, New Testament rhetoric. He employs an esoteric style, suffused with Gospel references, that challenges the individual reader to penetrate the mystery himself or herself: "He who has ears to hear, let him hear" (*Wer Ohren hat zu hören der höre*) (FA 1.18: 137).[19] In fact this entreaty from Matthew (13:9) comes directly after the parable of the sower (Matt. 13:3–8), with its message that only some seeds will take root, and thus it plays too into the organic metaphor running throughout the essay.

But the pastor's emphasis is on an individual experience that can simultaneously participate in universal meaning. The Pentecostal speech represents an originary moment where individuality and universality coincide. For on the one hand, he describes it as "that *simple, universal* speech" (*jene* einfache, allgemeine *Sprache*) that can be understood by diverse peoples, and nevertheless surpasses the limited human understanding (italics in original, FA 1.18: 138). But on the other hand, the channel for this universal spirit is the individual soul or heart: "If the spirit subsequently came over a soul, then that was the exhalation of its abundance, the first, most essential breath of a highly prized heart" (*Kam in der Folge der Geist über eine Seele, so war das Aushauchen seiner Fülle, das erste notwendigste Atmen eines so gewürdigten Herzens*) (FA 1.18: 138). Indeed, the description of the speaker as a mere conduit accords with the young Goethe's conception of artistic genius in early poems such as "May Song" (*Mailied*).

And yet this convergence of universal and individual is unstable, for, he asserts, no human being can sustain such heights of feeling. Therefore the gift of tongues is vulnerable to dangers and misuse. The apostles, he imagines, must have remembered and longed to regain the experience. They turned inwards, brooded, and tried to stir up the depths inside, but to no avail: the result was but meaningless, unedifying babble. Paul had to admonish the Corinthian congregation because of their excessive, unproductive ecstatic utterances (FA 1.18: 139)

In his reading of Paul, the pastor stresses the importance of mediation between the spirit residing in individuals and the communicable meaning or teachings. Once again, he turns to plant metaphors. Drawing on Paul (1 Cor. 14:14), he stresses that the language of pure spirit alone bears no fruit: "For if I pray with the language of depth, my spirit prays, but my understanding bears no fruit" (*So ich mit der tiefen Sprache bete, betet mein Geist, mein Sinn bringt niemanden Frucht*) (FA 1.18: 140).[20] But the soul moved by the spirit, he contends, can give rise to tranquil meaning, like a seed gives rise to a plant (FA 1.18: 139).

This connection between spirit and meaning or doctrine has failed, however, in the present; thus the pastor concludes his analysis of the gift of tongues with a lament and a critique of the contemporary church. The running stream of the spirit, he claims, has dispersed into swamps avoided by respectable people, and any productive irrigation has gone underground: "Here and there it waters a meadow in secret" (*Hier und da wässert er eine Wiese ins Geheim*) (FA 1.18: 140). He continues, "For our theological cameralists have the principle that one must dam up all such places, pass roads through and construct promenades" (*Denn unsre theologische Kameralisten haben das Prinzipium, man müßte dergleichen Flecke all einteichen, Landstraßen durchführen und Spaziergänge darauf anlegen*) (FA 1.18: 140). Few rich wetlands remain.

The metaphor of theological cameralists hindering the free watering of ground links this section on Christianity to the analysis of Judaism. Cameralism, or the science of statecraft, suggests Moses's enterprise, as the pastor depicts it, of founding a state. The deprivation of proper nourishment to a meadow by Christian cameralists seems connected to the image of Judaism as an unfruitful trunk.

If, in the pastor's analysis, the original Pentecostal experience represents a moment when universality and individuality were intimately conjoined, when a common spirit allowed communication between individuals as individuals, the fate of Christianity, even in its early days, was to lose this equilibrium. And the present church is in danger of replicating what the pastor attributes to Judaism: a collective particularism. Indeed, the Exodus section also ends with a warning to the present church. The church has preserved the error about the passages concerning the covenant, "and has drawn many disastrous conclusions from it" (*und [hat] viele fatale Konsequenzen draus gezogen*) (FA 1.18: 137). Thus the church is the inheritor more of Mosaic law than of the Pentecostal speech.

After completing his analysis of both questions, the pastor ends with an admonition to his correspondent to continue faithfully in his pastoral work. But he nevertheless holds out the possibility of a reemergence of the Holy Spirit:

> Should the eternal spirit cast a glance of its wisdom, a spark of its love to a chosen one, let him arise and babble forth his feelings.
>
> May he arise! And we wish to honor him. Thou art blessed, regardless of whence thou comest, thou who art a light unto the pagans, thou who bringest warmth to the nations.

> Wirft aber der ewige Geist einen Blick seiner Weisheit, einen Funken seiner Liebe einem Erwählten zu, der trete auf, und lalle sein Gefühl.
>
> Er tret auf! Und wir wollen ihn ehren! Gesegnet seist du, woher du auch kommst! Der du die Heiden erleuchtest! Der du die Völker erwärmst! (FA 1.18: 140)

An inspired individual or genius, described here in Christological terms, is summoned to reintroduce a true community. The end of "On German Architecture" also calls upon a new savior, but in the terms of Greek myth.[21] There the new genius is cast as the Promethean mediator who brings the fire of the gods to humans (FA 1.18: 118).

In this way, the vision of a new Christianity restoring the Pentecostal community is linked to the vision of a new German art restoring Erwin's legacy. At the core of the cultural and religious visions of all three essays is the promise of a new mediation between individual and whole—an individualized universality or a universal individuality. These Herderian visions are framed by their opposite—a collectivized particularity or a particularistic collective—attributed to the brand of Judaism introduced by Moses on Sinai. Of course, the polemical subtext throughout is that a desiccated uniformity, a political, cultural, and spiritual absolutism, is precisely what characterizes both the church and Germany in the present. Goethe has attributed to Judaism precisely what he wishes to criticize and overcome within his own culture.

Part Two: Moses in the 1790s

A quarter of a century later, Goethe came to associate the Exodus with a new European turning point—the French Revolution. Goethe's first direct encounter with the Revolutionary French was during the First Coalition War, when he accompanied Duke Karl August on the Prussian campaign in France. When the new citizen army of the French turned back the Prussian assault at Valmy in September 1792, Goethe claimed to have recognized the dawning of a new epoch in world history (FA 1.16: 436). Goethe's own German national enthusiasm had peaked in the early 1770s, supplanted by his growing aristocratic elitism: now his experience of the French Revolution cemented his wariness toward popular movements of all kinds.

The French Revolution and its fallout prompted a renewed thinking about both the ancient Israelites and modern Jews—from two opposed angles. First, the French Revolution and later the Napoleonic forces advanced the cause of Jewish emancipation, to which Goethe stood staunchly opposed. In this respect he associated Jews seeking civic liberties with French revolutionaries and read Exodus as itself an ominous popular uprising. Second, and conversely, the new French republic, which Goethe also deplored, heightened an alternative model in his mind, rooted in a now promising analogy between Germany and the Jewish "nation." In Goethe's logic, both peoples must depend upon a cultural or textual tradition rather than a unified political state for their survival. Here too Exodus became a key text, for, as I will argue, Goethe viewed it as a national epic, an essential component of a nation's cultural resources. Thus Exodus occupies a pivotal position in

Goethe's reflections about post-Revolutionary nationhood, standing at the center of analogies between both the French and Jews, and the Germans and Jews. Meanwhile, as we will see below, it provides a surprising link between two quite disparate texts from this era—his biblical critical essay "Israel in the Desert" ("Israel in der Wüste") and his verse epic *Hermann and Dorothea* (*Herrmann und Dorothea*).

German Epic / Jewish Epic

In 1797 while he was completing *Hermann and Dorothea*, Goethe tried his hand once again at a critical analysis of the Exodus story. Based on textual evidence, he argues, the Israelite journey through the wilderness could not have lasted forty years. He eventually set the essay aside, unfinished, for nearly fifteen years, picking it up to add a new opening in 1812.[22] It appeared finally in 1819 under the title "Israel in the Desert" in Goethe's disparate companion to the *West-Eastern Divan* (*West-östlicher Divan*) "Notes and Essays for Better Understanding" ("Noten und Abhandlungen zum besseren Verständnis"), where it lies sandwiched between a catalog of ideas for a future divan and a compendium of famous journeys to the East. In this location, the essay's detailed textual analysis can seem arcane, even quaint. Goethe himself suggests that the interest of the piece lies largely in its testimony to his earlier preoccupation with the books of Moses (FA 1.3.1: 229). But "Israel in the Desert" is anything but narrowly philological in its concerns. It embodies a broad and disconcerting cultural agenda, which only becomes fully legible when re-situated in its primary compositional context in the late 1790s.

It is no accident that Goethe's new biblical essay coincided in 1797 with his work on *Hermann and Dorothea*: both are outgrowths of his interest at that juncture in the genre of epic. Further, both "Israel in the Desert" and *Hermann and Dorothea* take the biblical Exodus from Egypt as the original model of a founding cultural narrative or national epic.[23] And yet the works appropriate this biblical material in the service of very different visions of nation. *Hermann and Dorothea* employs its Exodus analogy to suggest the possibility of an integrative, adaptive modern German cultural consciousness, while "Israel in the Desert" reads out of the Exodus story a highly negative prefiguration of a volatile modern Judaism, by analogy with the French. Indeed, I show that this essay of biblical criticism amounts to a barely concealed polemic against Jewish emancipation. These two works, taken together, illustrate Goethe's complex analogies linking Jews and the French, on the one hand, and Jews and Germans, on the other, while encapsulating the peculiar dynamic of rejection and dependence at work in his relationship to Judaism more generally.[24]

But before turning to the two works at hand, we need to elucidate Goethe's underlying conception of a *national epic* by looking at the circumstances and lines of thought that shaped it.

Theory of the National Epic

Events in 1796 sharply accentuated the tensions in Goethe's thinking about Germany and Germanness. Certainly, renewed French incursions on German territory lent urgency to the question of a trans-regional German identity. In July 1796 Frankfurt, still home to Goethe's mother, was bombarded and then occupied by the French. In their correspondence, Schiller and Goethe concern themselves not only with the fate of both Frankfurt and Schiller's Swabian homeland, but also with the possibility of a future French advance on Saxony and Thuringia.[25] In early September 1796, just days after the French were successfully expelled from Frankfurt, Goethe began *Hermann and Dorothea*, the epic German love story about a young man and woman who, in the shadow of French aggression, surmount regional differences.[26]

Yet even the advance of the French could not erode the deep skepticism Goethe had developed towards the German people. In his 1795 essay "Response to a Literary Rabble-Rouser" ("Literarischer Sansculottismus"), Goethe laments the conditions under which the German writer must labor, including "a mass public without taste that devours the good and the bad with equal relish" (*ein großes Publikum ohne Geschmack, das das Schlechte nach dem Guten mit eben demselben Vergnügen verschlingt*) (CW 3: 191; FA 1.18: 321). Hence it was as much domestic antagonism as foreign threat that set the stage for Goethe's engagement with epic. The publication in autumn 1796 of Goethe and Schiller's *Xenia* (*Xenien*), in which the two friends ruthlessly pilloried contemporaries, brought a public scandal that only further intensified Goethe's sense of alienation from the German public.[27] In December Goethe formulated an artistic self-defense in the form of an elegy, also entitled "Hermann and Dorothea" ("Herrmann und Dorothea"), which served as a poetic advertisement for his epic-in-progress. The poem portrays the task facing the modern epic poet. The poet situates himself in a domestic scene of recitation but also within a tradition that reaches back through the ages to the guild of the Homeridae.[28] His context is national neither in a provincial nor in a populist sense. He rejects the crude rabble (*Pöbel*) who, in turn, perceives only rabble in him (FA 1.1: 622). Yet his subject is indeed German: "To the Germans themselves I would lead you" (*Deutschen selber führ' ich euch zu . . .*) and his aim ultimately cultural self-knowledge: "We became acquainted with people and nations; so let us, knowing our own heart, be glad of it" (*Menschen lernten wir kennen und Nationen; so laßt uns, Unser eigenes Herz kennend, uns dessen erfreun*) (FA 1.1: 623).

Epic offered a fitting framework for Goethe's exploration of nation precisely because, by the end of the eighteenth century, it was increasingly understood as a national genre, a work for and about a people.[29] Virgil's *Aeneid* established a clear prototype of the epic as a founding narrative of a society; medieval epics seemed to advance the model by presenting heroic, watershed events in the vernacular. In the mid-eighteenth century (1755), the rediscovery of the

Nibelungenlied enabled Germans to boast of their own native epic tradition, a point that J. J. Bodmer rushed to underscore by translating the work into hexameter (1757). Writing years later in *Poetry and Truth*, Goethe asserts that a nation, to be worth anything, needs an epic: "every nation, if it wants any prestige, must possess an epic, though not necessarily in the form of an epic poem" (*jede Nation [muß], wenn sie für irgend etwas gelten will, eine Epopee besitzen, wozu nicht gerade die Form des epischen Gedichts nötig ist*) (*CW* 4: 212; FA 1.14: 306). I contend that a corollary is also at work in Goethe's thinking: not only does a nation need an epic, but the specific character of an epic is linked to the specific character of the nation.

Meanwhile, by the end of the eighteenth century, it was also no stretch to classify the biblical Exodus material as an epic. Klopstock ranked Moses, presumed author of the Pentateuch, with Homer and Milton as an exemplary epic poet.[30] Herder identified Exodus as "the first, most ancient, simplest epic that we have" (*SW* 32: 205).[31] Moreover, as we have seen, Herder stressed the *national* character of the Hebrew Bible material.

The emerging historical critical philology reinforced the treatment of Exodus as an epic by linking the Old Testament and Homer as the chief objects of its new methodology. The most important Homeric critic of the era, F. A. Wolf, was deeply influenced in his approach by the Old Testament critic J. G. Eichhorn.[32] Indeed, in a letter to Schiller of April 19, 1797, Goethe reports that he is reading Homer, the Bible, Eichhorn, and Wolf in conjunction with each other: "I am studying now in great hurry the Old Testament and Homer, and am reading simultaneously Eichhorn's introduction to the former and Wolf's Progelomena to the latter" (*Ich studiere jetzt in großer Eile das alte Testament und Homer, lese zugleich Eichhorns Einleitung ins erste und Wolfs Prolegomena zu dem letzten*) (FA 2.4: 319).

Goethe's simultaneous study of the Bible, Homer, and their respective critics in 1797 points unmistakably to the analogy between these works that operates in *Hermann and Dorothea*. But it also suggests his interest in a specific dimension of epic. Both Eichhorn and Wolf arrive at views of their respective works as composite texts shaped by later redaction. (We located this emerging view of both Homer and the Pentateuch already in Goethe's earlier essays.) In the same letter to Schiller, Goethe muses about the impulse to rationalize and make uniform that clearly drove the later editors of the Odyssey material; he observes the same impulse in his own editorial emendations to *Hermann and Dorothea*. In an earlier letter to Schiller, he remarks upon the composite character of the Pentateuch: "once again I haven't been able to get enough of the confusion and contraditions of the Five Books of Moses, which of course, as is known, may be composed of hundreds of written and oral traditions" (*[ich] habe mich aufs neue nicht genug über die Konfusion und die Widersprüche der fünf Bücher Mosis verwundern können, die denn freilich wie bekannt aus hunderterlei schriftlichen und mündlichen Traditionen zusammengestellt sein mögen*) (FA 2.4: 316–17). As we will see, this question of compositional layering stands at the heart of his essay on the Exodus narrative. Crucial here is that for Goethe the methodological question of what is original and what is later editorial intervention links the Bible in a central way to the epic tradition.

In 1797 Goethe and Schiller began to formulate their own definition of epic, first in their correspondence and eventually in their joint essay "On Epic and Dramatic Poetry" ("Über epische und dramatische Dichtung"). Goethe's April 19 letter to Schiller touches upon what he takes to be a central issue: retarding motifs that slow the forward movement of the plot. He writes, "A chief characteristic of the epic poem is that it always goes forward and backwards, therefore all retarding motives are epic. There may not be actual obstacles however, which actually belong in drama" (*Eine Haupteigenschaft des epischen Gedichts ist daß es immer vor und zurück geht, daher sind alle retardierende Motive episch. Es dürfen aber keine eigentliche* Hindernisse *sein welche eigentlich ins Drama gehören*) (FA 2.4: 320).[33] Elsewhere in his correspondence he locates this generic feature both in Homer and *Hermann and Dorothea*;[34] in his Exodus essay, he will bring the issue of narrative delay to bear on his evaluation of what is original and what is a later accretion in the Exodus narrative. He indeed employs the term "retardation" to describe what he considers a reasonable delay on the Israelite journey through the wilderness (FA 1.3.1: 241).

The essay "On Epic and Dramatic Poetry," which had at last taken form by the end of 1797, notes a further feature of epic that, as we will see, plays a role in Goethe's Exodus essay. At the center of the epic, in the authors' view, stands an individual acting on the external world in an expansive manner: "The epic poem depicts man's *physical interaction with the world*: battles, journeys, or any kind of enterprise which requires broad, descriptive treatment" (*das epische Gedicht [stellt] den* außer sich wirkenden *Menschen [vor]: Schlachten, Reisen, jede Art von Unternehmung, die eine gewisse sinnliche Breite fordert*) (emphasis in original, added in translation, *CW* 3: 193; FA 1.18: 445–46). The question of Moses's character, the proper direction of his energies, becomes another crux of Goethe's biblical critical analysis.

Thus we see the contours of Goethe's conception of epic in the late 1790s as it bears on his use of the Exodus material. Certain generic criteria figure above all in his historical critical essay. Epics—at least the ancient prototypes—are compositionally layered, with editorial afterthoughts intruding upon the original material. Pacing is a key issue for the epic: retarding motifs must delay the action without hindering it. The epic hero is externally directed and expansive in his relationship to the world. But the crucial assumption underlying both *Hermann and Dorothea* and "Israel in the Desert" is that epic has national import—it is a genre about and for a people, with a potentially formative cultural function. That Goethe conceives the Exodus narrative in both *Hermann and Dorothea* and in "Israel in the Desert" in national terms is unmistakable. But its meaning for German culture and its legacy for Jewish culture diverge vastly in Goethe's vision.

Hermann and Dorothea

Goethe's epic *Hermann and Dorothea* is a love story set in the immediate present of the late 1790s about a young village man, Hermann, and a refugee maiden, Dorothea, who, with others, has crossed the Rhine to flee French occupation. From its earliest reception by Wilhelm von Humboldt and August Wilhelm von Schlegel, and up to its apotheosis in the Nazi era, *Hermann and Dorothea* was interpreted as a national epic.[35] A letter to Schiller suggests Goethe anticipated this patriotic reception: "In Hermann and Dorothea, as far as the material goes, I have finally done the will of the Germans and they are exceedingly satisfied" (*In Herrmann und Dorothea habe ich, was das Material betrifft, den Deutschen einmal ihren Willen getan, und nun sind sie äußerst zufrieden*) (FA 2.4: 473). But with his qualification "as far as the material goes," he indicates that the "Germans" in their enthusiasm may be missing something. And indeed the criticism of the last several decades has been well attuned to the ample irony in the work. Still, it must be stressed that the irony relativizes, but does not necessarily negate, a German cultural agenda.[36] The ironic treatment of Hermann and his village belongs to the conception of an internally diverse, integrative national culture in this work. Goethe's complex, multivalent deployment of the Exodus material in his epic contributes to a vision at once cosmopolitan and domestic.

The allusion to Exodus is most explicit in the fifth and sixth cantos. Two of the villagers, the pastor and apothecary, encounter a wise old man who acts as a leader of the refugees and who is identified as "the Judge" (*der Richter*), a title suggestive of a biblical prototype—the leaders in the post-Exodus period.[37] Further, the pastor recognizes in the judge a resemblance to Joshua and Moses, the two preceding generations of commander in the Israelite campaign for Canaan: "Yes, when I see you today I take you for one of those ancient / Leaders of exiled people through wildernesses and wandering: / For I feel I am speaking to Joshua or to Moses" (*Ja, Ihr erscheint mir heut' als einer der ältesten Führer, / Die durch Wüsten und Irren vertriebene Völker geleitet. / Denk' ich doch eben, ich rede mit Josua oder mit Moses*) (CW 8: 279; FA 1.8: 847). The judge accepts and develops the Exodus comparison but also extends its reach:

> Truly, our times may well be compared with the rarest of epochs / That human history, sacred or worldly, has ever recorded. / For any man who has lived through these last few days has already / lived through many a year: thus all stories crowd together. (trans. altered, *CW* 8: 279)

> Wahrlich unsere Zeit vergleicht sich den seltesten Zeiten, / Die die Geschichte bemerkt, die heilige wie die gemeine./ Denn wer gestern und heut' in diesen Tagen gelebt hat, / Hat schon Jahre gelebt: so drängen sich alle Geschichten. (FA 1.8: 847)[38]

In the experience of these refugees, then, there converge not only generations of Israelite history but indeed all the epochs of human history. The judge employs the Exodus story in a paradigmatic sense, granting it a nearly universal human significance.

But the Exodus comparison in the judge's account has both positive and negative connotations. At first the Germans from the west bank of the Rhine are caught up in the revolutionary fervor, and identify with the French invaders, the emissaries of the Revolution. The story begins with the thrill of liberation. The nations seem emancipated, like slaves from the chains of arbitrary rule: "and the bondage / Which enslaved so many a people, which idle self-interest / Had imposed and maintained, now seemed at last to be easing" (*es schien sich / Aufzulösen das Band, das viele Länder umstrickte,/ Das der Müßiggang und der Eigennutz in der Hand hielt*) (CW 8: 280; FA 1.8: 848). But soon a sort of political idolatry sets in. The revolutionary leaders become like gods: "Were not the names of those men who had first proclaimed the new message / Highly exalted and praised to the stars as the equals of any?" (*Waren nicht jener Männer, der ersten Verkünder der Botschaft / Namen den höchsten gleich, die unter die Sterne gesetzt sind?*) (CW 8: 280; FA 1.8: 848). In a description reminiscent of the dance, or "Reigen" in Luther's translation, celebrating the golden calf (Exod. 32:19), the judge describes the adoration of the new flag: "Gleeful dancing began all around the new tricolour standard" (*Und der muntere Tanz begann um die neue Standarte*) (CW 8: 280; FA 1.8: 849). The French revolutionary spirit quickly spreads to the Germans, who come to share in the idolatrous error that "the highest" (*das Höchste*) is "near and attainable" (*nah und erreichbar*) (FA 1.8: 849).[39] These revolutionary ideals then degenerate into chaos and violence on all sides. The judge recounts, "They murdered each other and oppressed the new neighbors and brothers" (*Sie ermordeten sich und unterdrückten die neuen / Nachbarn und Brüder*) (FA 1.8: 849), thus echoing the fallout of the golden calf episode in Exodus where the Levites are ordered to "slay brother, neighbor, and kin" (Exod. 32:27). In an allusion to the bitter waters of Mara in the Sinai wilderness (Exod. 15:23), the judge laments their prolonged suffering: "not short are our sufferings; / for we have drunk the bitterness of all these years" (*nicht kurz sind unsere Leiden; / Denn wir haben das Bittre der sämtlichen Jahre getrunken*) (FA 1.8: 848).

The judge's account reveals the peril intrinsic to an uprooted condition. In describing the outrages they have suffered at the hands of retreating French soldiers, he cautions, "a fleeing person knows no law" (*der Flüchtige kennt kein Gesetz*) (FA 1.8: 850). This generalized warning about refugees cannot but apply to his own refugee people. Indeed a dangerous ambiguity lurks in the double analogy between the judge and the two biblical leaders, Moses and Joshua. The crossing of the Rhine, described as a divinely guarded border by Hermann's father (FA 1.8: 814), takes on very different meanings in these two analogies. If the judge is like Moses, then crossing the Rhine would be like the Israelites' miraculous crossing of the Sea of Reeds; if the judge is like Joshua, crossing the Rhine would be like crossing the Jordan into Canaan.

In the first case, if the judge is Moses, the French, who at points in the narrative embody the emancipatory impulse of the ancient Israelites, also become the hostile Egyptians repelled by the watery border. Hermann's village might then represent the welcoming Midianites, who receive Moses on his first flight from Egypt and help him again during the Exodus. Indeed, just as Moses finds his Midianite wife Zipporah at a well, Dorothea and Hermann meet at a well. But Midianite liaisons do not fare so well as the biblical narrative advances. Later the Israelites massacre a settlement of Midianites because their women have seduced Israelite men (Num. 31). Other peoples, such as the Amorites, who refuse to let the Israelites pass through their land, fare no better (Num. 21:21–32).

In the second comparison, between the judge and Joshua, these more ominous aspects of the story come to the foreground. In this case, crossing the Rhine becomes like crossing the Jordan, where a similar miraculous rolling back of the waters occurs (Josh. 3). Joshua leads his people into Canaan in order to fulfill God's lethal command: "In the towns of the latter peoples, however, which the Lord your God is giving you as heritage, you shall not let a soul remain alive" (Deut. 20:16). If the refugees are like the Israelites having crossed into Canaan, Hermann's village ought perhaps to be on its guard.

Yet the connotations of the Exodus subtext are at least as positive as they are negative. If one consequence of uprootedness is destruction and violence, another consequence is the opportunity for new, productive alliances such as marriage. With prompting from the pastor, the judge acknowledges that danger and hardship can bring out the best in people. He describes the sublimity of the refugee experience: just as God appeared to the Israelites through cloud by day and fire by night (Exod. 13.21): "he has appeared before us in clouds and in pillars of fire too" (*auch uns erschien er in Wolken und Feuer*) (CW 8: 279; FA 1.8: 847). It is revealed early on that Hermann's own mother and father also came together through a catastrophe—a fire that left both families homeless and eliminated the border separating them: "So we stood there, pensive and sad, and looked at each other; / For the boundary wall between our two houses had fallen" (*Also standen wir gegeneinander, bedenklich und traurig; / Denn die Wand war gefallen, die unsere Höfe geschieden*) (CW 8: 258; FA 1.8: 820). The trespassing of limits there means the advent of a new family. In addition, the revolutionary and refugee experiences identified with the biblical Exodus clearly give Dorothea a sense of uncertainty and fragility about human life and institutions, cultivate in her an appreciation of what is essential, and allow her to prove her capacity for commitment and even heroism. Both through her own experience and through her commemoration of a lost fiancé, who was indeed a revolutionary, Dorothea brings a widened, deepened perspective to the comically provincial village into which she marries.[40]

But the Israelite analogy—in both its negative and positive valences—applies not only to the refugees but to the villagers as well. In a less direct fashion than the judge, Hermann is also compared to Moses. Just as Moses protects Midianite maidens at the well from the intimidation of shepherds, Hermann defends the neighbor girls at the village well from the wildness of local boys (FA 1.8: 823). But while Moses wins his bride Zipporah this way, the neighbor girls reject Hermann because of his quaint, unfashionable ways. They laugh as their father mockingly inquires, "Are Adam and Eve the last couple you've heard of?" (*[er] kennt nur Adam und Eva?*) (*CW* 8: 260; FA 1.8: 824). Like Moses, Hermann wants to serve his fatherland, but his professed desire to become a soldier in order to do so militarily turns out to be just a cover for his apparently futile feelings of love for Dorothea (FA 1. 8: 834–35). Like Moses, Hermann has a slow tongue. But while Moses overcomes his speech defect to plead the case of his nation, Hermann overcomes his only to plead the case of love and marriage (FA 1.8: 842–43; Exod. 4:10). To the extent that Hermann is a national founding figure like Moses, his realm is his family. The covenant (*Bund*) that he proclaims in the end is the covenant of marriage (FA 1.8: 882).

And the complications of the biblical subtext only multiply. Hermann's more domestic inclinations suggest further admixture: he is a Moses, the protagonist of Exodus crossed with the patriarchal heroes of Genesis, especially Isaac and Jacob.[41] For Goethe, as we have seen, the first two books of Moses, Genesis and Exodus, stand in stark opposition, separated indeed by a great chasm (FA 1.14: 556). While in Genesis, national and collective meaning is entirely focalized through an individual or through family relationships, in Exodus, the nation emerges through grand political and military events resonant with modern times. Hermann, as much domestic patriarch as national defender, mediates, at least potentially, this dichotomy.

Thus both within the figure of Hermann and between Hermann and Dorothea, we see a drive in this epic for integration. The epic weaves together the patriarchal and idyllic themes of Genesis with the national and military themes of Exodus. It explores both the productive and destructive aspects of an Exodus-like uprootedness and change, and combines, in its vision of a national culture, stability and transformation, family and politics, individual action and historical forces.

And yet at the same time that Goethe was appropriating the Exodus material to fashion this vision of an adaptive, integrative German culture, he was also reinterpreting the same biblical material to suggest why Jews should be excluded from this very culture. Just as Goethe positions *Hermann and Dorothea* to shape a modern German consciousness, he implies that the Exodus story (in his highly idiosyncratic reading of it) has had a formative impact on modern Jewish consciousness.

"Israel in the Desert"

Goethe's argument in "Israel in the Desert" has two focal points: the character of Moses and the length of the journey through the wilderness.

> There are thus two things to which I wish to direct the attention of my reader: first, the development of the entire event of this strange migration from the character of the general who initially does not appear in the most favorable light; and second, the conjecture that the migration lasted not forty years but barely two.
>
> Zwey Dinge sind es daher, auf die ich die Aufmerksamkeit meiner Leser zu richten wünschte. Erstlich, auf die Entwickelung der ganzen Begebenheit dieses wunderlichen Zugs aus dem Charakter des Feldherrn, der Anfangs nicht in dem günstigsten Lichte erscheint, und zweytens auf die Vermuthung, daß der Zug keine vierzig, sondern kaum zwey Jahre gedauert. (FA 1.3.1: 231–32)

These two contentions, about plot pacing and character, turn out to be closely related. By cutting thirty-eight years off the journey, Goethe claims to do greater justice to the character of Moses.

Goethe's assertion that the Israelites could not have wandered forty years through the wilderness dates back, according to *Poetry and Truth*, to a discovery that he made in the early 1770s, presumably around the time of his earlier Exodus essay (FA 1.14: 557). Goethe's justification for this claim is textually complex. He calls the forty-year time span into question by comparing the narrative accounts in Exodus, Leviticus, Numbers, and Deuteronomy with the summary of all the stations of the journey in Numbers, chapter 33. The *narrative* account in Numbers mentions two locations with the name Kadesh: Kadesh in the wilderness of Paran (Num. 13:26) and Kadesh in the wilderness of Zin (Num. 19:1). The *list* of stations mentions only the latter, Kadesh in the wilderness of Zin, while meanwhile containing an extensive catalog of place names between Sinai and Kadesh unaccounted for in the narrative. Goethe's contention is that there was only one Kadesh, which the Israelites reached in the second year of the journey and after which in fairly short order they would have reached the River Jordan. The long catalog of locations in Numbers 33 must therefore be an attempt to fill out a forty-year time span, but it is unjustified either geographically or in terms of the narrative chronology.

But in the late 1790s, purportedly a quarter of a century after the original discovery, could Goethe really be concerned just to correct a historical fact in the Bible? As a politely laconic response by Schiller in a letter makes clear, a challenge to the historical accuracy of the Bible carries at this point minimal news value.[42] Certainly there were numerous precedents for historicizing and demythologizing accounts of the Exodus story, including one by Schiller himself.[43] I argue, then, that Goethe's ultimate concern as a critic is not to alight upon historical truth in this matter, but to achieve internal textual consistency (*innere Wahrscheinlichkeit*) (FA 1.3.1: 623). In a sketch for the essay he acknowledges that truth is to be found only in the *meaning*, not in the so-called *facts* in such amalgamated traditional texts. But, he makes clear, there are good and bad sorts of textual fabrication. He distinguishes between two kinds of "fable"—a poetic sort that might contradict the laws of nature and a prosaic sort that offends the laws of a healthy human understanding. The latter, the prosaic inventions, are usually "intentionally inserted . . . in order to conceal certain insufficiencies, fill in holes, and promote certain hypotheses" (*absichtlich eingeschoben . . . um gewisse Blößen zu decken gewisse Lücken zu füllen gewisse Hypothesen zu begünstigen*) (FA 1.3.1: 622). In identifying and purging "these circumstances that were imposed later" (*diese spät nacherfundene Verhältnisse*) (FA 1.3.1: 622), Goethe's aim is clearly not to get back to an original *event*, but to return to an original *poetic foundation.*

And that poetic foundation, it should now be clear, is an epic. The entire framework of his analysis—the presuppositions about editorial practices, the question of plot retardation, the discussion of aspects of Moses's character—all suggest this categorization. Now, as I argued earlier, for Goethe, the genre of epic carries with it the question of nation. Horst Lange has identified very clearly the critique of nationalism at the heart of "Israel in the Desert." But while Lange views the Jewish people as a prototypical case for Goethe's generalized critique, I maintain Goethe's aim is very culturally specific.[44] Through his textual criticism, Goethe seeks to illuminate the constitutive text of a particular people—the modern Jews.

Again, the clear political context in 1797 for this essay, as for *Hermann and Dorothea*, is the export of revolution from France. In Goethe's notes for this essay penned in 1797, the revolutionary theme is explicit, "Comparison with the modern French" (*Vergleichung mit den neuern Franzosen*) he writes (FA 1.3.1: 620). But on the heels of revolution came of course the specter of Jewish emancipation, for France had granted Jews the right of citizenship in 1791. Indeed, in precisely the period when Goethe wrote *Hermann und Dorothea* and was drafting his "Israel" essay, the possibility of emancipation suddenly became quite concrete. The destruction of the Frankfurt ghetto in a French assault led to an emergency integration of its Jewish inhabitants. Goethe suggested his desire to see the ghetto rebuilt (FA 1.16: 120). It is thus very telling that when Goethe finally picks up his Exodus essay again at the end of March 1812, to add its introductory paragraphs, it is approximately two weeks after the Prussian Edict of Emancipation granting Jews civil equality and the right to military service. This essay may target nationalism and revolution in general but it also targets, quite specifically, Jewish emancipation. Through his exposé of this supposed Jewish national epic, Goethe suggests that, far from being a model *Kulturnation*, the Jewish people are at heart something much closer to, indeed perhaps even more dangerous than, their new political-revolutionary ally France.

To discern Goethe's veiled polemic against modern Jewish emancipation we have to turn to his analysis of Moses, out of whose character, according to Goethe, the entire Exodus episode develops (FA 1.3.1: 232). Goethe eliminates virtually all divine agency in the story and makes even God a projection of Moses's all-determining personality: "like the man, so his God" (*wie der Mann so auch sein Gott*) (FA 1.3.1: 246). And just as an epic hero is supposed to act on the external world (FA 1.18: 445), so Goethe characterizes Moses as primarily a man of action "who, not born to think and reflect, merely strives for deeds" (*der nicht zum Denken und Ueberlegen geboren, bloß nach That strebt*) (FA 1.3.1: 233). He inherits his rash, active personality from the violent tribe of Levi, from which he descends (FA 1.3.1: 232).

But while Moses's impulse is to act and command unreservedly, he is constantly constrained in the external expression of his energies, both by circumstance as well as by his own resources. He is incapable of planning, negotiating, or, due to his speech defect, communicating effectively (FA 1.3.1: 233). With such channels of action cut off, Moses emerges as a closed-up (*verschlossen*) personality (FA 1.3.1: 232, 233, 236). Indeed, Goethe's characterization of Moses resembles a symptomology of the melancholic. He has a gloomy cast of mind (*trübsinnig*) (FA 1.3.1: 236). His strong nature turns inward and consumes itself (*sich selbst verzehrte*) (FA 1.3.1: 233). He is hampered by doubt and hesitation (*Zweifel und Zögern*) (FA 1.3.1: 233).[45] When he does act, it is often secretly, in a backhanded and deceitful rather than direct way. Goethe describes Moses's killing of an Egyptian for abusing an Israelite slave as an assassination (*patriotischer Meuchelmord*) done secretly (*heimlich*) (FA 1.3.1: 232).[46] Later, he implies that Moses is responsible for the death of his sister Miriam and the disappearance of his brother Aaron, soon after both of them rebelled against him (FA 1.3.1: 239). Moses's melancholy is thus of a dangerous, volatile sort.

Goethe's diagnosis of Moses as constrained, melancholic, and therefore dangerous applies as well to the Israelites and by implication to the modern Jews. Much of the analysis is organized around a contrast between the original freedom of the patriarchs and a stifling social and cultural constraint that, he suggests, has shaped Judaism ever since. The essay begins with the words of forgetting that introduce the book of Exodus, alluding again to what he views as the chasm separating the first two books of Moses. "There arose a new King in Egypt who knew nothing of Joseph. For the people, as for the ruler, the memory of their benefactor had disappeared" (*Da kam ein neuer König auf in Egypten, der wußte nichts von Joseph. Wie dem Herrscher so auch dem Volke war das Andenken seines Wohltäters verschwunden*) (FA 1.3.1: 229).[47] In his 1797 notes for the essay, Goethe nonetheless looks back to the story of Joseph's activity at Pharaoh's court in a way that anticipates the role of early modern court Jews as the procurers of royal wealth: Joseph not only rescued the Egyptions from famine through "prudence and cleverness" (*Vorsicht und Klugheit*) but he also procured the entire land as the property of the king "through an unheard-of speculation" (*durch eine unerhörte Speculation*) (FA 1.3.1: 633). Once confined to slavery in Egypt, the Israelites, this previously free, nomadic people, are forced "to build with their own hands fortified cities, which obviously are intended for them as places of enslavement and imprisonment" (*mit eignen Händen feste Städte zu bauen, welche offenbar zu Zwing- und Kerkerplätzen für sie bestimmt sind*) (FA 1.3.1: 230). Goethe alters the biblical account here in order to evoke modern ghettos. The garrison cities that the ancient Israelites were compelled to build for Pharaoh (Exod. 1:11) are in Goethe's account intended to imprison the Israelites themselves.

The essay repeatedly emphasizes the moral consequences of the exchange of the open nomadic life of the patriarchs for residence and then slavery in Egypt. Instead of the endless stars of the night sky with which the Lord had compared Abraham's descendants (Gen. 15:5), Israel has become "an innumerable people" that moves "sullenly in a sad wildnerness" (*ein unzählbares Volk [bewegt sich] mißmuthig in einer traurigen Wüste*) (FA 1.3.1: 235). He contrasts this stifled people with the free, nomadic Midianites: "A people like the Midianites that freely pursues its destiny and finds opportunity to exercise its powers, must be more developed than one which lives under a foreign yoke in eternal conflict with itself and circumstances" (*Ein Volk wie die Midianiter, das frey seiner Bestimmung nachgeht, und seine Kräfte in Uebung zu setzen Gelegenheit findet, muß gebildeter seyn als ein solches, das, unter fremdem Joche, in ewigem Widerstreit mit sich selbst und den Umständen lebt*) (FA 1.3.1: 236).

The narrowed horizons of the Israelites are clearly linked in Goethe's analysis with the theme of belief and unbelief. Goethe sees the "conflict of unbelief and belief" (*Conflict des Unglaubens und Glaubens*) as the preeminent theme in human history, with the triumph of faith serving as the theme of Genesis and lack of faith as the theme of the other four books of Moses (FA 1.8.1: 230). But Goethe employs these terms in his own distinctive fashion. Since the essay provides rationalistic explanations for divine events such as the killing of first-born Egyptians, and makes it clear that God is a projection of Moses's mindset, this hindering lack of faith should not be understood in a theological sense. In chapter 1, I argued that Goethe distinguished this Abrahamic or "Old Testament" faith from Christian assent to metaphysical doctrine: he seems instead to have in mind the confidence required to act. He gives, as an example of unbelief, the people's refusal to enter Canaan after scouts bring back reports of frightening inhabitants (FA 1.3.1: 237). Unbelief retards narrative progress in a narrow and "petty" (*kleinlich*) way, blocking faith "step by step" (*Schritt zu Schritt*) (FA 1.3.1: 230). Thus the conflict between belief and unbelief amounts to a Hamlet-like indecision about whether to proceed. In fact, within this essay the free Midianites emerge as better representatives of belief than the formerly enslaved, eternally conflicted Israelites.

The term "petty" (*kleinlich*) also links the Israelites' narrowed horizons and unfree mindset to what Goethe sees as a rabbinical or priestly sensibility in the last four books of Moses. He complains about the way ceremonial laws hinder progress of the journey:

> One cannot see why, with such a massive military campaign that already faced so many obstacles, they were so intently and *petty-mindedly* concerned to multiply the religious ceremonial baggage *through which any progress must be made infinitely more difficult.*
>
> Man sieht nicht ein, warum bey einem so ungeheuren Feldzuge, dem ohnehin so viel im Wege stand, man sich recht absichtlich und *kleinlich* bemüht, das religiöse Ceremonien-Gepäck zu vervielfältigen, *wodurch jedes Vorwärtskommen unendlich erschwert werden muß.* (FA 1.3.1: 231, my emphasis)

He suggests further that the promulgation of these laws, which have no immediate bearing on the present, are an excuse for inaction "where every day, every hour there is a dearth of advice and action" (*wo es jeden Tag, jede Stunde an Rath und That gebricht*) (FA 1.3.1: 231). He directly conjoins the terms "petty" (*kleinlich*) and "rabbinical" (*Rabinisch*) in a notation from this period about the composition of Genesis (FA 1.3.1: 630).

It is hard to miss a warning in Goethe's descriptions of the ancient Israelites, written at a time when German Jews were seeking liberation from figurative and literal ghettos. In a conception reminiscent of Schiller's critique of the French Revolution, political liberation does not entail *true* human freedom. The ancient Israelites in their urge for independence are lacking in all principle, "in the hopes of independence and self-rule, the Hebrew people recognizes no further obligations" (*in Hoffnung der Unabhängigkeit und Selbstbeherrschung, erkennt [das hebräische Volk] keine weiteren Pflichten*) (FA 1.3.1: 234). In fact, Goethe seems to side with the Egyptians. He describes the plague against the Egyptian first-born as a mass murder, not by an angel of God, but by the Israelites themselves, not of their Egyptian *enslavers*, but of their Egyptian *hosts*, "the foreigner murders the native, the guest murders the host" (*der Fremde ermordet den Einheimischen, der Gast den Wirth*) (FA 1.3.1: 234). He describes further the danger to other peoples in their path, and their ruthless annihilation of any resistance. He warns of the danger of an uprooted, refugee people, driven only by the "right of conquest" (*Eroberungsrecht*) and crushing any resistance: "anyone who defends what is his is an enemy, whom one can exterminate without mercy" (*wer das Seinige vertheidigt ist ein Feind, den man ohne Schonung vertilgen kann*) (FA 1.3.1: 236). Implicit in this characterization are the perils of Jewish emancipation for the German "hosts."

Epic Reform

And yet Goethe's polemic against Jewish emancipation is woven together with a strange literary-cultural reform agenda for Jews, directed back towards Genesis, his deeply influential and highly positive literary model. Goethe claims through his analysis in this essay to have restored to the Exodus story something of the patriarchal spirit that characterizes both Genesis as well as some of the later books, Joshua and Judges (FA 1.3.1: 246). He also claims, implicitly at least, to have made Judaism more fruitful. As we have seen, the metaphor of Judaism as an unfruitful tree has origins in both the Hebrew Bible (Jer. 11.16) and in Paul (Rom. 11.17–18) and comes up repeatedly in Goethe's characterizations of Jews and Judaism (see FA 1.14: 467, and FA 1.18: 133). Here he asserts that the forty years in the wilderness are "fruitless," and the many stations of the journey "unfruitful" (FA 1.3.1: 246). Meanwhile, he describes periods of belief (*Glaube*) as "fruitful for contemporaries and posterity" (*fruchtbar für Mitwelt und Nachwelt*) (FA 1.3.1: 230). Thus Goethe, by removing the long wandering, the worst symptom of Mosaic melancholy, can claim to render Moses's life more meaningful and in turn to restore the honor of "the national God" (*der Nationalgott*) (FA 1.3.1: 232). Through textual criticism he seeks to excise the "unfruitful" aspects of the account and make the barren Jewish trunk bear fruit again. In the broadest sense he is aiming to remove from Exodus those aspects that he associates with later rabbinic Judaism in order to reconnect Judaism to what he sees as the freer, more individualistic sensibility of Genesis. He seeks to reform Judaism by reshaping and purifying its epic.

And yet certainly the overall impact of Goethe's critical intervention on this central Jewish religious and cultural text is devastating. Goethe has turned Moses into the clandestine murderer of his own brother and sister and portrayed him as the largely incompetent leader of the first two years of the journey, even after the additional thirty-eight years are subtracted. Goethe suggests further that because of this ineptitude, Moses may have been secretly murdered by Joshua and Caleb, the new generation of leaders (FA 1.3.1: 239).[48]

More to the point, the essay purges the biblical account of its most profound and far-reaching thematic material. The experience of being a stranger in a foreign land is an explicit source of morality in Exodus, as in this injunction: "You shall not oppress a stranger [Luther: "Fremdling"], for you know the feelings of the stranger, having yourselves been strangers in the land of Egypt" (Exod. 23:9). In the concluding passages of *Hermann and Dorothea*, the recollected words of the lost fiancé echo this insight—that the experience of being a stranger connects us to others: "Man is only a stranger on earth, it has rightly been said so / And as never before we are strangers now in these last days" (*Nur ein Fremdling, sagt man mit Recht, ist der Mensch hier auf Erden. / Mehr ein Fremdling als jemals, ist nun ein jeder geworden*) (CW 8:

306; FA 1.8: 881).[49] In that epic, as I have indicated, the value of place is held in tension with the value of uprootedness. Indeed, as we will explore in the next chapter, Goethe's continuing sense of the ethical and existential significance of dislocation leads him to propose in 1808 that the Germans would be better off if they were dispersed into the world like the Jews (FA 2.6: 428). Yet in the Exodus essay, his most direct treatment of this biblical source as a Jewish text, he elides the thematic material that carries such weight in his own thinking. As he casts Jews in the mold of a revolutionary political body, he imagines Germany as the new cultural Israel.

To summarize, both *Hermann and Dorothea* and "Israel in the Desert" embody a programmatic cultural agenda born from the atmosphere of revolution in the 1790s. Both represent Goethe's efforts through the genre of epic to analyze and reshape national identity. But in effect what he excises from the Jewish biblical epic—a sense of the importance of displacement, of a history of wandering, as a component of collective consciousness—he gives to his German epic. Meanwhile he makes his position absolutely clear that Jews are unsuited for integration within German society.

Nevertheless, despite this anti-emancipatory cultural agenda, these works from the 1790s do reveal a more complicated reception of the Exodus material than the essays from the 1770s, where Moses represents legalism, statism, and cultural dessication. The further stage in Goethe's ambivalent, multifaceted reception of Moses is the figure of Faust, as will be laid out in chapter 5. And in fact, Goethe returned to his Faust project shortly after his work on the Exodus essay in 1797. The philosopher and critic Hermann Levin Goldschmidt sees a clear connection between the scathing depiction of Moses in the "Israel" essay and the emergence of Faust-Moses. According to Goldschmidt, in imagining Moses's murder by his own people, Goethe dispenses with the Jewish Moses and in turn clears the way for a new Faustian one. Goldschmidt writes, "Moses is murdered! In the next moment this Moses bursts anew, with large, indeed outsized dimensions, out of Goethe himself."[50] In broad terms, Goethe's vision of a German *Kulturnation* involves a similar act of destruction and reanimation of a Jewish cultural legacy.

Chapter 3

✦

The People of the Book

Goethe's *Volksbuch* Project and the *Journeyman Years*

The previous chapter considered Goethe's use and abuse of the Exodus narrative in his attempts to shape a modern German cultural identity according to his own image. In this chapter Goethe draws more broadly on the formal features and narrative content of the Hebrew Bible in an attempt to create a constitutive German book. Here again Goethe's reception of Judaism involves a complex mix of dependence and deprecation. Goethe builds on, and makes a bid to supersede his Jewish sources for the sake of his own conception of a dynamic, adaptive national community.

While the last chapter left off with Goethe's literary response to the military upheavals of the 1790s, this chapter picks up in the year 1808, in the wake of the humiliating French conquest and occupation of Prussia, which fed an emergent German nationalism. The war had now touched Goethe directly: in 1806, French troops sacked Weimar and set it afire. Marauding soldiers threatened Goethe's life and nearly plundered his home. His brother-in-law's young wife was raped.[1] And yet despite these high personal stakes, Goethe had an extremely ambivalent relationship to the German nationalist discourses aimed against the French invaders. He had a personal audience with Napoleon at the Erfurt Congress in 1808 and maintained a complex admiration for the general through most of his life, his typical aversion to the French Revolution apparently offset by his fascination with Napoleon's personality. Meanwhile Goethe seems to have begun accommodating himself to the new political reality. Already in 1807 he reached the decision that his son August should study law, that is, the Napoleonic Code, in Heidelberg in order to participate in building this new, more cosmopolitan society.[2] In 1813, at the price of his son's public humiliation and disgrace, he prevented him from joining the patriotic Weimar volunteer militia that had been organized to fight for German liberation.[3]

While rejecting the wave of anti-French German popular nationalism, Goethe tried to articulate a positive vision for German culture under the new order. Once again he drew on an analogy between a politically fragmented Germany and stateless Jews. In a conversation with Müller in 1808, he projected a paradoxical cultural survival for both peoples through diaspora: "The Germans must become transplanted and dispersed into the whole world like the Jews, in order to develop, for the well-being of all nations, the mass of good that lies in them" (*Verpflanzt und zerstreut wie die Juden in alle Welt müssen die Deutschen werden, um die Masse des Guten ganz und zum Heile aller Nationen zu entwickeln, die in ihnen liegt*) (WA 5.2: 231–32). I argue that in 1808 this analogy also informed Goethe's short-lived but far-reaching *Volksbuch* (literally: people's book) project—his cultural vision for Napoleonic Germany.

Goethe's *Volksbuch*

In August 1808 Goethe received a letter from the philosopher Immanuel Niethammer, who had recently become chief inspector of education for the Bavarian Ministry of the Interior. On behalf of the Bavarian kingdom, Niethammer wrote to Goethe to enlist his help on a project to promote the cultural and spiritual formation (*Bildung*) of the German nation: he hoped to commission Goethe to create a national book (*Nationalbuch*), a collection of classic German works that could serve as a standard, unifying pedagogical text for a fragmented Germany. It was a critical moment for German culture, in the midst of the Napoleon occupation, just weeks in fact before Goethe would meet Napoleon at the Erfurt Congress.

Perhaps somewhat surprisingly, Goethe said yes. Two concepts survive: extensive, but fragmentary notes, penned apparently on August 9, for a historical *Volksbuch* (*Volksbuch historischen Inhalts*), which would represent history through excerpts from diverse sources, and a proposal for a lyrical *Volksbuch*. The latter proposal he actually sent to Niethammer on August 19 (WA I.42.2: 397).[4] It is unclear whether Goethe ever really intended two volumes—a historical and a poetic one—or whether one conception displaced the other in his thinking.[5] Hans Dietrich Dahnke surmises that Goethe started with the historical plan, turned to the poetry collection in order to conform more closely to Niethammer's request, and then came back to the historical plan, ultimately abandoning it last.[6] Whatever the precise chronology, I believe the sketchy, yet highly ambitious historical plan has particularly long legs in his thinking.

In both plans it is clear that Goethe had his own ideas about the project, beginning with his choice of the term *Volksbuch* over Niethammer's term *Nationalbuch*.[7] The term *Volksbuch* traditionally referred to chapbooks—essentially early modern pulp fiction printed cheaply and available for pennies from street vendors.[8] But by this time, the word *Volksbuch* had begun to take on a more nationalist implication with an emphasis on the *Volk*. In a preface to a collection of *Volksbuch* legends in 1807 the Romantic writer Josef Görres depicts these stories as organic expressions of a sacred spirit inhering in a people.[9]

But Goethe defines *Volk* rather unromantically as "an uneducated, educable mass" (*eine ungebildete bildungsfähige Menge*) (WA I.42.2: 414), which can coincide with all or merely part of a nation. As this definition makes clear, his use of the term *Volk* instead of *Nation* is not intended to evoke some organic mystical community but simply to avoid the potentially political implications of a nation. Goethe also diverges from Niethammer's reverential attitude toward this national text. Niethammer ambitiously proposes that a *Nationalbuch* could mean to contemporary Germany what Homer meant to the Greeks and what the Lutheran Bible, in earlier (less secular) times, meant to the German Protestants (WA I.42.2: 405). But at a time when both Homeric and biblical criticism were transforming views of these texts, Niethammer advocates an explicitly non-critical approach to his proposed canon of German classic work. He laments "that obsessive appetite for dissection and criticism of spiritual works of art" (*jene Sucht des Zergliederns und Bekrittelns der geistigen Kunstwerke*) (WA I.42.2: 402), and imagines these literary models will convey in unmediated fashion a capacity to discern the beautiful, noble, and sublime, the good and the bad (*das Verwerfliche*) (WA I.42.2: 402). A national book is for Niethammer indeed something holy, "a gift of God" (*ein Geschenk Gottes*) (WA I.42.2: 405).

In laying out his plan for a prose, historical *Volksbuch*, Goethe too refers to Homer as a model, but with a difference. He alludes once again to the new critical conception, put forth by Friedrich August Wolf in his *Prolegomena ad Homerum*, that Homeric texts were the composite production of a guild of poets. He comments,

> To author a *Volksbuch* we need a large inventory. Material diverse in meaning that earlier was esteemed, honored, marveled at, then transmitted, finally collected, ordered, redacted and reviewed. In recent times we have become convinced that this is the case with Homer.
>
> Ein Volksbuch zu verfassen gehört ein großer Vorrath. Mannigfaltig bedeutendes das früher geachtet, verehrt, bewundert worden, dann fortgepflanzt, endlich gesammelt, geordnet, redigiert und rezensirt worden. Wir haben uns in der letzten Zeit überzeugt daß dies mit Homer der Fall sey. (WA I.42.2: 418)

But he immediately dismisses the possibility of matching Homer. A nation, he asserts, can no longer hope for such fortuitous content.

Instead he offers another model of a heterogeneous edited collection: the Bible. For, according to Goethe, while we have convinced ourselves recently of the composite character of Homer, "as regards the Bible, it's perfectly obvious" (*Was die Bibel betrifft, so liegt es am Tage*) (WA I.42.2: 418). This assertion matches his characterization of the Bible in *Poetry and Truth* as "a collective work that had come into existence little by little, with revisions at various times" (*ein zusammengetragenes, nach und nach entstandenes, zu verschiedenen Zeiten überarbeitetes Werk*) (CW 4: 377; FA 1.14: 554). Moreover, Goethe's *Volksbuch* aims not only to imitate the Bible but also to *compete* with it. He continues, "A great, meaningful content, that competes with the content of the Bible lies before us. It depends on our convincing ourselves of it, our seizing it and appropriating it for the German people" (*Ein großer bedeutender [Gehalt] der mit dem biblischen wetteifert liegt vor uns. Es kommt darauf an daß wir uns von ihm überzeugen, ihn ergreifen, ihn dem deutschen Volcke zu eignen*) (WA I.42.2: 419). Thus, unlike what we saw in Niethammer, Goethe, in striking an analogy between his *Volksbuch* and the Bible, is neither engaging in a rhetoric of the sacred nor proposing a devotional, non-critical relationship to his *Volksbuch*.

I maintain that when he writes of the Bible in this context, he is alluding chiefly, if not exclusively, to the Hebrew Bible. How is this evident? First of all, this new textual paradigm of the Bible as a diverse redacted text was pioneered on and, at this point, remained largely confined to the Old Testament. Goethe presumably has Eichhorn's work on the Old Testament specifically in mind. His parallel between the Bible and Homer is a clear allusion to the methodological connection between Wolf's *Prolegomena* and Eichhorn's *Introduction to the Old Testament*, which had served as inspiration for Wolf. As noted in the previous chapter, Goethe read the two works in conjunction with each other in 1797. He even includes Eichhorn's name among his notes for the historical *Volksbuch* under the heading "Groundwork" ("Vorarbeiten") (WA I.42.2: 427). Furthermore, *Introduction to the Old Testament* may well have been the source for Goethe's notion of the Hebrew Bible as *Volksbuch*, for Eichhorn employs the term *Volksbuch* to describe the role the written Mosaic law played as the foundation for all subsequent Hebrew literature, comparing it to the role the Lutheran Bible played for Germans, Homer played for the Greeks, Arabic poetry and later the Koran played for the Arabs.[10]

Second, Goethe's description of the textual disparateness of his proposed *Volksbuch* is simply a better match for the Hebrew Scriptures. His intended juxtaposition of "sacred" (*Heiliges*) and "secular" (*Weltliches*), "ideal" (*ideele*) and "real" (*reale*) segments certainly suggests the generic range and narrative diversity of the Hebrew Bible, which, among other genres, encompasses sacred and erotic poetry, a body of laws, historical narratives, first-person prophetic texts, comedy (as some have categorized Esther), and idyll (as Goethe himself termed the book of Ruth).[11] The phrases he uses to describe the form of his historical *Volksbuch*, such as "analogy of a mosaic" (*Gleichnis der Mosaick*), "incongruent parts" (*incongruente Theile*) (FA 1.42.2: 426) seem apt characterizations of the "bumpiness" that Alter identifies in the Hebrew Bible.[12] Goethe's notations "side-by-side" (*Neben einander*) and "few connecting words" (*wenige Verbindungsworte*) suggest the parallelism and paratactic syntax that is so characteristic of the Hebrew Bible in particular (FA 1.42.2: 426).

But the strongest evidence that the "Bible" here means primarily the *Hebrew* Bible is the further content of his notes, which are structured largely around parallels between German and Jewish history. Just as the Germans are the *Volk* in his proposed *Volksbuch*, the Jews are the implied *Volk* in his biblical model. A further implication is then also clear: Goethe's analogy and competition extend not only between his *Volksbuch* and the Bible but also between Germans and Jews.

Goethe's project to create a representative German book introduces the question of what is indeed authentically or originally German. In his essay on the lyrical *Volksbuch*, Goethe fleshes out a claim that also appears in his notes for the historical one: that Germans do not need to be ashamed about the extent of foreign influence on their culture:

> When one thinks, that so few nations in general, particularly none of the new ones, can make a claim to absolute originality, a German does not need to be ashamed, who, because of his location, found himself in such circumstances, that he received his education externally and, particularly as concerns poetry, took the form and content from foreign influences.
>
> Bedenkt man, daß so wenig Nationen überhaupt, besonders keine neuere, Anspruch an absolute Originalität machen kann; so braucht sich der Deutsche nicht zu schämen, der seiner Lage nach in den Fall kam, seine Bildung von außen zu erhalten, und besonders was Poesie betrifft, Gehalt und Form von Fremden genommen hat. (WA I.42.2: 417)

The question of the originality of the ancient Hebrews was similarly at issue as the new historical criticism strove to place the Old Testament within broader geographical and ethnographical frameworks. Indeed, the very status of the Israelites as the founders of monotheism came into question. For example, Carl Leonhard Reinhold's essay, "The Hebrew Mysteries or the Oldest Religious Freemasonry" ("Die Hebräischen Mysterien oder die älteste religiöse Freymauerey"; 1787), which became the basis of Schiller's essay "The Mission of Moses" ("Die Sendung Moses"; 1790), asserts that Mosaic law and religion were essentially a transplant of Egyptian mystery religion onto the Hebrew people.[13] Again Eichhorn may well have been a resource in Goethe's thinking about this issue. For Eichhorn concedes that if originality were understood as complete self-creation in isolation then of course the Hebrews are not an original people: even from their earliest history as nomads; they had contact with, and came under the influence of, other tribes.[14] But Eichhorn dismisses such a rigid notion of originality as absurd and redefines it to include creative cultural exchange. It is enough to qualify as original, he explains, if one takes what is borrowed and foreign and mixes it in such a way as to create an integral whole; transforms the foreign material into one's own; or imprints one's own resolutely preserved character upon it. He concludes, "And in this sense the Hebrews were in their customs and laws, in their religious and political constitution and in their entire literature, as far as we know it, original to the highest degree."[15]

Eichhorn's conception of originality resonates in Goethe's notes where "external education" (*Bildung von außen*) appears paradoxically under the rubric "properly German" (*Deutsches Eignes*) (WA I.42.2: 420). Thus his German *Volksbuch* will include translated sources, indeed it will represent "that which was important from all times and places for human beings of all kinds and eras" (*Was aus allen Zeiten und Orten für Menschen aller Zeiten und Arten wichtig war*) (WA I.42.2: 421). And in this context, for a second time, he asserts the primacy of the Bible as his model: "We find the highest form of such a collection in the Bible" (*Die höchste Form einer solchen Samml[ung] finden wir in der Bibel*) (WA I.42.2: 421).[16]

From here he turns to the topic of Jewish history with the notation: "The Jewish people as the most appropriate people for constructing a world history in our sense" (*Das iudische Volck als günstigstes um eine Weltgeschichte in unserm Sinne anzureihen*) (WA I.42.2: 422). He outlines Jewish history in a series of general phrases and keywords that could also suggest some more general patterns of world history. He refers, for example, to the people's inconstancy with regard to both religious and political principle, their dissolution occasioned by both internal and external developments, their recovery through tenacity and endurance, their further conflict, stubbornness, decline, the deliberate annihilation of the people and their condition "cast into the world" (*Verschlagen in die Weltmasse*) (WA I.42.2: 422). Yet, his outline continues, the people reemerges and continues to have an impact: "And yet resurfacing again. / still living on. Continuing to influence" (*Und doch wieder auftauchend. / Noch fortlebend. Fortwirkend*) (WA I.42.2: 422). Goethe's notes then turn to a second, more specific outline, which puts his intercultural model in further relief. He lists the various stages of foreign cultural influences on the ancient Hebrews (Egyptian, Phoenician, Greek, etc.) and ends with the decline of the Jewish people and emergence of Christianity, which he treats briefly as if a mere postscript to Jewish history.

He then turns to the Germans: "Emergence of the Germans" ("Hervortreten der Deutschen") (WA I.42.2: 424). The basic point of the comparison is clear: both the Germans and the Jews emerged through interaction with foreign influences. About the Germans, Goethe writes, "no nation, less so the newer ones, perhaps least of all the German nation, formed itself out of itself" (*keine Nation, weniger die Neuern, am wenigsten vielleicht die Deutsche, hat sich aus sich selbst gebildet*) (WA I.42.2: 420). In short, sometimes cryptic phrases he now traces German history from Tacitus to the eighteenth century and then gestures toward the future. And here, below the phrase "Outlook towards the future" ("Aussichten auf die Zukunft"), appears the notation "New Jerusalem" ("Neues Jerusalem") (WA I.42.2: 426).

"New Jerusalem" is a term laden with biblical significance. It appears in the New Testament book of Revelation, where it alludes to, and transforms, a passage from the Hebrew scriptures: Ezekiel's vision of the temple restored after its destruction by the Babylonians (Ezek. 40–48).[17] While the prophet Ezekiel refers to this specific historical catastrophe (from the sixth century B.C.E.), John, the voice of Revelation, describes a universal, apocalyptic destruction, "the first heaven and the first earth had passed away and the sea was no more" (Rev. 21:1). While Ezekiel describes the new temple in exhaustive, architectural detail, John's New Jerusalem has no temple: "for its temple is the Lord God the Almighty and the Lamb" (Rev. 21:22).[18] Indeed, John's "New Jerusalem" clearly no longer refers to an earthly, historical city of Jerusalem, but to a universal, spiritual, eschatological community, that is, Christianity. While Goethe's use of the term almost certainly does not imply the Christian apocalyptic meaning, it does imply the figural framework. That is, Goethe's project refashions this familiar Old Testament/New Testament construct within a secular, historical context. His use of this term suggests, whether ironically or not, a new typological relationship between Jewish history as source and German history as horizon.

Thus we see that Goethe models his own *Volksbuch* on the Hebrew Bible as a matter of both form (he aims for a disparate mosaic of sources of different age and provenance) and content (he conceives German cultural history according to the intercultural patterns of Jewish history, where originality emerges through intercultural contact, even disunity and dispersal). Furthermore, he borrows the Christian figural framework to suggest that German culture can supersede its Judaic model.

Reconfiguration of the *Volksbuch* Project

But where did his *Volksbuch* conception end up after 1808? According to Niethammer's documents, by summer 1811 Goethe had communicated his abandonment of the project and he had presumably given up on it long before (WA I.42.2: 410). My hypothesis is that the historical *Volksbuch* was one of the important tributaries that flowed into one of Goethe's most radically modern projects—*Wilhelm Meister's Journeyman Years*, which Goethe had indeed begun in 1807 and picked up again in 1809.[19] One doesn't have to look far to discover formal parallels between Goethe's novel and this new critical conception of the Hebrew Bible. The novel is a fictional textual archive comprising diverse sources and voices, widely disparate genres and subject matters, much like Goethe's biblically inspired *Volksbuch*.[20] The archive metaphor is yet another link: as Jonathan Sheehan has explored, the conception of the Bible as an archive of an ancient civilization was current among prominent eighteenth-century critics such as Eichhorn and Lavater.[21]

Perhaps the clearest hint that Goethe was actually working with this analogy is a rich description of the Jewish holy books by Wilhelm's guide in the Pedagogical Province.

> "A principal strength," the sage replied, "is the splendid collection of its sacred books. They fit together so well that out of the most disparate elements a plausible whole can be constructed. They are sufficiently complete to be satisfying, sufficiently fragmentary to be intriguing, sufficiently barbaric to be challenging, sufficiently subtle to be soothing; and how many other paradoxical qualities can be celebrated in these books, in this book!" (*CW* 10: 207)

> "Ein Hauptvorteil," versetzte jener, "Ist die treffliche Sammlung ihrer heiligen Bücher. Sie stehen so glücklich beisammen, daß aus den fremdesten Elementen ein täuschendes Ganze entgegentritt. Sie sind vollständig genug, um zu befriedigen, fragmentarisch genug, um anzureizen; hinlänglich barbarisch, um aufzufordern, hinlänglich zart, um zu besänftigen; und wie manche andere entgegengesetzte Eigenschaften sind an diesen Büchern, an diesem Buche zu rühmen!" (FA 1. 10: 426)

This quotation is at once clearly applicable to the generically disparate, aggregate novel of which it is part and recalls Goethe's plans for his *Volksbuch* as a heterogeneous compilation.

The novel also includes an embedded representation of Jewish history in a gallery of murals in the Pedagogical Province. Just as, in the *Volksbuch* plan, Jewish history is to serve as a paradigm for world history (WA I.2.2: 422), so, here as well, Jewish history serves an exemplary role: "That is why we have presented it here as a model, as the central subject, which the others only serve to frame" (*Wir haben es daher als Musterbild aufgestellt, als Hauptbild, dem die andern nur zum Rahmen dienen*) (*CW* 10: 207; FA 1.10: 425).

Certainly the *Journeyman Years* as a whole works out the intercultural and diasporic model of national identity that emerged in the *Volksbuch* plan. The novel serves as Goethe's most sustained exploration of wandering as a multi-dimensional historical, cultural, aesthetic, and existential paradigm. Its predecessor novel, *Wilhelm Meister's Apprenticeship*, introduces a fluid, self-ironizing model of community in its Tower Society; the *Journeyman Years* radicalizes this vision in its thoroughgoing renunciation of permanence in social institutions and associations. The novel is centripetal in its motion, ultimately dispersing its characters into new projects and even into the new world, through immigration to America. Thus the fate of the Tower Society could aptly be summed up with phrases from the *Volksbuch* plan cited earlier describing the Jewish diaspora: "Cast into the world. / And yet resurfacing again. / still living on. Continuing to influence" (WA I.42.2: 422). Likewise the novel seems to embody Goethe's 1808 pronouncement, also cited above, that Germans should be, like Jews, transplanted and strewn throughout the world for the good of all.

Further, the diasporic network in the *Journeyman Years* has a discernible, if qualified, utopian trajectory that links it to the "New Jerusalem," the horizon of German history in the *Volksbuch*. (To be sure, the novel's utopian quality resides more in the opportunities it suggests for diverse experimentation and creative refashioning than in any solidified conception.) Montan, the new name the Tower Society member Jarno assumes in the *Journeyman Years*, could also suggest this project of a New Jerusalem. The name "Montan" is usually assumed to refer to "montanus," the Latin adjective related to "mountain," because of the character's geological pursuits. But Montan also serves as the Tower's prophet of renunciation, and in this respect this new alias could simultaneously refer to the second-century heretic Montanus. As Goethe would have read in Gottfried Arnold's *Impartial History of the Church and of Heretics (Unparteyische Kirchen- und Ketzer-historie)*, Montanus preached "discipline and moderation," accepted women as prophets and teachers (like Makarie in the novel) and proclaimed a New Jerusalem in Asia Minor.[22] But like so many other modern attempts to establish a New Jerusalem, the novelistic one looks west, to the new space of America.[23]

Far more important than any specific content that might be associated with Goethe's cryptic term "New Jerusalem" is the underlying typological structure it implies, both for the *Volksbuch* plan and, as I will now argue, for the novel that succeeds it. My thesis is that Goethe not only draws inspiration from the Hebrew Bible and the motifs of Jewish history for his novel but, in the novel, as in the *Volksbuch* plan, adopts a logic of competition and overcoming toward this source. The typological construct upon which the *Journeyman Years* rests has multiple, complex implications: the novel positions itself toward the earlier *Apprenticeship* as New Testament to Old Testament.[24] In doing so, it also effectively presents itself as an alternative, secular New Testament and thereby contains a critique and revision of Christianity. But these relationships—to the earlier novel, to Christian narratives—are both predicated on a paradigm of supersession toward Judaism and the Hebrew Bible. And in the 1829 novel, that model takes on a darker exclusionary cast than in the *Volksbuch* plan.

Adoptive Fathers

The self-positioning of the *Journeyman Years* as an ersatz New Testament is hinted at by the biblical allusions at the junctures between the *Apprenticeship* and *Journeyman Years*. The *Apprenticeship* ends with a comparison between

Wilhelm and the Israelite king Saul. In a reference to 1 Samuel, Friedrich asserts, "You seem to me like Saul, the son of Kish, who went in search of his father's asses, and found a kingdom" (*du kommst mir vor wie Saul der Sohn Kis, der ausging seines Vaters Eselinnen zu suchen, und ein Königreich fand*) (*CW* 9: 373; FA 1.9: 992). In sharp contrast, the *Journeyman Years* opens with a New Testament scenario, a chapter entitled "The Flight into Egypt" ("Die Flucht nach Ägypten") in which Wilhelm and Felix encounter a strange apparition—a man accompanying a blue-berobed woman upon a donkey with an infant in arms, all as if taken directly from images of the holy family in religious painting. The man, who is known as St. Joseph the Second, lives out his life in self-conscious imitation of the adoptive father of Jesus.

The opening exploration of the role of the foster father seems an oblique reflection on the novel's own program as a creative act of *reception*, rather than *conception*. As we saw, heterogeneous cultural reception is key to the *Volksbuch* plan, which relativizes any claim to national originality. The novel is correspondingly broad in its integration of other sources (including the nearly whole-cloth insertion of a French novella). Thus, among the disparate sources that compose the texture of the *Journeyman Years*, the Bible is not even dominant; but as the highest form of a textual compilation according to the *Volksbuch* plan (WA I 42.2: 421), the Bible serves as a kind of meta-source for the whole project.

If we pursue Goethe's adoption metaphor, we can discern multiple layers of adoption at work in the opening of the novel. The biblical Joseph adopts the Christ child; Wilhelm's contemporary, the young St. Joseph II, adopts certain versions of this adoptive relationship as a model within his own life; Wilhelm, listening to this story, identifies so strongly with its teller that he adopts it in a certain sense for himself, putting his words in St. Joseph's mouth in a letter to his wife Natalie (*SW* 1.10: 30). One can similarly refer to multiple layers of adoption or reception in the *Volksbuch / Journeyman Years* conception. At the first level, the Hebrew Bible integrates disparate sources, constructing itself, in Goethe's view, "out of the most disparate elements" (*CW* 10: 207; FA 1.10: 426). At the next level, Christianity, in its core typological move, adopts the Hebrew Bible into its own rhetorical and theological program.[25] Finally, Goethe's novel as self-consciously modern, secular fiction adopts the Hebrew Bible (and indeed a broader conception of Judaism) and thereby positions itself as *like* Christianity. In this third sense, the novel simultaneously adapts Christianity for its own purposes, creating, as Goethe describes in *Poetry and Truth*, a version of the religion "for my own private use" (*CW* 4: 466; FA 1.14: 692). In short, then, the novel not only adopts and modifies the model of the Hebrew Bible and Judaism, but adopts and modifies Christianity's relationship to these sources, thus in turn purveying its own revised, modernized brand of Christianity. And yet the metaphor of adoption with which the novel opens is far too benign to capture the full dynamic of reception and appropriation of Judaism at work, whether concerning Christianity's historical relationship to Judaism or Goethe's peculiar construction of Judaism in the service of his own literary and religious modernity. (Of course, at closer look, the models of father-son relationships in the novel are also anything but benign, but this theme in the novel falls outside of the scope of this discussion.)

Competing Wanderers

Another motif perhaps better illuminates the more radical logic of supersession operating in the novel: the Wandering Jew. As discussed in chapter 1, Goethe reports that he became acquainted early on with the traditional legend of the Wandering Jew as told in the old chapbooks and later began, but never finished, his own epic of the Wandering Jew (FA 1.14: 42; 692–94). To review: in the chapbook version of 1602, Ahasverus is a shoemaker in Jerusalem who curses Christ when Christ leans up against his house while carrying the cross on his way to his crucifixion. Ahasverus is then condemned to leave his wife and child and wander through the ages seeking redemption and testifying to Christ's suffering.[26] According to later versions of the myth, Ahasverus is not able to stay in one place more than three days.[27]

Wilhelm explicitly compares himself to a Wandering Jew because of the relentless mobility imposed upon him by the Society of Renunciants (FA 1.10: 408). Like Ahasverus, he is separated from his wife and—for most of the novel—his child. As in popular versions of the myth, he is not permitted to stay in one place more than three days. While obviously no supernatural or divine curse is at work, the requirement of constant movement is cast in vaguely religious terms. These commandments (*Gebote*) (FA 1.10: 268) are both self-imposed and issued by the Tower Society, as represented by a figure known only by his religious title—the "Abbé." While no specific sin is identified that has condemned Wilhelm to this itinerant way of life, the terms of his letter to Natalie suggest past mistakes and a vague underlying guilt. He regards the document that bears the conditions of his wandering as "this record of my last confession, my last absolution" (*Zeugnis meiner letzten Beichte, meiner letzten Absolution*) (CW 10: 100; FA 1.10: 268). In a letter to the Abbé, he asks to be relieved of the condition "that stamped him as a Wandering Jew" (*die ihn zum ewigen Juden stempelte*) (CW 10: 194; FA 1.10: 408). Thus one arc of the novel concerns Wilhelm's liberation from this condition of directionless wandering into a more intentional, meaningful form of motion and activity.

This motif of the redemption of the Wandering Jew also places the *Journeyman Years* in a typological relationship to the *Apprenticeship*, even if the "typos" here is drawn from legend rather than the Bible. As has been recognized, the Harpist in the *Apprenticeship* is an implicit Wandering Jew.[28] When he is first introduced, his strange apparition leads to a debate among guests at a tavern "whether the old man was a priest or a Jew" (*ob es ein*

Pfaffe oder ein Jude sei) (CW 9: 72; FA 1.9: 482). His mysterious utterance about a terrible guilt and fate imposed upon him by a higher judge also casts him in the mold of Ahasverus: "The vengeance that pursues me is not of any earthly judge. I am caught up in inexorable fate. I cannot remain here, for I dare not" (*Die Rache, die mich verfolgt, ist nicht des irdischen Richters; ich gehöre einem unerbittlichen Schicksale; ich kann nicht bleiben und ich darf nicht*) (CW 9: 122; FA 1.9: 569–70). The Harpist's guilt, as it turns out, concerns Mignon, his daughter born of incest. Wilhelm's pilgrimage to Mignon's birthplace in the middle of the *Journeyman Years* suggests that his unspecified guilt also concerns, at least in part, this child. Indeed his failure in the *Apprenticeship* to comprehend and sympathize with her suffering appears to hasten her illness and death. In this case, Wilhelm's sin appears to be, like the sin of Ahasverus, a failure of compassion.

As seen in chapter 1, Goethe's plans for his own epic on the Wandering Jew reveal a great deal of ambiguity. On the one hand, he signals his clear identification with the figure of the Wandering Jew through autobiographical clues such as the planned encounter with Spinoza; on the other, he signals his rejection by employing conventional Christian-Jewish typologies, such as spirit versus letter, sympathy versus propriety (FA 1.14: 730). In his précis, Goethe repeatedly represents Ahasverus as a stationary figure in front of his workshop, while Christ is among the passersby (FA 1.14: 692). Ahasverus even tries to discourage Christ's transient way of life, urging him not to wander around with idle types or draw people away from their work (FA 1.14: 692–93). This polyvalent sketch seems to offer, as an alternative to Ahasverus, a positively constructed model of wandering associated with Christ.

Certainly the later novel develops this association of wandering with Christianity. The term "wanderer" first appears in the novel in reference to the journeying family consciously styling themselves as Joseph and Mary with baby Jesus (FA 1.10: 265). Later, in the Pedagogical Province, the boarding school to which Wilhelm entrusts his son, Christ's conduct or life journey (*Wandel*) is held up as an explicit model for human behavior (FA.1.10: 429). Most importantly, Wilhelm's liberation from his status as a Wandering Jew by becoming a surgeon (*Wundarzt*) is cast in Christian terms. Once freed from this relentless mobility, he is able to undertake surgical training that allows him to achieve a more profound relationship to suffering, temporality, and other human beings—a new outlook on life that I argue, the novel associates with Christianity. For example, the Pedagogical Province characterizes Christianity as a reverence for that which lies below us, including the adoration "of the repulsive, the hated, the shunned" (*des Widerwärtigen, Verhaßten, Fliehenswerten*) (CW 10: 210; FA 1.10: 430), and emphasizes Christ's attention to sickness, suffering, and pain. Clearly, Wilhelm's care of wounded bodies expresses a commitment to compassion in its most concrete and practical form and therefore serves as a form of redemption from the original sin of the Wandering Jew. Wilhelm's final act in the novel of resurrecting the dead (his own son who appears lifeless after falling into the river) completes his transformation from Wandering Jew to a wanderer in a Goethean-Christian mode.

The potential for competition with the Jews over the status of wanderer is made quite explicit in Lenardo's speech to the League of Emigrants. The league's ideal of wandering must be set apart from the eternal wandering of the Jews, which is aimed, he claims, to trick and surpass others:

> But what shall I say of the race which above all others has adopted the role of the eternal wanderer, and, through constant movement and activity, contrives to outsmart settled shopkeepers and outdo its fellow itinerants? We may speak neither good nor evil of it: not good, because the league is on its guard against them, not evil because the wanderer is obligated to treat everyone he meets in friendly fashion, and be mindful of mutual advantage. (*CW* 10: 366)
>
> Was soll ich aber nun von dem Volke sagen, das den Segen des ewigen Wanderns vor allen andern sich zueignet und durch seine bewegliche Tätigkeit die Ruhenden zu überlisten und die Mitwandernden zu überschreiten versteht? Wir dürfen weder Gutes noch Böses von ihnen sprechen; nichts Gutes, weil sich unser Bund vor ihnen hütet, nichts Böses, weil der Wanderer jeden Begegnenden freundlich zu behandeln, wechselseitigen Vorteils eingedenk, verpflichtet ist. (FA 1.10: 668)

Thus, while Lenardo's ideal of wandering claims an ethical orientation directed toward the mutual advantage of all, Jewish wandering is represented as hostile and competitive, amounting to a mere mobile activity. Jews, acccording to Wilhelm's guide in the Pedagogical Province, have few virtues as a people other than sheer persistence: they are "the most persistent people on earth" (*das beharrlichste Volk der Erde*) (*CW* 10: 207; FA 1.10: 425). Elsewhere the novel holds out the danger of a deficient, radically disoriented, even destructive sort of wandering, identified with terms such as error (*Irrtum*), aberrancy (*Verirrung*), and confusion (*Verwirrung*). For example, in the collection of aphorisms "Reflections in the Spirit of the Wanderers": "Truth is constructive. From error nothing comes; it only entangles us" (*Das Wahre fördert; aus dem Irrtum entwickelt sich nichts, er verwickelt uns nur*) (*CW* 10: 310; FA 1.10: 581).[29] The motif of the Jewish wanderer or Wandering Jew clearly belongs to this category within the novel of a deficient, non-developmental wandering.[30]

This casting of Jewish wandering as a condition to be overcome culminates in one of the most disturbing moments in Goethe's oeuvre, the ultimate exclusion of all Jews from the Society of Emigrants: "we tolerate no Jew among us" (*[Wir] dulden keinen Juden unter uns*) (*CW* 10: 378; FA 1.10:

687). Critics have long struggled with the challenges presented by this pronouncement, representing the collective decision of the Emigrant group, in the midst of such a systematically complex and ironic work.

On the one hand, Goethe's record of opposing the social integration of Jews bears consideration: in his account of his travels to Switzerland in 1797 he presents the town of Heilbronn as a model of civic culture, adding in a strikingly similar formulation, "No Jews are suffered here" (*Es werden keine Juden hier gelitten*) (FA 2.4: 405). He also praises the exclusion of Jews closer to home: as previously cited, in an 1816 letter he refers to the law that no Jews may spend the night in Jena as a "praiseworthy decree" (*löbliche Anordnung*) (FA 2.8:19).

On the other hand, a high degree of caution is indeed called for with this text. Interpreters of the *Journeyman Years* have rightfully been wary of any readings that seek to cut across the contradictory contexts, disparate perspectives, and whimsical insertions—what Swales calls the novel's "postmodern universe of pantextuality"[31]—to arrive at some singular programmatic meaning. Jane Brown's reading of the novel is exemplary in its illumination of playful and parodistic elements as well as shifting perspectives. She points out that the society that will tolerate no Jew also bans reading libraries.[32] Meanwhile Benjamin Bennett stands out in his effort to integrate these disturbingly anti-Jewish passages into a view of the novel's overarching ironic strategies. Bennett understands the novel as radically subversive, in fact as "*nothing but subversive* with respect to anything that might be claimed as its content" (emphasis in original).[33] The logical outcome of this all-pervasive irony is a reversal—our ultimate identification as readers with the excluded category—the Jews."[34] Yet Bennett's charitable reading cannot allay the blunt force of this and other anti-Jewish passages scattered through the novel.

Clearly, within the context of this complicated novel, one must walk a careful line, taking seriously Goethe's representational sophistication and perspectivism on the one hand and the raw impact of this and other anti-Jewish pronouncements on the other.[35] My point is precisely that the anti-Jewish moments and the narrative complexity of the novel are not at odds, but rather deeply entwined. For even the novel's irony, its semiotic indeterminacy, its perspectivism, anti-essentialism, and cosmopolitanism fall under the trope of wandering. But as Lenardo's speech asserts, this true, cosmopolitan culture of wandering—friendly, receptive, even-handed—is exemplified by his league, not by the Jews who claim it as their legacy. In the logic of the novel, irony is tied to the overcoming of "Jewish wandering" in the name of a modern, relativistic, Goethean-Christian wandering.

Refashioning Christianity

In order to highlight more precisely the peculiarly modern attributes Goethe assigns to his own vision of a Christian wandering we should first review his critique of his own contemporary Christian culture (previously sketched out in the introduction). Most of Goethe's distaste for the Christianity of his time concerns its tendency toward the kind of fallacies that Kant labels dogmatic metaphysics. This form of thinking is embodied in particular by Goethe's friend Lavater, whose aggressive evangelism annoyed Goethe to the point that he was prepared to choose atheism over Lavater's brand of Christianity (FA 1.14: 661). One of the errors that Goethe identifies in Lavater is essentially semiotic. In his physiognomic system Lavater conflates sensory and spiritual realms, individual visage with moral character (FA 1.14: 818). Lavater's tendency to collapse sign and signified ties into the broader theme of *idolatry* in Goethe's work. Perhaps Goethe's most scandalous example of an idol is the crucifix (FA 1. 38.1: 509). His rejection of the doctrine of Christ's divinity as, in his words, a "piece of crap" may also belong to his eschewal of any dogmatic fixation of the eternal (FA 2.1: 451).

A further form of Christian dogmatic metaphysics that Goethe pillories is its tendency toward otherworldly visions. Lavater once again embodies this category error in his fantasies of the next life as a mere extension of one's current life under less onerous conditions (FA 1. 14: 818). This sort of morbid delusion, in fact, helps drive Werther's suicide. By contrast, Goethe's entire oeuvre evinces a core commitment to this world and a respect for time and finitude. Goethe also concerns himself with the ethical consequences of this otherworldly, metaphysical orientation in Christianity. The emphasis on faith over works, on internal contemplation of truths unseen over active engagement in the world, results in an ethical passivity best exemplified by the Beautiful Soul in the *Apprenticeship*. His hope for Christianity at the end of his life is that it might place action over belief. In a conversation with Eckermann in 1832, he projects, "And we will all, by and by, increasingly move from a Christianity of the Word and of faith to a Christianity of ethos and deed!" (*Auch werden wir alle nach und nach aus einem Christentum des Wortes und Glaubens immer mehr zu einem Christentum der Gesinnung und Tat kommen!*) (FA 2.12: 749).

Thus the novel projects an idiosyncratic Goethean Christianity that is cultural and existential rather than theological and metaphysical in its orientation. To do so it attempts to supersede—and simultaneously appropriate—a signifying tradition, an ethical orientation, and a temporal-historic outlook to which Judaism can lay claim.

The Anti-Idolatrous Sign

The Christianity Goethe develops in the novel is closely related to his conception of symbolic meaning. The paradigmatic Goethean symbol in the novel, so frequently cited by critics, is the casket (*Kästchen*) which reappears throughout the main plot of the novel and also emerges in different guises in a couple of the interpolated novellas. The collector, with whom Wilhelm confers about having the casket forcibly opened, suggests Wilhelm wait to see if a key turns up. In making this argument, he compares the casket to a piece of an old crucifix he once owned, to which the other missing pieces eventually surfaced. The collector sees in this happy coincidence the fate of the Christian religion, "which often enough dismembered and dispersed, must in the end always come together again around the Cross" (*die oft genug zergliedert und zerstreut, sich doch endlich immer wieder am Kreuze zusammenfinden muß*) (CW 10: 197; FA 1.10: 412).

Crucial to the symbolic character of the casket is that it withholds any final meaning or epiphany. When at last the key turns up, and a goldsmith, who understands the mechanism, successfully opens the box, he immediately presses it closed again with the comment that it is better to leave such secrets be. If one pursues the collector's analogy between the casket and the fate of Christianity, this is also a Christianity without final epiphany. Dismembered and dispersed elements collect together around the *cross*—the image of earthly suffering; they are not necessarily made whole in an ultimate scene of resurrection or apotheosis. Indeed, when Wilhelm revives his own son in the final scene, this resurrection is but a moment in an inevitable sequence of new injuries and new recoveries: "'You are always brought forth anew, glorious image of God!' [Wilhelm] exclaimed, 'and are always injured again straight away, wounded from within or without!'" (*"Wirst du doch immer aufs neue hervorgebracht, herrlich Ebenbild Gottes!" rief [Wilhelm] aus, "und wirst sogleich wieder beschädigt, verletzt von innen oder von außen"*) (CW 10: 417; FA 1.10: 745). The Christianity identified with symbolic meaning in this novel contents itself with local injuries and local resurrections, renouncing any immanent metaphysical wholeness or chiliastic fulfillment. At the very heart of the novel's semiotics, its version of Christianity, stands, then, this negation, this renunciation.

A closer look at the structure of Goethe's symbol will reveal the operation of this negation. Todorov identifies two aspects or "phases" in the Goethean symbol. First, the symbol has its own being. It is in this sense opaque and intransitive. (The particular body, one might say, is a particular body.) Yet, to quote Todorov further: "[The symbol] is and it signifies at the same time."[36] In the second phase, the symbol points to something ineffable and inexpressible beyond itself.

The *Journeyman Years* is full of this semiotic motion, which Blackall aptly calls "contrapuntal."[37] Some of the contrapuntal pairs identified by Blackall are movement and rest, stones and stars, and particular and general.[38] To Blackall's pairs, one could add: inner and outer, center and periphery, coming together and coming apart, matter and spirit. Through these oppositions, the novel constantly alternates between a focus on local, concrete experience and a gesture toward something larger, even ineffable. In a crucial scene in the very center of the novel, this contrapuntal motion becomes focused into the rhythm of a rocking boat (*schaukeln*). Rocking refers to both the physical motion of the renunciant friends in a boat on Lake Maggiore as well as their emotional states as they find themselves alternately drawn together and pulled apart (FA 1.10: 504).

This contrapuntal dynamic is also associated with Christ. Wilhelm's guide in the Pedagogical Province emphasizes the juxtaposition between stasis and movement: "[Christ] holds steadfastly to his principles; he travels his road undismayed" (*[Christus] steht auf seinem Punkte fest; er wandelt seine Straße unverrückt . . .*) (CW 10: 209; FA 1.10: 429). The guide continues with a description of Christ's twofold orientation toward both the lowly and the divine: he raises up the poor, the sick and ignorant and equates himself (*sich gleichstellen*) with them; yet he also equates himself (*sich gleichstellen*) with God (FA 1.10: 429). The guide does not simply assert that Christ *is* divine or *is* human, but attributes to Christ himself an active self-positioning. Through this oscillatory movement between materiality and the infinite, the description avoids any static absolute.

And yet the oscillatory semiotics that Goethe here associates with Christianity he elsewhere connects with Judaism. As laid out in chapter 1, Goethe's myth of creation in book 8 of *Poetry and Truth* suggests a kabbalistic origin for his model of contraction and expansion as the fundamental pulse of the universe. His reading of Genesis in book 4—material that is primal for Goethe both in terms of its position in the biblical canon and its acknowledged role in his own creative development—also brings out an underlying rhythm of contraction and expansion.

But more to the point, in this period, similar forms of signification involving negation were explicitly associated with the Jewish ban on images. Kant's sublime, for example, has a negative structure: the imagination, confronted with its own inadequacy in the estimation of nature, gives way to the powers of reason, to which no sensory intuition is adequate. As mentioned earlier, Kant explicity compares the sublime to the Jewish ban on graven images. Hegel too, in his "Lectures on Aesthetics" under the category of "The Symbolism of the Sublime," explores a two-pronged symbolic dynamic, which he identifies with Judaism.[39] On the one hand, according to Hegel, the sublime sign points beyond itself to an independent meaning. This incommensurability between sign and signified is in effect the content of the sublime: "nothing comes into the representation except as this transcendence [*Hinaussein*] and superiority [*Hinausgehen*]."[40] On the other hand, the sublime brings with it a new emphasis on finitude: "existence both natural and human now acquires the new position of being a representation of the Divine only because its finitude appears on its own surface [*an ihr selber*]."[41] For Hegel, the two elements that would be united in a genuine symbol remain separate in the sublime—the abstract independence (*Fürsichsein*) of God and the concrete existence (*Dasein*) of the world.[42] While Hegel's contrastive dynamic of individuality/materiality versus transcendent meaning may not be identical to the contrapuntal movement observed in Goethe's novel, it is certainly akin. Like Kant, Hegel connects this two-phase form of signification with the Jewish ban on images, which denies that any material image is adequate to represent God.

Thus it would seem difficult to distinguish between the Christian symbolism operating in the novel and Jewish-identified traditions of signification. And yet the novel does undertake to draw this distinction. For according to the guide in the Pedagogical Province, allegory is the appropriate mode for representing Jewish history after the fall of the temple (FA 1.10: 427). Goethe's notion of the symbol is, of course, based on an opposition with allegory. It is, therefore, necessary to consider what it would mean for Judaism to be associated with allegory in opposition to Christian symbolism. In one of his most famous formulations, dating from 1822, Goethe describes the different relationships that symbol and allegory strike between the particular and general.

> It makes a difference whether the poet seeks the particular to stand for the general or whether the poet sees in the particular the general. From the former arises allegory, where the particular serves as but an instance, an example of the general; the latter is actually the nature of poetry. It expresses a particular, without thinking of, or pointing to the general.
>
> Es ist ein großer Unterschied, ob der Dichter zum Allgemeinen das Besondere sucht oder im Besondern das Allgemeine schaut. Aus jener Art entsteht Allegorie, wo das Besondere nur als Beyspiel, als Exempel des Allgemeinen gilt; die letztere aber ist eigentlich die Natur der Poesie, sie spricht ein Besonderes aus, ohne ans Allgemeine zu denken oder darauf hinzuweisen. (FA 1.13: 368)

While poetry resides in the particular character of the symbolic sign, the particularity of the allegorical sign is of little consequence. To use Todorov's term, the allegorical sign is transitive: "In allegory there is an instantaneous passage through the signifying face of the sign toward knowledge of what is signified."[43] A later pronouncement by Goethe contrasts what the two signs are capable of signifying: symbol reaches toward an inexpressible idea, whereas allegory designates a mere concept.[44]

And yet, Goethe's opposition between symbol and allegory, like his implicit distinction between Christian and Jewish wandering, is distinctly unstable. Walter Benjamin, for example, demonstrated that the allegorical sign, precisely in its arbitrariness and subordinate position, can appear as estranged materiality and particularity. Furthermore, in its radical concreteness and disjunction, allegory can function paradoxically as a negative sign of something ineffable. By foregrounding its own semiotic deficiency, the allegorical sign can gesture to that which lies outside the sphere of representation. Thus, allegory, too, can operate in two phases—the sign is radically particular; and the sign, in its estrangement and insufficiency, points beyond itself.

It is evident by now that any semiotic distinction between Judaism and Christianity must slice through very complex and murky territory. Even if one were to treat as stable Goethe's 1822 equation of symbol with particularity and allegory with the general, it remains very difficult to pin these terms on to Christianity and Judaism, as Jeffrey Librett points out:

> Hence, one finds oneself confronted with the following apparent undecidability. Allegory seems Jewish because its abstract character coincides with the abstraction with which Judaism is identified insofar as Judaism is seen as a radically anti-idolatrous monotheism. Accordingly, symbol seems Christian because, just as symbolic art privileges concretion, so does Christianity (in the forms of the embodiment of God in humanity, the Eucharist, the iconic traditions, and so forth). On the other hand, allegory seems Christian because it, like Christianity, is radically spiritual; and symbol thus seems Jewish because of the worldly materiality and even literal realism it shares with the ostensibly Jewish fetishism of the legalistic letter.[45]

I argue that *Wilhelm Meister's Journeyman Years* simplifies the task of constructing a Christian semiotics by misrepresenting its competition with Judaism. The images in the halls of the Pedagogical Province amount to a systematic degradation of the Jewish ban on images. On the whole, Judaism is relegated to a concrete and literal realm without capacity to signify something higher or greater. In the Pedagogical Province, Judaism is identified as an ethnic and moreover *pagan* religion. The characterization of Judaism as pagan is debasing precisely because it carries the implication of idolatry. The guide concedes, however, that *among all the pagan religions* Judaism has the greatest advantages, one of which is its prohibition on embodying God in any form. The guide continues: "[the Israelite religion] leaves us free to give Him an exalted human form and also, in contrast, to depict wicked idolatry in the form of animals and monsters" (*[die isrealitische Religion läßt] uns die Freiheit, [Gott] eine würdige Menschengestalt zu geben, auch im Gegensatz die schlechte Abgötterei durch Tier- und Untiergestalten zu bezeichnen*) (CW 10: 207; FA 1.10: 426). The Jewish ban on images amounts, then, to little more than an intermediate step—a refusal to represent the divine in animal or monster form as other pagan religions do, thus paving the way for Christianity to represent God as human. The sublimity of mind that Hegel, and before him Kant, associate with the Jewish ban on images is completely denied.

The murals concerning Judaism also differ in kind from those of Christianity in the next gallery. They are described as sensuous (*sinnlich*) and lacking the inwardness (*Inneres*) of the Christian murals (FA 1.10: 426, 427). Wilhelm is glad to think that for his son, who will be raised among the murals, these exemplary events in Jewish history might become real and alive (FA 1.10: 426). They do not evoke something inexpressibly deeper or higher, as do the representations of Christian miracles and parables in the next gallery. Goethe denies Judaism here any kind of greater signifying trajectory and confines it to the literal realm. As noted, in the gallery devoted to Judaism, events after the destruction of the temple are represented through allegory, which in Goethe's lexicon is already a degraded form of representation. Allegory, the guide explains, is appropriate here, because the events depicted would fall outside the limits of true art (FA 1.10: 427). This amounts to an inversion of the traditional ban on images: the referent is too lowly, not too lofty to allow for a direct representation.

Still, the leaders of the Pedagogical Province come closest to associating something like a Goethean symbol with Jews when they praise the Hebrew holy books in the passage quoted earlier. But even here the rhetoric seems at most proto-symbolic The most foreign elements create a whole described as "täuschend," which Winston translates as "plausible" but also has the sense of "illusory" or even "deceptive" (*CW* 10: 207; FA 1.10: 426), thereby suggesting superficial sensory effects. The described impact of the Hebrew Bible on its reader also draws on a rhetoric that is more physiological than profound: the holy books are complete enough to satisfy (*befriedigen*), fragmentary enough to stimulate (*anreizen*), barbaric enough to challenge (*auffordern*), and tender enough to calm (*besänftigen*) (FA 1.10: 426). The Hebrew Bible, while described here in positive terms, can nevertheless be surpassed by the "new world" (*neue Welt*) (FA 1.10: 427) of Christianity, with its internal content, as presented in the final gallery on Wilhelm's tour.

Ethical Action

The semiotic contrast between Christianity and Judaism corresponds to an ethical opposition, in which again Jews come up short. Lenardo, as previously mentioned, characterizes Jewish wandering as an attempt to trick and outmaneuver others. Wilhelm's guide in the Pedagogical Province prefaces his praise for the toughness and persistence of the Jews with the claim: "the people of Israel was never worth much, as it was a thousand times admonished by its leaders, judges, chiefs, and prophets. It possesses few virtues and most of the faults of other peoples" (*CW* 10: 207) (*Das isrealitische Volk hat niemals viel getaugt, wie es ihm seine Anführer, Richter, Vorsteher, Propheten tausendmal vorgeworfen haben; es besitzt wenig Tugenden und die meisten Fehler anderer Völker*) (FA 1.10: 425).

Meanwhile, the novel develops a practical ethics linked to Christianity's reverence for the earthly and to Christ as healer. As Wilhelm frees himself from his status as Wandering Jew and acquires the practical surgical training to aid suffering bodies, he becomes a kind of secular, non-metaphysical Christ figure. Both Muenzer and Redfield have pointed out that technical knowledge and local action in the novel take on a semiotic character. Redfield writes, "Technics is knowledge derived from the renunciation of knowledge, and this renunciation of knowledge links technical prowess to the transcendental unknowability of the symbol."[46] The practical activity of the surgeon is a negation of, and thereby a reference to, an unknowable universal truth. Again, Goethe is suggesting here a pragmatic Christianity wrested free of all theological claims.

Yet Goethe's link between ethical action and epistemological renunciation was arguably anticipated in Goethe's era by the Jewish philosopher Moses Mendelssohn.[47] In his autobiography Goethe expresses identification with Mendelssohn as, like himself, a target of Lavater's evangelistic zeal (FA 1.14: 660). In response to Lavater's public demands that he convert, Mendelssohn wrote his programmatic defense of Judaism as a religion compatible with Enlightenment and tolerance, *Jerusalem, or On Religious Power and Judaism* (*Jerusalem oder über religiöse Macht und Judentum*; 1783). Here Mendelssohn offers the ritual action prescribed by Jewish law—*thou shalt do*—as an alternative form of religious devotion to the faith in revealed doctrine demanded by Christianity—*thou shalt believe*.[48] At the heart of Mendelssohn's critique of doctrinal revelation is, of course, the ban on images. Ritual actions are less likely than signs to lead to idolatry because they are themselves ephemeral and temporal. These actions are supposed to give rise to thinking about eternal truths but in no way claim to represent what is in principle unrepresentable. While, in a narrow sense, Mendelssohn's discussion concerns ceremonial laws and practices, in a broader sense, he attributes to Judaism a fundamentally social and practical orientation. Indeed, because of their transitory character, ceremonial rites promote social interaction:

> Human actions are transitory and have no constant and enduring character, which, like pictographs, can lead, through misuse or misconception, to idolatry. They have the advantage over symbolic alphabets that they do not isolate a person and make him into a solitary creature brooding over writings and books. Instead they impel interaction, imitation and a vital, oral form of instruction.[49]

To be sure, significant differences exist between Mendelssohn and Goethe's treatment of religion: Mendelssohn sees reason as a reliable source of eternal truth shared by all religions and all human beings. Without this ultimate appeal to reason, Goethe's skepticism towards revelation leads him into deeper, potentially agnostic territory. Yet, the anti-idolatrous, ethical orientation of Goethe's version of Christianity still converges in significant ways with Mendelssohn's portrayal of Judaism.

And even if Goethe somehow never read Mendelssohn's treatise—which is hard to imagine given its connection to Goethe's problematic friend Lavater—he could have derived the same point from Lessing's play *Nathan the Wise* (*Nathan der Weise*) with its thinly veiled portrait of Mendelssohn as the title character. The play makes a clear connection between Nathan's concern for ethical social action and his refusal to engage in metaphysical speculation. In the first act, Nathan's daughter Recha has become convinced—with the encouragement of her fanatical Christian nursemaid Daja—that the being who rescued her from a burning house was no mere mortal but an angel. To conflate sensory objects or persons with the supersensible realm in this way is a clear example of dogmatic metaphysics.[50] Indeed, Nathan strives to convince his daughter that this fantasy runs the risk of "blasphemy."[51] In attributing divine powers to this human being, Recha also overlooks her rescuer's concrete needs and the real aid she can offer him. Nathan seeks to make Recha aware of the distinction between an idolatrous enthusiasm (*Schwärmen*) and a practical action (Handeln): "But do you realize, how much easier it is to enthuse devoutly than to do good?"[52] Recha's *Jewish* mentor Nathan teaches her to hold rigorously to the ethical demands of life in this world, while her *Christian* mentor Daja allows her to sink into otherworldly dreams. Lessing thus shares with Goethe the complaint that Christianity substitutes metaphysical speculation (i.e., idolatry) for ethical engagement, but holds out Judaism as an alternative.[53]

Time and History

Wilhelm's new ideal of wandering promises a more active, existential, and intentional relationship to time and history. This new ideal rejects both the traditional Christian emphasis on an otherworldly, eschatological eternity and the unending succession that he associates with "eternal" Jewish wandering. In short, this third category concerns the competition over modernity per se.

When Wilhelm is relieved of the conditions that "stamp him as a Wandering Jew," time acquires meaning for him in relationship to a purpose: "Wilhelm now gave Montan an account of how he had employed his time since receiving the dispensation to arrange his assigned journey not by days and hours but in accordance with his true goal of obtaining thorough training" (*[Wilhelm] gab nunmehr Rechenschaft von der Anwendung seiner Zeit, seitdem er die Vergünstigung erlangt, die auferlegte Wanderschaft nicht nach Tagen und Stunden, sondern dem wahren Zweck einer vollständigen Ausbildung gemäß einzuteilen und zu benutzen*) (CW 10: 281; FA 1.10: 537). By implication, then, time was marked off in the previous stage in repetitive units—in days and hours—without orientation towards a goal, in the empty, relentless duration of the Wandering Jew. One can find this interpretation of the myth of the Wandering Jew clearly articulated in a contemporary source, in Göschel's 1824 book on Goethe's *Faust*. According to Göschel, the legend points to "the insubstantiality of things past . . . the nothingness of the *present time* . . . the fathomless emptiness of the *future*."[54]

This view of the temporal condition of the Wandering Jew is echoed in the novel's representations of Jewish history. As previously noted, in the Pedagogical Province Jews are praised, in the absence of any other virtue, for their historical perseverance. Jewish history is represented in these galleries as a series of real, external events belonging to the annals of world history, but without any connection to the events of Christ's life and teaching. When Wilhelm wonders why Christ is missing from the chain of events depicted before the destruction of the temple, his guide explains:

> What publicly befalls entire peoples and their members belongs to world history, and to that world religion which we consider the first. What privately befalls the individual belongs to the second religion, to the religion of the sages; it was such a religion that Christ preached and practiced, for the time he was on earth. That is why the outward religion comes to an end here, and I shall now reveal the inward one to you. (CW 10: 208)

> Was Völkermassen und ihren Gliedern öffentlich begegnet, gehört der Weltgeschichte, der Weltreligion, welche wir für die erste [Religion] halten. Was dem Einzelnen innerlich begegnet, gehört zur zweiten Religion, zur Religion der Weisen: eine solche war die, welche Christus lehrte und übte, so lange er auf der Erde umherging. Deswegen ist hier das äußere abgeschlossen und ich eröffne euch nun das Innere. (FA 1.10: 427)

And thus the guide opens for Wilhelm a new gallery of an entirely different character, reflecting a new inner orientation.[55]

The experience of the past as an incessant chain of external events, here attributed to Jews, ties in to a persistent anxiety in the *Journeyman Years* about the trajectory of modernity. This uneasiness is most apparent in the section "Reflections in the Spirit of the Wanderers" ("Betrachtungen im Sinne der Wanderer"). An aphorism on the culture of journalism laments that "our" time lets nothing ripen but rather consumes the present in incessant activity: "each day is squandered in the next, and so we live perpetually from hand to mouth, without ever producing anything" (*man [verspeis't] im nächsten Augenblick den vorhergehenden, [vertut] den Tag im Tage, und so immer [lebt] aus der Hand in den Mund, ohne irgend etwas vor sich zu bringen*) (CW 10: 298; FA 1.10: 563). In the subsequent aphorism, this relentless modern velocity is cast in economic terms: "The liveliness of commerce, the continual rustle of paper money, the increase in debts to pay off other debts—all these are frightful elements that the young man of the present confronts" (*Die Lebhaftigkeit des Handels, das Durchrauschen des Papiergelds, das Anschwellen der Schulden, um Schulden zu bezahlen, das alles sind die ungeheuern Elemente, auf die gegenwärtig ein junger Mann gesetzt ist*) (*CW* 10: 298; FA 1.10: 563). While there is no allusion to Judaism or Jews in these passages, the description of vicious cycles of debt and credit easily plays into long-worn anti-Semitic stereotypes of usurious Jewish financiers. The mention of paper money too is significant: I will argue in chapter 5 that the paper money episode in *Part Two* has the biblical Exodus story as a strong subtext. Further, as we have seen, Lenardo distances his group of wanderers from the Jews precisely because of their ruthless pace, through which they strive to trick and out-step their fellow wanderers (FA 1.10: 668). Thus the novel, while developing an ideal of an adaptive, pragmatic, existential wandering, opposes itself to a frenetic, disoriented, modern acceleration, which is tied implicitly and/or explicitly to the Jews.

Wilhelm's task as Renunciant is indeed to overcome both the heavy burden of the past and the persistent pressure toward the future. Jarno reminds Wilhelm that the Renunciants are obligated to speak neither of the past nor the future but to focus entirely on the present (FA 1.10: 296). After his visit with Makarie's astronomer friend, Wilhelm announces how one can counter the pull of an infinite time with a focus on the present:

> Have you the right even to imagine yourself in the midst of this eternally living order if there does not immediately manifest itself inside you something in continuous motion, revolving around a pure center? And even if it would be difficult for you to find this center in your own breast, you would recognize it because a benevolent, beneficent effect emanates from it and testifies to its existence. (*CW* 10: 177)

> Wie kann sich der Mensch gegen das Unendliche stellen, als wenn er alle geistigen Kräfte, die nach vielen Seiten hingezogen werden, in seinem Innersten, Tiefsten versammelt, wenn er sich fragt: "Darfst du dich in der Mitte dieser ewig lebendigen Ordnung auch nur denken, sobald sich nicht gleichfalls in dir ein beharrlich Bewegtes, um seinen reinen Mittelpunkt kreisend, hervortut? Und selbst wenn es dir schwer würde, diesen Mittelpunkt in deinem Busen aufzufinden, so würdest du ihn daran erkennen, daß eine wohlwollende, wohltätige Wirkung von ihm ausgeht und von ihm Zeugnis gibt." (FA 1.10: 382–83)

Wilhelm's solution to the relentless passing of time is for each individual to find and define his center of orientation. This internal orientation is also offered in the aphorisms cited above as the antidote to modern temporality: a measured, calm sense, or guiding will can counter this restless "spirit of the day" (*Tagesgeist*) (*CW* 10: 298; FA 1.10: 563). As Wilhelm's guide in the Pedagogical Province explained, the expression of inwardness is precisely what distinguishes the images in the Christian galleries from those in the Jewish ones.

It is important, however, to note Wilhelm's agnosticism about the nature of this internal center. In the above quote, Wilhelm allows that it may be difficult to discover this center in oneself: only its outward, beneficial effects make it manifest. Thus, Wilhelm avoids the inward retreat of the devoutly Christian "Beautiful Soul" from the *Apprenticeship*. The guiding internal principle retains the status of hypothesis: one gains access to it only through outward-directed activity. The self, therefore, remains thoroughly temporal in character even as it resists the all-engulfing press of time.[56]

Once again, to the extent that a concept of Christianity is in play here, it is a deeply existential one. That is precisely what places it in competition with Judaism: as earlier quoted, in a maxim on "Jewish nature," Goethe explicitly identifies Jews with endeavors that are earthly, temporal, and directed toward the present moment (FA 1.13: 273).[57] Consequently, what stands out in this novel is a drive to distinguish a productive focus on life in this world claimed for Christianity, from an earthly temporality associated with the Jews. Goethe achieves this, I contend, by trivializing the role of history for Jews.

This emphasis on the role of history is evident in the passage in which the emigrant leaders conclude that no Jews will be tolerated in their colony. This declaration is not attributed to one character but presented as a more or less consensual outcome of a conversation between Friedrich and Wilhelm, which presumably involved previous consultation with Lenardo and others. The logic that leads to this pronouncement is deeply perplexing:

> We adhere firmly to [the Christian] religion, but in a peculiar way; we teach our children from youth on about the great benefits it has brought us; only much later, however, do we acquaint them with its origin and history. Only then do we come to love and value its founder, and any account that refers to Him becomes sacred. In this sense, which might perhaps be called pedantic, but whose consistency must be acknowledged, we tolerate no Jews among us. How can we grant them participation in the highest culture when they repudiate its origin and source? (CW 10: 378)

> An [der christlichen] Religion halten wir fest, aber auf eine eigne Weise; wir unterrichten unsere Kinder von Jugend auf von den großen Vorteilen, die sie uns gebracht hat; dagegen von ihrem Ursprung, von ihrem Verlauf geben wir zuletzt Kenntnis. Alsdann wird uns der Urheber erst lieb und wert, und alle Nachricht, die sich auf ihn bezieht, wird heilig. In diesem Sinne, den man vielleicht pedantisch nennen mag, aber doch als folgerecht anerkennen muß, dulden wir keinen

> Juden unter uns, denn wie sollten wir ihm den Anteil an der höchsten Kulter vergönnen, deren Ursprung und Herkommen er verleugnet? (FA 1.10: 686–87)

According to this pedagogical strategy, Christianity is taught to children first as a set of values—faith, hope, love, endurance of suffering—rather than as historical revelation. Early instruction brackets out the figure of Christ as the originator of the Christian religion.

Indeed, throughout the novel and in many variations, origins appear ambiguous, inaccessible, or subordinate to a more pragmatic perspective. For example, at the miners' festival, Wilhelm listens to a lively debate about the origin of the world. He hears many geological hypotheses and wonders about their relationship to the biblical account of the earth's genesis. When he turns to his friend Montan for an opinion, Montan shows no interest in arriving at the true answer. He concerns himself only with the present character of the mountains: "How these mountains here came to be, I do not know, nor do I care to. But I seek continually to wrest from them the secret of their individuality" (*Wie diese Gebirge hier entstanden sind, weiß ich nicht, will's auch nicht wissen; aber ich trachte täglich ihnen ihre Eigentümlichkeit abzugewinnen*) (*CW* 10: 281; FA 1.10: 536).

And yet, even though the emigrants' approach to religion seems to share this more pragmatic orientation, it ultimately bans Jews on the basis of biblical origins. According to the above strategy, once youth have learned the advantages of Christianity, they come to love and cherish its founder, and regard the gospel of his life as "holy." Because Jews deny this religious origin and genealogy, they must be excluded from the colony's "highest culture." Given the apparent subordination of Christian origins to practical Christian values in the passage, this categorical exclusion of Jews seems gratuitous and unmotivated. The group acknowledges the pedantry of its logic, even while insisting on its consistency.

What are we to make of this strange justification for religious intolerance? Is the forced logic of this passage simply intended to draw our attention to the arbitrariness of the whole emigrant undertaking? Bennett views the "logical failure" in this passage as indeed self-conscious. In his view, it serves as further evidence of the deep and thoroughgoing irony of the novel, including its attitude toward Jews.[58] For Bennett, this failure consists in the fact that the valuable religious principles that the emigrants hope to gain from Christianity originate in the Hebrew Bible, in Ecclesiastes: "The allusions to Ecclesiastes, in fact, remind us that even that supposedly Christian 'reverence' (if we think back to the pedagogical province, and think of Ecclesiastes as a whole) can be derived from *Jewish* writings."[59] Yet Bennett's own observation here could serve as a further instance of the pattern that I am identifying: attributing to Christianity principles and perspectives to which Judaism has a prior claim.

I read the emigrant group's argument not as self-canceling but as indeed—as the passage maintains—logically consistent (*folgerecht*). This logic works, however, rather indirectly. The exclusion of the Jews, I contend, is not entailed by the pragmatic "Christian" view of origins endorsed by the colony and developed elsewhere in the novel; it is a consequence rather of the literalist conception of history that the novel attributes by contrast to the Jews. That is to say, the group judges the Jews incapable of participating in the highest culture of the colony, not just because they deny the historical Christ, but implicitly because *they* are so peculiarly and narrowly attached to historical events. As the guide in the Pedagogical Province explains, "ethnic religions" such as Judaism are directly bound to history: "The import [of ethnic religion] can be found in world history, as its husk can be found in individual events" (*Der Gehalt [der ethnischen Religion] findet sich in der Weltgeschichte, so wie die Hülle derselben in den Begebenheiten*) (CW 10: 206; FA 1.10: 424). The emigrants thus have it both ways: they retain for Christianity a sophisticated irony toward history *and* reject Jews for their skepticism toward the revelatory claims of Christian history. Christianity, thereby, assumes the mantle of tolerance: indeed, Lenardo emphasizes in his speech his group's strong commitment to honor all forms of religious worship (FA 1.10: 672)—by which he apparently means all forms of Christianity.

The emigrants' argument against the Jews hardly merits refutation. Nevertheless, one need only cast another glance toward Mendelssohn to find a very different Jewish conception of history that supports tolerance and exchange across religious faiths. (A version of this interfaith model was widely popularized in Lessing's "Parable of the Ring" in *Nathan the Wise*.) In *Jerusalem*, Mendelssohn distinguishes between the role of historical and eternal truths in Judaism. Historical truths rest on evidence, cultural transmission, and authority and may involve revelations that are constitutive for a people, but they do not prescribe doctrine. Eternal truths are rational, according to Mendelssohn, and thus equally accessible to all human beings, regardless of culture or creed. One can certainly recognize in this division the logic of the ban on images, that an eternal, universal absolute does not appear incarnate in human history. History is not, however, thereby devoid of meaning. Mendelssohn makes it clear that precisely because truth eludes permanent fixation in human signs, it is proper for religion to evolve historically through interpersonal transmission.[60] One could perhaps go a step beyond Mendelssohn's argument to further suggest why a history without final epiphany could nonetheless assume religious weight: as we saw in the paradoxical dynamic of the sublime described by Hegel, precisely through its negative and renunciatory relationship toward the absolute, finitude takes on meaning as a counterpart to the unrepresentable.

Mendelssohn's argument allows him to remain deeply committed to his own cultural history and tradition without insisting upon its absolute character. Separate cultures can thus share common ground and mutual respect.

Mendelssohn quotes Rabbi Hillel's one-line summary of the Jewish law, "Love your neighbor as yourself" (*Liebe deinen Nächsten wie dich selbst*),[61] which Jesus also identifies as a core commandment (Matt. 22:39). Moreover, as Hess argues, in *Jerusalem* Mendelssohn paints Jesus as an essentially Jewish thinker who supports the continued authority of Jewish law *for those born into it*. That is to say, according to Mendelssohn, Jesus does not overcome Judaism but rather endorses its continued existence. In this view, Jesus stands for precisely the Jewish model of religious tolerance that Mendelssohn himself advances.[62]

There is a further historical irony to the emigrant argument against the Jews, of which Goethe must have been aware. The group's logic rests on the supposition that a sophisticated Christian stance toward origins is incompatible with the dogmatic historical literalism of the Jews. In the Lavater affair, these two religions occupied opposite positions. Lavater seized upon an occasion on which Mendelssohn privately expressed philosophical and moral respect for Christ to try publicly to force Mendelssohn to convert. In this well-known instance, then, *Jewish openness* toward the founding figure of Christianity was met with aggressive and relentless *Christian dogmatism*. As pointed out earlier, on this occasion, Goethe identified with Mendelssohn.

Thus we recognize the recurring pattern in Goethe's work: at the root of the anti-Judaism in this novel there appears to lie a distorted identification with Jews. Goethe's vision in the *Journeyman Years* of epistemological renunciation and existential orientation brings him awkwardly close to traditions within Judaism that he knew or to which he had access. Yet, just as Wilhelm strives to overcome his status as Wandering Jew, the novel strives to supersede its relationship to Judaism with its own brand of Christian existentialism. The novel achieves this by systematically downplaying the profound meaning of the Jewish ban on images for semiotics, ethics, and historical consciousness. Meanwhile, the negativity of the ban on images is recuperated within the novel's own philosophy of renunciation. Thus, the exclusion of Jews from the novel's fundamental ideal of an ontological wandering does not seem accidental or merely ironic. Rather, it appears to be the foundation upon which the novel's own anti-foundationalism rests.

In the path from the *Volksbuch* to the *Journeyman Years* we see the double-edged nature of Goethe's very modern reception of the Hebrew Bible. The Hebrew Bible, conceived as the representative text of the Jewish people, serves indeed as a foundation for his vision of modern German literature. But in a sense, the subordinate position of the Old Testament within Christianity (and by extension of Jewish history and the Jewish people) is conserved in Goethe's now secular scheme. In his *Volksbuch* outline, Jewish history is succeeded by German history with an ultimate outlook toward a "New Jerusalem." The *Journeyman Years* is very much in the spirit of his abandoned project, taking its inspiration from the Hebrew Bible while ultimately supplanting Judaism.

Chapter 4

✦

Faust as Keeper of the Covenant

Part One of the Tragedy

The *Journeymen Years*, with its particularly ominous treatment of Judaism, is neither Goethe's last nor his most significant variation on his theme of Jewish wandering and wandering Jews. In my view, the two parts of *Faust*, which he worked on intermittently for sixty years, offer a more complex, profound, and sustained exploration both of wandering as the modern condition and of the Hebrew Bible as a modern text. To understand the figure of Faust we can think again of Goethe's description of his early encounter with the patriarchs of Genesis in book 4 of *Poetry and Truth*: their heroism consisted not in virtuous behavior, but in their faithfulness toward their existential covenant. In Goethe's reading, their nomadic wanderings assume a pattern of expansion and contraction, anomy and nomos, which mirrors what he identifies in his kabbalistic cosmology in book 8 as the very pulse of the universe.[1] Faust's challenge is similarly to keep in motion, to avoid, by persistent striving, the risk of over-contraction, whether through self-satisfaction, static meanings, or idolatrous absolutes of any kind. Faust's wanderings are of course governed by his pact with Mephistopheles, which Goethe sets up through an analogy that is at once outrageous and surprisingly sympathetic: Faust's pact functions like the covenants that bind the heroes of the Hebrew Bible, referred to collectively in the Christian Scriptures as the "Old Covenant" in distinction to the Christian "New Covenant."[2] Thus Goethe casts his Faust as *like* a member of the older covenant, that is as *like* a Jew

To be clear, I do not read Faust as literally Jewish or crypto-Jewish within the fictional world of the drama. Clearly, on the face of it, he is not. Rather, he is positioned typologically as standing outside, as a matter of choice and commitment, the salvific promises of Christianity. Now if one were to assume an overarching Christian perspective in the work, as many commentators do, Faust's refusal of Christianity would be his failing. But I argue quite to the contrary that Faust's loyalty to a prior, more this-worldly covenant and his rejection of the otherworldly promises of Christianity is for Goethe the mark of a certain existential integrity. Meanwhile, it is important to stress that Goethe's take on Hebrew Bible covenants is distinctly his own. He is less concerned with the precise content of the successive biblical formulations of the covenant—for example, circumcision in the Abrahamic covenant, the laws of the Mosaic covenant—than in a certain covenantal faithfulness per se. Finally, the biblical analogy must be understood as simply one valence of a spectacularly multivalent drama. Goethe's masterpiece cannot be reduced to an allegory of the relationship between Christianity and Judaism: central conflicts in the drama are nevertheless inflected in these religious terms.

While the ubiquity of biblical references in *Faust* has often been noted, either single themes or references are treated in isolation or the "Bible" is regarded as a whole cloth; rarely have critics attended to the significance of the Hebrew Bible in distinction to the Christian Bible or the interplay between Old and New typologies within the work.[3] I will focus by contrast on how biblical references create key lines of demarcation in the drama that illuminate Faust's commitments. Goethe develops parallels between the Faust of *Part One* and two Hebrew Bible figures, both of whom invest Faust's striving with new significance and even heroism—Job and Solomon. The analogy with Job bears on the nature and the meaning of the pact; the analogy with Solomon elucidates the inevitability of error in even the most faithful forms of striving. In casting Faust in the mold of heroes of the so-called Old Covenant, Goethe shifts the entire meaning of the legend. Nevertheless Goethe's Jewish inflection of the figure of Faustus is not without precedent.

Doctor Faustus and Early Modern Representations of Jews

Goethe did not need to invent links between Faust and Judaism: they were latent in the Faust material he inherited. While the Faustus of Spiess's 1587 chapbook is explicitly not Jewish—in fact one of his many tricks involves cheating a Jewish moneylender out of his money—nevertheless, the legend converges with early modern representations of Jews within the general sphere of mysterious, occult, and heretical practices.[4] Goethe's work picks up on these strains, exploits and transforms them.

For example, the legendary Doctor Faustus has a clear kinship with the legendary Wandering Jew. Both accounts belong to the same popular, chapbook genre, bear a strong imprint of the Lutheran Reformation, and were published within fifteen years of each other.[5] Both Faustus and Ahasverus are unredeemed, supernatural wanderers whose stories spin themselves out in an in-between time, before a pending damnation or salvation. While the Faustus of legend renounces Christianity and, after twenty-four years of devilish adventure, is forever damned, Ahasverus, after rejecting Christ himself on the road to his crucifixion, is condemned, despite his repentance and baptism, to wander until Christ's Second Coming when he presumably will be saved. While Faustus's twenty-four years provide occasion in the chapbook for plenty of entertaining travels, tricks, and encounters with historical figures before the moral of the story comes due, the same potential for adventure and entertainment in the Ahasverus material is only brought out in the eighteenth and nineteenth centuries in a slew of popular literary reworkings. Indeed, Goethe's own sketches, which date from around the same time as his work on his earliest Faust conception, suggests a more episodic treatment of the material and thus bring Ahasverus closer to Faustus as a vehicle for wide-ranging adventures. Goethe casts his Faust as a kind of Ahasverus in a speech in "Forest and Cavern" (*Wald und Höhle*) where Faust characterizes himself as "the fugitive" (*der Flüchtling*), "the unhoused" (*der Unbehauste*), "the aimless, restless reprobate" (*Der Unmensch ohne Zweck und Ruh*), and "I whom God had cursed" (*der Gottverhaßte*) (Luke, *Faust Part One*, 3348, 3349, 3356). The comparison has not been lost on critics over the years, including one of Goethe's contemporaries. In 1824, the Right Hegelian thinker Karl Friedrich Göschel published a work linking Goethe's Faust with his planned epic history of the Wandering Jew.[6]

Faustus's supposed profession as physician also links him with early modern typologies of Jews. According to Spiess's chapbook, he presented himself as a medical doctor, a "D. Medicinae," and initially helped many people with his various herbs, roots, tonics, and clysters.[7] The practice of medicine was surrounded generally by a whiff of magic and demonology in the medieval and early modern periods: it was also one of the few professions open to Jews. Jewish physicians, perhaps in part because of their knowledge of ancient medical traditions transmitted in Arabic, Greek, and Hebrew, were admired and sought after in the courts of Christian rulers. But this prominence led to Christian resentment and suspicion. With some Christians dependent in matters of life and death on Jewish doctors, the ground was fertile for conspiracy theories.[8] Luther, for example, warned Christians concerning the malevolent intentions of Jewish doctors.[9] Such allegations persisted into the eighteenth century. Two infamous Christian "exposés," of Judaism, J. A. Eisenmenger's *Judaism Revealed* (*Entdecktes Judenthum*; 1700) and J. J. Schudt's *Jewish Peculiarities* (*Jüdische Merckwürdigkeiten*; 1714), both belonging to the library of Goethe's father, claim specifically that rabbinical sources allow Jewish doctors to experiment with risky, untried medicines on non-Jews.[10] In reference to Jewish doctors, Schudt quotes Plinius, "Only doctors have the freedom to kill people with impunity for the earth covers their mistakes."[11] Goethe not only has his Faust study medicine, as in the chapbook, but adds his own twist that Faust and his father experimented with an alchemical concoction that killed rather than healed its patients, all with impunity: "The medicine was there, and though the patients died, Nobody questioned: who got well?" (*Hier war die Arzenei, die Patienten starben, Und niemand fragte: wer genas?*) (Kaufman, *Goethe's Faust*, 1048–49). In this way, Goethe goes a step further than the chapbook to associate Faust's practice of medicine with allegations specifically concerning Jewish doctors.

Even more definitively, Dr. Faustus's practice of magic brings him into proximity with legends surrounding Jewish magicians. The early modern Christian image of the Jewish magician (*Zauberjude*) was knit together from a variety of prejudices and outright fabrications such as the "blood libel" alleging the Jewish ritual use of Christian blood or communion host.[12] Suspicions surrounding the magical arts also became deeply interwoven with popular mystifications concerning Kabbalah. As the defamatory book by Schudt defined it, the practical Kabbalah (as opposed to the theoretical Kabbalah) involves employing words and phrases from the Old Testament in order to do things such as conjure devils, heal sickness, extinguish fire, and drive out devils. He concludes that it is "nothing but the black arts and devilish magic."[13]

Within Schudt's long catalog of Jewish kabbalistic activities appear accounts of magically procured wine. Schudt provides two stories of Jewish Kabbalists who invoke the "Schem" or divine name, plunge a sharp object into the wall (an awl in one case, a knife in the other). Out of the hole runs wine as if out of the tap of a barrel.[14] While this particular magic trick may have circulated in many forms as a versatile equivalent of an urban legend of its day, it serves as a further link between Jewish magicians and Goethe's Faust.[15] To be sure, the Faustus chapbook already contains the famous episode in which Faust wins a great volume of wine for some students by betting with the owner that he could bring a large wine barrel out of a cellar and then riding it out like a horse. But while Goethe's version makes a nod to the chapbook by inserting the barrel ride as a means of exit at the end of the scene, Mephistopheles's chief trick is procuring wine for the patrons of Auerbach's Tavern by drilling into the table, from which it then pours. Here again, then, Goethe moves the Faustus material into even closer proximity to legends surrounding Jews.

Schudt actually makes a direct comparison between the Faust of legend and Jewish kabbalists. He cites a report about a certain Jew, who used his kabbalistic arts to summon the most beautiful female figures including the Queen of Sheba. Schudt indeed compares this feat to Faustus's summoning of the historical Alexander and his wife to the imperial court.[16] In the second part of the drama, Goethe's Faust also summons a historical couple at court, but it is not Alexander, as in the chapbook, but, as in the tale of the kabbalist, a paragon of beauty—Helena—along with Paris.[17]

Alchemy too belongs to the broader network of kabbalistic and Jewish associations from which Goethe draws his portrait of Faust. In a detailed study, Gershom Scholem shows that while alchemy in fact never played a central role in *Jewish* Kabbalah, the presumed connection is ubiquitous within the *Christian* reception of Kabbalah, "For more than four hundred years, the terms alchemy and Kabbalah have been synonymous among the Christian theosophists and alchemists of Europe."[18] Kabbalistic and alchemical conceptions are thoroughly entangled in a strange theosophical treatise that fascinated Goethe as a young man: Welling's *Opus Mago-Cabbalisticum et Theosophicum*. Schudt's *Judaism Revealed* aims to prove Jewish dealings in alchemy by appending a purportedly Jewish alchemical treatise.[19]

Goethe weaves together alchemical and kabbalistic traditions for example in the scene "Witch's Kitchen." If the youth potion Faust drinks can be understood as the alchemical *aurum potabile*,[20] the "witches one-times-one" that the witch recites before its consumption has a strong kabbalistic ring.[21] The poem is organized around the number ten, beginning: "This you must know! / From one make ten" (*Du mußt verstehn! / Aus Eins mach' Zehn*) (Kaufman, *Goethe's Faust*, 2540–41) and returning to ten at the end: "And nine is one, / And ten is one, That is the witch's arithmetic" (*Und Neun ist Eins / Und Zehn ist keins. / Das ist das Hexen-Einmal-Eins!*) (2550–52). As the number of the Sephiroth, the divine emanations, ten is a highly significant number in Kabbalah.[22] In his polemical depiction of kabbalistic "nonsense and absurdity," Herder pokes fun at the ubiquity of the number ten, which appears "in all figurations, meanings and forms" (*SW* 6: 484, 486). The form of the witches' incantation may itself suggest an admixture of kabbalistic and alchemical traditions. Gershom Scholem identifies a "kind of witches' one-times-one" from the most prominent kabbalistic work, the Zohar ("One ascends to one side, one descends to the other, one enters between two. Two crown themselves in three, three enter into one") and likens it to alchemical mystery words attributed to the fictional Maria the Jewess.[23]

Furthermore, within the underground culture of magical and occult practices in the seventeenth and eighteenth centuries, Faustus emerges as a close cousin of the great biblical king Solomon. The association of King Solomon with magical knowledge and demonology was widespread and ancient, referred to for example in Flavius Josephus's first century *Judean Antiquities*: "He composed incantations by which illnesses are relieved, and left behind exorcistic practices with which those binding demons expel them so that they return no more."[24] Solomon's magical knowledge and command of practical kabbalah were purportedly preserved in the *Key of Solomon*, or *Clavicula Salmonis*, a magic manual of obscure origin, but with a strong underground circulation well into the eighteenth century.[25] The book proffered various forms of secret knowledge such as how to conjure and control spirits and make magic pentacles.[26]

But the *Key of Solomon* is very close in content and may have been a source for a series of works attributed to the legendary Dr. Faustus himself, for example, *Faust's Coercion of Hell*, which was also in underground circulation since the seventeenth century.[27] The similarities between these two grimoires were so clear that the *Key of Solomon* and Faust's *Coercion of Hell* were often named in the same breath. For example, Georg von Welling lumps them together with others of their "infernal ilk."[28] And Johann Christoph Adelung published both the *Key* and the *The Coercion of Hell* in an attempt to destroy the high-priced market in these "magic books that lurk around in the dark."[29] Through these books and less well-known offshoots, Solomon and Faust clearly emerge as the two most prominent magicians of the grimoire genre. As an early nineteenth-century German study of magic observes: "Solomon plays an approximately similar role in the ancient Jewish art of magic as Faust in modern European Christian [magic].[30] In the early twentieth century Carl Kiesewetter calls Solomon "the Jews' Faust" (*Faust der Juden*)."[31]

Goethe exploits this connection through a curious detail. After an excursion beyond the city gates, Faust watches as a mysterious dog, which has followed him home, begins to shift shapes, first into a hippo and eventually into the figure of Mephistopheles. In the midst of this transformation, Faust reaches for aid from a magic handbook, the *Key of Solomon*: "With this hybrid half-brood of hell / King Solomon's Key works very well" (*Für solche halbe Höllenbrut / Ist Salomonis Schlüssel gut*) (Luke, *Faust Part One*, 1257–58). Scholars have questioned why the author of *Faust's Coercion of Hell* would turn to a similar book by another magician.[32] My answer is that Goethe here highlights a comparison that underlies the entire first part of the drama—between Faust and Solomon in biblical and post-biblical tradition.[33]

Faust's recourse, earlier in the same scene, to a book by Nostradamus is another peculiar detail through which Goethe appears to accentuate latent Jewish associations in the Faust material. Critics are often perplexed why Goethe has Faust consult an occult book by Nostradamus, since no such book existed, and Paracelsus, or Agrippa might be more obvious magician-authors for Faust to turn to. But in fact, Nostradamus is another figure in whom magical arts, medicine, and purported Jewishness come together. In a polemical portrait of Nostradamus published in 1789, Johann Christoph Adelung interprets Nostradamus's claim that the gift of prophecy was a family inheritance as a reference to the family's known Jewish origin.[34] Adelung supposes that Nostradamus's paternal grandfather was the original convert, a man who, like the grandson, was a physician by profession.[35] According to Adelung, Nostradamus embraced his Jewish background, making no attempt to hide it, but rather counting it as an honor.[36] Further, as a physician, Adelung suggests, he was a "quack" and a "charlatan."[37]

Finally, the very notion of a Faustian pact has a remote Hebrew Bible echo that Goethe's version magnifies. Almut Neumann has traced the evolution of the cultural topos of a "pact with the devil" from the Hebrew Bible conception of a covenant with God.[38] The role of blood in the Faustian pact could recall this religious history.[39] Animal blood seals the Mosaic covenant with Israel: Moses took the blood and dashed it on the people and said, "This is the blood of the covenant that the LORD now makes with you concerning all these commands" (Exod. 24:7–8). In the New Testament, Jesus's offering of the communion cup as "the new covenant in my blood" also echoes this tradition (Luke 22:20). While the Faustus of the chapbook composes the contract in his own blood, in Goethe's version, Mephistopheles's request for a signature in blood appears silly, a mere "game" (*Fratze*) to Faust, to which Mephistopheles responds, "Blood is a very special juice" (*Blut ist ein ganz besonderer Saft*) (Kaufman, *Goethe's Faust*, 1739, 1740). In this way, Goethe's version draws attention to, and insists upon, an archaic connection with a covenantal past.

Testamental Divide

While Goethe clearly positions his Faust within a network of early modern Jewish characterizations and associations, the tests of Faust's status come in moments of religious decision within the drama. Goethe repeatedly sets up situations that highlight the divide between the Christian and Jewish scriptures and locates Faust on the non-Christian side of that divide. These critical moments include Faust's near-suicide, his translation of the book of John, and his ultimate parting from Gretchen. But these passages also reveal a complicated and ambiguous relationship to Christianity rather than a simple rejection. Christianity serves as an inspiration or temptation that ultimately helps keep Faust in motion, sustaining the fundamental rhythm of contraction and expansion in his striving.

The most densely typologically laden of these passages, and the one to which I will devote the most space, is Faust's near-suicide at the end of "Night" where he is inclined to drink a cup filled with a "distilment of all drowsy syrups" (*Inbegriff der holden Schlummersäfte*) (Luke, *Faust Part One*, 693), presumably a lethal dose of opiates.[40] As he contemplates this act he envisions a chariot of fire sweeping down toward him: "A fiery chariot on light wings descends / And hovers by me! I will set forth here / On a new journey to the heaven's ends, / To pure activity in a new sphere!" (*Ein Feuerwagen schwebt auf leichten Schwingen / An mich heran! Ich fühle mich bereit, / Auf neuer Bahn den Äther zu durchdringen, / zu neuen Sphären reiner Tätigkeit*) (Luke, *Faust Part One*, 702–5). Commentaries usually identify the *fiery chariot* with Elijah's ascent into the heavens in 2 Kings 2:11: "As they kept on walking and talking, a fiery chariot with fiery horses suddenly appeared and separated one from the other; and Elijah went up to heaven in a whirlwind."[41] (Goethe's term *Feuerwagen* unquestionably echoes Luther's term *feuriger Wagen* in this passage.) But according to exegetical traditions, Elijah does not die in this episode.[42] Faust, in his Elijah fantasy, is not imagining his own death and eternal life in heaven but simply his continued existence elsewhere.

At stake for the drama at this juncture is precisely the question of an eternal afterlife. The notion that the Old Testament does not evince a doctrine of immortality was common currency in the Enlightenment.[43] The Deist thinker Reimarus, in an essay published by Lessing, argues at great length that Judaism had no conception of eternal life, at least not until it came into contact with other peoples during the Babylonian Captivity.[44] Any attempt to see intimations of immortality in Old Testament passages, he claims, is but a false projection of Christian doctrine.[45] Elijah's ascension in the chariot of fire serves Reimarus as a case in point: nowhere, he argues, does the text indicate that Elijah lives forever either corporeally or spiritually.[46]

Lessing, despite his friend Mendelssohn's spirited efforts to argue for an assurance of immortality in the Hebrew scriptures,[47] affirms Reimarus's claim: in *Education of the Human Race* (*Erziehung des Menschengeschlechts*; 1780) he argues that the Old Testament has only "allusions and cues," but no real conception of an immortal soul.[48] But Lessing makes an interesting point about what it means *not* to believe in an eternal life of rewards or punishments, especially if one can also not count on just rewards or just punishments in this life either. It can amount to a kind of "heroic obedience": "Let us admit that it is a heroic obedience to observe the laws of God, simply because they are God's laws and not because God has promised here and there to reward the observer of them."[49] In fact, when, in his essay, Lessing comes around to describing a future humanity *beyond* Christianity, he recalls this aspect of Judaism. The human being will pursue good for its own sake, not because of future rewards, the promise of which can, at best, only serve a pedagogical function.[50]

But if Goethe too affirms the heroism of a this-sided orientation, here it is clear that Faust is falling prey to an illusion. In his fantasy of the chariot of fire, he imagines that, rather than facing death from his toxic elixir, he is on the verge of a deathless *transcendence*, a transport to a higher realm of *experience*. And indeed the image of a chariot has to be understood within a complex web of imagery of overcoming in the play. Certainly it links into a progression of images of flight in the first few scenes, echoing Faust's opening fantasy of flying low between earth and sky (392–97) and anticipating his later intended or unintended invocation of Mephistopheles: "If there be spirits in the air / That hold their sway between the earth and sky, / Descend out of the golden vapors there / And sweep me into iridescent life" (*O gibt es Geister in der Luft, / Die zwischen Erd' und Himmel herrschend weben, / So steiget nieder aus dem goldnen Duft /Und führt mich weg, zu neuem buntem Leben!*) (Kaufman, *Goethe's Faust*, 1118–21). Further, as Schöne points out, the vision of the fiery chariot seems to correspond to Mephisto's later mode of transport, his flying coat propelled by "fiery air" (*Feuerluft*) (Kaufman, *Goethe's Faust*, 2060; Schöne, 226).

The fiery chariot is also an answer to Faust's philosophical conundrum. What Faust seems to seek in his flirtation with suicide is a suspension of the conditions of consciousness that have led to his despair. In an echo of Kantian dualism, neither activity nor receptivity enables him to grasp the whole of life: "Alas, not only pain, even activity / Itself can stop our life's advance" (*Ach! Unsre Taten selbst, so gut als unsre Leiden, Sie hemmen unsres Lebens Gang*) (Luke, *Faust Part One*, 632–33). He seems attracted to the poison vial precisely because it seems to anesthetize both sides—*both* active and passive inclinations, *both* striving and suffering (696–97). The climax of this passage in the vision of fiery chariot suggests a suspension of these cognitive conditions and access to a realm of being in which one could, in effect, perceive and grasp all, to achieve—to return to Kantian terms—the "intellectual intuition" not otherwise available to mortal minds.

The reference in the passage to wings (*Schwingen*) also suggests a second possible allusion to the Hebrew Bible: Ezekiel's vision of God's throne chariot, which is accompanied by winged creatures and surrounded by flashing, radiant fire (Ezek. 1). Goethe's logic in connecting the visions of Ezekiel and Elijah could have been primed through his early childhood fascination with the illustrations in the family Bible, for Merian's engravings of Elijah's ascent and Ezekiel's vision are clearly parallel in their presentations.[51] But while according to traditional interpretations Elijah is swept into a divine sphere, transcending earthly boundaries without suffering death, the example of Ezekiel's vision of the throne chariot and its occupant is even more bold: it is nothing short of a divine theophany, and indeed gave rise to the ancient tradition within Judaism of Merkabah (or chariot) mysticism.[52]

The analogy to Ezekiel's theophany signals that Faust has entered risky territory. Indeed, in the Hebrew Bible any vision of the divine is inherently dangerous: as God says to Moses, "you cannot see My face, for man may not see Me and live" (Exod. 33:20).[53] Thus, as Maimonides describes in *The Guide for the Perplexed*, the mysteries of Ezekiel's vision have to be closely guarded: "[Our Sages] have clearly stated that the Divine Chariot includes matters too deep and too profound for the ordinary intellect."[54] Further, even the representation of the divine risks breaking the commandment banning graven images (Exod. 20:4). In his "Scattered Leaves" ("Zerstreute Blätter"), Herder adapts a Haggadic story concerning the divine throne chariot that well illustrates its inherent danger. A pious man becomes too absorbed in visions of the divine so that he neglects the necessary burdens of a mortal human being (*SW* 26: 356). In three successive dreams, he has visions of the chariot and its winged bearers, but longs to see more clearly the divine throne, until a Seraphim warns him not to dare to try to see that which even the heavenly hosts cannot. The man finally learns the lesson of his own mortality when he wakes up to witness a moth become scorched as it dares come too close to the flame of his lamp.

Thus, for Faust, the encounter heralded by the chariot of fire would presumably far surpass in power and danger his already failed encounter with the powerful earth spirit (*Erdgeist*). Faust himself foresees the possibility of his own extinction, the "risk of utter dissolution" (*Gefahr, ins Nichts dahinzufließen*) (Kaufman, *Goethe's Faust*, 719). Crucial here is that *nothingness* (*Nichts*) rather than eternal salvation or damnation stands on the other side of death, should Faust fail.

Yet just as Faust embarks upon this deadly step, raising the glass to his lips, the New Testament asserts itself. He is interrupted by the Easter message.

Chorus and bells ring out, recalling Christianity's New Covenant: "Is this already, choirs, the sweet consoling hymn / That was first sung around his tomb by cherubim, / Confirming the new covenant?" (*Ihr Chöre, singt ihr schon den tröstlichen Gesang, / Der einst, um Grabes Nacht, von Engelslippen klang, / Gewißheit einem neuen Bunde?*) (Kaufman, *Goethe's Faust*, 746–48). Much rests symbolically and thematically upon this concluding term of his pivotal Easter morning speech. In its newness, the "New Covenant" contrasts and supervenes an old typology, here the chariot of fire. As a covenant (*Bund*), it looks forward to, and suggests an alternative to the later, very different compact (*Bündnis*) (1741), which Faust will seal with Mephistopheles.

In his juxtaposition with the near-suicide scene, Goethe also draws on the Christian theological meaning of the New Covenant. In the Christian scriptures, it is associated with the communion cup. "This cup that is poured out for you is the new covenant in my blood" (Luke 22:20). The communion cup thus promises human community—in contrast to Faust's solitude. More to the point, this drink is associated not with death, as in the vial of opiates, but with life, indeed, in the New Testament Letter to the Hebrews, with *eternal* life: "For this reason [Christ] is the mediator of a new covenant, so that those who are called may receive the promised eternal inheritance, because a death has occurred that redeems them from the transgressions under the first covenant" (Heb. 9:15).

Nevertheless it becomes immediately apparent as the scene continues that Faust's response to the Easter morning does *not* involve an affirmation of the Christian metaphysical claims of eternal life: "Although I hear your gospel, I lack your faith" (*Die Botschaft hör' ich wohl, allein mir fehlt der Glaube*) (Atkins, *Faust I & II*, 765), he says. And faith is of course precisely that which, according to the Gospel of John, secures eternal life (John 3:15). Thus Faust's emotional response to the Easter message ends not with a statement of conversion but only with the assertion that "I am earth's again!" (*Die Erde hat mich wieder!*) (Atkins, 784). In fact, he formulates his response as a *restoration* of his former condition: the *earth*—not the heavenly kingdom—has him *again*.

And yet while he decisively rejects Christian metaphysics, the Christian celebration of Easter, especially the emphasis on earth and community, offers a positive impulse that, at a critical moment, turns him from a dangerous idolatry verging towards death. In this way, Christianity seems to play the role of keeping Faust in motion. He recalls in his youth how the sound of bells reached him "in sabbath's solemn quiet" (*in ernster Sabbatstille*) (Atkins, *Faust I & II*, 772) and drove him into a communion with nature: "An unbelievably sweet yearning / Drove me to roam through wood and lea, / Crying, and as my eyes were burning, / I felt a new world grow in me" (*Ein unbegreiflich holdes Sehnen / Trieb mich durch Wald und Wiesen hinzugehn, / Und unter tausend heißen Tränen / Fühlt' ich mir eine Welt entstehn*) (Kaufman,

Goethe's Faust, 775–78). The term "sabbath quiet" (*Sabbatstille*) could certainly be applied to Christian observation of quiet on Sunday, but its primary definition according to Grimms' dictionary is the Jewish one.[55] And at closer look within this passage "sabbath quiet" has a clear typological meaning. The Pentateuch contains repeated injunctions concerning rest on the Sabbath. For example, "Let everyone remain where he is: let no one leave his place on the seventh day" (Exod. 16:29); the Gospels, by contrast, are full of accounts of how Jesus broke the Sabbath law. For example, he and his disciples go through the fields and pick grain (Mark 2:23, Matt. 12:1, Luke 6:1). Faust's memory of movement from solemn Sabbath stillness to movement through the fields thus encapsulates a movement from the Old Testament to the New.

But predictably the Easter morning offers no permanent solution for Faust. The pronoun "he" in the proclamation of Christ's resurrection at the end of this scene, "For you *he* is here!" (*Euch ist* er *da!*) (Kaufman, *Goethe's Faust*, 807, emphasis mine), is carried over into a profane context in the next scene. A young woman outside the city gate exclaims, "We'll find *him* at the poplars, I'm certain it is true" (*Wir finden* ihn *gewiß bei jenen Pappeln stehen*) (Kaufman, *Goethe's Faust*, 821, emphasis mine), recalling perhaps Mary Magdalene looking for the risen Christ (see Matt. 28, Mark 16, John 20) among poplars, trees with biblical associations (see Gen. 30:37). But in fact the "him" she seeks is but her lover and dance partner. Faust himself fully adopts a secular and naturalistic interpretation of the Easter scene: "Out of the hollow gloomy gate / Surges and scatters a motley horde. / All seek sunshine. They celebrate / The resurrection of the Lord. / For they themselves are resurrected" (*Aus dem hohlen finstern Tor / Dringt ein buntes Gewimmel hervor / Jeder sonnt sich heute so gern. / Sie feiern die Auferstehung des Herrn, / Denn sie sind selber auferstanden*) (Kaufman, *Goethe's Faust*, 918–22). But even this more secular sense of communion with nature and with others, his confidence in humanity—"Here I am human, here it's allowed!" (*Hier bin ich Mensch, hier darf ich's sein*) (Luke, *Faust Part One*, 940)—turns out to be but another false idol. After remembering how his medicinal experiments led to widespread deaths, he finds himself in a "sea of errors" (*Meer des Irrtums*) (Kaufman, *Goethe's Faust*, 1065). Thus even the more metaphorical understanding of the Easter message—springtime rejuvenation, human community—offers no more of a permanent solution for Faust than any other stage. And yet Faust continuously falls prey to such illusory conceptions of fullness and completion within life. He seeks to have it all, to attain an absolute *within* time and in that sense he longs, in spite of himself, to suspend time.

To summarize, the Easter message serves as a crucial stage, but a stage among a succession of stages. The bells and chorus intervene at a moment when Faust is tending toward a dangerous idolatry, when he envisions the approach of the divine chariot, and is at risk of falling into stasis, for it clearly portends his death. But the Christian Easter impulse falls into a pattern of impulses and inspirations that include the magic book with its sign of the macrocosm and the encounter with the earth spirit. These visions set Faust in motion when he has become fixated or edges toward despair. They offer a temporary rejuvenation and the promise of a breakthrough into a new, freer sphere of activity (see 430–46, 462–67, 699–705). But then each of these moments turns out to be, in its way, deceptive or dangerous. None provides a permanent solution, but as each fails, it gives way to a new impulse and motion, in short to further forms of contraction and expansion. More primary and more far-reaching than Faust's encounter with Christianity, then, is his more general commitment to *this* life. And that commitment, in the logic of the drama, is akin to the covenant of the patriarchs.

Two further brief examples can establish the pattern of Faust's decisive self-positioning outside Christianity. Faust seems again to verge on Christianity and then retreat in the scene in which he translates the opening of the Gospel of John. He prefaces the attempt by praising the "holy" New Testament (1222), where he hopes to find the "supernatural realm" (*das Überirdische*) and "revelation" (*Offenbarung*) (Kaufman, *Goethe's Faust*, 1216–18). And yet his successive translations for the Greek word *logos* as "word" (*Wort*), "mind" (*Sinn*), "force" (*Kraft*), and "act" (*Tat*) are revealing (Kaufman, *Goethe's Faust*, 1224, 1229, 1233, 1237). Gerhard Kaiser observes that in his list of possible translations, he conspicuously fails to offer the word "love," a word that Kaiser points out would be distinctly New Testament in spirit and that would point forward to the Eternal Feminine.[56] In this sense Faust appears to fail a Christian litmus test. To further press the point, the translation for logos that Faust does end up with, "act," is, at least according to Christian typologies, distinctly *Old* Testament, suggesting as it does a concrete realm of works as opposed to spirit. (See for example Rom. 3:27, which contrasts the law of works with the law of faith.) According to this logic, Faust effectively translates John's line about creation back into a Hebrew Bible context. Once again he edges towards Christianity but remains decisively outside of it.

Perhaps the most emphatic declaration of Faust's outsider position in relation to Christianity comes from Gretchen, who feels their relationship is askew, "for you have no Christianity" (*Denn du hast kein Christentum*) (Kaufman, *Goethe's Faust*, 3468). As Faust acknowledges, Christian belief is the only path to salvation in her eyes (3531–32). And Goethe could hardly have created a more compelling representative of traditional Christian faith than Gretchen. For this faith sustains her even in moments of extreme mental agony. As her desperate situation dawns on her, she still clings to the familiar form of the Mater Dolorosa prayer as a vehicle that imparts shape and meaning to her suffering (3587–19). Faust, by contrast, evades any attempt to confine the divine within a name or concept, referring in his conversation with Gretchen to "the All-Embracing / The All-Sustaining" (*Der Allumfasser, / Der Allerhalter*), (Kaufman, *Goethe's Faust*, 3438, 3439). The religious divide between Faust and Gretchen becomes unbridgeable in the final scene where Gretchen rejects Faust's attempts to save her from execution and receives instead assurance of ultimate salvation from a theatrical voice on high: "is saved" (*Ist gerettet*) (Kaufman, *Goethe's Faust*, 4612). Meanwhile Mephistopheles wrenches Faust away to continue his itinerant existence, which assumes the place of hell or damnation in the original legend.

Arnd Böhm has suggested that Faust's whole tragedy lies in his failure to follow Gretchen and join the community of the Christian faithful.[57] Of course one has to acknowledge Faust's utter moral failing toward Gretchen, his inability to recognize her as another subject rather than an object of his striving. Nevertheless, to see Faust's problem as a failure to accept Christianity's promise of eternal life is to overlook the positive commitments he keeps. For in the same scene, as his penultimate line, he utters the phrase "That I had never been born!" (*O wäre ich nie geboren*) (Kaufman, *Goethe's Faust*, 4596), echoing Job's long speech cursing the day of his birth (Job 3:1–19). Faust thus reminds us in the final moments of the agonizing conclusion to *Part One* that he is not simply a sinful, failed Christian, but Job, a faithful hero of the Hebrew Bible.

Mein Knecht: Faust as Job

The analogy between Faust and Job is fundamental to understanding the entire dramatic structure established through the pact.[58] Goethe himself openly acknowledged the parallel he set up through the play's exposition (FA 2.12: 140). The "Prologue in Heaven," which precedes the main action in *Faust*, corresponds to the first two chapters of Job, which even in Goethe's time was referred to as its "prologue." (Furthermore, the core of Job was often seen as a "drama.")[59] Both prologues, Jobian and Faustian, involve a discourse in heaven—between the Lord and Satan or Mephistopheles, where the Lord draws attention to a particular man. In the Bible, the Lord asks the Adversary, "Have you noticed My servant Job? (Job 1:7–8). In Goethe's parallel passage, the Lord asks, "Do you know Faust?" (*Kennst du den Faust?*). To Mephisto's quizzical reply, "The doctor?" (*Den Doktor?*), the Lord responds, "Aye, my servant" (*Meinen Knecht!*) (Kaufman, *Goethe's Faust*, 299). Two things are of immediate significance in this comparison: the status of Mephistopheles as, like Satan, a member of the divine court, and the status of Faust as the Lord's "servant" (*Knecht*), in both Goethe's text and Luther's translation.

Goethe's Job-like frame establishes Mephistopheles from the first as a far more complex figure than countenanced by the legend. *Satan* in ancient Hebrew sources referred, according to Elaine Pagels, to "any one of the angels sent by God for the specific purpose of blocking or obstructing human activity."[60] Regardless of whether the Satan harms or helps the individual human being, he is acting on behalf of God.[61] Goethe's contemporaries were well aware of the gap between Job's Satan and the Christian devil. Eichhorn, whose *Introduction to the Old Testament* Goethe had read before he added the "Prologue," asserts that Satan in Job has nothing to do with Christian or even Chaldean notions of the devil, but operates at the direct behest of God. All that Job has to go through "conspicuously originates only from God."[62]

Admittedly, the opening analogy with the Satan of Job does not exhaust Mephistopheles's role within the drama. From the prologue to the penultimate scene of *Part Two*, Mephistopheles reveals multiple shifting and evolving dimensions, embodying Jewish and Christian as well as pagan conceptions. Herder, Goethe's early mentor in biblical criticism, notes the historical transformation of the devil within the Bible from divine agent of death and destruction, member of the divine council, and accuser of human beings in the ancient Hebrew context, to an independently acting liar, seducer, and agent of moral evil in the later Christian one (HW 5: 167–75). Certainly when Mephistopheles defines himself to Faust as "part of that force which would / Do evil evermore, and yet creates the good" (*Ein Teil von jener Kraft, Die stets das Böse will und stets das Gute schafft*) (Kaufman, *Goethe's Faust*, 1335–36), he locates himself between these two traditions, as both subordinate to divine purposes and independently willing destruction.[63] Regardless of what Mephistopheles wills and works at various points throughout the drama, he takes care not to rupture his precarious relationship to the Lord: "I like to see him sometimes and take care / not to fall out with him" (*Von Zeit zu Zeit sehe' ich den Alten gern, / Und hüte mich, mit ihm zu brechen*) (350–51).[64] His initial engagement with Faust is, in turn, an expression of this original connection to the divine. Much like Satan in the book of Job, Mephistopheles serves the Lord in an adversarial role by testing the Lord's claim that Faust is his servant.

But Mephistopheles's dealings with Faust are predicated not just on *his own* relationship to the Lord but also on an implicit prior relationship binding *Faust* to the Lord. Whether one regards Faust's ultimate contract with Mephistopheles as a pact or a bet, Faust's prior commitment as *Knecht* is the starting point. And the very term "Knecht" has far-reaching biblical implications beyond the book of Job. As Schöne points out, the Lord's use of the term "Knecht" puts Faust not only into the company of Job, but also of Abraham, Moses, and David.[65] The term "servant" in the Hebrew Bible context "designates the relation of the weaker partner to the stronger in a covenant."[66] The *Bündnis* with Mephistopheles (1741) thus rests on a prior *Bund*, a covenantal relationship with the Lord.

In the Bible, Job's relationship to the covenantal tradition is complex. To begin with, Job is often taken to be an Edomite, rather than an Israelite, because of his homeland Uz.[67] But more to the point, the story of Job seems to test the very boundaries of the human/divine contract that, in other instances, involves the expectation of blessings for the righteous. In particular it appears to challenge the reciprocity of the Mosaic covenant, as formulated especially in Deuteronomy. There, Israel is affirmed as a treasured people and enjoined to observe the Lord's laws and commandments (Deut. 26:17–19). This affirmation is followed by a list of detailed consequences for Israel's success or failure to uphold its end of the covenant. Blessings will ensue "if you will but heed the word of the LORD your God" (Deut. 28:2); curses will follow "if you do not obey the LORD your God to observe faithfully all His commandments and laws" (Deut. 28:15).

The stability of a covenantal relationship based on rewards and punishments is then precisely what the prologue to the book of Job seems to call into question. When, in the prologue, the Lord expresses his pleasure in his servant, the Adversary suggests that Job's righteousness will continue only as long as he reaps benefits:

> The Adversary answered the LORD, "Does Job not have good reason to fear God? Why, it is You who have fenced him round, him and his household and all that he has. You have blessed his efforts so that his possessions spread out in the land. But lay Your hand upon all that he has and he will surely blaspheme You to Your face. (Job 1:9–11)

Thus Satan suggests a test of Job's genuine, uncompensated commitment to the Lord.[68]

But if Job's righteous commitment brings no rewards but only suffering, just what *is* the point of it all? The book of Job can seem to hold out the possibility of an answer to this question—the promise, that is, of a theodicy. And yet readers are often disappointed. Mayer Gruber puts Job's "inconclusive conclusion" in the following way: "There is no way of understanding the meaning of suffering. That is, in the LORD'S argument, the reasons for suffering—if there are any—are simply beyond human comprehension."[69]

In Goethe's era, Eichhorn read the book of Job as internally at odds over the question of innocent suffering. The Lord's speech provides no answers, for he asserts only his own unfathomability. Thus a distinct prologue and epilogue were added "in order to solve the problem, that is not easily solved in the drama [*Stück*] itself."[70] The prologue in the heavenly court suggests, according to Eichhorn, that a crisis motivates the testing of Job, while the epilogue abruptly reverses all of Job's misfortunes.[71] For example, Job receives ten replacement children for the ones crushed to death earlier (Job 42:13). But in a later, revised edition of his famous study, Eichhorn acknowledges an apparent problem with this view of the epilogue: it seems to undermine the central argument of the middle of the book, that righteousness does not guarantee a lack of suffering.[72]

And yet this epilogue, which can seem to reverse the meaning of the book, becomes key to the Christian reception of Job. The New Testament book of James describes Job as the patient one ultimately rewarded by God: "You have heard of Job's perseverance and have seen what the Lord finally brought about" (James 5:11). In context, the passage suggests that, just as Job's virtue of patience reaped rewards, so will patient Christians be rewarded with the second coming of Christ. In an episode in his autobiography, Goethe offers an implicit critique of the antithetical Christian reception of Job as guaranteeing relief for innocent suffering. When his friend, the extremely devout Christian Jung-Stilling, undergoes great shame as an eye doctor after bungling an operation, and struggles to make sense of his situation, he gets the meaning of the book of Job backwards. Goethe reports, "we played out this Job-like drama from start to finish, with the honest man himself in the role of the scolding friends" (*wir spielten das unerfreuliche Drama Hiobs von Anfang bis zu Ende durch, da denn der treue Mann sich die Rolle der scheltenden Freunde selbst übernahm*) (CW 5: 533; FA 1.14: 744). The friends in the book of Job insist that somehow misfortune must be divine punishment for vice. And yet the Lord himself explicitly declares Job's scolding friends to be wrong—"you have not spoken the truth about Me" (Job 42:7). The pious Christian Jung-Stilling, having missed the central point of Job, remains fixated on the expectation that God indeed exacts punishments and grants rewards based on individual human behavior.[73]

In the figure of Faust, then, Goethe insists upon the more difficult, non-Christian aspects of Job. In particular, his representation of Faust-as-Job emphatically challenges the New Testament characterization of Job as patient. As many commentators have pointed out, Job is anything but patient through most of the book.[74] Before arriving at his final affirmation of God's majesty, Job openly and powerfully challenges God's justice, asserting: "I insist on arguing with God" (Job 13:3). Goethe brings home this point through Faust's long list of curses in the second "Study" scene that are reminiscent of Job's curses in the third chapter. As Schöne notes, Faust curses three of the core Christian virtues named by Paul: faith, hope and love (1 Cor. 13:13; Schöne, 257). Furthermore, Faust ends his long chain of deprecations with a final rejection of precisely the virtue that the Christian epistle James assigns to Job: "but cursed be patience most of all!" (*Und Fluch vor allen der Geduld!*) (Atkins, *Faust I & II*, 1606). Neither Faust nor Job passively accept their condition.

Perhaps the key point of Goethe's comparison is the failure of any justification of suffering. Unlike the transaction that seems to be promised in Deuteronomy, the relationship between the Lord and Job is completely non-reciprocal: while Job must be tested or justified, the Lord never justifies himself. Here we can take a cue from Muenzer's observation of an affinity between Goethe's reading of Job and his understanding of Spinoza: in both, Muenzer argues, Goethe found an ever self-transforming, immanent God-in-nature.[75] Moreover, Goethe explicitly encountered in Spinoza—as in Job—a non-reciprocity in the human-divine relationship. In *Poetry and Truth* he writes: "That curious statement, 'He who loves God rightly must not require

God to love him in return,' with all the premises on which it rests and all the results issuing from it, pervaded my meditations" (*[Jenes wunderliche Wort] "Wer Gott recht liebt, muß nicht verlangen, daß Gott ihn wieder liebe" mit allen den Vordersätzen worauf es ruht, mit allen den Folgen die daraus entspringen, erfüllte mein ganzes Nachdenken*) (*CW* 4: 459; FA 1.14: 681).

Thus we come to the crux: as the Lord's servant, by analogy with Job, and perhaps filtered through Spinoza, Faust is bound in a relationship that guarantees neither life after death, nor rewards in this life. Despite the appearance of the Lord as a dramatis persona, Goethe's conception of the divine is not personal. Faust himself does not encounter the Lord, but is the Lord's servant despite himself, almost without realizing it.[76] Faust finds himself in a covenant, not with a personal God, but with *this existence* and all it implies: flux, temporality, no guarantees, and a sense of a whole always beyond one's reach.

Ultimately, then, the contract Faust enters into with Mephistopheles is but a new proviso imposed upon the original commitment to this life. That the terms of his agreement have not changed the basic character of an original commitment is clear from Faust's own formulations: if he fails "then I will gladly be destroyed!" (*Dann will ich gern zu Grunde gehn!*) (Atkins, *Faust I & II*, 1702). The threat of damnation means nothing to him: "With the Beyond I cannot be much bothered" (*Das Drüben kann mich wenig kümmern*) (Atkins, 1660). For his concern is only with the joys and tribulations of this life: "This earth's the source of all my joys, / and this sun shines upon my sorrows" (*Aus dieser Erde quillen meine Freuden / Und diese Erde scheinet meinen Leiden*) (Atkins, 1663–64).

The terms of the pact reflect the drama's vision of a dynamic universe, unfolded for example in the evolving, competing cosmologies of the archangels' songs in the "Prologue in Heaven" (243–70). The risk for Faust, according to the Lord, is to become fixed in place: "Human activity slackens all too easily, / and people soon are prone to rest on any terms" (*Des Menschen Tätigkeit kann allzuleicht erschlaffen / Er liebt sich bald die unbedingte Ruh*) (Atkins, *Faust I & II*, 340–41). And thus Faust formulates the wager in very similar terms. He loses should he stop moving: "If on a bed of sloth I ever lie contented" (*Werd' ich beruhigt je mich auf ein Faulbett legen*) (Atkins, 1692) or "If I should ever say to any moment: Tarry—remain! you are so fair!" (*Werd' ich zum Augenblicke sagen: Verweile doch du bist so schön!*) (Atkins, 1699–1700). Consequently, he rejects all that in this life provides a false sense of permanence, comfort, or repose. In his Job-like list of curses cited earlier, Faust includes all that bind us to this life: "enticements" "cheating visions" (*Lock- und Gaukelwerk*) and "powers of persuasion and deception" (*Blend- und Schmeichelkräfte*) (Atkins, 1587–90). His catalog of deceptive lures includes "high pretenses" (*die hohe Meinung*), "deluded senses" (*das Blenden der Erscheinung*) "dreams of fame, honor and a lasting name" (*des Ruhms, der Namensdauer Trug*) "vain property" (*Besitz*) including in the form of "wife and child" (*Weib und Kind*), and finally, money or "mammon" (*Mammon*) (Luke, *Faust Part One*, 1591–99). In short, as the term "Mammon" suggests,[77] Faust rejects all forms of idolatry.

But just as the drive for expansion is always offset by the drive for contraction (and vice versa), striving always leads to erring in Goethe's conception. As the Lord says, "Man errs as long as he will strive" (*Es irrt der Mensch, solang' er strebt*) (Kaufman, *Goethe's Faust*, 317). Mephistopheles hopes that precisely through relentless activity, he can get Faust stuck: "Through dissipation I will drag him / Through shallow insignificance, / I'll have him sticking, writhing, flagging" (*Den schlepp' ich durch das wilde Leben, / Durch flache Unbedeutenheit, / Er soll mir zappeln, starren, kleben*) (Arndt, *Faust: A Tragedy*, 1860–62). As in the Hebrew Bible, the temptations of idolatry always reemerge. This theme is the basis of a second, fundamental biblical analogy in *Part One*: Faust and Solomon.

Solomon: Natural Philosopher, Idolater, Lover

Faust's analogy with Solomon is actually earlier than the one with Job, dating back to the *Urfaust*. Indeed, in the precise period when Goethe was working on his earliest Faust sketches, he was also occupied with Solomon. In a letter dated October 7, 1775, Goethe notes his current work on two projects: a translation of the Song of Songs, the biblical love poetry attributed to Solomon, and *Faust* (FA 2.1: 483). Goethe only added the Job frame in the "Prologue" about a quarter of a century later.

But the one biblical hero did not displace the other in Goethe's conception: Job and Solomon would have seemed a good fit for each other as consonant, indeed philosophically and theologically parallel figures. Eichhorn notes that Solomon was sometimes thought to be the author of the book of Job.[78] Job falls in the category of wisdom literature along with two books attributed to Solomon, Ecclesiastes and Proverbs. Both Job and Solomon were occasionally labeled philosophical skeptics.[79] In *Poetry and Truth*, Goethe groups Job with two Solomonic books (Song of Songs and Proverbs) as examples of ancient sources that unite poetry, religion, and philosophy (FA 1.14: 243). A particularly strong affinity lies between Job and Ecclesiastes, a book ascribed to Solomon under the name Koholeth. Like Job, Koholeth/Solomon provides no assurances of rewards and punishments in this life, nor certainly in an afterlife.[80] In Eichhorn's words, Ecclesiastes "seems to deny moral providence and life after death."[81] And yet Solomon and Job also share the designation that Goethe applies to Faust, "servant of God" (1 Kings 3:7).

Even more than Job, Solomon is a figure of nearly kaleidoscopic complexity and variability.[82] His life is narrated in two biblical books, 1 Kings and 2 Chronicles, and is the object of countless legends and accounts within Judaism, Christianity, and Islam. He is the purported author of three canonical books, Ecclesiastes, the Song of Songs, and Proverbs; one apocryphal book, the Wisdom of Solomon; and many pseudoepigraphical works. In addition to his kingly role he emerges as philosopher, natural scientist, magician, demonologist, and lover par excellence. He is at once one of the great heroes of the Bible—builder of the Temple—and a great sinner, because, at the end of his life, he is lured by his many foreign wives and concubines to break the covenant and commit the sin of idolatry.

Goethe had access to, and clearly knew, many of the diverse sources on Solomon. His literary efforts involving Solomon in the mid-1770s already reveal his active investigation of the figure. Around the same time as he translated the Song of Songs, Goethe wrote a Solomon-inspired prose piece, "The Golden Words of Solomon, the King of Israel and Judea, on the Cedar to the Hyssop" ("Salomons Königs von Israel und Juda Güldne Worte von der Ceder biss zum Issop"), a short collection of tree and plant parables with Solomon as fictional author. Some commentators see Goethe's inspiration for his Solomonic parables in the biblical verse: "[Solomon] discoursed about trees, from the cedar in Lebanon to the hyssop that grows out of the wall; and he discoursed about beasts, birds, creeping things and fishes" (1 Kings 5:13).[83] Yet for Goethe's choice of the parable form, another source seems likely: Flavius Josephus's portrait of Solomon in his *Judean Antiquities*, to which Goethe would have had easy access in his father's library. Josephus reports "[Solomon] spoke a parable about each kind of tree from the hyssop to the cedar."[84] Further, Goethe's Solomonic parables are consonant with the dark vision in Ecclesiastes of the flux and vanity of all things.[85] Clearly, already in his early career, Goethe was working to piece together an image of Solomon from multiple sources.

But the canonical books of the Hebrew Bible and Josephus's first-century historical account are just the beginning of the exotic buffet of materials on Solomon to which Goethe had access. Goethe was well acquainted with the biblical Apocrypha (FA 2.12: 746), and therefore certainly knew the Wisdom of Solomon. In his study of the Koran in the early 1770s, he would also have come across a number of references to Solomon, including references to devils in Solomon's service.[86] Rabbinical sources were indirectly available to him in his father's library through Johann Andreas Eisenmenger's account in *Judaism Revealed*. Because of its authorship by a professor of Oriental languages, this highly distorting, anti-Jewish representation of Jewish beliefs and practices served as an authoritative representation of the Talmud for non-Jews.[87] Herder's adaptations of Jewish legends, although published first in 1787, could be a further source, one that drew in turn on several early eighteenth-century compendia of Talmudic material, including Eisenmenger.[88] One of the most extensive reference works on Solomonic traditions was J. A. Fabricius's codex of Old Testament pseudepigrapha which devotes well over 100 pages to summaries and excerpts from a great number of sources either about or supposedly by Solomon."[89] Masonic culture played on myths surrounding the architecture of Solomon's temple and contributed to the general aura of mystery and esoteric wisdom associated with Solomon (Goethe became an apprentice in the Amalia lodge in 1780). Meanwhile, Zedler's lengthy entry on Solomon in his 1742 lexicon includes a partially annotated list of twenty-four works that he deems falsely attributed to the biblical king. In addition to the *Key of Solomon* already mentioned, Zedler's list includes works of medicine, alchemy, wisdom, psalms, and especially magic and conjuration.[90] On the literary front, Klopstock's tragedy *Salomo* (1765) imagines a crucial episode in Solomon's life not elaborated in the Bible—his veneration of idols. Klopstock portrays Solomon's worship of the Ammonite god Moloch, and implicates him in child sacrifice.

From this colorful array of Solomonic sources and traditions, three aspects converge with Goethe's portrayal of Faust: Faust as seeker (philosopher, scientist, magician, and conjurer of demons), Faust as lover, and, bound treacherously close to the first two, Faust as idolater. While many of the specific allusions to Solomon in *Faust* have been noted before, they are usually read in isolation. I argue that Goethe weaves the thematic connections together to underscore the broader logic of his tragedy.[91]

Faust as Solomon

In the opening monologue of "Night," penned presumably during the same Frankfurt years when Goethe occupied himself with Solomon, we encounter a Faust powerfully reminiscent of Koholeth (a.k.a. Solomon), the voice of Ecclesiastes.[92] Both Faust's opening speech and the opening chapter of Ecclesiastes describe a drive to know all. Says Faust: "I've studied now, to my regret, / Philosophy, Law, Medicine, / and—what is worst—Theology / from end to end with diligence" (*Habe nun, ach! Philosophie, / Juristerei und Medizin, / Und leider auch Theologie / Durchaus studiert, mit heißem Bemühn*) (Atkins, *Faust I & II*, 355–58); says Koholeth: "I set my mind to study and to probe with wisdom all that happens under the sun" (Eccl. 1:13). But for both Koholeth and for Faust, the search for wisdom ends in heartache: "To increase learning is to increase heartache," says Koholeth. (Eccl. 1:18); "We can know nothing. It burns my heart" (*Und sehe, daß wir nichts wissen können! Das will mir schier das Herz verbrennen*) (Kaufman, *Goethe's Faust*, 364–65), says Faust. According to tradition, Ecclesiastes is associated with a juncture in Solomon's life—after his decline into old age—that matches Faust's at the outset of the play.[93] Like the character Faust, Koholeth is brimming with self-contradictions including, in Eichhorn's view, "a great inconstancy in principles, an inconsistency in contemplation of the world and in the experiences therein."[94] And both Faust and Koheleth share what one is tempted to call an existential outlook—a focus on the joys, sorrows, and exigencies of this life "under the sun"—the signature phrase of Ecclesiastes.

But in *Faust*, as in broader traditions surrounding Solomon, the philosopher and seeker of wisdom turns to magic and even demonology. Faust resorts to magic in a pious yet precarious urge to grasp "what secret force / Hides in the world and rules its course" (*was die Welt / Im Innersten zusammenhält*) (Kaufman, *Goethe's Faust*, 382–83). And thereby, as we have seen, he reaches specifically for the *Key of Solomon*. But of course, as the scene "Night" progresses, it becomes clear that what Faust seeks is nothing short of a theophany—a vision of an eternal All, which takes the form alternately of the sign of the macrocosm, the encounter with the Earth Spirit, and finally with the vial of poison. In all three cases, the theophanic vision comes apart, either as false fantasy (454), as exceeding Faust's powers of perception and comprehension (485), or as potentially fatal (719). At last he turns to the devil to facilitate his further searching.

Solomon's magic places him on a similar trajectory. As described by the first-century Jewish historian Josephus, Solomon's magic is a mere version of natural philosophy and his knowledge of demons is exorcistic:

> God also enabled him to learn the technique against demons for the benefit and healing of humans. He composed incantations by which illnesses are relieved, and left behind exorcistic practices with which those binding demons expel them so that they return no more."[95]

But within the body of Solomonic sources that came down to Goethe, these practices glide easily from pious undertaking to dangerous transgressions including idolatry. Solomon's greatest achievement is the building of the Great Temple. He declares to the Lord "I have now built for You / A stately House, / A place where You / May dwell forever" (1 Kings 8:13). Yet according to a rabbinical legend included in Eisenmenger, Solomon is supposed to have used supernatural means, including demons, in order to achieve his goal.[96] In doing so, he quickly gets in over his head with the king of the demons Asmodeus and falls into disgrace.[97] Thus while in the canonical account foreign wives lead Solomon astray, this legend suggests that in the temple project itself—which God commanded Solomon to undertake—lie the hazards of sin. Even in the canonical biblical account, Solomon seems to question the whole attempt to house God. "But will God really dwell on earth? Even the heavens to their uttermost reaches cannot contain You, how much less this House that I have built?" (1 Kings 8:27). Josephus suggests furthermore, that some of the temple ornamentation was itself idolatrous.[98]

Perhaps the source that best links Faust and Solomon on the slippery ride from pious search for wisdom to idolatry is the book "Wisdom of Solomon," which is contained in the Luther Bible under "Apocrypha." The Wisdom of Solomon provides a succinct description of the way in which the seeker and lover of beauty and nature falls prey to idolatry—a description that also seems to match Faust's problem. The presumptive author Solomon here observes that the things of beauty in the world, which should lead us to think of the God who creates them, become mistaken for gods: "but they supposed that either fire or wind or swift air, or the circle of the stars, or turbulent water, or the luminaries of heaven were the gods that rule the world" (Wis. 13:2). The author both defends and criticizes those who are "led astray" through this idolatrous short-circuit in thought.

> Yet these people are little to be blamed, for perhaps they go astray while seeking God and desiring to find him. For while they live among his works, they keep searching, and they trust in what they see, because the things that are seen are beautiful. Yet again, not even they are to be excused; for if they had the power to know so much that they could investigate the world, how did they fail to find sooner the Lord of these things? (Wis. 13:6–9)

In his translation of this passage, Luther uses the verb "irren" to describe this manner of going astray. It is of course the same word used by the Lord in the "Prologue in Heaven": "Man errs [*irrt*] as long as he will strive" (317). The pitfall described in the passage, as in the Faustian pact, is that one lingers with things that are beautiful. Even the most searching human mind is itself finite and tempted to rest with a finite image of beauty, thus betraying its own commitments to the endless fluidity of this life.

Equally illuminating for Faust's dilemma is the analogy linking him to Solomon as lover. Both Koholeth and Faust turn to erotic and other earthly pursuits after recognizing the futility of knowledge. Koholeth praises enjoyment as the only good a man can have under the sun (Eccl. 8:15). He proclaims, "Enjoy happiness with a woman you love all the fleeting days of life that have been granted to you under the sun—all your fleeting days. For that alone is what you can get out of life and out of the means you acquire under the sun" (Eccl. 9:9). Faust, an old man despairing of coherence and internally conflicted, also experiments with the path of mere enjoyment facilitated by Mephistopheles, or "shallow insignificance" (*flache Unbedeutenheit*) (1861) in Mephisto's words. And this path leads him to Gretchen.

Connections between Gretchen and the Shulamite, the beloved woman in the Song of Songs, are well established. Over a century ago, Pniower argued for parallels in the first "Garden" scene and in Gretchen's song at the spinning wheel.[99] A particularly striking allusion to the Song of Songs in the Garden scene is Gretchen's exclamation when Faust takes her hands, "I'm trembling" (*Mich überläuft's*) (3187), a somewhat unusual construction that Pniower links to "mich überliefs," the Shulamite's response to the approach of her lover in Goethe's own translation of the Song of Songs (FA 1.12: 368).[100] Between the Song of Songs and Gretchen's spinning wheel song, Pniower finds multiple parallels: in the list of the lover's attributes (Song 5:11–13, compare 3394–3401); in the urge to clasp and hold on to the lover (Song

3:4, compare 3408–9); and in the climactic, almost violent longing in the final stanzas, which echoes the biblical verses with which Goethe ended his translation (Song 8:6–7; compare 3406–13).[101]

But in fact the Song of Songs subtext, by inserting Gretchen into the broader, disparate Solomonic tradition, lends a stunning complexity and indeterminacy to her encounter with Faust. For example, the celebration of the lovers' blissful devotion to each other in the Song of Songs stands in jarring juxtaposition to the report in 1 Kings, that Solomon had seven hundred wives and three hundred concubines. By analogy, the reader of Faust must hold in mind that Faust's meeting with Gretchen is prefaced by the prediction that he will find "in every woman a Helen of Troy" (*Bald Helenen im jedem Weibe*) (Atkins, *Faust I & II*, 2604). Further, the contiguity between the Shulamite and more ambivalent female typologies in the Solomonic material troubles the analogy with Gretchen. In the book of Proverbs, there are two female figures that stand in sharp contrast. One is the "foreign woman," a prostitute or adulteress, who leads the man astray: "Her feet go down to Death" (Prov. 5:5). She is described in sensuous terms similar to the Shulamite; compare: "Your lips drop sweetness like the honeycomb, my bride" (Song 4:11) and "for through the lips of an adulteress drip honey" (Prov. 5:3).[102] And further, this adulterous female stranger, guilty of forgetting the covenant (Prov. 2:17), recalls the pagan wives and concubines in 1 Kings who lure Solomon away from the covenant into idolatry (1 Kings 11:11). In the post-biblical tradition about Solomon, dangerous female figures multiply. Significant among them is the demon Lilith, supposedly Adam's first wife, who goes on to kill newborn children. Lilith appears in Walpurgis Night (4119) in, according to Albrecht Schöne, "Analogy-Antithesis" to Gretchen, as a figure capable of ensnaring and detaining Faust (Schöne, 355). Among the diverse sources connecting Lilith and Solomon, the one most accessible to Goethe would have been the Talmudic legend recounted in Eisenmenger's *Judaism Revealed*.[103] Lilith and three other female demons—all previously servants of Solomon—are said to gather with their host during the solstices from sundown to midnight on the mountain Nischpa, near the mountain of darkness.[104] Eisenmenger's account could well have contributed to Goethe's depiction of "Walpurgis Night."

Thus questions emerge concerning where Gretchen fits into the narrative of covenant-breaking and covenant-keeping within this Solomonic subtext. If Gretchen is to be read as an entrapping figure like Lilith or the foreign wives, the temptation with which she tries to lure Faust might well be Christianity.[105] Goethe makes this connection between a devout Christian (Catholic) woman and the seductions of idolatry in a poem of 1815, "Sweet Child, The Rows of Pearls" ("Süßes Kind, die Perlenreihen"), which was preserved in his papers, but was clearly too controversial to publish. The poet's beloved comes to him wearing a crucifix for which she demands homage, but which he views as an idol. The poet lists Abraham, Moses, David, Mohammed, and interestingly Jesus himself all as true monotheists who resisted idolatry, for he says, he who turns Jesus into a god injures Jesus's own sacred will. He cites Solomon alone as one who gives in to idol worship through the seduction of his many wives. And so at last the poet capitulates to his beloved: "And I'll not claim to be better / When it happens to me / Solomon forswore his [God] / My God I have denied" (*Und ich will nicht besser scheinen / Als es sich mit mir ereugnet, / Salomo verschwur den seinen, / Meinen Gott hab ich verleugnet*) (FA 1.3.1: 509).

But if the comparison with Solomon suggests on the one hand that Faust's erotic entanglements are dangerous, drawing him toward stasis, idolatry and defeat, it also suggests the very opposite, that his love of Gretchen moves him forward. For Proverbs contrasts the dangerous foreign woman with the female figure of wisdom. In this Solomonic book, Wisdom appears as an eternal personality, co-dwelling with God prior to all creation (Prov. 8:22–23).[106] In the Wisdom of Solomon (10–11) she is described as a rescuing, delivering spirit guiding the righteous through history. Certainly this Solomonic eternal female figure of Wisdom ranks among the many sources evoked by "the Eternal Feminine" who draws us onward in the final lines of *Part Two*. As I will consider in the final chapter, the female imagery in the final scene is also highly Christianized, creating further ambiguity about what it is that traps Faust and what it is that keeps him in motion.

The allusions to the Song of Songs thus introduce Gretchen into a nearly undecidable nexus of meanings and narratives. Is she, like the Shulamite, a loving and beloved woman, concretely present to Faust as a sensuous being? Or is she a Mephistophelean diversion leading him from his pact like the adulterous woman, the idolatrous wife or concubine, the infanticidal Lilith? Or is she the personification of the ideal of wisdom that draws Faust ever onward to keep his existential covenant? Or does she perhaps embody all these things and therefore present for Faust the tragic paradox—that it is nearly impossible for him to strive in time without longing to negate time? To love Gretchen is at once to live in the moment, to become attached to the beautiful moment, and then to wish the conditions of time away. The truly striving "servant" almost inevitably becomes ensnared in life. The dilemma is encapsulated in the passage from the apocryphal Wisdom of Solomon quoted earlier: people should not be greatly blamed when, in the course of their earnest searching, they are captivated by the beauty they encounter in the world.

And yet, as that same passage continues, such people are also not to be excused for their errors. Neither does Goethe justify Faust's atrocious crimes—his responsibility in the deaths of Gretchen, their child, her mother, and her brother. Faust's failings certainly include his lack, at least up until the final scene, of any intersubjective recognition. That is, in his own striving, he fails to grasp Gretchen's perspective at all, or to understand her as more than the aim of his striving, as indeed like him, a striving being.[107] The misogynistic typologies—witch, prostitute, demon—imposed so jarringly upon this adolescent girl only heighten that sense of failed reciprocity. In this respect, perhaps the worst, most destructive idol of all is Faust's own subjectivity.

Part One thereby ends in tragedy but not damnation. Neither the suffering that Faust causes, nor the suffering that he undergoes, receive justification within the universe Goethe represents. But in the end, Faust remains, like Job and Solomon, a "servant," bound by commitments that persist through all tribulation and error. *Part Two* extends both the reach of Faust's wanderings and the magnitude of his error.

Chapter 5

✦

Faust and the Promised Land

Part Two of the Tragedy

The Chasm

The break and shift between *Part One* and *Part Two* recalls in many ways the transition between *Wilhelm Meister's Apprenticeship* and *Wilhelm Meister's Journeyman Years*. We move from the earlier works that, for all their innovations, still have a graspable shape and scope, to the later works that, in their sheer representational range and formal heterogeneity, seem to anticipate the experiments of high modernism. And yet I contend that underlying the transitions between the two *Meister* novels as well as the two parts of *Faust* are biblical paradigms. Chapter 3 argued that the *Journeyman Years* positions itself as an alternative New Testament in relationship to the *Apprenticeship* as Old Testament. But with the two parts of Faust, a different kind of biblical break is at work: the "chasm" (*Kluft*) Goethe describes between the plots of parts 1 and 2 of *Faust* is parallel to the "chasm" he experienced between the first and second books of the Hebrew Bible, that is between the patriarchal settings of Genesis and the narrative swath of Exodus.[1] The two biblical models—Old Testament/New Testament, Genesis/Exodus—have very different implications for the kind of modernity they herald. The Testamental model holds out the possibility, however qualified and ironized, of utopian transformations—of a "New Jerusalem" as the *Volksbuch* sketch calls it, or "a new world" as revealed in the Christian murals in the Pedagogical Province. The Pentateuchal model suggests for Goethe a very different paradigm of historical change. Goethe employs the Exodus narrative both as a way to expose the violence inherent in utopian projects, and to come to terms with the inevitably contingent and compromising forces of history.

But how does this claim that the two parts of *Faust* reflect the Genesis-Exodus divide square with the argument in the previous chapter that the dominant Hebrew Bible models in *Part One* of the drama were Job and Solomon? What do Job and Solomon have to do with Genesis? The book of Job, despite its canonical placement far from the book of Genesis and its setting remote from Canaan, has often been viewed as evocative of the patriarchal period. In the view of modern biblical criticism, Job's "archaizing" presentation makes it seem older than it presumably is.[2] In fact, in Goethe's day, Eichhorn argued that the book of Job truly had the most ancient origins of all.[3] Herder also found in Job "a strong echo of the first ages of the world and of the natural wisdom of the elders and patriarchs, which was simple, innocent, and, in its very poverty, rich" (*SW* 10: 131). For Goethe's definition of patriarchal, then, a perceived tone or spirit matters more than any historical or geographical locus. He notes "ein reineres patriarchalisches Wesen" in Joshua, Judges, and even later books (FA 1.3.1: 246),[4] and associates "patriarchal life" with the world of Homer (FA 1.8: 59). The poem "Hegire," which prefaces Goethe's *West-östlicher Divan*, contrasts a Europe coming apart through wars and revolutions—"Thrones burst, kingdoms shake" (*Throne bersten, Reiche zittern*)—with the patriarchal environment of the East in general: "Flee, to savor patriarchal air in the pure East" (*Flüchte du, im reinen Osten / Patriarchenluft zu kosten*) (FA 1.3.1: 12). Thus "patriarchal" implies traditional forms of authority, pastoral or small-scale settings, and a focus on individual relationships, rather than on political or legal systems and mass movements. In this respect, despite their location in a much later period of Israel's history, the Solomonic stories would also have had something of this freer, more individual appeal for him, for the Israelite people take a clear back seat to the philosophy, love affairs, and character strengths and weaknesses of their king. In particular the Song of Songs takes place, Goethe notes, in a "rural, familiar setting" (*ländlich trauliche Verhältnisse*) (FA 1.3.1: 141). In my reading then, *Part One*, with its Jobian and Solomonic subtexts, embodies this patriarchal spirit; *Part Two* takes on the narrative trappings of Exodus.

But to be more precise, the patriarchal-Exodus divide falls not just between the parts, but between the opening scene of *Part Two*, "Charming Landscape" ("Anmutige Gegend"), and the main action of the play, beginning in the emperor's court. Functioning as a kind of prologue or entr'acte introducing *Part Two*, "Charming Landscape" offers a succinct recap of the opening chapters of Genesis.

Renewal of the Covenant

Like Genesis, the scene "Charming Landscape" represents a beginning. It opens in an in-between time, in the moments before dawn as spirits attend to, and soothe, Faust, lying restively asleep in a meadow. The first light of day then arrives with a great sound and fanfare as if it were the first instant of creation. Strong parallels have been noted between the break of day in this scene and Herder's description of the daily repetition of the creation story in each sunrise.[5] Faust's opening speech then progresses through an individual version of the first books of Genesis—the story of creation and the fall. As he emerges from sleep, he notes the animation of the earth around him, "all that surrounds me forms a paradise" (*Ein Paradies wird um mich her die Runde*) (Atkins, *Faust I & II*, 4694). In Jane Brown's formulation, Faust "rises as a new Adam in Paradise."[6] This earthly paradise as described by Faust awakens the resolve to strive to the highest form of existence: "You [earth] rouse and stir a vigorous resolve / to strive henceforth towards being's highest form—" (*Du [Erde] regst und rührst ein kräftiges Beschließen, / Zum höchsten Dasein immerfort zu streben*) (Atkins, 4684–85).

But the activation of "striving" in "paradise" should make us wary: next will undoubtedly come transgression and catastrophe. But exactly who or what will destroy this paradise? *Whose* resolve to strive is stirred in the lines just quoted? The indefinite article here, *a* forceful resolve, creates a key ambiguity: does the resolve inhere in nature itself, or only within Faust, or in both Faust and nature?

In fact, our narrative expectation of a fall is soon met. Faust describes a position on the verge of fulfillment: "eager hope" (*sehnend Hoffen*), fixed on its highest goal, finds "the portals of fulfillment open wide" (*Erfüllungspforten findet flügeloffen*) (Atkins, *Faust I & II*, 4704, 4706). These lines suggest a position already outside of paradise, for fulfillment implies an intervening deficit and promise. But then the fulfillment is hindered by a sudden burst of flame as the sun breaks over the horizon, forcing Faust to turn away in pain: "From those unfathomed depths a sudden mass / Of fire bursts forth, we stand amazed" (*Nun aber bricht aus jenen ewigen Gründen / Ein Flammenübermaß, wir stehn betroffen*) (Luke, *Faust Part Two*, 4704–8). The fire could recall the biblical fiery sword blocking reentry to the Garden of Eden: "[The Lord] drove the man out, and stationed east of the garden of Eden the cherubim and the fiery ever-turning sword, to guard the way to the tree of life" (Gen. 3:24). The language at the end of the stanza evokes further consequences of the biblical expulsion, the new task to tend to the soil (Gen. 3:23) and the introduction of clothing (Gen. 3:7, 21): "We look back earthwards, hiding from this blaze / Behind a youthful veil of awestruck shame" (*So daß wir wieder nach der Erde blicken, / Zu bergen uns in jugendlichstem Schleier*) (Luke, *Faust Part Two* 4713–14).

Notable, then, given the context of the drama, is that no devilish temptations or machinations play a role in this fall. The eager hope seeking its highest goal, which seems to accompany or precipitate the break, echoes the earlier description of the earth's awakening of the resolve "to strive on still towards supreme existence" (*Zum höchsten Dasein immerfort zu streben*) (Luke, *Faust Part Two*, 4685). And if the origin of the striving remains somewhat ambiguous, the suggestion is strong that it lies in nature itself rather than in an arbitrary act of human free will. The fall would thus be a built-in paradox of nature: the earth stirs the resolve to strive and the sun punishes the striver.

Faust's speech then skips ahead to, and closes with, a reference to the story of the deluge in Genesis. In the final stanza of his speech, Faust describes the violent rush of water through a waterfall. Out of this storm (*Sturm*) emerges at last a rainbow (4721). Within the narration of sunrise, the rainbow offers a reflected, mediated, optical phenomenon through which to apprehend the morning sunlight that had been so blindingly intense moments before.[7] But in the biblical context the rainbow also alludes to the sign of the covenant with which the episode of the great flood ends. God announces: "This is the sign that I set for the covenant between Me and you, and every living creature with you, for all ages to come" (Gen. 9:12).[8]

As in the "Prologue in Heaven," Faust's covenant with life thus appears as prior to, and far more fundamental than, the pact with Mephistopheles. In fact, in this scene, Mephistopheles plays no role at all, signaling clearly that the pact with the devil is ancillary to a more fundamental existential covenant. Mephistopheles is not a primary party in Faust's enterprise, but an agent of the Lord. According to Anderegg he is a principle inherent in human affairs: "Mephistopheles or the Mephistophelian is always present—corresponding to the Lord's provision—when the human being acts as a human being."[9]

Of course in this scene the Lord is also not present as the other party to the covenant. But his absence seems compatible with what Faust here affirms: the reflected, mediated conditions of human life and consciousness, the impossibility of a direct, divine encounter. "[This rainbow] mirrors all aspiring human action / On this your mind for clearer insight fasten: That life is ours by colorful refraction" (Der [*Bogen*] *spiegelt ab das menschliche Bestreben / Ihm sinne nach und du begreifst genauer: / Am farbigen Abglanz haben wir das Leben*) (Arndt, *Faust: A Tragedy*, 4725–27). The rainbow defines the human condition by mediating between intrinsic human striving and the unsustainable absolute. It is poised between earth and sky and thereby addresses Faust's repeated fantasies in *Part One* to fly through this middle space (392–97, 1074–88, 1118–19). As a product of sunlight and water vapor, the rainbow introduces the imagery of interacting elements.[10] The elements that converge in the rainbow—fire and earth, water and air—play a pervasive thematic role throughout *Part Two*. The character and interaction of the elements is thematized explicitly, for example, in the Classical Walpurgisnight of act 2, which culminates with another rainbow-like blending of the elements in the encounter between the fiery flying vial of Homonculus and the sea-borne mussel shell bearing the goddess Galatea. At the end of this festival of the sea a general chorus proclaims "To you four, O Elements, / here we offer solemn praise!" (*Hochgefeiert seid allhier, / Element' ihr alle vier!*) (8486–87).[11]

Of particular significance in the sign of the rainbow is that it consists in an enduring flux (*Wechseldauer*) (4722). The rainbow is a refracted representation of the divine absolute, and yet it is ephemeral and fluid "now purely limned and now in air dissolving" (*bald rein gezeichnet, bald in Luft zerfließend*) (4723). The theme of an enduring flux reaches deep into many aspects of Goethe's thinking, but is clearly intimately tied to Jewish sources, as he understands them. We saw it in the pattern of focus and dispersal, settlement and wandering, in Goethe's reading of Genesis in book 4 of *Poetry and Truth*, and again in the rhythm of contraction and expansion that he lays out in his kabbalistic narrative of creation in book 8. Opposed to enduring flux in Goethe's thinking is the risk of over-concentration or hypostatization, what I am calling "idolatry."

The theme of idolatry emerged in association with the Faust and Solomon analogy in *Part One*: in *Part Two*, it gains even greater programmatic significance. The dynamic beauty of the rainbow represents an anti-idolatrous ideal that is echoed in other moments and phenomena throughout the play. Helena for example is described by Chiron as a being "that flows with joy and love of life" (*Das froh und lebenslustig quilt*) as opposed to a "rigid image" (*starres Bild*) (7400, 7402). Helena herself sees the danger of becoming a dead image (*ein Idol*) (8881)."[12] Throughout the work, this risk of rigid absolutism or idolatrous calcification is related to the German word *Erstarrung* (rigidification, torpor).

But again it must be stressed that the anti-idolatrous covenant, renewed through the symbol of the rainbow, does not guarantee virtuous future behavior. Nor does the appearance of the rainbow suggest a forgiveness of Faust's previous sins.[13] Within Genesis, the Lord's decision not to flood the world again is based less on sins forgiven or atoned than on an acceptance of human nature in all its depravity: "Never again will I doom the earth because of man, since the devisings of man's mind are evil from his youth; nor will I ever again destroy every living being, as I have done" (Gen. 8:21). In the next biblical verse, the Lord affirms the unceasing, alternating pattern of earthly life: "So long as the earth endures, / Seed time and harvest, / Cold and heat, / Summer and winter, / Day and night / Shall not cease" (Gen. 8:22) The outcome of the biblical episode seems to be that despite the human inclination to sin, "the rhythm of human life goes on."[14] This affirmation of an alternating rhythm of human life—rather than the removal of sin—is very much in the spirit of Goethe's drama.

Even more provocative than the notion that Faust's moral failings will go unpunished is the complementary suggestion that the divine (or nature) does not conform to human notions of morality at all. The striving implicated in the figurative fall from Paradise is an intrinsic characteristic of creation itself. In Faust's speech, just after the point in his account corresponding to the expulsion from Paradise and the appearance of the flaming sword, he feels nearly consumed by fire and questions whether he is encountering a force of love or hate: "We only meant to kindle up life's torches, / And flames engulf us, seas of torrid blazes! / Love? Hatred? Which? envelops us and scorches" (*Des Lebens Fackel wollten wir entzünden, / Ein Feuermeer umschlingt uns, welch ein Feuer! Ist's Lieb? Ist's Haß? die glühend uns umwinden?*) (Arndt, *Faust: A Tragedy*, 4709–11). These lines raise again the problem of evil, which for Goethe, as I argued in chapter 1, the Hebrew Bible entertained in a more challenging way than the New Testament. While the explanation of creation in the first article of his Lutheran catechism presented the young Goethe with a God who was wise, merciful, and fatherly, in reports of the Lisbon earthquake and its aftermath he saw just the opposite—a God who consigned just and unjust to the same ruin (FA 1.14: 37). The idea of an ultimate moral purpose to creation was, according to Herder, among the doctrines that Christianity has falsely imposed upon the book of Genesis: "That God created everything for his own glory and for the greatest good of human beings, is probably not the chief meaning of the poem" (HW 5: 169–70). Goethe found further support for the view of creation as beyond conventional human conceptions of good and evil in Spinoza, who refuted the anthropocentric fallacy that all nature exists and all events transpire for the benefit of humankind: "that God has made everything for man's sake and has made man so that he should worship God."[15]

Thus Goethe's version of the Genesis narrative here provides no moral explanation for the fact that a striving apparently inherent in nature leads to suffering, where one is blinded by the sun and expelled from Paradise. This sense of a theodicy thwarted returns us also perhaps to the book of Job, for the rhetorical question Faust poses here—is it love or hate?—recalls the dominant rhetorical mode of that biblical book. Job's many questions probing and protesting his afflictions go unanswered: "I cry out to You, but You do not answer me" (Job 30:20), until at last the Lord responds with his own barrage of rhetorical questions intended to assert divine might and unfathomability. After all, "Who is wise enough to give an account of the heavens?" (Job 38:37). The answer in the book of Job, such as it is, is a catalog of natural phenomena, and magnificent and terrible creatures such as the behemoth and the leviathan, in lieu of a rational justification or theodicy. Here the answer to the unanswerable question is the rainbow. This beautiful transitory convergence of the disparate elements seems to affirm the value of life in all its paradoxes. Within the play, the covenantal rainbow thus serves as an ideal of human existence, to which all of Faust's experiences bear imperfect, sometimes tragic relation.

From Noah to Moses

After Faust gazes on the symbol of the Noahic covenant in his opening speech, he transitions, so I contend, into a troubled, modern Moses. Noah and Moses are strongly linked within covenantal history: the Noahic covenant, which is first and universal, sealed with all living creatures for all the ages (Gen. 9:12), is followed by the Abrahamic covenant embracing all of Abraham's offspring, including some non-Israelite descendants (Gen. 17:7)[16] and then by the Mosaic or Sinaitic covenant with the children of Israel specifically (Exod. 34:28). The gift of the law on Sinai—both the oral and written—is, of course, of the greatest import in Judaism, as "the defining and seminal moment in

Israel's relationship to God."[17] But Goethe, certainly standing in a long tradition of Christian denigration of the Jewish law, grasps the history of Moses as a falling away from the patriarchal ideals of Genesis.

As we saw in chapter 2, Goethe conceives of Moses as a crafter of the modern legal administrative state, a view in fact anticipated by both Luther and Spinoza;[18] in the post-Revolutionary era, of equal importance for Goethe's thinking are the mass dimensions of the biblical migration.The Sinaitic covenant applies no longer to a nomadic clan, as the Abrahamic one did, but to a massive migrating people numbering more than six hundred thousand men according to the Book of Numbers (Num. 1:46). Goethe's own descriptions of the transition to Exodus place a strong emphasis on the word "Volk." In *Poetry and Truth,* he describes how "the *people*, countless as the stars in the sky" (*das* Volk, *wie die Sterne des Himmels unzählbar*), had forgotten their own covenantal history (*CW* 4: 378; FA 1.14: 556). In his "Israel" essay, he paints a gloomy picture of the migrating populations, "an innumerable *people* moves sullenly in a sad wilderness" (*ein unzählbares* Volk *bewegt sich mißmuthig in einer traurigen Wüste*) (emphasis mine, FA 1.3.1: 235).

Part Two of *Faust* evinces an analogous shift from individual toward the collective, which can even be charted statistically. According to Schöne, Faust's speeches account for 30 percent of *Part One* but only 13 percent of *Part Two*. Meanwhile, group or choral speech makes up only 7 percent of *Part One*, but 20 percent of *Part Two* (Schöne, 388). The term "Volk" (including various compound versions of the word) comes up with twice the frequency in *Part Two* than in *Part One*.[19] And so the Faust of *Part Two* experiences a modernity of a whole different magnitude. He contends not only with his own existential conundrums, but with vast collective challenges such as economic crisis, war, technological transgression, and environmental destruction. Faust becomes the representative of an age spinning quickly out of control.

The case for an analogy between Faust and Moses was made in extensive detail and at substantial length by Konrad Burdach, in his classic three-part 1912 study "Faust and Moses." Burdach's argument develops from parallels between the death of Faust at the end of *Part Two* and the death of Moses in biblical depictions and rabbinical traditions that were known to Goethe. Both Moses and Faust die after a vision (literally in the one case, figuratively in the other) of a future land; and after their deaths, angels and demons contend for the body and/or soul before the Lord claims it. These and other parallels will come under discussion later in the chapter.

While my thesis takes off from Burdach's and profits from his enormous store of evidence, it differs in fundamental ways. Burdach argues for a much more pervasive analogy between Faust and Moses in both parts of the tragedy, reaching back, for example, to the appearance of the earth spirit in *Part One*, as well as to Faust's blinding encounter with the sun in "Charming Landscape," as symbolic burning bushes. By contrast, I see a clear predominance of the Moses analogy in *Part Two*.

For Burdach, Goethe's Moses is moreover a national hero, although one somehow removed from a specifically Jewish context.[20] Burdach casts Goethe's Moses as a kind of oriental prophet, mystical seer, magician, and priest, as Moses appears especially in Neoplatonic, theosophical traditions. His nationalistically tinged, pre-World War I reading resolutely emphasizes Goethe's positive identification with this titanic version of Moses. As Burdach has it, Goethe himself gradually becomes like Moses "a leader, priest, prophet of his people, founder of a new covenant with God and a national culture."[21] The attribution to Goethe of an unproblematic identification with Moses as a national leader ignores the pervasive suspicion of *Volk* that runs through both text and subtext of this work, and through Goethe's work generally.

And yet, while this book has traced Goethe's negative associations with Moses from the period of enlightened absolutism to the French Revolution, nevertheless the Moses-Faust analogy does finally suggest a far more complicated view that clearly evolved over the course of his life.[22] Perhaps the connection that best underscores Goethe's relationship to Moses in *Part Two* is a further analogy at work between Faust and yet another military commander and lawgiver, Napoleon. Gustav Seibt has traced Goethe's complex admiration for Napoleon through its phases, and sees a clear echo of Napoleon in the second part of *Faust*. In 1815 Goethe wrote to Boisereé, "Faust leads me to how I think and have thought about Napoleon" (*Faust bringt mich dazu, wie ich von Napoleon denke und gedacht habe*).[23] Among Goethe's unpublished "Tame Xenia" ("Zahme Xenien") is a poem depicting Napoleon on Judgment Day: when Satan wants to makes off with Napoleon to hell, the Holy Spirit challenges the devil to try to catch the man. This scenario in which the sinful protagonist nevertheless slips away from the devil's grip can be read, according to Seibt, as "the shortest version of the end of *Faust*."[24] It is also precisely the scenario—a dispute between the devil and the heavenly hosts—that most closely connects Faust with the traditions concerning Moses, as we will discuss later in the chapter. Thus we can discern an implicit transitive logic in Goethe's thinking: if Faust is like Napoleon and Napoleon is like Moses, then Faust is like Moses. Further, Seibt suggests Goethe's peculiar brand of Bonapartism lies in his recognition of a recalcitrantly amoral dimension to reality.[25] For Goethe, Moses and Faust represent an incontrovertible aspect of modernity that cannot be reversed or even simply condemned.

The conception of Moses that structures *Part Two* is therefore fashioned neither from pure sympathy nor from simple antipathy. I will show that Goethe employs the Moses subtext rather to highlight characteristically modern idols—*Volk* or nation, capital, progress, revolution. But he also brings out here the fundamental alternating rhythm between idolatry and wandering, stasis and striving, contraction and expansion that we have highlighted elsewhere in his work. We turn now to consider how Goethe weaves this theme of stasis and movement together with an imagery of earth, fire, water, and air that also draws, in turn, on the biblical account of Moses's life.

Moses and the Elements

Whereas Faust's ideal of the rainbow in the opening scene embodies a fluid exchange of the elements, on his subsequent Mosaic adventures, he encounters the elements in a more polarized condition, with fire and water in conflict, in particular. Clues to the nature of this conflict within the drama can be found in the disputation between the Greek philosophers Anaxagoras and Thales in the "Classical Walpurgisnight." In their speeches (which echo the Plutonist/Neptunist controversy in Goethe's era), the Greek philosophers argue whether the earth was formed by water or fire. The forces of fire and earth are identified with violence and revolution, whereas water and air emerge as more gradualistic, vitalistic forces (see, for example, 7861–64). Indeed, throughout the drama, fire corresponds to an eternal but annihilating absolute. It is conjoined with mountains, seismic depths, and gold—all that is fixed and rigid, "starr," or "erstarrt." Meanwhile water, which is conjoined with air and clouds, represents fluidity, transience, diffusion, and dispersal. But despite his use of the two Greek philosophers as spokesmen, Goethe's sources for these meanings are as much biblical as classical.

Within the Exodus narrative, both mountains and fire are associated with divine theophany. From a burning bush on Mount Horeb, Moses receives his assignment to free the Israelites enslaved in Egypt (Exod. 3:2). Through fire, the Lord helps guide the Israelites in their escape: "The Lord went before them in a pillar of cloud by day, to guide them along the way, and in a pillar of fire by night, to give them light, that they might travel day and night" (Exod. 13:21). Once the Israelites have crossed into Sinai, Moses ascends Mount Sinai (presumed to be the same mountain as Horeb) to receive further directions from God, who has descended upon it as fire (Exod. 19:18), and appears as fire to the Israelites below (Exod. 24:17). The Lord's rage often expresses itself as fiery punishments and threats (Lev. 10:2; Num. 11:1, 16:35). Fire is associated with proper veneration of the Lord (through burnt offerings), but also with transgression, for example when the sons of Aaron bring an unauthorized fire to the Lord (Lev. 10:1). The greatest transgression of the Israelites, the creation of the idol of the golden calf, also involves fire. Aaron explains, "So I said to them, 'Whoever has gold, take it off!' They gave it to me and I hurled it into the fire and out came this calf!" (Exod. 32:24).

While a transgressive, human fire gives rise to the golden calf, Moses's solution is to liquefy it: to melt it, turn it to powder, dissolve it into water, and give it to the Israelites to drink (Exod. 32:20). But in post-biblical traditions the golden calf episode links Moses to alchemy, that is, the enterprise of marrying the elements to produce an eternal gold. Zedler's *Universal Lexicon* article on Moses, for example, mentions the conclusion by scholars "that Moses must have been experienced in chemistry because without this science, he could not have pulverized the golden calf."[26] Indeed, according to Burdach, the alchemical notion of a drinkable gold, "aurum potabile," derives from this account of Moses.[27] In effect, this tradition of Moses as alchemist, as a synthesizer of gold, reverses the biblical account of his pulverization and destruction of the gold idol. The long association of Moses with alchemy plays neatly into Goethe's theme of idolatry, for as Binswanger points out, alchemy is driven by the attempt to create permanence out of transitoriness.[28]

Thus despite Moses's status in Exodus as a rigorously anti-idolatrous monotheist, Goethe is able to draw on a counter-tradition linking him to metallurgy and the fashioning of idols. One of the engravings in the family Bible that Goethe contemplated as a small child depicts an idol fashioned by Moses and destroyed by a Judaean king. In the book of Numbers, the Lord commands Moses to mount a serpent figure on a pole so that anyone bitten by a snake could look at it and survive (Num. 21:8–9). But according to 2 Kings, the snake, although originally commissioned by the Lord, began, over time, to serve as an object of worship. In the scene depicted by Merian, King Hezekiah has the bronze serpent demolished along with other idols in his realm. In this familiar image from his childhood, Goethe would have found support for his representation of Faust-Moses as repeatedly, tragically vulnerable to the slippage from fiery mountaintop theophany to cold metal idol.

Water and vapor act in *Faust* as the fluid counterforces to this calcifying tendency. And here too Goethe's Faust can draw on a store of biblical imagery. No less than fire and earth, water plays "a decisive thematic role in Moses's career" according to Robert Alter.[29] Furthermore, recurring water imagery establishes crucial connections and contrasts between Exodus and Genesis.

Goethe found in the opening passages of Genesis a reflection of his own view that the earth's formations emerged out of the sea. In 1806, in his notes concerning the formation of the earth, he wrote, "The emergence of the world out of the waters was pronounced in the holy books of the Jews. Similarly the return of the waters in that which is called the deluge. Old accounts of other peoples agreed" (*Das Hervortreten der Welt aus den Wassern war in den heiligen Büchern der Juden ausgesprochen. Ebenso das Zurückkommen der Wasser, in dem, was man Sündfluth nannte. Alte Nachrichten anderer Völker stimmten damit überein*) (FA 1.25: 534). Goethe presumably refers here to the first creation account in the first verse of Genesis: "When God began to create heaven and earth—the earth being unformed and void, with darkness over the surface of the deep and a wind from God sweeping over the water—God said, 'Let there be light' " (Gen. 1:1). In contrast to the second account of creation in Genesis 2, this passage does not seem to support the doctrine of a creation ex nihilo but rather suggests a creation from, or at least in the midst of, primordial waters.[30] Contemporary biblical scholarship also corroborates Goethe's observation of parallels between the Genesis story and other ancient myths: Levenson, for example, elaborates the parallels between the Hebrew account and the combat myth in the Babylonian *Enuma elish* according to which the god Marduk forms the world out of the divided body of the goddess of the sea, Tiamat.[31]

This combat myth of creation has significant echoes later on in the book of Job. The Lord speaks from the tempest, describing how he set a limit to the waters in the moment of creation. The watery chaos has gushed from a primordial womb ("mutterleibe" in Luther's translation).

> Who closed the sea behind the doors
> When it gushed forth out of the womb,
> When I clothed it in clouds,
> Swaddled it in dense clouds,
> When I made breakers My limit for it
> And set up its bars and doors,
> And said, "You may come so far and no farther;
> Here your surging waves will stop"? (Job 38:8–11)[32]

As James van der Laan has also noted, this description of creation as the delimitation of female watery force is highly suggestive for *Part Two of the Tragedy*.[33] Like the Lord in this passage, both Faust and Moses claim land from the sea. In crossing the Sea of Reeds, Moses holds out his arm and the Lord creates a dry path between wall-like boundaries:

> Then Moses held out his arm over the sea and the Lord drove back the sea with a strong east wind all that night, and turned the sea into dry ground. The waters were split, and the Israelites went in the sea on dry ground, the waters forming a wall for them on the right and on their left. (Exod. 14:21–22)

Levenson sees here another instance of the "pattern of cosmogonic victory over lethal waters, the salvific appearance of dry land, and the construction of the sanctuary."[34] The same objective is echoed in Faust's wish to delimit the sea: "to bar the shore to the imperious sea, / narrow the limits of the ocean's great expanse, / and force the waters back into themselves" (*Das herrische Meer vom Ufer auszuschließen, / Der feuchten Breite Grenzen zu verengen / Und, weit hinein, sie in sich selbst zu drängen*) (Atkins, *Faust I & II*, 10228–30).[35]

And yet, as Goethe observes in his note on the formation of the earth quoted above, the primordial waters tend to return, for example in the flood story. In the flood account, the water seems to break through a limit set for it: "All the fountains of the great deep burst apart, / And the floodgates of the sky broke open" (Gen. 7:11). Furthermore, as Goethe presumably would have recognized, Noah's survival in the flood story is connected to the infant Moses's survival through a *tevah*, the Hebrew word for ark. In what Alter calls a "a pointed allusion to the Flood story," Moses's mother saves her infant son by setting him afloat on the river Nile in a little wicker ark, a *tevah*, the only other appearance of this word in the Bible.[36] Alter continues,

"As the ark in Genesis bears on the water the saving remnant of humankind, the child borne on the waters here will save his imperiled people."[37] These two arks perhaps suggest a more fragile relation of dependence on the watery substrate of life.

Water, then, emerges as both threatening and sustaining in these biblical sources. Moses wins his wife Zipporah at a well when he rescues her and her sisters from hostile shepherds and draws water for her flock (Exod. 2:16–19). He punishes Pharaoh for his hard-heartedness by turning all the water in Egypt into blood so that all fish die and people have nothing to drink (Exod. 7:17–21). In the wilderness he saves the people from their thirst by turning bitter waters sweet (Exod. 15:25) and making water issue from rock (Exod. 17:6; compare Num. 20:11). In this way, the Exodus narrative bears out an exclamation made by Goethe's Thales in act 2, "Water sustains all things that exist" (*Alles wird durch das Wasser erhalten!*) (Atkins, *Faust I & II*, 8435).

Even Moses's name suggests the significance of water, for it is said to refer to the fact that he was pulled from the water: "[Pharaoh's daughter] named him Moses, explaining, 'I drew him out of the water'" (Exod. 2:10). The Jewish commentary *Etz Hayim* points out that Moses is actually an Egyptian name associated here with a Hebrew verb:

> Through wordplay, the Egyptian *Mose* is connected with Hebrew *Moshe,* "to draw up/out (of water)." Note the ironic wordplay. She intended it as "the one who is drawn out (of the water)." *Moshe* is active in form and means "one who draws out," a name that fits his future situation better than his present.[38]

Regardless of whether Goethe would have been alert to this ambiguity created by the voice of the Hebrew verb, he would have found in Luther's translation similar issues of agency. Luther has Pharaoh's daughter employ the verb *ziehen* transitively to mean "pull" or "draw": "Jch *habe* jn aus dem wasser *gezogen*" (my emphasis, Exod. 2:10). Later in the narrative Luther repeatedly uses the term "ziehen" intransitively to mean "move out or forth." For example, "Also *zogen aus* die kinder Jsrael von Raemses" (my emphasis, Exod. 12:37). Thus Moses's active role in leading this migration (*ziehen*) is preceded by his passivity as the object pulled (*gezogen werden*). And in this primal event, memorialized in his very name, he is beholden to both water and a woman. This ambiguity concerning agency—does one independently move along or is one pulled forth?—is certainly a central question in Goethe's *Faust*. Indeed, in the final scene of his drama, in which female figures predominate, Goethe also employs the same verb "ziehen" to suggest that the ever-striving Faust is actually drawn along: "The Eternal-Feminine / *draws* us on high" (*Das Ewig-Weibliche* zieht *uns hinan*) (my emphasis, 12110–11). In this way, Faust's association with Moses underscores the primordial flux to which both characters are beholden.

Act One

The Exodus subtext commences in the second scene of act 1 as Faust and Mephistopheles show up in the court of the emperor much like Moses and Aaron appearing before Pharaoh.[39] Just as we saw in *Hermann and Dorothea* in chapter 2, here too the Exodus subtext is applied with a broad brush, and its narrative chronology is not strictly followed. The biblical associations are multivalent. Roles shift—the Kaiser is positioned like Pharaoh but later has a vision of himself as Moses. The magic introduced by the strange court visitors (i.e., paper currency) simultaneously functions as a plague *and* as liberation or exodus. The positive and negative aspects of their intervention are thus woven together: the revolution that promises to transform this kingdom and free it of its corruption also issues in a new idolatry of permanent economic progress, state, and *Volk*.

The court scene that Goethe sets up is loosely based on the chapbook version of the legend. In the chapbook, Faust visits the Emperor Charles V, who requests that he conjure Alexander the Great and his consort, which Faust does; in a later episode he also conjures Helen of Troy for some students. In *Part Two* Goethe combines these two chapbook adventures: Faust conjures for the Emperor *not* Alexander and his wife, but Helen of Troy *and* Paris. As noted in chapter 4, Schudt compares the tales of Faust's conjurations to a similar report of the conjuration of the Queen of Sheba by a Jew, and attributes the trick to kabbalistic arts.[40]

While Goethe assigns his Emperor no historical identity in the ultimate version, in an 1816 plan he identifies him as Maximilian I, thus diverging from the chapbook account where the emperor is Maximilian's grandson Charles V (FA 1.7.1: 593). The choice of Maximilian is suggestive, for, as the so-called "last knight" among emperors, he is usually viewed as a figure at the end of the Middle Ages, on the cusp, therefore, of a new age. In his play *Götz*, Goethe represents Maximilian's rule as the transition from a more variegated social fabric to a modern administrative state through the imposition of the Perpetual Public Peace (1495), which replaced a more individualistic (and heroic) system of private feuds with uniform law. Certainly this shift recalls Goethe's Pentateuchal "chasm," the leap from patriarchs to laws. But if Goethe was an admirer of the older order, he represents this court as nevertheless fully ripe for revolution.[41]

The court is mired in financial trouble. Like his historical model Maximilian, Goethe's Emperor has accrued great debt (Schöne, 398). And yet while Maximilian's great creditor was famously Jakob Fugger, from the wealthy Catholic merchant family, Goethe adds a gratuitous anti-Jewish angle. The Steward complains about a Jewish creditor: "The Jew will squeeze as hard as he is able; / I get advances from him, years ahead. / We buy tomorrow what we eat today" (*Der Jude wird mich nicht verschonen / Der schafft Antizipationen, / Die speisen Jahr um Jahr voraus*) (Luke, *Faust Part Two*, 4870–72).[42]

In a later scene, when the court's financial problems seem solved, the Steward declares, "The claws of usury have been appeased" (*Die Wucherklauen sind beschwichtigt*) (Atkins, *Faust I & II*, 6042). Clearly this statement also trades in anti-Semitic stereotypes, as it joins both the term "Wucher" (usury)—a term Goethe explicitly associates elsewhere with Jews[43]—with subhuman "Klauen" (claws). In addition, this history of Jewish financial speculation links the court of the fictional Emperor in act 1 to Goethe's representation of the Egyptian empire in his "Israel" essay. As observed in chapter 2, Goethe's 1797 sketch for the essay casts the Israelite Joseph as a clever financier in the Egyptian court. The actual biblical backstory to Exodus includes the patriarch Joseph's efforts on an earlier Pharaoh's behalf: Joseph simultaneously saves the Egyptian people from a famine and consolidates Pharaoh's power and property by selling the people bread in exchange for their land and possessions (Gen. 47). But Goethe casts this transaction in modern terms, with Joseph in the mold of an early modern "court Jew" engaging in "an outrageous speculation" (*eine unerhörte Speculation*) (FA 1.3.1: 633).

Thus Goethe's scenario in the Emperor's court in act 1 recalls his version of Exodus from the earlier essay in several respects. A pair of visitors (Faust and Mephistopheles, like Moses and Aaron) arrives in a court that has relied in the past on an (anti-Semitically cast) Jewish financial "speculator." In both cases, unrest is brewing—in the "Israel" essay there is "agitation in the populace" (*Gärung im Volke*) among the Israelites (FA 1.3.1: 233); in *Faust*, there is "sedition's growing turmoil" (*Des Aufruhrs wachsendes Gewühl*) (Atkins, *Faust I & II*, 4793–94). The Emperor's court in *Faust* differs from the account in the essay in that here there is no distinction between peoples—no Egyptians and Hebrews—just a single throng ripe for revolution. The "Murmurs from the Crowd" (*Gemurmel der Menge*), voiced five times in the scene "Imperial Palace—Throne Room," echo Luther's synonymic "Murren" (grumbling) of the Israelites during their journey in more than a dozen passages in Exodus and Numbers.[44]

In this volatile situation, Faust and Mephistopheles offer an economic emancipation or exodus. Mephistopheles proposes paper money secured by gold—gold not yet discovered, but presumed to be left buried underground in times of great migration. Binswanger, drawing on the rhetoric employed in the scene, interprets the introduction of paper money in the court as a kind of alchemy.[45] Binswanger understands alchemy as the defiance of the conditions of time, "man's attempt to break out of time while still in time—his bid to break free of transitoriness while still in this life."[46] Alchemy in Binswanger's sense is thus related to what I am calling idolatry, an absolutism that defies the conditions of time and the limits of human existence.

Here then is Goethe's characteristic twist on the Exodus story: Faust and Mephistopheles offer an alchemical emancipation that in fact produces its own idols. Mephistopheles describes the gold that will emerge from the ground as golden calves, suggesting again his identification with the biblical

Aaron. He promises: "and from the soil you'll liberate / a herd of golden calves" (*Und eine Herde goldner Kälber, / Sie reißen sich vom Boden los*) (5041–42). According to the terms of Mephistopheles's descriptions, his plan draws solidity (gold) out of an underlying fluidity in history. Floods of refugees will have left behind buried treasures that can be raised from the soil: "Still, bear in mind how often in those days of terror, / when human tides submerged entire nations / people, despite all fear and trembling, / would hide what they most prized somewhere or other" (*Bedenkt doch nur: in jenen Schreckensläuften, / wo Menschenfluten Land und Volk ersäuften, / Wie der und der, so sehr es ihn erschreckte / Sein Liebstes da- und dortwohin versteckte*) (Atkins, *Faust I & II*, 4931–34). As already noted, the golden calf is itself an important alchemical symbol, because of Moses's reported incineration of the calf to create a drinkable gold potion. Mephistopheles reverses the biblical image: instead of the gold being reduced to fluidity, here floods of human history will yield up the gold.

But the golden calves in Mephistopheles's description give way to an important further transmutation. As Binswanger persuasively argues, Goethe suggests here a very modern take on traditional alchemy, for the gold that presumably lies hidden underground will serve as the hypothetical guarantee for paper money. Gold itself remains static and frozen (again, Goethe uses the word *erstarrt*): "The abundance of treasure buried deep / Under your lands lies *frozen* and asleep" (*Das Übermaß der Schätze, das* erstarrt, */ In deinen Landen tief im Boden harrt / Liegt ungenutzt*) (my emphasis; Luke, *Faust Part Two*, 6111–13). Yet the illiquidity of this underground gold is to be transformed into the new permanent, absolute liquidity of currency.[47] The new absolutism then becomes the insistence upon infinite expansion and progress. Binswanger writes: "Thus the economy gains the transcendental character (i.e., surpassing all limits) formerly sought in religion. It is not belief in a hereafter but economic activity in the here and now, that opens up modern man's perspective on eternity."[48] To cast Binswanger's analysis of alchemy in terms of idolatry, the old idol of gold, as permanent value, becomes a new modern idol, the permanently expanding potential of capital.

Corresponding to this idol of endless economic expansion for Goethe is an idol of political and social redemption. In the midst of the carnival, the Emperor signs the authorization for paper money in order to achieve, in the Chancellor's words, the "salvation of the people" (*des Volkes Heil*) (6070). This monetary transformation—which aims at the deliverance of a people—is parallel to the theatrical and indeed parodistic transformation of the traditional carnival procession into a modern exodus. Admittedly, the carnival masque is notoriously difficult to interpret. Its allegorical valences are disparate and at points obscure. The scattered references to the Exodus that I will highlight do not reliably organize the multitude of characters and actions into a unitary meaning, but provide nevertheless a strong interpretive thread. And again, it is important to emphasize that Goethe employs Exodus here in a counterintuitive, provocative way: as a story of political idolatry despite the explicitly anti-idolatrous thrust of the biblical account. As we saw in the Exodus subtext in *Hermann and Dorothea*, the revolutionary impulse becomes idolatrous for Goethe when the people believe that "the highest" is "near and attainable" (FA 1.8: 849).

The carnival masque is itself another liminal phenomenon, an ultimately unsustainable premodern form on the threshold of modernity. The pre-Lenten festivities in the scene "A Great Hall" are clearly reminiscient of the Easter procession into the countryside in the scene "Outside the City Gate" in part 1.[49] Both festive scenes offer an unidealized vision of human life and society as diverse and variable, involving plenty of sexuality, discord, and drinking. Amidst all the social injustices and flaws, these colorful, manifold social spectacles exert their own attraction, much as the flower girls describe their artificial flowers: "Each one variously pleases. / But the whole is harmony" (*Mögt ihr Stück für Stück bewitzeln / Doch das Ganze zieht euch an*) (Luke, *Faust Part Two*, 5102–3).

But despite their aesthetic appeal, the societies represented in "Outside the City Gate" and in "A Great Hall" are, from the perspective of the drama, superannuated. Faust, as the estranged modern scholar, finds himself a mere observer of the Easter festivities, unable to commune with the people because of his own secret guilt concerning his medical experiments during the plague. The pre-Lenten carnival masque in "A Great Hall" is already deeply ironized, as a courtly allegory of the society rather than a snapshot of the society itself. With its thematization of greed, artificiality, commodification, "of empty appearances uninformed by spirit" in Brown's phrase,[50] the imperial society emerges here again as very much an ancien regime primed for revolution. Goethe's depiction of the carnival masque precludes nostalgia even as its represented alternative—an exodus—is equally rife with hazards.

The revolutionary pressure comes to bear with the arrival of Zoilo-Thersites—often assumed to be Mephistopheles in disguise.[51] Now the masque gives way to an "anti-masque."[52] The figure of Zoilo-Thersites introduces a Homeric subtext into the mix, for the name combines two figures who are antagonistic toward heroic Greek culture: Zoilos, an Athenian critic of Homer in the second century B.C.E., and Thersites, a character in the *Iliad* who lambasts King Agamemnon for undertaking the war against Troy.

Zoilo-Thersites and the Herald of the masque play out a scene from book 2 of the *Iliad*. Odysseus there receives from Agamemnon a royal staff with which he serves as the defender of royal authority, guarding against rabble-rousers in the Greek forces, and warning: "Surely not all of us Achaians can be as kings here. Lordship for many is no good thing."[53] When Odysseus encounters Thersites's incendiary railings against the king, he roundly beats him with his staff. Similarly, in this scene in *Faust*, when Zoilo-Thersities disrupts the festivities, the Herald smites him with his staff: "Why then, my sacred staff, you low- / Born cur, shall strike a master-blow" (*So treffe dich, du*

Lumpenhund, / Des frommen Stabes Meisterstreich!) (Luke, *Faust Part Two*, 5471–72). However, Zoilo-Thersites, unlike the Homeric Thersites, does not cower or cry, but rather undergoes a repulsive metamorphosis into an egg, out of which emerge a bat and otter. The disruption succeeds. The spectators respond with fear and loathing: "What was fun is spoiled completely—" (*Ganz verdorben ist der Spaß—*) (Atkins, *Faust I & II*, 5492).

This revolutionary, anti-Homeric anti-masque—which no aristocratic-Odysseus figure can quell—is, in turn, loosely identified with Exodus and the Hebrew Bible. Once again we find a version of the Genesis-Exodus "chasm," but here Homer, associated in *Werther* with "patriarchal life" (FA 1.8: 59), stands in for Genesis, while the revolutionary-political themes associated with Exodus are attributed more broadly to the Hebrew Bible. For when Zoilo-Thersites, the implicit opponent of Homeric ideals, breaks in and criticizes the masque, he paraphrases the prophet Isaiah: "When I exalt what's base, degrade what's grand / put crooked straight what's straight askew / then, and only then, do I feel elated / for that is how I want things here on earth" (*Das Tiefe hoch, das Hohe tief, / Das Schiefe grad, das Grade schief, / Das ganz allein macht mich gesund, / So will ich's auf dem Erdenrund*) (Atkins, *Faust I & II*, 5467–70).[54]

The Moses analogy comes to the fore in the magic antics that now ensue. The Herald's "pious" (*fromm*) staff (5732), initially reminiscent of Odysseus's rod, falls into the hands of Faust (disguised as Plutus) and becomes like the "holy" (5972) staff of Moses. In the biblical account, Moses's staff works spectacular miracles at the Egyptian court in order to persuade Pharaoh to liberate the Israelites. Moses's wonder-working staff indeed led classical authors such as Pliny the Elder and Apuleius to view him as the first magician.[55] In a letter, Goethe also casually refers to Moses's staff as his "magic wand" (*Zauberstab*) (WA 4.5: 323).

Plutus's first trick with the staff is to open containers of gold. At the touch of the rod, the locks magically open. Treasures seem to surge in iron kettles with golden blood (*wallt von goldnem Blute*) (5712). Gold coins seethe as if alive, writhing (*sich wälzen*), rolling (*kollern*), and hopping (*hüpfen*) (5718, 5722, 5719). The threatening description could recall some of the plagues brought on by Moses's staff in the Bible: blood that fills rivers and streams, even vessels of wood and stone (Exod. 8:19); and frogs that swarm from the Nile into every home, every bed and oven (Exod. 7:27–29). Moses also commands fire with his staff: "So Moses held out his rod toward the sky, and the LORD sent thunder and hail, and fire streamed down to the ground" (Exod. 9:23). Similarly, when the people scramble for the gold, Plutus turns the staff into a glowing, flaring torch with which to drive them off: "Whoever has too rashly neared / At once is mercilessly seared" (*Wer sich zu nah herangedrängt, / Ist unbarmherzig gleich versengt*) (Arndt, *Faust: A Tragedy*, 5745–46). Plutus's syntax here echoes a Pentateuchal prohibition against approaching the Tabernacle: "Everyone who so much as ventures near the LORD's Tabernacle must die" (In Luther's translation: *Wer sich nahet zu der Wonung des HERRN, der stirbt*) (Num. 17:28).[56] Goethe employs the prohibition against approaching the tabernacle metaphorically elsewhere in his writings.[57]

Once fire has ignited the Emperor's beard and spread into a general conflagration, Plutus/Faust strikes the ground with his staff and brings water vapors to extinguish the flames. As already observed, Moses's staff also controls water, when, held aloft, it parts the Sea of Reeds (Exod. 14), or struck against a rock, it brings forth water (Exod. 17:6; Num. 20).

Thus the carnival masque compresses and conflates the various aspects of the biblical narrative so that exodus and idolatry are of a piece. Faust/Plutus, as well as Mephistopheles in his guises, appear as Moses and Aaron figures, introducing spectacular tricks, apparently in order to prime the Emperor and his court for the authorization for paper money for "the salvation of the people." But at the same time, the illusions staged also dramatize the vulnerability of the people to an idolatrous relationship to gold and money. The people scramble for the gold coins revealed by Plutus until Plutus threatens them with his fiery staff. Just as Aaron fashions the golden calf for the Israelites (Exod. 32:4), Mephistopheles treats the gold as a pliable medium to shape into his own icon—a golden phallus, with which to frighten the women (5781–82). The gnomes who mine the gold warn that it leads to theft, adultery, and murder, as well as to the breaking of the remaining Ten Commandments—including, implicitly, the ban on idolatry: "whoever breaks these three Commandments / will pay no heed to all the rest" (*Und wer die drei Gebot' veracht't, / Sich auch nichts aus den andern macht*) (Arndt, *Faust: A Tragedy*, 5860–61).

As the festival devolves, the distinction between Moses and Pharaoh, Faust and Emperor, seems to collapse. While initially Faust seems to occupy the position of Moses and the Emperor that of Pharaoh, now the Emperor shades into an alter ego of Faust, serving, as Hamlin puts it, "as an analogue to Faust himself."[58] In "Palace Garden," the scene following the carnival masque, the Emperor describes his experience of the fire and its extinguishing, but he imagines himself now as Pluto/Faust: "Suddenly it seemed / That I was Pluto" (*Es schien mir fast, als ob ich Pluto wäre*) (Luke, *Faust Part Two*, 5990). In this vision his encounter with fire and water contains references to the Exodus story. Indeed, the jointly narrated visions of the Emperor and Mephistopheles distill the spectacular effects in the biblical account—the appearance of a pillar of fire and the crossing of the Sea of Reeds.

In his vision, the Emperor describes long rows of people among columns of fire. "In this vast space I saw my peoples, in long lines, / move past its twisted fiery pillars" (*Durch fernen Raum gewundner Feuersäulen / Sah ich bewegt der Völker lange Zeilen*) (Atkins, *Faust I & II*, 5997–98). He thus uses Luther's term for the pillar of fire in which the Lord appears to lead the children of Israel by night out of Egypt and through the wilderness.[59] And yet the Emperor envisions not *one* people following a single column of fire, but multiple peoples among multiple fiery columns. Moreover, the peoples do not seem to be following the columns somewhere, but rather circling around the Emperor to render homage: "They thronged towards me, circling far and near, And all, as hitherto, paid homage here" (*Sie drängten sich im weiten Kreis heran / Und huldigten, wie sie es stets getan*) (Luke, *Faust Part Two*, 5999–6000). Thus at the center of the ring of devotees, the Emperor ultimately finds himself in the position of the golden calf. Luther refers to this worship-dance as "circle dance" (*Reigen*) (Exod. 32:19); and this circling form of homage has a long pictorial tradition, including the illustrations in the Lutheran Bible supplied originally by the workshop of Cranach the Elder and later by Matthäus Merian.[60] After serving as an emancipator, then, the emperor has undergone a further transformation into an idol.

Mephistopheles now takes over the vision and describes a kind of dry crossing through the sea.

> Next plunge into the sea at its most savage, / And scarcely do you tread its pearly ground / When all about you forms a glorious round / For undulating nile-green swells, upwelling / With coral edges, mold a splendored dwelling / With you for center. Every step you do / The glassy palaces advance with you. (Arndt, *Faust: A Tragedy*)

> Wirf dich ins Meer, wo es am wildsten tobt, / Und kaum betrittst du perlenreichen Grund, / So bildet wallend sich ein herrlich Rund; / Siehst auf und ab lichtgrüne schwanke Wellen, / Mit Purpursaum, zur schönsten Wohnung schwellen / Um dich, den Mittelpunkt. Bei jedem Schritt, / Wohin du gehst, gehn die Paläste mit. (6006–6012)

In the biblical account of the crossing of the Sea of Reeds, the Israelites traverse dry ground while the water forms walls (Luther: *Mauern*) on both sides (Exod. 14:22, 29). The water then turns back, falls upon, and drowns the pursuing Egyptians. Mephistopheles turns this scenario into a dazzling vision, as if the emperor were encased in a dynamic aquarium. Behind the "watery walls" (*Wände*, 6013) spectacular sea life is visible, including golden-scaled dragons and sharks with gaping jaws. The treatment of this miraculous crossing as an occasion to peer into the wonders of the depths also has precedent. Compare Calderón's description of the event in *The Great Stage of the World*: "And by the watery pile / The sun shall see that day / The strangest depths it ever / Beheld in any age."[61]

This scene again suggests the idolization of the Emperor. Instead of the sea merely closing in again, as it does for the Israelites, Mephistopheles conceives it as something of a vortex, "a glorious round" (6008) surrounding the Emperor on all sides. For a second time, the Emperor finds himself in the center point of a circular spectacle, now at once both Moses and the golden calf. As Mephistopheles continues his speech, he adds Greek nymphs to the underwater marvels and then tempts the Emperor with a seat on Mount

Olympus (6027). But the Emperor responds in a way that one might expect from Faust, thus strengthening the analogy between them: he rejects this godlike apotheosis in favor of life on earth: "You need not bother with ethereal regions— / the throne up there is all too soon ascended" (*Die luft'gen Räume, die erlass' ich dir: / Noch früh genug besteigt man jenen Thron*) (6028–29). Here again then Goethe's implicit use of a Moses analogy is not entirely negative. Goethe's Moses is repeatedly vulnerable to idolatry and yet also repeatedly returns to his anti-idolatrous commitments.

Furthermore, even the carnival masque reveals a positive potential in its modern, emancipatory transformation. Jane Brown sees in the "anti-masque" introduced by Zoilo-Thersites an "allegory of creativity." In this part of the masque, Plutus/Faust, the god of wealth, mediates between two further figures—the Boy Charioteer and Greed (Mephistopheles in disguise), who represent respectively spirit and nature, according to Brown. The Boy-Charioteer identifies himself explicitly as the spirit of poetry while Greed, as a "sign maker," is, in Brown's view, also a kind of poet. Thus the three-part constellation, Boy Charioteer—Plutus/Faust—Greed, suggests the possibility of integrating creative forces within the social order.[62] Again, one might speculate that the complexity and ambivalence in Goethe's assessment of a transformative modern order, the sense of artistic elements at work in statecraft in this late work, could stem from his complex, even admiring relationship to Napoleon.

The conception of a creative moment or potential within the new social order is also reinforced by Goethe's ironic use of inter-testamental typologies to link Plutus, as god of wealth, to the Boy Charioteer, as offspring. Plutus plays first on a line from Genesis, "[You are] spirit of my spirit" (*Bist Geist von meinem Geiste*) and then on a line from the Gospel of Mark, "Beloved son, I am well pleased in you" (*Mein lieber Sohn, an dir hab' ich Gefallen*) to suggest that poetry is part and parcel of his own surfeit (Luke, *Faust Part Two*, 5623, 5629).[63] The subsequent speech of the Boy Charioteer draws specifically on a New Testament episode, which, as we have seen, is linked typologically to the story of Moses: the gift of the spirit on Pentecost which manifested itself as tongues of fire resting on each person (Acts 2:3).[64] "See how I've scattered all about / the greatest gifts I can bestow. / Above the heads of some among you / there glows a spark that I ignited" (*Die größten Gaben meiner Hand, / Seht, hab' ich rings umher gesandt. / Auf dem und jenem Kopfe glüht / Ein Flämmchen, das ich angesprüht*) (Atkins, *Faust I & II*, 5630–33). As discussed in chapter 2, this Christian event falls upon—and, within the Christian calendar, replaces—the Jewish festival of Shavuot, celebrating the giving of the Law on Mount Sinai. But surely in this context, Goethe employs this imagery lightly. He does not suggest that the Boy Charioteer's poetry, his lavish gifts of the spirit, supersedes the new economic and social order represented by Plutus and the Emperor. Indeed, the Boy Charioteer is an ephemeral phenomenon; he disappears as abruptly as he first appears. Goethe's point, again, seems to be that the modern revolutionary transformation is accompanied by a creative, dynamic moment along with an inevitable risk of absolutism and idolatry.

We also see the positive, anti-idolatrous dimension of the Moses metaphor in the subsequent "Mothers" scenes. Just as Moses dissolves the golden calf into water given to the Israelites to drink, here too Faust leans toward the dissolution of things solid. He seeks no salvation (*Heil*) in rigidification (*Erstarren)* (6271) but descends now, in search of Helena, into a frighteningly fluid realm, the realm of the Mothers. This cloud-like region without place of orientation or rest is described as "wilderness" (*Wildernis*), as "untrodden territory" (*das Unbetretene*), and as "wasteland and solitude" (*Öd' und Einsamkeit*) (6236, 6223, 6227). Faust's descent therefore recalls Moses's foray into the wilderness.

In summary, Goethe employs the Moses analogy in act 1 to suggest an alternating inclination in Faust. Faust leans toward idolatry and then rejects it; is tempted away from the existential covenant and then reaffirms it. In this way, the Moses analogy emphasizes the basic life pulse of contraction and expansion that Goethe found to be so prominent in the Hebrew Bible and that became a key component in his thinking generally.

Act Four: The Post-Exodus History

The allusions to Moses largely fade in acts 2 and 3 as Faust is transported to a mythological Greek realm of Classical Walpurgisnight, and then travels to ancient Sparta, wins the legendary Helena, experiences a brief domestic idyll with her and their son Euphorion, and then loses both wife and child. But the beginning of act 4 signals the return of the Exodus analogy as a hallmark narrative of European modernity. Recalling the association of clouds with the female that we saw in the realm of the Mothers, Faust is conveyed onto a mountaintop by a cloud that then dissolves and floats away in the forms of both Helena and Gretchen. Moses too reaches the top of Mount Sinai in a cloud: "Moses went inside the cloud and ascended the mountain" (Exod. 24:18). But whereas Moses receives the law for Israel for all ages to come on Mount Sinai, Faust receives no divine revelation on his rocky summit. Nevertheless his mountaintop represents a social turn that Goethe may have meant as an analogy to Moses's charge to impose a civil social order, for here he first expresses his wish to limit the sea which, in act 5, he articulates further as a vision for a future society—a free people on free ground (11580).

It is easy to overlook the Moses reference here because this scene includes a reference to an episode from the Christian scriptures—where the devil takes Christ to a mountaintop and tempts him. (Indeed, Goethe annotates his own text with the chapter reference to Matthew 4.) Here Mephistopheles offers Faust, as the devil offers Christ, "the kingdoms of the world and all their glory" (*die Reiche der Welt und ihre Herrlichkeiten*) (Atkins, *Faust I & II*, 10131).[65] Yet Faust plays the Christ role poorly, because unlike Christ, he accepts the offer, asserting his specific wish to control and roll back the sea.[66]

This scene also deals in the elemental alternations between cloud/water and earth/fire that run throughout *Part Two*. His vaporous transport—associated with his female lovers—gives way to the rocky vantage point—described as *starr* (rigid) like the root word we have seen in *Erstarren (*to become solid or fixed). From this fixed place, Faust longs to defeat the fluctuating sea: "To lock the imperious ocean from the coast, / To shrink the borders of the damp expanse, / And gorge it, far off, on its own advance" (*Das herrische Meer vom Ufer auszuschließen, / Der feuchten Breite Grenzen zu verengen / Und, weit hinein, sie in sich selbst zu drängen)* (Arndt, *Faust: A Tragedy*, 10229–31). As already suggested, this imagery converges with the Lord's description in the book of Job of his original creative act, where he set a limit to the sea. It also recalls Moses's parting of the Sea of Reeds in the escape from Egypt in Exodus. In fact, the same miracle of parted waters occurs as the Israelites cross the Jordan into Canaan in the book of Joshua. There too the waters roll back to allow human traffic, as Joshua here foretells: "the waters of the Jordan, the waters coming from upstream—will be cut off and will stand in a single heap" (Josh. 3:13). Thus the rolling back of the sea provides the precondition not only for the Exodus but for the settlement of the Promised Land.

What follows Faust's mountaintop resolution to tame the sea in act 4 is of course war. Mephistopheles and Faust help the Emperor put down a revolt by a rival claimant to the throne in order to gain, as reward, the shoreline that Faust wishes to extend. In this way, the war explicitly serves Faust's land reclamation project.

Extensive war also follows the biblical Exodus. The procession through the wilderness described in the Pentateuch and the conquest of Canaan in Joshua and Judges involve many battles. The monarchical period recounted in the books of Samuel and Kings is also torn by violent rivalries and civil war. Indeed, various allusions in act 4 as well as in act 5 suggest, in a deliberately conflating, non-chronological way, a sweeping post-Exodus history of the establishment and early years of Israel. Faust's project of a free people on free ground is compared to the dream and realities of establishing a new state in the Promised Land.

The most explicit reference to post-Exodus history—explicit because, here again, Goethe appends a reference to chapter and verse—are the three strong men in the service of Mephistopheles. These three plundering, violent thugs help the Emperor win the civil war in act 4 and then, in an attempt to forcibly remove the elderly couple Philemon and Baucis, cause their death and the death of their guest in a fire that consumes their home. Goethe's own biblical citation links them to David's warriors in his battle against the Philistines (2 Sam. 23:8).[67] Nothing in the account in the book of Samuel of David's warriors, other than their daring feats and prowess in battle, would seem to motivate this insidious comparison with Mephistopheles's henchmen. But the immediately preceding several verses in Samuel, which recount David's final words, suggest a connection between David's divine covenant ("Bund" in Luther's translation) and the violent destruction of one's opponents: "For he has granted me an eternal pact, / Drawn up in full and secured. / Will He not cause all my success / And [my] every desire to blossom?" (brackets in original, 2 Sam 23:5). David continues that his opponents will be destroyed like thistles and in addition—in striking parallel to the death of Philemon and Baucis—consumed by fire in their dwelling.[68] This passage, applied to Faust, seems to implicate the pact itself in the violence—not just the pact with Mephistopheles but what I am calling the existential covenant, with its recurring potential for severe error amidst the striving.

The condition of civil war in act 4, where the Emperor is challenged by a counter-emperor, also resonates with the recurring divides in early Israel, as recounted in the books of Samuel and Kings. Civil war erupts in the wake of Saul's death between David, who becomes anointed king of Judah, and Saul's son Ish-bosheth, who assumes the kingship of the remaining tribes of Israel (2 Sam. 2–4). After Ish-bosheth is assassinated (without David's authorization), David becomes king over all the tribes. But David's own son, Absalom, raises a revolt against him. After Absalom is murdered, David reunites the kingdom and bequeaths it to his son Solomon, who rules largely in peace. But in punishment for Solomon's sin of idolatry under the influence of his foreign wives, the Lord divides the kingdom again after Solomon's death. Solomon's son Rehoboam becomes king of Judah while the rival Jeroboam becomes king of Israel and henceforth "there was continual war between Rehoboam and Jeroboam" (1 Kings 14:30). Thus begins the long history of the divided monarchy.

Reinforcing the link between the contest of two emperors in act 4 and the divisions within Israel are two references to psalms. The emperor echoes Psalm 110 when he imagines wreaking his wrath on his rival: "His proud head as my footstool he will see" (*so möchte ich . . . das stolze Haupt in Schemeltritt verwandeln*) (Luke, *Faust Part Two*, 10486; Schöne, 681). In the psalm, the Lord similarly promises to make "your enemies your footstool" (Luther: "zum schemel deiner Füsse") (Ps. 110:1). But the counter-emperor is also associated with a psalm. As the empire first falls into anarchy, many give up on the emperor and cast their lots with a new one, who they trust will wed peace and justice (*Fried' und Gerechtigkeit vermählen*) (10284). This metaphorical marriage echoes the hope in Psalm 85 that God will bring about a realm in which justice and peace kiss (Luther: "Gerechtigkeit vnd Friede sich küssen") (Ps. 85:11).[69] While the association of psalms with both the emperor and his rival suggests their essential similarity, Goethe's choice of particular psalms highlights original divisions even within the biblical text. Psalm 110, paraphrased by the emperor, is attributed to David; Psalm 85, associated with the counter-emperor, is attributed to the sons of Korah. Moreover, these two psalms reflect a much greater biblical dividing line that stretches back to the opening chapters of Genesis and which Goethe knew well: Psalm 110 belongs to the group of psalms that uses Jehovah as the name for God; Psalm 85 belongs to the group of psalms that uses the name Elohim. The analysis of the Hebrew Bible into Jehovah-sources and Elohim-sources was, as has been repeatedly stressed, a starting point for the new biblical criticism in the eighteenth century. Goethe perhaps draws on this divide to reinforce his anti-idolatrous theme, suggesting that fault lines, whether open or latent, run through any construct, whether a text or an empire.

Act Five: The Temptation of Paradise

Faust, now having been granted the shoreline for his help in battle, moves ahead with his project to reclaim land from the sea. The diffuse allusions to post-Exodus Israel continue in this act, and at the same time his project is represented as an attempted reintroduction of "paradise" (11086, 11569). But in order to win this new free land on which a free people will dwell, he has to first eliminate the current inhabitants, Philemon and Baucis.

In commenting on the removal of the elderly couple, Mephistopheles explicitly alludes to another episode from the period of the divided monarchy: "What passes here is far from new; There once was Naboth's vineyard too" (*Auch hier geschieht, was längst geschah, / Denn Naboths Weinberg war schon da*) (Arndt, *Faust: A Tragedy*, 11286–87). Goethe once again supplies the citation: 1 Kings 21. The story of Naboth's vineyard falls under the reign of King Ahab over the northern kingdom of Israel. Ahab "did what was displeasing to the Lord, more than all who preceded him" (1 Kings 16:30), including worship of Baal. Like Solomon before him, he is led to idol worship through a liaison with a foreign woman, his wife Jezebel. Ahab desires to take possession of the vineyard neighboring his palace for a vegetable garden. When its owner Naboth refuses the king, the latter becomes sullen and dejected, so his wife Jezebel offers to take care of the matter. Just as Mephistopheles usually fulfills Faust's wishes with his own perverse twist, Jezebel fulfills Ahab's wishes in a murderous fashion, arranging for the stoning death of Naboth. The prophet Elijah confronts Ahab and foretells divine punishment. A parenthetical insertion at this juncture condemns again Ahab's extreme degree of sinfulness, especially noting his worship of idols (1 Kings 21:25–26). Thus, through textual juxtaposition, Ahab's obsession with this piece of property, even at the expense of human life, is associated with a more primary sin—the sin of idolatry. As goes Ahab, so goes Faust.

And yet other passages in act 5 seem to allude to an earlier period in the post-Exodus establishment of Israel—the conquest of Canaan. When Faust contemplates his expanse of land, he is furious to spy that which is not his: a small church, a linden tree, and the home of Philemon and Baucis. These blots on his otherwise endless vista are like "thorns to the eyes and thorns to the soles" (*Dorn den Augen, Dorn den Sohlen*) (11161). As commentators have pointed out, this phrase echoes a passage in Numbers as the Israelites are encamped on the plains of Moab prior to the crossing of the Jordan into Canaan. The Lord gives Moses instructions on how to settle the Promised Land, including the dispossession of its current inhabitants, warning, "But if you do not dispossess the inhabitants of the land, those whom you allow to remain shall be stings in your eyes and thorns in your side" (Num. 33:50–55).[70] By summoning the biblical context, Faust implicity justifies his destruction of existing habitation through the grander significance of his own utopian project.

But Goethe figures the inhabitants to be removed in act 5 less as members of an unfamiliar people (the Canaanites) than as the original patriarchs. As Trunz points out, the tale of Philemon and Baucis in Ovid, where guests treated graciously by the couple turn out to be the gods in disguise, invites comparison with a story about Abraham and Sarah in Genesis 18, where the Lord appears to the couple as a stranger and is likewise received with great hospitality.[71] Indeed Herder, in his reading of the visitation episode in Genesis, comments, "One feels as if one is reading the story of Philemon and Baucis" (*SW* 11: 411). References to "paradise" in act 5 also suggest that Faust's project involves an attempted return to the opening of Genesis. Philemon describes the new, artificially extended landscape as "an image of paradise" (*ein paradiesisch Bild*) (11086); Faust himself describes this territory as if it were freshly created, as "the newest earth" and "a paradisal land" (*d[ie] neuste[ ] Erde, ein paradiesisch Land*) (11566, 11569). Philemon's exhortation that, in the face of the strange new goings-on, they "trust the *old* god" (*dem* alten *Gott vertrauen*) (emphasis mine, 11142), underscores Goethe's demarcation between the old ways of Genesis and the new ways of Exodus.

Act 5 connects, furthermore, with the imagery of paradise in Faust's opening speech in the beginning of *Part Two*: while he there describes a fall from paradise, here he attempts its recovery. The biblical subtext suggests an attempted return in both time and space—from Exodus back to Genesis, from Egypt back to Canaan. In this scenario, Moses (Faust) returns to Canaan to dispossess Abraham and Sarah (Philemon and Baucis). Yet the episode implies that the return to Paradise, or Genesis, is, at last, impossible and the attempt yields only violence. Still, in this work that served as his final literary testament, Goethe does not ultimately condemn the individual agent of this historical drive.

The Death of Faust / Moses

Now we turn to the death of Faust—the starting point for Burdach's comparison between Faust and Moses. Burdach notes five parallels between Goethe's depiction of the end of Faust and various legends and traditions concerning the death of Moses: (1) the struggle between Mephistopheles's devils and the angels over Faust's soul in "Entombment" recalls rabbinic traditions, according to which beneficient and adversarial forces fight over Moses's body and/or soul; (2) in both *Faust* and in some legends involving Moses, spirits help prepare the grave; (3) both men, despite their extreme age (Faust is 100, Moses 120), resist death; (4) both men die with their (real or mental) gaze fixed on a future, hoped-for land; and (5) both men die after speaking their own testament or legacy (*Vermächtnis*).[72] Burdach draws on an extraordinarily rich store of primary sources that support these parallels. The most obvious parallel, noted indeed by commentators prior to Burdach, is between rabbinical traditions surrounding the death of Moses and the scene "Entombment," where Mephistopheles fights with the angels over possession of Faust's soul.[73] Goethe would have known this tradition from a brief mention in the New Testament Letter of Jude (1:9), from Herder's literary variations on Jewish stories and legends in his "Scattered Leaves," and potentially from a diverse set of other sources.[74] Goethe's familiarity with this legend is clear from at least two sources: his reference to the legend in his "Tame Xenia": "over Moses's corpse fought blessed ones with accursed demons" (*Über Moses' Leichnam stritten Selige mit Fluchdämonen*) (FA 1.12: 675); and his reaction, in a letter, to a depiction of the death of Moses by Friedrich (Maler) Müller.

The letter refers to the rabbinic legend concerning "the fight of both spirits over the corpse of Moses" (*Der Streit beider Geister über den Leichnam Mosis*), which he casts disparagingly as "a silly Jewish fable" (*eine alberne Judenfabel*). Goethe takes issue with Müller's treatment of the subject, where the deceased Moses, having just seen the Promised Land, and still with the "reflection of glory" (*Abglanz der Herrlichkeit*) in his countentance, nevertheless ends up under the foot of the devil. This depiction, he asserts, makes one angry with the angel for not hurrying more quickly to take possession of Moses's remains in an honorable fashion. Goethe continues with his own vision in which the devil is thwarted:

> If one wants indeed to treat this subject, it seems to me it couldn't be done otherwise than in the following way: the holy one [Moses], still full of the delightful vision of the promised land, passes away in rapture and angels are engaged in lifting him away in glory. For the phrase, "the Lord buried him" grants us the most beautiful prospects, and here Satan could at most stand in contrast, with his dark shoulders, in a corner of the foreground and, without laying a hand on the Lord's anointed one, could merely look around to see if there isn't something he might be able get for himself.

> Wenn man doch dieses Sujet behandeln wollte, so konnte es, dünkt mich, nicht anders geschehen, als daß der Heilige [Moses], noch voll von dem anmuthigen Gesichte des gelobten Landes, entzückt

> verscheidet und Engel ihn in einer Glorie wegzuheben beschäftigt sind; denn das Wort: "Der Herr begrub ihn," läßt uns zu den schönsten Aussichten Raum, und hier könnte Satan höchstens nur in einer Ecke des Vorgrundes mit seinen schwarzen Schultern kontrastiren und, ohne Hand an den Gesalbten des Herrn zu legen, sich höchstens nur umsehen, ob nicht auch für ihn etwas hier zu erwerben sein möchte. (FA 2.2: 354–55)

Thus Goethe's concept for a painting of the legend contains many of the elements he included in the final scenes of his drama: the hero's recent ecstatic vision of a future land, a defeated devil, and angels lifting the deceased away in glory.

Nevertheless, for Goethe, the chief attraction of the store of extra-biblical stories concerning the death of Moses might well have lain in their very ambiguity and controversy. Eisenmenger recounts a legend according to which Moses repeatedly resists death, including by pleading with the Lord to allow him to continue to live and see the world, even if it means living like an animal of the field or like a bird in the wind.[75] At last the Lord himself gently takes Moses's soul from his body through a kiss, and then the Lord himself weeps.[76] Eisenmenger expresses his outrage at this legend that stands so opposed to the honor of the Lord and the glory of Moses, since it should be clear that Moses should prefer the afterlife to life on this earth: "How should Moses have so preferred the life of this world over heavenly delight, that he would have rather wanted to live like a wild animal or a bird than to be transported into eternal blessedness and total joy?"[77] But of course Eisenmenger's criticism is precisely Goethe's point. Faust's commitments, like Moses's in the legend, are fully to this life: "Let him stand firm and look at what's around him: / no good and able man finds this world mute! / What need has he to float into eternity—" (*Er stehe fest und sehe hier sich um; / Dem Tüchtigen ist diese Welt nicht stumm. / Was braucht er in die Ewigkeit zu schweifen?*) (Atkins, *Faust I & II*, 11445–47).

The article on Moses in Zedler's *Universal Lexicon* points to controversies concerning Moses's death that seem to anticipate interpretive problems concerning Faust's death. Zedler presents claims that were contested by scholastic authors: some maintained that Moses had never died but rather had been transported alive to heaven; others argued that Moses was unredeemed because of his lack of faith in the episode concerning the waters of Meribah, and his apparent lack of repentance or penance.[78] In opposition to the view that Moses was unredeemed, Zedler cites the fact that the Lord after all called Moses his servant (*Knecht*).[79] The death of Faust, also a designated servant of the Lord (299), likewise leaves plenty of room for controvery. Could Faust, the unrepentant criminal, really be redeemed, and if so, why or in what sense?

Few critics today opt for an un-ironic reading of the final scene with its strikingly Christian, indeed Catholic, imagery—"the clearcut

Christian-ecclesiastical figures" (*die scharf umrissenen christlich-kirchlichen Figuren*) (FA 2.12: 489). But critics take very different measure of that irony: some see it as essentially a species of Romantic irony that reflects upon the inadequacy of its own representations; others regard it as a more radical form of satire.[80] But perhaps the ambiguity surrounding Faust's death is precisely the point for Goethe. As Jane Brown writes, "Like everything else in this play the cosmic framework can appear positive or negative, profound or ridiculous, depending on the point of view. The reader must be prepared to encompass both points of view."[81] I will thus offer two opposed readings of this final scene in relationship to the biblical subtexts, with which I have been operating throughout.

The first reading takes seriously the specifically Christian figuration of the final scene. Given the strong Hebrew Bible subtext throughout the drama, the heavy-handed Christianity at the end could introduce a final supersessory twist. The supersessory typologies become especially pronounced in the speeches of the three penitent women who address the Mater Gloriosa in the highest of the three spheres in "Mountain Gorges," and precede the appearance of Gretchen. The first two figures are drawn from Gospel anecdotes that showcase Jesus's sympathy and forgiveness toward sinful, especially sexually transgressive, women. But Goethe underscores another aspect of these Gospel passages: they implicitly draw the line between Christianity and Judaism.

The speech of the "Magna Peccatrix" refers explicitly (according to Goethe's scriptural gloss) to a story in Luke 7. Presumably a prostitute, she seeks Jesus out where he is dining at the home of a Pharisee, weeps upon his feet, anoints them with oil, and wipes them with her own hair. But with the phrase "scorn of Pharisees defying" (*Trotz des Pharisäerhohnes*) (12040), Goethe highlights a key point of the Luke passage: the penitent woman serves as a foil for the Pharisee, who is made to seem arrogant, uncomprehending, and a poor host. Pharisees, upon whose traditions later rabbinic Judaism was based, serve as ubiquitous Jewish villains in the Gospels, referred to close to one hundred times. Indeed, the story of the sinful woman in Luke comes in the wake of several anti-Pharisaic statements and anecdotes in the preceding chapters, including references to their emerging plot against Jesus (Luke 6:11) and their rejection of God's purpose for them (Luke 7:30). Thus following the New Testament example, the speech of the "Magna Peccatrix" conjoins her acceptance by these heavenly hosts with an overcoming of (a caricatured) "Judaism," the Pharasaic scorn.

The speech of his second pentitent, "Mulier Samaritana," draws on another key episode in Christianity's dissociation of itself from Judaism (in John 4, as indicated in Goethe's own gloss). Here Jesus encounters a Samaritan woman at a well that is described as having once belonged to the patriarch Jacob. Jesus asks the Samaritan woman for a drink and she responds with surprise, "Jews do not share a thing in common with Samaritans" (John 4:9). Jesus engages in a conversation with her despite the cultural and religious customs separating them, and despite the woman's sinfulness, for Jesus discloses his knowledge of her marital and sexual history. Because of this mysterious knowledge, she comes away convinced he is the savior; and many Samaritans, after listening to her testimony and hearing Jesus themselves, also become convinced. This is a crucial encounter because it represents an expansion of Jesus's ministry beyond Judaism, which is depicted within the passage as too narrow in its scope. Amy-Jill Levine delineates the construction of a "bad Judaism" in this story:

> John's account of Jesus and the Samaritan woman lends itself to readings that offer the "bad Judaism" versus "good Jesus" mode of interpretation, for it fits the view that Jesus breaks down barriers between men and women, Jews and Gentiles. In this scenario, "Judaism" again becomes the system that erects and seeks to maintain those barriers, and the Samaritan woman represents the ultimate "Outsider" who finds, with Jesus, her place on the inside.[82]

Goethe conspicuously brings out this theme of overcoming Jewish barriers through a repeated, expanding image of water. The Mulier Samaritana's speech arcs from the well, to which Abram (Abraham) led his flock, to the vessel from which the Saviour drank, to the pure, rich (clearly spiritual) source that pours forth and flows throughout the world (12045–52). As Faust commentators have noted, two things are curious here. First, Goethe identifies the well with the covenantal patriarch Abraham rather than his son Jacob, who is explicitly associated with it in the biblical passage. Second, Goethe employs Abraham's original, pre-covenantal name Abram (Schöne, 808). The appearance of Abram here then serves to emphasize the boundary created by the covenant of circumcision, the point at which the nomadic chieftain Abram is proclaimed to be the "father of a multitude"—the meaning of his God-given new name, Abraham (Gen. 17:5).

The status of the Abrahamic covenant is indeed a crucial issue for the New Testament. Some Gospel passages seems to affirm the distinct standing of Jews as the children of Abraham (see Luke 19:9), while others appear to contest it. For example, John the Baptist preaches, "Do not begin to say to yourselves, 'We have Abraham as our ancestor'; for I tell you, God is able from these stones to raise up children to Abraham" (Luke 3:8, see also Matt. 3:9). The Gospel of John, from which the story of the Samaritan woman is taken, is most virulent in this regard. In a polemical exchange with "Jews" (as if Jesus were not a Jew), Jesus responds to the assertion "Abraham is our father" with "You are from your father the devil" (John 8:39, 44). In this same passage, "the Jews" suggest that Jesus is in fact a Samaritan. Given the broader New Testament contexts for both the Samaritan woman and the figure of Abraham, there is nothing innocent about the appearance of the name Abram here. The Mulier Samaritana's speech suggests a genealogy that circumvents one of the foundational covenants of Judaism and makes the patriarch instead the ancestor of a universalistic Christianity.

As Goethe notes, the source for the third penitential woman "Maria Aegyptiaca" is the Acts of the Saints. According to legends, Mary of Egypt was a prostitute in Alexandria who made a trip to Jerusalem merely for pleasure. But when she tried to enter the Church of the Holy Sepulchre on the day when the holy cross was displayed, a secret power prevented her entry. She then prayed to an image of the Virgin and was able to enter. After leaving the church, a voice told her to cross the Jordan. She did so and then spent the next forty-seven years in the wilderness of Perea. Toward the end of her life she encountered a monk who brought her the Eucharist at Easter time.[83] When she died she left him a message in the sand requesting a Christian burial (Schöne, 808).

As with the prior two anecdotes drawn from the Gospels, the legend of Maria Aegyptiaca can suggest Christianity's elision or supersession of Judaism. Indeed, Auerbach offers the legend of Maria Aegyptiaca as an example of medieval figural interpretation, suggesting she may have served in Christian art as a "figure of the people of Israel going out of Egypt."[84] While he does not sketch out this interpretation in detail, it is not hard to work out a reading that indeed lines up with other tendencies in the representations of Jews. Just as the dishonored, often blindfolded female figure of Synagoga departing from the scene of the crucifixion is a frequent allegorical representative of Judaism in medieval Christian art,[85] Maria of Egypt, in her early sinful life, could represent an unredeemed Israel that has rejected Christ and is therefore excluded from the church and the sight of the redemptive cross. After she has repented, Maria must return across the Jordan to reenact Israel's wandering in the wilderness, but now as a penitent Christian, until she at last finds eternal rest and redemption in a Christian burial. Thus her legend also bears similarities to the myth of the Wandering Jew who must wander in penitence until Judgment Day, and, in general, to a conception of Jews as a "witness people," whose suffering bears witness to the truth of the gospel.

Is Goethe suggesting a Christian typological reading for his Maria Aegyptiaca? Certainly the Exodus subtext, which I have argued pervades *Part Two*, would prime a reader to understand Maria in this light. Furthermore, Goethe turns the saint's forty-seven years in the desert into the forty years that the children of Israel were to have wandered in the wilderness.

But perhaps the most typologically charged aspect of the final scene is its portrayal of redemptive, intercessory love. Just as the three pentitents plead to Mater Gloriosa to grant forgiveness for Gretchen (12065–68), Gretchen pleads on behalf of Faust (12092). Variations on the word "love" (*Liebe*) come up fifteen times in the final scene, including evocations of all-powerful love (11873), eternal love (11865, 11924, 11964), and love from above (11938–39). In the assessment of the Christian theologian Hans Hübner, "Faust II thus ends . . . with an apotheosis of love!"[86] Love is of course a keyword in the Gospels, especially the Gospel of John. Meanwhile it is made clear that the Jewish leaders, by contrast, are deficient in love (John 5:42, 8:42; see also Luke 11:42). The contrast between the so-called Old Testament God of Wrath and the New Testament God of Love is an old and pervasive one in Christianity.[87] Indeed, as discussed in chapter 1, these paradigms structured the thinking of the young Goethe as he struggled to make sense of the Lisbon earthquake. Goethe indulges in this sort of typing of Jews as somehow loveless in a remark reported by Riemer: "'A person who feels no love must learn to flatter, otherwise he doesn't get by,' noted Goethe when the conversation concerned the character of the Jews" (*"Wer keine Liebe fühlt, muß schmeicheln lernen, sonst kommt er nicht aus," bemerkte Goethe, als vom Charakter der Juden die Rede war*).[88]

Even the claim, made most prominently by Schöne, that the final scene enacts a version of *apokatastasis panton* (*Wiederbringung aller*), a universal redemption and restoration, does not rule out the supersessionist reading, for the claim to universality belongs to the Christian conception of its superiority over Judaism. According to Schöne, Goethe would have learned of this doctrine through Gottfried Arnold's account of the church father Origen (Schöne, 788). And while *apokatastasis panton* in fact bears similarities to the Jewish kabbalistic conception of *tikkun olam*, I argued in chapter 2 that in his early essay "Brief des Pastors . . ." Goethe has his Pastor embrace this notion as a Christian universalistic heresy in contradistinction to his conception of Jewish particularism.

The Christian reading of this final scene would therefore be that Faust, this now blind old man embodying the "Old Covenant," reminiscent perhaps of the blinded "Synagoga," that denigratory symbol of a "people that walked in darkness" (Isa. 9:2), is saved at last, in spite of himself. His redemption comes through the grace of a universalistic Christian love represented as a female principle, the Eternal Feminine. But there is good reason to resist this reading: it would be a repudiation of everything that the drama otherwise appears to be about.

Above all, to take "Mountain Gorges" as an ultimate revelation in a Christian vein would be to abandon the anti-idolatrous ideal that is affirmed by Faust—despite his repeated shortcomings—up until the end of his life. It is worth remembering that the ban on dogmatic metaphysics—on inventing versions of ourselves in transcendent realms—is not merely Goethe's obsession but a chief tenet of the entire age of Kant. Shortly before his death, Faust still resolutely refuses to imagine the beyond: "The yonder view is blocked to mortal ken / A fool who squints beyond with blinking eyes, / Imagining his like above the skies" (*Nach drüben ist die Aussicht uns verrannt; / Tor, wer dorthin die Augen blinzelnd richtet, / Sich über Wolken seinesgleichen dichtet!*) (Arndt, *Faust: A Tragedy*, 11442–44). But this ban on metaphysical scenes is violated in "Mountain Gorges" where human figures appear in the highest atmosphere and where the "view" (*Aussicht*) is not "blocked" (*verrant*) but rather, according to Doctor Marianus, "free" (*frei*) (11989). Indeed, the potential for idolatry seems to increase as the scene progresses and reaches the highest regions.

The natural setting at the beginning of the scene implies an encounter of opposites that could recall the fluid existential ideals elsewhere in the drama. Mountain (*Berg*) converges here with gorge (*Schlucht*), perhaps implicitly representing male and female. A mountain gorge landscape also already played a role in "Classical Walpurgisnight" culminating in the erotic encounter between Homonculus and Galatea (6954). The lower regions of "Mountain Gorges" also introduce a mixture of fire and water reminiscent of the Noahic rainbow from "Charming Landscape." Pater Ecstaticus, for example, describes an experience that is at once glowing (*glühend*), seething (*siedend*), and foaming (*schäumend*) (11855–57). Pater Profundis describes a waterfall down rocks, in a dynamic process with air and lightning (11866–11871).

But if the lower regions recall the mediated rainbow ideal in "Charming Landscape," the higher regions offer unmediated encounter: whereas Faust averts his eyes from the sun to contemplate a mere "colorful refraction" in "Charming Landscape," by the end of "Mountain Gorges" Doctor Marianus implores all to look indeed directly at the revealed Mater Gloriosa: "Look up to salvation's eyes" (*Blicket auf zum Retterblick*) (Atkins, *Faust I & II*, 12096).

What alternative does a reader have to accepting this vision as revelation? It has not been lost on commentators that the Job frame, established at the beginning of *Part One*, resurfaces at the very end of *Part Two*, providing perhaps an alternative vantage point from which to understand the Christian imagery in "Mountain Gorges." The laments of Mephistopheles, as he is teased and tricked by the angels in the penultimate scene "Entombment," alert us to the reemerging significance of Job: from their tossed roses Mephistopheles suffers boils "Job-like" (*Hiobsartig*) (11809). Like Job, he frames his distress as a legal complaint in rhetorical questions: "From whom can I now seek redress? / Who will procure me what I've duly earned" (*Bei wem soll ich mich nun beklagen? / Wer schafft mir mein erworbenes Recht*) (Atkins, *Faust I & II*, 11832–33).[89] But while Mephistopheles may be just setting out on a Jobian odyssey, the implications of which are unclear, Faust apparently has come to the end of his.

These textual allusions can recall the important structural parallels between Faust and the book of Job. Job has a clear and distinct epilogue that, like its prologue, is distinguished by its prose form, in contrast to the poetic core of the book. This abrupt epilogue (Job 42:7–17) contains a sudden happy ending to Job's ordeal: all of Job's fortunes are restored. Children crushed to death at the beginning are replaced by new offspring in the end. As Eichhorn attests, it is difficult to know what to make of the epilogue, for it undermines the book's central argument that virtue guarantees no divine rewards; indeed, by the eighteenth century its authenticity already stood in question.[90] Goethe himself clearly had a rich sense of the incongruity of the epilogue: he once characterized the divinity that compensates Job so richly in the end as "humorous" (*humoristisch*) (WA 4.39: 237). Certainly critics have long been struck by the artifice, theatricality, and even oddly funny character of the ending of Faust.[91] Nicholas Rennie, for example, draws a comparison between the internal disjunction in the two texts: the disjunction in Job between the dramatic, poetic core of the book (with its unanswered questions) and its folk tale frame (providing explanation and resolution); and the disjunction in *Faust* between the tragedy at the core and the theodicy offered by the frame.[92] By analogy with the epilogue of Job, then, the conclusion of *Faust* seems an arbitrary undoing of the drama's rigorous focus on this life without heavenly guarantees.

The heavy Christian imagery in the concluding scene actually underscores this analogy with the epilogue of Job. For while the epilogue in Job is certainly not Christian in origin, Goethe would have had good reason to view it in the context of its Christian reception, as if it functioned as a Christian coda to a Hebrew Bible narrative. Johannes Anderegg has argued that the ending of *Faust* draws specifically on Christianizing traditions surrounding Job.[93] A striking example of this Christianization, cited by Anderegg, is the tendentious translation of Job 19:25 in the Vulgate, the fourth-century Latin translation of the Bible, which was picked up by Luther: "ABER ICH WEIS DAS MEIN ERLÖSER LEBET / VND ER WIRD MICH HERNACH AUS DER ERDEN AUFFWECKEN" and rendered similarly in the King James Version, "For I know that my redeemer liveth, and that he shall stand at the latter day upon the earth" (Job 19:25). Luther capitalizes this passage to point to its salvational significance and glosses the term "redeemer" (*Erlöser*) with an explicit reference to Christ.[94] But according to Mayer Gruber, the Hebrew word in question, "go'el," is understood in its historical context as a kinsman tasked with avenging the murder of a family member, and Job's hoped-for remedy is a legal one. Hence the passage reads in the Tanakh translation: "But I know that my Vindicator lives; / In the end He will testify on earth—" (Job 19:25).[95] While exposed primarily to the Lutheran translation, Goethe would have been alert to the discrepancy from his early adolescent biblical studies with the exegetical commentary commonly referred to as *das englische Bibelwerk*.[96] Anderegg notes other passages, including James 5, in which Job's purported patience is held up as an example for a Christian community awaiting Christ's return, and also explores conventions linking Job to Christ in visual art. He concludes that in the Christian reception, Job becomes a "paradigm for salvation and resurrection, more precisely, for the longing for, and belief in, resurrection."[97]

Goethe may further allude to the Christianizing reception of Job in a crucial, much-debated passage from "Mountain Gorges" concerning Faust's redemption. The angels carrying Faust's soul intone: "'for him whose striving never ceases / we can provide redemption;' / and if a higher love as well / has shown an interest in him, / the hosts of heaven come and greet him with a cordial welcome" (*"Wer immer strebend sich bemüht, / Den können wir erlösen." / Und hat in ihm die Liebe gar / Von oben teilgenommen, / Begegnet ihm die selige Schar / Mit herzlichem Willkommen*) (Atkins, *Faust I & II*, 11936–41).[98] Critics argue over the logic of this passage: is the person who strives redeemed *because* he strove?[99] And how is that striving related in the next sentence to the love from above that guarantees a welcome from the heavenly host? Has the striver personally earned his heavenly rewards? The quotation marks around the first two lines seem to invite us to seek an external source. Compare then the famous passage from James about Job (with key terms inserted in Luther's German):

> Indeed we call blessed [*wir preisen selig*] those who showed endurance [*erduldet haben*]. You have heard of the endurance [*gedult*] of Job, and you have seen the purpose [*das ende*] of the Lord, how the Lord is compassionate and merciful. (James 5:11)

Luther's German phrase "wir preisen selig" means to praise as blessed but here it also could suggest that Job has been saved. Has he been saved because of his faithful endurance? The structure of this sentence from James—*we call blessed, those who have endured*—seems mirrored in inverted form in the line from *Faust—whoever strives, we can redeem*. In distilled form: whoever persists/strives, we can redeem (Faust); we call redeemed those who persist/endure (Job). Both could *seem* to ground salvation in persistent activity—whether striving or enduring—but in neither is the causal relationship certain. Both passages continue with a logically ambiguous, merely additive "and" (*und*), introducing divine mercy or love and rewards that, again, may or may not be linked to the activity of the hero. If one takes this parallel seriously, the angelic pronouncement of redemption for Faust is like James's Christianizing gloss on Job: it serves at best as a rhetorically ambiguous patch on a story that, at its core, offers no answers, no guarantees, and certainly no theodicy. In a broader sense, the relationship of the redemptive ending to the rest of the Faust drama parallels the appendage of Christian promises of eternal life to the Hebrew Bible narratives of a faithful wandering.

Thus Goethe lets the reader decide what status to grant the final vision. One can take it seriously as a Christian revelation that fulfills and supersedes all that has come before. The speeches of the three penitents in particular encapsulate this traditional stance of Christianity toward Judaism. In this reading, a saving Christian love and eternal life always awaited Faust if only he had had the capacity to perceive it. As Arnd Bohm argues about *Part One*, tragedy could have been averted if Faust had simply heard and responded to Gretchen's call welcoming him into the community of the Christian faithful.[100] Alternatively, one can see the redemption at the end as self-conscious artifice, a superimposed happy ending that stands at odds with the spirit of the drama as a whole. In this reading the scene offers mere wishful thinking

(*Wunschbilder*) concerning immortality.[101] And these images tend again towards the idolatry that Faust has struggled against throughout his life.

In fact, Goethe clearly builds this dual perspective into the final lines of the work. Does this passage claim to be offering a revelation or a potentially deceptive image of something unrepresentable? "All that is transitory / is but a parable; / the unattainable / here is seen done; / what's indescribable / here becomes fact; / The Eternal Feminine / draws us along" (*Alles Vergängliche / Ist nur ein Gleichnis; / Das Unzulängliche, /Hier wird's Ereignis / Das Unbeschreibliche, / Hier ist's getan; Das Ewig-Weibliche / Zieht uns hinan*) (12104–11).[102] The plainer meaning is the epiphanic one where the scene "Mountain Gorges" reveals eternal, heavenly truths. In this reading, "the transitory" that remains "but a parable" describes the core of the play, Faust's temporal odyssey prior to his ultimate salvation. The subsequent verses would then affirm that in this scene all that is otherwise unattainable and indescribable is *here* (i.e., in this eternal realm) achieved. In this reading, the Eternal Feminine that draws us onward would seem to refer to the Mater Gloriosa, the figure of eternal Christian love, who serves as the spiritual destination in the scene and who urges Gretchen to lift herself to higher spheres (12094).

The alternative approach is to take the scene itself as a mere representation or "parable." In a reading sketched out by Schöne, following Schlaffer, the *here* in these verses refers to the stage itself, where the unattainable and indescribable are nevertheless signified, if only provisionally and incompletely (Schöne, 815). The final vision is therefore not an ultimate revelation but only a representation and, as with all representations, in danger of calcification and deception. In this reading, the Mater Gloriosa would be only one imperfect approximation of the Eternal Feminine, no more decisive and final than, say, the ambiguous mothers in act 1. Perhaps indeed the best definition of the Eternal Feminine is simply *that which draws us along*. It embodies the principle of expansion in the fundamental rhythm of expansion and contraction that Goethe describes in *Poetry and Truth* and that we saw at work in his reading of Genesis. Not only, then, should the Eternal Feminine not be limited to a Christian context, but its very Christianization would represent a version of the inevitable error that comes with striving.[103]

In this sense, even this apparent Christian apotheosis does not cancel Goethe's identification with the Hebrew Bible characters with whom he wrestled his whole life. We return again to Goethe's 1815 poem "Sweet Child, the String of Pearls," in which the poet resists the idolatrous veneration of the crucifix: "Shall I indeed sing of stick across stick, so rigid" (*Soll ich wohl, in seiner Starrheit, / Hölzchen quer auf Hölzchen singen?*) (FA 1.3.1: 508). He recalls all the religious heroes who opposed idol worship—Abraham, Moses, David, Mohammed, and even Jesus himself. But in the end, the poet identifies with Solomon who fell into idolatry for the sake of his beloved: "And I'll not claim to be better /When it happens to me. Solomon forswore his [God] My God I have denied" (FA 1.3.1: 509). Perhaps in the culminating scene of this, his final literary testament, Goethe is likewise revealing himself to be an unsteady keeper of the existential covenant, a relapsing idolater. Less than two years before his death, he may be acknowledging with irony the lure of the "beneficially limiting form and solidity" (*wohltätig beschränkende Form und Festigkeit*) of this Catholic iconography (FA 2.12: 489), and the irresistible desire for ultimate scenes and revelations. But even here, the Hebrew Bible remains Goethe's fundamental narrative inspiration and model.

Conclusion

This book has had little to say about the social, economic, political, and interpersonal circumstances surrounding Goethe's actual interactions with his Jewish contemporaries. Instead it has sought out underlying, formative, and pervasive tropes and typologies that inform his entire literary program. Goethe's version of Judaism involves wandering, ineluctable cycles of sin and idolatry, a this-worldly bent, and a tolerance for a morally impenetrable universe. His conceptions are mediated through popular accounts, history and legend, kabbalistic and philosophical traditions but above all, and most profoundly, through the Hebrew Bible. As I have shown, the Hebrew Bible is no remote or quaint document for Goethe: it is a challenging, resonant, polyvocal compilation that in many ways becomes his template for modern literature.

But Goethe's deep admiration for the Hebrew Bible is double-edged. On the one hand, his engaged reading from a young age as well as his embrace of the emerging biblical criticism allows him to see the Hebrew Bible in a distinctive, new light, no longer overshadowed by Christian theology. On the other hand, his appropriation of the material entails a disappropriation of the people he considered its unworthy heirs. Hence Goethe's relationship to Judaism is pervaded by his sense of a "contrast between the forefathers and the descendants that makes us confused and displeased" (*Contrast zwischen den Ahnherren und den Enkeln, der uns irre macht und verstimmt*) (FA 2.7: 67).[1] Furthermore, he seeks the roots of the purported decline in the descendants within the Hebrew Bible itself, and perceives fault lines—most pronouncedly in the transition from Genesis and Exodus—between a free and sublime patriarchal outlook and what he takes to be the narrow mindset of modern rabbinical Judaism. This contrast maps on to broader paradigms of modernity in his work: a good modernity that is individual, exploratory, free of dogmatic metaphysics, and a destructive modernity that is collectivist, unmoored, and vulnerable to dangerous absolutisms.

Beyond this variable appropriation of material within the Hebrew Bible, Goethe makes a more sweeping move: he overturns the traditional New Testament/Old Testament hierarchy only to reinstate a new literary hierarchy: now a secular, modern German literature that rests on and supersedes the Hebrew Bible. This pattern is clearest in the trajectory that leads from the *Volksbuch* project to the *Journeyman Years*. The logic of supersession expresses itself most malevolently in the segregationist stance of the Society of Emigrants, who will tolerate no Jew among them. But certainly Goethe's relationship to Judaism cannot be reduced to this one virulent position, nor does he seem to reach a consistent or unitary position at all. Rather the relationship is a shifting, troubled, implicating mix of admiration, sympathy, debt, resentment, condescension, and rejection. My book has tried to capture that fluctuating dynamic with its alternations between more generally positive examples of reception (in chapters 1, 4, and 5) and more clearly negative ones (in chapters 2 and 3). But my conclusion remains that, despite Goethe's complex sympathies and secular, critical turn, his literary appropriations of the Hebrew Bible bear forward the disfiguring figural hermeneutic that defined Jewish-Christian history from its earliest eras.

What impact Goethe's representations had on the subsequent course of German-Jewish history is not easy to assess and is not the subject of this book. Nevertheless, here at the end, a look deserves to be cast toward the catastrophic events of the twentieth century. In lieu of speculations and generalizations, I offer simply the testimony of Paul Celan's "Deathfugue" ("Todesfuge"). Embedded within this powerful poetic monument to the murdered Jews of Europe is a compressed commentary on Goethe's legacy.

In paratactic, repetitive phrases, Celan distills a deadly typological logic at work in the Holocaust. The poem is set in a concentration camp in which Jews are simultaneously forced to work to death through digging and to accompany this labor with music; they are overseen by a man who is at once murderous and spiritually-aesthetically inclined. Woven throughout are references to canonical German authors, Goethe prominent among them.[2] For example, the figure of death, embodied by the overseer, is identified as "a master [*Meister*] from Deutschland"; among many possible referents, Felstiner suggests Goethe's Wilhelm Meister.[3]

But far more multivalent are the poem's references to *Faust*. Celan would have had little reason, in his early life, to see *Faust* as antithetical to his Jewish upbringing; indeed, he received a copy as a Bar Mitzvah present.[4] He likely would have been acquainted with the substantial role of the Hebrew Bible within *Faust*, for the biblical parallels were firmly established in the scholarship of the early twentieth century.[5] Celan thus deploys *Faust* to instantiate, but also to complicate and make agonizingly intimate, the poem's German-Jewish dichotomy.

One of the parallels between the poem and *Faust* concerns the work of digging. As Schöne observes, the forced digging of the inmates in "Deathfugue" recalls Faust's utopian project of land reclamation, for which he orders that workers, if necessary, be pressed into service digging ditches (*Graben*) (11554).[6] But what Faust believes is the construction of a ditch, advancing his utopian vision, is in fact his grave (*Grab*). As Mephistopheles comments in a low voice, "One talks, if my ears still behave / Not of a groove, but of a grave" (*Man spricht, wie man mir Nachricht gab, / Von keinem Graben, doch vom Grab*) (Kaufman, *Goethe's Faust*, 11556–57). Celan's poem takes up and multiplies the link between death and utopia in *Faust*. The Jewish laborers are digging "a grave [*Grab*] in the ground" which cannot in fact be their literal grave, for they will be borne as cremated ash into a grave in the sky: "you'll have a grave then in the clouds." The earthly ditch they dig thus advances some Nazi project, while the grave in the clouds belongs, through an association of imagery, to the overseer's dream of transcendence and Romantic longings. In the images of both earth and sky, then, the death of Jews is conjoined with transcendence for a German.

The dependence of German signification upon Jewish mortification is precisely the conceit of the poem. In this way, the poem serves as a chilling human enactment of the figural hermeneutic. Like the living spirit of Christianity arising from the supposed dead Jewish letter of the Old Testament, here the spiritual elevation of the overseer requires the reduction of the Jews to ash and dust. The poem's fugue-like texture, evoked in the title, plays out this relation on a formal level, where contrasting voices offset each other in a pattern of themes and counter-themes. As in a Bach fugue, the dissonance enhances the uplifting, sacralizing effect, but here with entirely sinister implications.

Celan's most direct and devastating allusion to both Goethe and the Christian typological tradition is the juxtaposition of the Shulamite (here: Shulamith) from the Song of Songs and Margarete from *Faust*. Gretchen's golden hair is offset by Shulamith's hair described as the color of ash, as if burned in the crematorium. And yet what many commentaries on the poem overlook is that the comparison between the two women is not fundamentally dichotomous, because, as we saw in chapter 4, Goethe's depiction of Margarete contains repeated, unmistakable allusions to the Shulamite. When Celan concludes his poem by separating these two figures unbridgeably onto two separates lines,

> dein goldenes Haar Margarete
> dein aschenes Haar Sulamith,

he thereby suggests a merciless division of things deeply entwined, an intimate act of violence.[7] This violence may be the legacy of Goethe, but it is certainly also the legacy of the original break between Christianity and Judaism with its brutal textual-typological divides within deeply connected traditions.

The *Faust* reference contributes one further twist. To return to the scene of digging in the final act, the ditch, as noted, turns out to be Faust's grave. By analogy, the ditch ordered dug in the poem signals not only the death of the diggers but also of the dreamer. This reading lines up with another very obvious subtext for the poem, Heine's "The Silesian Weavers," where the exploited, starving weavers working themselves to death simultaneously weave Germany's funeral shroud. But Celan's allusion to Goethe's figure of Faust, a character so clearly indebted, in turn, to the figures of Job, Solomon, and Moses, makes the entanglement of destinies far more personal. The poem's Romantic murderer cannot extricate himself at last from the fate of the murdered, upon whom his transcendence depends. And so Celan's poem projects a hope, however faint, for the demise of the whole semiotic apparatus that enlists Jewish suffering to signify German-Christian supremacy.

But the conventions of figural interpretation die hard. What Nietzsche once rejected as a "philological farce" remains deeply, often imperceptibly ingrained in many of the defining narratives of European and American culture, whether religious or secular. In its complex appraisal of Goethe, this book tries to draw attention to the diffuse power, persistence, and mutability of these Jewish-Christian typologies and, in some small way, help further loosen their grip.

NOTES

Introduction

1. See Willi Jasper, "Die Entstehung eines nationalen Goethe-Bildes im 19. Jahrhundert," in *"Außerdem waren sie ja auch Menschen": Goethes Begegnung mit Juden und Judentum*, ed. Annette Weber (Berlin: Philo, 2000), 133–44, especially 133–36; Ehrhard Bahr, "Goethe and the Concept of Bildung in Jewish Emancipation," in *Goethe in German-Jewish Culture*, ed. Klaus L. Berghahn and Jost Hermand (Rochester, N.Y.: Camden House, 2001), 16–17; and Hans Vaget, "The GDR Faust: A Literary Autopsy," *Oxford German Studies* 24, no. 1 (1995): 147.

2. See Baldur von Schirach, "Goethe-Rede," *Diskussionen Deutsch* 19 (1988): 153–56 (reprint of a speech delivered in 1937); Johann Wolfgang von Goethe, *Goethe als Kämpfer: Zitate*, ed. Benedikt Weiser, field post edition (Berlin: Mittler, 1942); Karl Justus Obenauer, "Goethe als Naturforscher," *Das deutsche Wort* 11, no. 34 (1935): 8–10; Günther Schulz, "Goethe und die bäuerliche Welt," *Odal: Monatsschrift für Blut und Boden* (1940): 929–32; Franz Koch, *Goethe und die Juden*, Publications of the Reich-Institute for the History of the New Germany (Hamburg: Hanseatische Verlagsanstalt, 1937).

3. Vaget, "GDR Faust," 151.

4. Barbara Hahn shows how Jewish *salonieres*, including Rahel von Varnhagen and Marianne Meyer, read Goethe in ways that allowed them to negotiate the cultural boundaries between "German" and "Jewish" identities. Hahn, "Demarcations and Projections: Goethe in the Berlin Salons," in Berghahn and Hermand, eds., *German-Jewish Culture*, 31–43.

5. Friedrich Wilhelm Riemer, *Mitteilungen über Goethe* (Leipzig: Insel-Verlag, 1921), 208.

6. Ludwig Börne, *Sämtliche Schriften*, 5 vols. (Düsseldorf: Melzer, 1964), 2: 857; Heinrich Heine, *The Romantic School and Other Essays*, The German Library (New York: Continuum, 1985), 36. See also Hans Otto Horch, "Die Juden und Goethe," in Weber, ed., *Goethes Begegnung mit Juden*, 117–31.

7. Horch, "Juden und Goethe," 117–18, 127.

8. Horch sees a shift in the portrayal of Goethe in the *Allgemeine Zeitung des Judentums* after 1890. Horch, "Juden und Goethe," 128. Ehrhard Bahr makes the distinction between Goethe's reception among German Jews before and after 1870. Bahr, "Goethe and the Concept of Bildung in Jewish Emancipation," in Berghahn and Hermand, *German-Jewish Culture*, 16–28.

9. Elon claims that "Rosenzweig was said to have derived his new theology mainly from Goethe rather than from the sages whom he cited." Elon cites as his source Anthony David Skinner on Salman Schocken. Amos Elon, *The Pity of It All: A Portrait of the German-Jewish Epoch, 1743–1933* (New York: Picador, 2002), 378, 427n.

10. See Gisela Hoecherl-Alden, "German-Jewish Goethe Scholars in U.S. Exile," in Berghahn and Hermand, eds., *German-Jewish Culture*, 123–35.

11. "Jews and Judaism in Goethe's Esthetical and Reactionary World: A Typological Study," *Revue des Études Juives* 162, no. 1–2 (January–June 2003): 144.

12. The most important contributions of the last several decades are the two previously cited essay collections: Weber, ed., *Goethes Begegnung mit Juden* and Berghahn and Hermand, eds., *German-Jewish Culture*. The former collection is particularly strong in providing historical context and documentation; the latter has a strong emphasis on the reception of Goethe. A number of these essays will be referenced individually. Over the last thirty years a number of other article-length surveys have considered the question of Goethe's relationship to Judaism. These include (in chronological order) Wilfried Barner, "150 Jahre nach seinem Tod: Goethe und die Juden," *Bulletin des Leo Baeck Instituts* no. 63 (1982): 75–82; Norbert Oellers, "Goethe und Schiller in ihrem Verhältnis zum Judentum," in *Conditio Judaica: Judentum, Antisemitismus und deutschsprachige Literatur vom 18. Jahrhundert bis zum Ersten Weltkrieg*, ed. Hans Otto Horch and Horst Denkler, 3 vols. (Tübingen: Niemeyer, 1988–93), 1: 108–30; Gunter Hartung, "Goethe und die Juden," *Weimarer Beiträge* 40, no. 3 (1994): 398–416; Jürgen Gidion, "Goethe und die Juden," *Neue Sammlung* 40 (2000): 537–54; Veltri, "Jews and Judaism"; Adolf Muschg, "War Goethe Antisemit?" in *Innenansichten aus Europa*, ed. Helmut Schmidt and Richard von Weizsäcker, *Die Neue Mittwochsgesellschaft* 4 (Munich: Beck, 2007), 46–88. What these articles have in common is that they cover a great deal of ground very briefly and come to general conclusions concerning Goethe's overall position toward Jews, but offer little in the way of sustained literary analysis. Indeed, Veltri makes the astounding claim that, while the reception of Goethe's relationship to Judaism is of the greatest consequence, there is nothing sufficiently interesting in Goethe's corpus itself to justify this much attention to the topic (144). A notable exception to the trend toward broad evaluation over close reading is the exemplary analysis of Goethe's "Judenpredigt" by Jürgen Stenzel and Oliver Höher, "'Die Verschrobenheit eines veralteten Unsinns': Goethes Judenpredigt," special printing, *Jahrbuch des freien deutschen Hochstifts* (2000): 1–26.

13. Compare Adolf Muschg: "The process in which Jews and Jewishness entangled Goethe reaches into the core of his beliefs, indeed of his person, and I think I have discerned there one of the most powerful driving forces in his productivity." Adolf Muschg, "Eine Ausnahme macht Adolf Muschg, Mehr Licht für ein Ärgernis: Goethe und die Juden: Eine Rede, gehalten im Goethehaus Frankfurt," *Frankfurter Allgemeine*, no. 223, September 26, 1987, quoted in Stenzel and Höher, "Verschrobenheit," 23–24.

14. I invoke Harold Bloom's term loosely to suggest the fraught dynamic of dependence and rejection at the heart of Goethe's reception of Judaism, particularly of the Hebrew Bible. Goethe's competition with the Hebrew Bible belongs to some degree to the peculiarly modern literary tradition Bloom describes "of anxiety and self-saving caricature, of distortion, of perverse, willful revisionism without which modern poetry as such could not exist" (30). But there are important limits to the appropriateness of Bloom's model for my analysis: (1) I do not celebrate Goethe for his "strong readings," given his concomitant denigration and disenfranchisement of Jews; (2) I do not refer to Bloom's taxonomy of literary strategies (Kenosis, Tessera, etc.); (3) Bloom in fact does not consider Goethe,

with his "appalling self-confidence," to have even suffered from the anxiety of influence. Bloom, *The Anxiety of Influence* (New York: Oxford University Press, 1973), 52. Compare Jane Brown, *Goethe's Allegories of Identity* (Philadelphia: University of Pennsylvania Press, 2014), 123, 202n.

15. Michael Hardt and Antonio Negri, *Empire* (Cambridge, Mass.: Harvard University Press, 2000), 71. This book is not otherwise informed by the work of Hardt and Negri, but those authors share with Goethe a significant debt to Spinoza.

16. Muschg, "War Goethe Antisemit?" 46.

17. Several of the articles that have been written in previous decades seem aimed above all at defending Goethe from charges of anti-Jewish prejudice, in particular: Oellers, Hartung, and Gidion. Oellers draws an untenable distinction between the older Goethe, to whom he attributes a lack of sympathy for the struggles and sufferings of Jews, and the younger Goethe, whom he sees as coming close to open opposition to anti-Semitism ("Goethe und Schiller," 123). Hartung provides a particularly thorough overview of the material and touches on key issues such as idolatry and nationalism in Goethe's conception of Judaism, but he explains away or willfully reinterprets even the most egregious examples of anti-Judaism on Goethe's part, simply denying that prejudice plays a role either in Goethe's relationship to contemporary Jewry or to the Hebrew Bible and Jewish religion ("Goethe und die Juden," 406). Gidion displays more generational and cultural introspection than either Oellers or Hartung. But despite a certain pathos in tone, he follows Hartung's identically titled article closely in both content and form. For example, just as Hartung sees Goethe's negative characterization of Jewish bankers and financiers as simply an instance of his general dislike of bankers and financiers (Hartung, "Goethe und die Juden," 400), Gidion dismisses Goethe's caricature of a rabbi as simply an instance of Goethe's enlightened critique of religious hierarchy and priestly classes (Gidion, "Goethe und die Juden," 544). Both critics seem deaf to the very specific anti-Jewish discourses in which Goethe participates.

18. Examples of this economic stereotype in Goethe's letters and writing can be found in his letter to Behrisch, November 10, 1767 (WA 4.1: 144); to Christiane Vulpius, January 3,1797: (WA 4.12: 4); to C. G. Voigt, October 18, 1799 (WA 4.14, 202); in the "Historic Part" of his *Theory of Colors*, he writes of the modern "business of haggling and usury among Abraham's descendants" (*schacher- und wucherbetrieb der nachkommen Abrahams*) (WA 2.3: 140).

19. See Martha Helfer's concise and illuminating discussion of the term "anti-Semitism" and her argument for retaining it in its plainest dictionary meaning to signify hostility and opposition to Jews. Helfer, *The Word Unheard: Legacies of Anti-Semitism in German Literature and Culture* (Evanston, Ill.: Northwestern University Press, 2011), xvii–xix.

20. Goethe maintained friendly contact with Felix Mendelssohn (who was born Jewish but baptized), David Friedländer, and Moritz Oppenheim, among others.

21. Mark Waldman, *Goethe and the Jews: A Challenge to Hitlerism* (New York: Putnam, 1934), xvi.

22. Alan Levenson, *Between Philosemitism and Antisemitism: Defenses of Jews and Judaism in Germany, 1871–1932* (Lincoln: University of Nebraska Press, 2004), 146.

23. Ibid., 147–48.

24. Hartung and Gidion also make this argument, although both seem to offer it as an excuse, as a lesser charge to acquit Goethe of a more serious anti-Jewish bias.

25. W. Daniel Wilson, "Goethes Haltung zur Judenemanzipation und jüdische Haltungen zu Goethe," in Weber, ed., *Goethes Begegnung mit Juden*, 34, 154n.

26. Wilson outlines the history of this opposition in the article cited above, "Goethes Haltung," as well as in "'Humanitätsalbader': Goethe's Distaste for Jewish Emancipation and Jewish Responses," in Berghahn and Hermand, eds., *Goethe in German-Jewish Culture*, 146–64.

27. Wilson, "Humanitätssalbader," 147. Wilson also discusses two episodes in which Goethe supported the legal rights of individual Jews, but points out that the duchy had a financial interest in supporting the Jews in question and that both cases involved the upholding of existing laws rather than the expansion of Jewish civil rights (148).

28. From Goethe's letter to Lavater, July 29, 1782 (FA 2.2: 436).

29. Riemer, *Mitteilungen*, 279. Ascribed to Goethe by Riemer and dated August 1, 1807.

30. Horst Lange, "Isaac, Iphigeneia, Christ: Human Sacrifice and the Semiotics of Divine Intentions in Goethe," *Publications of the English Goethe Society* 78, no. 3 (2009): 166–88, see esp. 184–88.

31. Quoted in Lange, "Isaac," 185, 184.

32. See Helmut Thielicke, *Goethe und das Christentum* (Munich: Piper, 1982). Thielicke, a theologian, observes many of the same areas of criticism in Goethe's conception of Christianity: the critique of religious passivity and of the dogmatic conception of the afterlife (45–50); the eschewal of a personal God and of an absolutist conception of Christ (59–66); as well as the rejection of a faith in miracles and of an orthodox approach to the Bible (66–72).

33. In her book on idolatry in Franz Rosenzweig's thought, Leora Batnitzky sees a source for Rosenzweig's conception in Moses Mendelssohn's essay "Jerusalem" (1783). According to Batnitzky, the Jewish ceremonial law is a prime example of anti-idolatrous representation for Mendelssohn because "it embodies the recognition of the need for continued interpretation and reinterpretation." Batnitzky, *Idolatry and Representation: The Philosophy of Franz Rosenzweig Reconsidered* (Princeton, N.J.: Princeton University Press, 2000), 33.

34. Immanuel Kant, *Critique of Judgement*, trans. James Creed Meredith (Oxford: Oxford University Press, 2007), 104.

35. A nascent notion of a Jewish *Kulturnation* can be seen, for example, in a review in 1771, where Goethe points to Jewish nationhood and patriotism as an example of the principle that a nation is constituted by its circumstances rather than its soil (FA 1.18: 28).

36. Goethe describes his admiration for the Jews as the producers of the Hebrew Bible in a conversation with Simon von Laemel in May 1812. Johann Wolfgang von Goethe, *Goethes Gespräche*, 10 vols. (Leipzig: F. W. v. Biedermann, 1889–96), 8: 315. Goethe describes the dilemmas of writing for an underdeveloped culture in his essay "Literarischer Sansculottismus" (FA 1.18: 319–24).

37. Andrew Cusack, *The Wanderer in Nineteenth-Century German Literature: Intellectual History and Cultural Criticism* (Rochester, N.Y.: Camden House, 2008). See esp. 222 and 230.

38. Ibid., 3, 1.

39. Elon, "Pity," 30.

40. Edward H. Flannery traces this notion of Jews as a "witness-people" back to Augustine. Flannery, *The Anguish of the Jews: Twenty-Three Centuries of Antisemitism*, rev. ed. (New York: Paulist, 1985), 52–53. See also James Hanson, "The Endangered and Reaffirmed Promises of God: A Fruitful Framework for Biblical Theology," *Biblical Theology Bulletin* 30, no. 3 (Fall 2000): 93.

41. Flannery, *Anguish*, 53. See also 307n. (Flannery refers to Augustine's commentary on Psalm 50, which seems to be an error. A comparison to Cain appears in his commentary to Psalm 40).

42. George K. Anderson, *The Legend of the Wandering Jew* (Providence, R.I.: Brown University Press, 1965), 46.

43. The connection was, for example, taken for granted by Goethe's contemporary, Karl Friedrich Göschel. See Göschel, *Ueber Göthe's Faust und dessen Fortsetzung: Nebst einem Anhange von dem ewigen Juden* (Leipzig: Hartmann, 1824).

44. See also Riemer, *Mittheilungen*, 208.

45. Quoted in Robert Alter, *The World of Biblical Literature* (New York: Basic Books, 1992), 48.

46. Friedrich Nietzsche, *Daybreak: Thoughts on the Prejudices of Morality*, trans. R. J. Hollingdale (Cambridge, Eng.: Cambridge University Press, 1982), 84.

47. Compare Aaron Gale on the Gospel of Matthew: "Matthew's Jesus is not only depicted as the 'new Moses,' who interprets Torah for the people of Israel, but he is also Moses' superior." Aaron Gale, "The Gospel According to Matthew," in *The Jewish Annotated New Testament*, ed. Amy-Jill Levine and Marc Zvi Brettler (Oxford: Oxford University Press, 2011), 2.

48. Erich Auerbach, *Scenes from the Drama of European Literature*, Theory and History of Literature (Minneapolis: University of Minnesota Press, 1984), 50.

49. Ibid., 50–51.

50. Ibid., 61.

51. See, for example, Albrecht Schöne, *Vom Betreten des Rasens: Siebzehn Reden über Literatur*, ed. Ulrich Joost, Jürgen Stenzel, and Ernst Peter Wieckenberg (Munich: Beck, 2005), 52–54. See also Jeffrey Librett, *The Rhetoric of Cultural Dialogue: Jews and Germans from Moses Mendelssohn to Richard Wagner and Beyond* (Stanford, Calif.: Stanford University Press, 2000).

52. Wüthrich mentions Michelangelo as one of Merian's artistic models. Lucas Heinrich Wüthrich, *Matthaeus Merian d. Ä, Eine Biographie* (Hamburg: Hoffmann und Campe, 2007), 142.

53. According to Lang, the source of this tradition is Martin Schubart's 1896 book about Thoranc, but the claim itself is unreliable. Bernhard Lang, *Joseph in Egypt: A Cultural Icon from Grotius to Goethe* (New Haven, Conn.: Yale University Press, 2009), 104–5. The historical fact of the matter—whether or not the visage of the young Wolfgang is actually reflected in the painting—may not be provable, but the likelihood of the boy's identification with the image remains strong. At age ten, he would have been about the same age as the boy Joseph in the painting and, by his own account, he was very invested in the production of the paintings. In his autobiography, Goethe strongly alludes to his own youthful identification with the figure of Joseph (FA 1.14: 155).

54. Lang suggests that Trautmann drew from illustrated bibles in his depiction of Joseph, and yet oddly doesn't suggest Merian as a possible source. Lang, "Joseph," 102.

55. Matthäus Merian, *Iconum Biblicarum* (Wenatchee, Wash.: AVB, 1981), 78. Merian's biblical engravings were published in four parts from 1625 to 1630 before they were published with the biblical text. About the history of the images, see Wüthrich, *Merian*, 132–36.

56. "Unser Osterlamb ist Christus für uns Geopffert." Merian, "Iconum," 89.

57. The text on the page facing the image makes explicit the comparison of the death of Simon to the crucifixion of Christ, names another child allegedly murdered by Jews, and comments generally on the threat and burden Jews represent to Christians. Johann Ludwig Gottfried, *Johann Ludwig Gottfrieds Historische Chronick oder Beschreibung der Merckwürdigsten Geschichte, So sich von Anfang der Welt bis auf den heutigen Tag zugetragen*, 3 vols. (Frankfurt am Main: Hutter, 1743–59), 1: 688.

58. Deutschländer, in his 1923 study, finds Hebrew Bible themes and motifs in nearly every significant work by Goethe with the possible exceptions of Clavigo, Tasso, and Reineke Fuchs. Leo Deutschländer, *Goethe und das Alte Testament* (Frankfurt am Main: Omonuth-Verlag, 1923). A late-nineteenth-century survey of biblical allusions in Goethe's work supports, if modestly, a preference for the Hebrew Bible. Gerhard Sauder, "Aufklärerische Bibelkritik und Bibelrezeption in Goethes Werk," *Goethe-Jahrbuch* 118 (2001): 122.

59. From an unpublished, relatively recently discovered manuscript composed between 1764 and 1769, "Über die ersten Urkunden des Menschlichen Geschlechts: Einige Anmerkungen." Because it is not included in Suphan's otherwise more comprehensive edition of Herder's works, I cite the DKV edition here.

60. Jonathan Sheehan, *The Enlightenment Bible: Translation, Scholarship, Culture* (Princeton, N.J.: Princeton University Press, 2005), 152, 178.

61. Robert Alter also warns against the pitfalls of projecting modern aesthetic values onto these ancient texts. Robert Alter, *The Art of Biblical Narrative* (New York: Basic Books, 1981), 131. I try here to focus upon the historical reception of the Hebrew Bible as modern rather than assuming its intrinsic modernity.

62. Erich Auerbach, *Mimesis: The Representation of Reality in Western Literature*, trans. Willard R. Trask (Princeton, N.J.: Princeton University Press, 1974), 20.

63. Gabriel Josipovici, "The Epistle to the Hebrews and the Catholic Epistles," in *The Literary Guide to the Bible*, ed. Robert Alter and Frank Kermode (Cambridge, Mass.: Belknap/Harvard University Press, 1987), 520.

64. Alter, *World*, 22.

65. John Updike, "The Great I Am: Robert Alter's new translation of the Pentateuch," *The New Yorker*, November 1, 2004: http://www.newyorker.com/archive/2004/11/01/041101crbo_books.

66. Franz Kafka, *Tagebücher 1910–1923* (Frankfurt am Main: Fischer, 1951), 545.

67. Clark S. Muenzer, "Das Buch Hiob und Goethes Naturbegriff," in *Goethe und die Bibel*, ed. Johannes Anderegg and Edith Anna Kunz (Stuttgart: Deutsche Bibelgesellschaft, 2005), 161–71.

68. Johann Gottfried Eichhorn, *Einleitung in das Alte Testament*, 3 vols., 2nd ed. (Leipzig: Weidmann, 1787), 2: 300–303.

69. J. G. Eichhorn, *Einleitung in das Neue Testament*, 5 vols., 3rd ed. (Leipzig: Weidmannische Buchhandlung, 1804), 1: vii.

70. Alter, 7, 20.

71. Marc Zvi Brettler, "Preface" in *The Jewish Study Bible: Tanakh Translation*, ed. Adele Berlin, Marc Zvi Brettler, and Michael Fishbane (Oxford: Oxford University Press, 2004), 7.

72. Riemer, *Mitteilungen*, 359.

73. See Robert Alter, *The Five Books of Moses: A Translation with Commentary* (New York: Norton, 2004), 301–2.

74. Martin Buber, "The Burning Bush (Exodus 3)," in *Exodus*, ed. Harold Bloom, *Modern Critical Interpretations* (New York: Chelsea House, 1987), 33. Buber nonetheless emphasizes the continuity between the two representations of the divine.

75. Compare Horst Lange: "Goethe . . . goes a long way toward reading at least the Pentateuch as a genuinely Jewish document." Lange, "Reconstructing a Nation's Birth: Monotheism, Nationalism, and Violence in Goethe's Reading of the Pentateuch," *Colloquia Germanica* 33, no. 2 (2000): 118n.

76. Sheehan, *Enlightenment Bible*, 180.

77. Both the "Jewish sermon" and the "Purim play" suggest an interest in Jewish culture and practices but also have a derisive bent. A possible source or inspiration for both is Johann Jacob Schudt's *Jüdische Merckwürdigkeiten*, a monumental anti-Jewish screed, which was nevertheless an important eighteenth-century source on Jewish history, religion, and customs and was owned by Goethe's father. See Stenzel and Höher, "Verschrobenheit," 12; and Yaacov Deutsch, "Johann Jacob Schudt—Der erste Ethnograph der jüdischen Gemeinde in Frankfurt am Main," in *Die Frankfurter Judengasse: Jüdisches Leben in der frühen Neuzeit*, ed. Fritz Backhaus (Frankfurt am Main: Societäts-Verlag, 2006), 67. In his review of Behr's "Poems by a Polish Jew," Goethe's expectation of intercultural encounter underlies his disappointment in a poet he finds as conventional as any Christian: "so it seems to us poorly done to make a fuss about his Jewishness" (*so ist es, deucht uns, übel getan, mit seiner Judenschaft ein Aufsehn zu machen*) (FA 1.18: 50).

Chapter 1

1. Augustine, *Confessions*, trans. R. S. Pine-Coffin (New York: Penguin, 1982), 53.

2. Ibid., 165.

3. David Hume, *Dialogues concerning Natural Religion and Other Writings*, ed. Dorothy Coleman (Cambridge, Eng.: Cambridge University Press, 2007), 74.

4. Augustine, *Confessions*, 2.

5. Ibid., 28.

6. Ibid., 47.

7. Peter L. Berger, *The Sacred Canopy: Elements of a Sociological Theory of Religion* (New York: Anchor, 1990), 53.

8. Ibid., 53.

9. Susan Neiman, *Evil in Modern Thought: An Alternative History of Philosophy* (Princeton, N.J.: Princeton University Press, 2002), 7.

10. Ibid., 7–8.

11. Paul Ricoeur, "Evil," in *Encyclopedia of Religion*, ed. Mircea Eliade, 16 vols. in 8 (New York: Simon and Schuster Macmillan, 1995), 5: 199.

12. Georges Gusdorf, "Conditions and Limits of Autobiography," trans. James Olney, in *Autobiography: Essays Theoretical and Critical*, ed. James Olney (Princeton, N.J.: Princeton University Press, 1980), 39. Originally published in 1956, Gusdorf's essay is dated in many respects, but aptly characterizes the religious roots of the genre.

13. Ibid., 33.

14. "The Romantic era, in its exaltation of genius, reintroduced the taste for autobiography." Ibid., 34.

15. Cusack, *Wanderer*, 28.

16. Jean-Jacques Rousseau, *Confessions*, trans. Angela Scholar (Oxford: Oxford University Press, 2000), 20.

17. Ricoeur, "Evil," 5: 203.

18. He also refers in a passage in book 2 to his doubts about God's benevolence at this time (FA 1.14: 55).

19. Later Goethe moderates his views, claiming to have reconciled himself again with "God or the gods" after having had the experience that there was much good to balance the bad. But this singular or plural conception is still a long way from that of a providential Christian God (FA 1.14: 178).

20. He had studied the *images* in the Merian Bible at an earlier age (FA 1.14: 41).

21. Luz-Maria Linder, *Goethes Bibelrezeption: Hermeneutische Reflexion, fiktionale Darstellung, historisch-kritische Bearbeitung* (Frankfurt: Lang, 1998), 98–99.

22. Baruch Spinoza, *Complete Works*, ed. Michael Morgan, trans. Samuel Shirley et al. (Indianapolis, Ind.: Hackett, 2002), 409. See T. M. Rudavsky, "Galileo and Spinoza: Heroes, Heretics, and Hermeneutics," *Journal of the History of Ideas* 62, no. 4 (2001): 611–31.

23. Nicolai places the Hebrew lessons between June 1762 and mid-1763. Goethe turned thirteen in August 1762. Heinz Nicolai, *Zeittafel zu Goethes Leben und Werk* (Munich: Beck, 1977), 8.

24. Gabriel Josipovici, "An Open Book: How the Bible Places Realism above Consolation," *Times Literary Supplement*, February 24, 2006, 13. Jon D. Levenson comments that God's promise to bless Abraham and make of him a great nation comes "like a bolt from the blue, an act of God's grace alone; no indication has been given as to why or even whether Abram merits them." Jon D. Levenson, "Genesis Introduction and Annotations," in Berlin, Brettler, and Fishbane, eds., *Jewish Study Bible*, 30.

25. FA 1. 14: 144. See Eichhorn, *Einleitung*, 2nd ed., 3: 301. The relevant biblical passage is Gen. 11:1–9.

26. I have altered this translation, adding "seem to" in the second sentence in order to match the verb "scheinen" in the original.

27. "Hail to the unknown / Loftier beings / Our minds prefigure! / Let man be like them: His example teach us / To believe those" (*Heil den unbekannten /*

Höhern Wesen, / Die wir ahnen! / Ihnen gleiche der Mensch! / Sein Beispiel lehr uns / Jene glauben) (*CW* 1: 79; FA 1.1: 333).

28. Emphasis in original. Moses Mendelssohn, *Gesammelte Schriften: Jubiläumsausgabe*, ed. Alexander Altmann, 25 vols. (Bad Cannstatt: Frommann-Holzboog, 1971–), 8.2: 166.

29. Wilhelm Friedrich Hezel, *Biblisches Real-Lexikon über biblische und die Bibel erläuternde alte Geschichte . . .*, 3 vols. (Leipzig: Weygandsche Buchhandlung, 1783), 1: 8.

30. Mendelssohn, *Schriften*, 8.2: 166.

31. Martin Buber, *Two Types of Faith: A Study of the Interpenetration of Judaism and Christianity*, trans. Norman P. Goldhawk (New York: Harper and Row, 1961), 170. Compare Jon D. Levenson's gloss on Gen. 15:6 in Berlin, Brettler, and Fishbane, *Jewish Study Bible*, 35. See also Goethe's discussion of faith elsewhere in his autobiography: FA 1.14: 668.

32. Goethe's own identification with this experience is highlighted in book 8 where he writes, "the truth of that old saying, 'Increase of knowledge is increase of disquiet' had hit me with full force" (*die Wahrheit jenes alten Worts, Zuwachs an Kenntnis ist Zuwachs an Unruhe, hatte mich mit ganzer Gewalt getroffen*) (*CW* 4: 243–44; FA 1.14: 354).

33. Goethe neglects to mention that Laban had made a dishonest attempt to withhold the part of the flock due to Jacob (Gen. 30:35–36)

34. Usually the linguistic mysticism ascribed to Kabbalah (rather than this cosmic narrative) is seen as its chief contribution to the poetics of this era. See the references in Detlef Kremer, "Kabbalistische Signaturen: Sprachmagie als Brennpunkt romantischer Imagination bei E.T.A. Hoffmann und Achim von Arnim," in *Kabbalah und die Literatur der Romantik: Zwischen Magie und Trope*, ed. Eveline Goodman-Thau, Gert Mattenklott, and Christoph Schulte (Tübingen: Niemeyer, 1999), 201n.

35. Erich Trunz's commentary, otherwise useful on Goethe's esoteric sources, gives short shrift to Kabbalah. He mentions Kabbalah as a source for Goethe's notion of contraction and expansion, but cites only Buhle's chapter on "kabbalistische Philosophie," specifically a passage on the *Christian* Kabbalah of Robert Fludd. Erich Trunz, commentary to *Goethes Werke*, by Johann Wolfgang von Goethe, 14 vols. (Munich: Beck, 1981), 9: 752, see also 759. Zimmermann places greater emphasis on the contribution of Kabbalah to Goethe's conception of contraction, exploring in particular the link through Oetinger. Zimmermann mentions Zimzum by name, but never its author, Luria. Rolf Christian Zimmermann, *Das Weltbild des jungen Goethe*, 2 vols. (Munich: Fink, 1969–1979), 1: 201–2.

36. Quoted in Gershom Scholem, "Die Wachtersche Kontroverse über den Spinozismus und ihre Folgen," in *Spinoza in der Frühzeit seiner religiösen Wirkung*, ed. Karlfield Gründer and Wilhelm Schmidt-Biggemann (Heidelberg: Lambert Schneider, 1984), 21.

37. Compare Christoph Schulte, who argues that the Lurianic conception of Zimzum is one of the very few elements in the wild theosophical mix in this era that remained distinctly Jewish. Christoph Schulte, "Zimzum bei Schelling," in *Kabbala und Romantik*, ed. Eveline Goodman-Thau, Gert Mattenklott, and Christoph Schulte (Tübingen: Niemeyer, 1994), 104.

38. Otto Betz, "Friedrich Christoph Oetinger und die Kabbala," in *Friedrich Christoph Oetinger*, ed. Gerhard Karl Schäfer and Martin Schmidt, 3 vols., *Texte zur Geschichte des Pietismus Abt.* 7 (Berlin: de Gruyter, 1999), 3.2: 6.

39. See Konrad Burdach, "Faust und Moses," pts. 1–3, *Sitzungsberichte der Preussischen Akademie der Wissenschaften: Philosophisch-Historische Klasse* nos. 23, 35, 38 (1912): 3: 739; and Franz Götting,"Die Bibliothek von Goethes Vater," *Nassauische Annalen* 24 (1953): 39.

40. Johann Gottlieb Buhle, *Geschichte der neuern Philosophie seit der Epoche der Wiederherstellung der Wissenschaften*, in Aetas Kantiana, 314 vols. (Brussels: Culture et civilisation, 1968–81), 52: 1–6. Originally published 1800–1805.

41. Trunz, *Goethes Werke*, 9: 752.

42. "Cabbalisten," in *Deutsche Encyclopädie oder Allgemeines Real-Wörterbuch aller Künste und Wissenschaften von einer Gesellschaft Gelehrten*, 23 vols. (Frankfurt am Main: 1778–1807), 4: 707–12.

43. Johann Georg Wachter, *Der Spinozismus im Judenthumb, oder, die von dem heutigen Judenthumb und dessen Geheimen Kabbala, vergötterte Welt . . .* (Amsterdam: Wolthers, 1699).

44. On the controversy surrounding Wachter and the relationship, whether real or imagined, of Spinoza to Kabbalah, see Gershom Scholem, introduction to *Das Buch Scha'ar Haschamajim oder Pforte des Himmels . . .*, by Abraham Cohen Herrera, trans. Friedrich Häußermann (Frankfurt: Suhrkamp, 1974), esp. 47–55; Scholem, "Wachtersche Kontroverse"; Richard Popkin, "Spinoza, Neoplatonic Kabbalist?" in *Neoplatonism and Jewish Thought*, ed. Lenn E. Goodman (Albany, N.Y.: SUNY Press, 1992), 387–409; and Rebecca Goldstein, *Betraying Spinoza: The Renegade Jew Who Gave Us Modernity* (New York: Schocken, 2006).

45. Solomon Maimon, *Salomon Maimons Lebensgeschichte: Von ihm selbst geschrieben und herausgegeben von Karl Philipp Moritz*, ed. Zwi Batscha (Frankfurt: Insel, 1984), 84; Friedrich Heinrich Jacobi, *Ueber die Lehre des Spinoza in Briefen an den Herrn Moses Mendelssohn*, in Aetas Kantiana, 116: 33–34; Jacob Brucker, *Kurtze Fragen aus der philosophischen Historie*, 7 vols. (Ulm, 1731–37), 4: 782n, 784, 805n, 917, 950; Dietrich Tiedemann, *Geist der spekulativen Philosophie*, in Aetas Kantiana, 274.6: 234; "Cabbalisten" in *Deutsche Encyclopädie*, 4: 707, 709. Mendelssohn's *Morgenstunden* is cited in Scholem, *Das Buch Scha'ar*, 56.

46. Gabriela Schlick, "Was Johann Wolfgang Goethe hätte sehen können . . . Die Judengasse in Frankfurt am Main," in Weber, ed., *Goethes Begegnung mit Juden*, 64.

47. Paul Arnsberg, *Die Geschichte der Frankfurter Juden seit der Französischen Revolution*, 3 vols. (Darmstadt: Eduard Roether, 1983), 3: 15–17; Rachel Elior, "R. Nathan Adler and the Frankfurt Pietists," in *Jüdische Kultur in Frankfurt am Main von den Anfängen bis zur Gegenwart*, ed. Karl E. Grözinger (Wiesbaden: Harrassowitz, 1997), 135–41.

48. R. Abraham Cohen Irira, "Porta Caelorum," in *Kabbala Denudata*, trans. and ed. Knorr von Rosenroth, 2 vols. (Sulzbach, 1677–84, repr. Hildesheim: Georg Olms, 1974), non-continuous pagination, 1: 51.

49. Gershom Scholem, *Major Trends in Jewish Mysticism* (New York: Schocken, 1995), 260.

50. R. Abraham Cohen Irira, in Knorr, ed., *Kabbala Denudata* 1: 70–71. Thanks to Rienk Vermij for help with translation from the Latin.

51. Brucker, *Kurtze Fragen*, 4: 553n.

52. Jacobi, *Ueber die Lehre des Spinoza*, 116: 33–34.

53. Buhle, *Geschichte der neuern Philosophie*, 52.2: 378.

54. Buhle criticizes this view as grounded in human observation of the workings of light and argues that the relationship of God to the world should be viewed as a transcendent matter, of which a theoretical, objective knowledge is impossible. Buhle, *Geschichte der neuern Philosophie*, 52.2: 381.

55. Scholem, *Major Trends*, 263.

56. Noted for example by Brucker, *Kurtze Fragen*, 4: 815.

57. Johann Jacob Brucker, *The History of Philosophy from the Earliest Periods: Drawn Up from Brucker's Historia Critica Philosophiae by William Enfield*, 2 vols. (Bristol: Thoemmes, 2000), 2: 416; Buhle too describes the inhabitants of this world as "malicious and material spirits" (*Geschichte der neuern Philosophie*, 2: 376).

58. Brucker, *Kurtze Fragen*, 4: 860.

59. Allison P. Coudert, *Impact of the Kabbalah in the Seventeenth Century: The Life and Thought of Francis Mercury van Helmont (1614–1698)* (Leiden: Brill, 1999), 340. According to Coudert, after its revival in the Renaissance, Pelagianism had a great impact on the development of a scientific and Enlightenment mentality. It was transmitted especially in kabbalistic, alchemical, Neoplatonic, and hermetic sources. Coudert, *Impact of the Kabbalah*, 339.

60. See Herrera, *Pforte des Himmels*, esp. 246–70.

61. Scholem, *Major Trends*, 246.

62. Brucker, *Kurtze Fragen*, 4: 889.

63. See Astrida Tantillo, *The Will to Create: Goethe's Philosophy of Nature* (Pittsburgh, Penn.: University of Pittsburgh Press, 2002), 20–27.

64. Brucker, *Kurtze Fragen*, 4: 555n.

65. Both Hartung ("Goethe und die Juden," 409), and Gidion ("Goethe und die Juden," 545) conclude that Goethe's conception for his Wandering Jew epic was free of the anti-Jewish tendencies contained in the original legend—an assessment that must be based more on the extant fragment than on the description in *Poetry and Truth*.

66. See, for example, Martin Bollacher, *Der junge Goethe und Spinoza: Studien zur Geschichte des Spinozimus in der Epoche des Sturms und Drangs* (Tübingen: Niemeyer, 1969), 62–65; Carsten Schapkow, *"Die Freiheit zu philosophieren": Jüdische Identität in der Moderne im Spiegel der Rezeption Baruch de Spinozas in der deutschsprachigen Literatur* (Bielefeld: Aisthesis Verlag, 2001), 82.

67. See, for example, Oellers, "Goethe und Schiller," 122. Bell emphasizes Goethe's connection of Spinoza with Christianity: David Bell, *Spinoza in Germany from 1670 to the Age of Goethe* (Leeds: Institute of Germanic Studies, 1984), 150. While Goethe did indeed describe Spinoza to Jacobi as "christianissimum" in a letter (FA 2.2: 583), one has to consider the context and the audience, that is, a defense of Spinoza to his fideistic Christian friend.

68. Goethe's version of Spinoza must be taken on its own terms. He doubts his own grasp of Spinoza's philosophy (FA 1.14: 680), and, as Lange has recently

analyzed, with good reason: Horst Lange, "Goethe and Spinoza: A Reconsideration," *Goethe Yearbook* 18 (2011): 11–33.

69. In the original, the words do not match as precisely: "Breite und Freiheit," "grosse und freie Aussicht" (FA 1.14: 150, 681).

70. There are precedents in the Hebrew Bible for the description of suffering, bitterness, and punishment as a cup (*Kelch*) that one must drink. See, for example, Isa. 51:17, 22. But the notion of a cup willingly drunk as a form of self-sacrifice is clearly a reference to these famous Gospel passages.

71. Spinoza defines providence as "nothing else than the *striving* which we find in the whole of Nature and its individual things to maintain and preserve their own existence" (Spinoza, *Works*, 53). This notion of providence has no moral content.

72. His appeal to the classical concept of the daemonic in the final book seems to reintroduce a personal, if not necessarily conscious or beneficent, principle guiding individual experience.

73. Spinoza, *Works*, 378.

74. See Scholem on the significant discrepancies between Wachter's source and Spinoza's regarding the purported pantheism of Lurianic Kabbalah. Wachter relied on a Latin translation of Herrera's Spanish book; Spinoza would have known a Hebrew translation of the same work. Scholem, "Wachtersche Kontroverse," 21.

75. Herrera's essay, as published in *Kabbala Denudata*, would have been the clearest source on the breaking of the vessels: see Cohen de Herrera, *Pforte des Himmels*, 254–59. Zimmermann points out that Goethe could have read about the "Kelipot," the broken shards or shells in Fabricius's *Bibliographia antiquaria*, which he quotes in his youthful notes (Zimmermann, *Weltbild des jungen Goethes*, 201). References to the "Kelipot" also exist in Brucker, who refers to them as "Schalen" (Brucker, *Kurtze Fragen*, 4: 874–76). See also Oetinger, 1:1: 134.

76. Cohen de Herrera, *Pforte des Himmels*, 241, 242.

77. Scholem, *Major Trends*, 268.

78. Ibid., 268–73.

79. The presumed source for Goethe's account is Bettina von Arnim's letter to Goethe of November 12, 1810, in which she recounts the story, as told to her by Goethe's mother. Bettina's version lacks the mythic character and language of a fall. Goethe's mother also figures more prominently in Bettina's reported account than in Goethe's. Bettina von Arnim, *Bettinas Briefwechsel mit Goethe*, ed. Reinhold Steig (Leipzig: Insel, 1922), 191.

Chapter 2

1. Elsewhere Herder suggests Samuel or a psalmist edited the Pentateuch (*SW* 32: 206).

2. See *CW* 3: 242n7.

3. "It marks the final critical stage in the extension of the Gospel and the expansion of the church." C. K. Barrett, *A Critical and Exegetical Commentary on the Acts of the Apostles*, 2 vols., International Critical Commentary, ed. J. A. Emerton, C. E. B. Cranfield, and G. N. Stanton (Edinburgh: T & T Clark, 1994), 1: 491.

4. Antoine Guenée, *Letters of Certain Jews to Monsieur Voltaire Containing an Apology for Their Own People and for the Old Testament*, trans. Philip Lefanu

(Philadelphia, 1795), 21, https://archive.org/stream/lettersofcertain00gu#page/n3/mode/2up. web.

5. Ibid., 38

6. Ibid., 39.

7. See Robert W. Wall, "The Acts of the Apostles: Introduction, Commentary, and Reflections," in *The New Interpreters Bible*, 12 vols. (Nashville, Tenn.: Abingdon, 2002), 10: 54.

8. Augustine, *The Works of St. Augustine*, ed. Boniface Ramsey, 50 vols. (Hyde Park, N.Y.: New City, 1990–), 1.23: 168, http://www.nlx.com/collections/148; Martin Luther, *Luther's Works*, ed. Jaroslav Pelikan and Helmut T. Lehmann, 55 vols. (Philadelphia: Muhlenberg, 1960), 35: 161; Johann Gottfried Herder, "Von der Gabe der Sprachen am ersten christlichen Pfingstfest," *SW* 19: 1–59.

9. Herder also employs the tree image to critique later Hebrew poetry, which he describes as a tree that suffocated in the temple dome (*SW* 11: 457).

10. Bernard Levinson, "Goethe's Analysis of Exodus 34 and Its Influence on Wellhausen: The *Pfropfung* of the Documentary Hypothesis," *Zeitschrift für die Alttestamentliche Wissenschaft* 114 (2002): 221.

11. Jeffrey H. Tigay, "Exodus: Introduction and Annotations," in Berlin, Brettler, and Fishbane, *Jewish Study Bible*, 145.

12. As Bernard Levinson has discussed, Goethe's claim that Exodus 34 is the original covenant has had long legs within pentateuchal criticism (Levinson, "Goethe's Anaysis," 220).

13. Karl Eibl, Fotis Jannidis, and Marianne Willems, eds., *Der junge Goethe in seiner Zeit*, by Johann Wolfgang von Goethe, 2 vols. and CD ROM (Frankfurt: Insel, 1998), 390; FA 1.18: 1116; and Willy Schottroff, "Goethe als Bibelwissenschaftler," in *Allerhand Goethe: Seine wissenschaftliche Sendung aus Anlaß des 150. Todestages und des 50. Namentages der Johann Wolfgang Goethe–Universität in Frankfurt am Main*, ed. Dieter Kimpel and Jörg Pompetzki (Frankfurt: Lang, 1985), 117–18.

14. See Bollacher, *Goethe und Spinoza*, 61.

15. Spinoza, *Complete Works*, 430–31.

16. Ibid., 440.

17. Tillmann misses this distinction between particular and individual and thus passes over Goethe's conspicuous attack against Judaism. Thomas Tillmann, "Vom Sprechen zum Lallen: Glossolalie und Prophetie in Goethes 'Zwo wichtige bisher unerörterte biblische Fragen,'" in *Goethe und die Bibel*, ed. Anderegg and Kunz, 31.

18. He uses the word "allgemein" to mean both general and universal.

19. The longer passage quotes both Matt. 13:9 and John 3:8. A third New Testament allusion from a parable in Luke, "You have Moses and the Prophets" (*Ihr habt Mosen und die Propheten*) (Luke 16:29) has, despite the apparent attribution of authority to the Hebrew scriptures, the same esoteric meaning in Goethe's context: the individual has all he needs to grasp the spiritual message, but some fail to do so, even, as the Luke passage continues in an oblique reference to Christ, if someone comes back from the dead to deliver it (Luke 16:31).

20. Goethe diverges from Luther's translation of this passage. Where Goethe has "mit der tiefen Sprache," Luther has "mit Zungen."

21. See Eibl, Jannidis, Willems, eds., *Der junge Goethe*, 2: 396.

22. I will not distinguish between the 1797 body of the essay and the introductory six paragraphs contributed in 1812 because the 1812 paragraphs seem very much in line with Goethe's 1797 agenda. Furthermore, according to Wilhelm Solms, the 1812 paragraphs may have been a reworking of earlier papers dating back to 1771–72. Wilhelm Solms, *Goethes Vorarbeiten um Divan*, Münchner Germanistische Beiträge (Munich: Fink, 1977), 223–24.

23. Goethe's description of *Hermann and Dorothea* as "my idyllic-epic poem" (*mein idyllisch-episches Gedicht*) (FA 2.4: 370) has led to many critical discussions of the relationship between idyll and epic in this work. See for example T. M. Holmes, who sees an "interdependence" of the two genres, "Goethe's Hermann und Dorothea: The Dissolution of the Embattled Idyll," *Modern Language Review* 82, no. 1 (January 1987): 110; or Günter Niggl, who views the poem as outgrowing the idyll to become an epic, *Studien zur Literatur der Goethezeit* (Berlin: Duncker & Humblot, 2001), 109. Klaus Detlef-Müller writes of an "Aufhebung der Idylle zum Epos" in "Den Krieg wegschreiben: *Hermann und Dorothea* und *die Unterhaltungen deutscher Ausgewanderten*," in *Ironische Propheten: Sprachbewußtsein und Humanität in der Literatur von Herder bis Heine*, ed. Markus Heilman and Birgit Wägenbaur (Tübingen: Gunter Narr, 2001), 91. I focus here on Goethe's epic framework, as reflected in the use of Exodus material, but I believe he draws on Genesis for idyllic elements. Thus the interaction between Genesis and Exodus motifs corresponds to some extent to the play of epic and idyllic genres.

24. Others have noted in passing Goethe's treatment of Exodus as an epic. Luz-María Linder notes the epic issue of plot retardation in the "Israel" essay and observes the analogy between Goethe's handling of the *Odyssey* and the Old Testament: *Goethes Bibelrezeption: Hermeneutische Reflexion, fiktionale Darstellung, historisch-kritische Bearbeitung*, Europäische Hochschulschriften Reihe I, Deutsche Sprache und Literatur (Frankfurt am Main: Lang, 1998), 174. Frank Zipfel briefly considers Moses's character in the "Israel" essay in relationship to Homeric heroes in "Überlegungen zu Goethes Moses-Bild in Israel in der Wüste," in Anderegg and Kunz, *Goethe und die Bibel*, 213. As for the literature on *Hermann and Dorothea*, the biblical subtext has typically played a tangential role, usually in the context of Goethe's other source materials, and not in relationship to the work's character as a national epic.

25. FA 2.4: 216; Friedrich Schiller, *Schillers Werke: Nationalausgabe*, ed. Julius Petersen et al., 42 vols. (Weimar: H. Böhlaus Nachfolger, 1943–), 28: 269.

26. According to a letter to Meyer, the epic is set in August 1796 (FA 2.4: 264).

27. See Goethe's letter to Schiller of December 7, 1796 (FA 2.4: 268).

28. Alluding to F. A. Wolf's theory that the *Iliad* and the *Odyssey* were shaped by a later guild of poets, the Homeridae, Goethe imagines himself as the last of this epic guild, "Doch Homeride zu sein, auch nur als letzter, ist schön" (FA 1.1: 623).

29. For example, in his *Critical Poetics* (1740) the Swiss critic J. J. Breitinger describes epic as a morally edifying representation of a great deed of *national* import. Josef Schmidt, ed., *Erläuterungen und Dokumente: Johann Wolfgang Goethe: "Hermann und Dorothea"* (Stuttgart: Reclam, 1970), 42.

30. In his Latin graduation address from Schulpforta. Wolf-Daniel Hartwich, *Die Sendung Moses: Von der Aufklarung bis Thomas Mann* (Munich: Fink, 1997), 29.

31. This quotation stems from an unpublished sketch, but see also the emphasis on the epic character of the Exodus story in "Vom Geist der hebräischen Poesie," which Goethe checked out of the ducal library in April 1797 (*SW* 11: 454; 12: 55–56); Werner Deetjen, ed. *Goethe als Benutzer der Weimarer Bibliothek: Ein Verzeichnis der von ihm entliehenen Werke* (Weimar: Böhlaus, 1931), 13.

32. Goethe also alludes to Wolf's theories in his elegy, "Hermann and Dorothea." On the closeness between the critical methodologies of Wolf and Eichhorn, see Anthony Grafton, Glenn W. Most, and James E. G. Zetzel, introduction to *Prolegomena to Homer*, by F. A. Wolf (Princeton, N.J.: Princeton University Press, 1985). On the historicism that provides the context for views of both the Bible and Homer see Sheehan, *Enlightenment Bible*, 211–13.

33. In the essay "Über epische und dramatische Dichtung," Schiller and Goethe will see retarding motifs as appropriate for both epic and drama (FA 1.18: 446).

34. Goethe ultimately wavers on the question of whether this work contains retarding motifs. Compare two letters: FA 2.4: 321, 466.

35. For a history of the reception of this work, see Peter Morgan, *The Critical Idyll: Traditional Values and the French Revolution in Goethe's "Hermann und Dorothea"* (Columbia S.C.: Camden House, 1991), 140–62; and Paul Michael Lützeler, *Geschichte in der Literatur: Studien zu Werken von Lessing bis Hebbel* (Munich: Piper, 1987), 86–96.

36. "Many recent critics sense a tension between idyllic form and ironic-parodic tone, and a weakness in the character of Hermann himself as the spokesman for a resurgent Germany." Peter Morgan, *The Critical Idyll: Traditional Values and the French Revolution in Goethe's "Hermann und Dorothea"* (Columbia, S.C.: Camden House, 1991), 156.

37. The judges, after whom the Book of Judges is named, rule after the death of Joshua and before the kingship of Saul (see FA 1.8: 1207).

38. I have altered the translation of the last clause, "so drängen sich alle Geschichten," replacing David Luke's "so thick and fast have events come," to better capture the sense of a general pronouncement, in the present tense, concerning the broader applicability of their experiences.

39. Gerhard Kaiser sees in the subsequent two lines an allusion to the New Testament Pentecost story. Kaiser, *Goethe—Nähe durch Abstand: Vorträge und Studien* (Jena: Verlag und Datenbank für Geisteswissenschaften, 2000), 68. As we have seen, Goethe indeed tends to draw on the traditional typological pairing of Pentecost and the giving of the Law.

40. See Kaiser, *Goethe—Nähe durch Abstand*, 75.

41. In his pursuit of marriage and family, Hermann is simultaneously identified with two Genesis patriarchs, Isaac and Jacob, both of whom emphatically loved their wives (Gen. 24:67; 29:20). Like Isaac, Hermann is an only child, and a notably weak figure in the shadow of his father. Both Abraham and Hermann's father appoint intermediaries to aid in the procuring of wives for their sons. Note the common language in Goethe's description of the biblical episode in *Poetry and Truth* (FA 1.4: 152) and in the parallel scene in the epic (FA 1.8: 843). Hermann is also like Jacob in his especially close relationship to his mother (FA 1.8: 843). Just as Rebekah cooks up the scheme by which Jacob steals his father's blessing (Gen. 27: 5–17), Hermann's mother is not averse to strategizing to win the father's approval for her son (FA 1.8: 835). Like Isaac's intermediary before him,

and Moses after him, Jacob meets the bride-to-be at a well (Gen. 29). Hermann too, has his decisive meeting with Dorothea at the well (FA 1.8: 861).

42. See Schiller's letter to Goethe, April 14, 1997: Schiller, *Schillers Werke*,29: 63.

43. According to Schiller's essay "Die Sendung Moses" (1790), Moses, educated in Egyptian wisdom or "the religion of reason," sees the necessity of conveying the truth to his people "in a mythical [*fabelhaft*] manner." Schiller thus suggests that Moses's miracles may not have been genuine miracles (Schiller, *Schillers Werke*, 17: 392, 394). Other demythologizing precedents include Reimarus's fragment calculating that a mass migration of such scale could not have been accomplished as represented, published by Lessing in 1777. Gotthold Ephraim Lessing, *Werke und Briefe*, ed. Wilfried Barner et al., 12 vols. (Frankfurt: Deutscher Klassiker Verlag, 1985–2003), 8: 236–46. Michaelis's notes to his translation of Exodus (1771) suggest that the rolling back of the Red Sea was a natural phenomenon involving low tides and a strong storm rather than a miracle (see discussion in Sheehan, *Enlightenment Bible*, 206). Spinoza's *Theological-Political Treatise* (1670), which, as it argues against miracles categorically, discusses the Exodus miracles specifically (Spinoza, *Works*, 451). Spinoza also contends that Moses's legislation aimed primarily to found a stable temporal commonwealth (chap. 5) and rejects Moses's authorship of the Torah (chap. 8).

44. Lange, "Reconstructing a Nation's Birth," 115.

45. See Schings's discussion of eighteenth-century theories of melancholy. Relevant here are the tendency to rebel, and the tendency to see God as a punishing figure. Hans-Jürgen Schings, *Melancholie und Aufklärung*: *Melancholiker und ihre Kritiker in Erfahrungseelenkunde und Literatur des 18. Jahrhunderts* (Stuttgart: Metzler, 1977), 48–52. Schings mentions a seventeenth-century treatise by Petrus Petitus that identifies Moses as a melancholic (378n66). Zipfel also notes the "melancholische Note" in the characterization of Moses ("Goethes Moses Bild," 201). Linder sees parallels with Hamlet (178).

46. Zipfel notes the implication of treachery (*Heimtücke*) in the term "Meuchelmord" ("Goethes Moses Bild," 191).

47. Compare Hermann Levin Goldschmidt, *Werkausgabe in neun Bänden*, ed. Willi Goetschel, 9 vols. (Vienna: Passagen, 1997), 4: 184.

48. Freud, citing Goethe, adopts the theory of the "killing of Moses by his own Jewish people." Sigmund Freud, *Der Mann Moses und die monotheistische Religion* (Frankfurt am Main: Fischer, 1992), 95.

49. This is a direct reference to another passage in the Hebrew Bible: Ps. 119:19 (FA 1.8: 1210). But Goethe has changed the word "Gast" in the Lutheran translation ("Ich bin ein Gast auf Erden) to "Fremdling" (stranger). In any case, the connection to a Hebrew biblical context is clear.

50. Goldschmidt, *Werkausgabe*, 189.

Chapter 3

1. Gustav Seibt, *Goethe und Napoleon: Eine historische Begegnung* (Munich: Beck, 2009), 10.

2. Ibid., 76.

3. Ibid., 204–7.

4. Because the documentation of the project is more complete in the Weimar Edition (WA), I cite it, rather than the Frankfurt edition.

5. According to the Weimar Edition, Goethe outlined first the general, historical *Volksbuch* and then worked on the conception of the poetry collection, which he understood to be Niethammer's vision (WA I.42.2: 397). Hans Joachim Kreutzer suggests that Goethe's own reference in 1830 to plans for two separate collections was a false memory and that the project evolved from the historical to the lyrical conception. Kreutzer, *Der Mythos vom Volksbuch: Studien zur Wirkungsgeschichte des frühen deutschen Romans seit der Romantik* (Stuttgart: Metzler, 1977), 63–64.

6. Hans-Dietrich Dahnke, "Das Recht, das Tüchtige aller Zeiten und Völker': Goethe und das Projekt eines 'deutschen Volksbuchs' im Jahre 1808," in *Schönheit, welche nach Wahrheit dürstet: Beiträge zur deutschen Literatur von der Aufklärung bis zur Gegenwart*, ed. Gerhard Kaiser and Heinrich Macher (Heidelberg: Universitätsverlag Winter, 2003), 98–99.

7. Dahnke, "Das Projekt eines 'deutschen Volksbuchs,' " 94.

8. "A book suitable for the masses, intelligible to all." *Deutsches Wörterbuch von Jacob Grimm und Wilhelm Grimm*, s.v. "Volksbuch" (1854–1960), 26: 475, dwb.uni-trier.de.

9. Görres refers to "this holy spirit that resides in the nation [*Volk*]." Joseph Görres, *Die teutschen Volksbücher* (New York: Hildesheim, Olms, 1982), 7.

10. Eichhorn, *das Alte Testament*, 2nd ed., 2: 216–17.

11. Compare Goethe's comic use of the Esther material in his *Jahrmarktsfest zu Plundersweilen*. Elsewhere he terms Ruth "epic and idyllic" (*episch und idyllisch*) (FA 1.3.1: 140).

12. Alter, *World of Biblical Literature*, 7, 20.

13. Jan Assmann treats in detail the history of this influential thesis concerning Moses as transmitter of Egyptian mysteries. Assmann, *Moses the Egyptian: The Memory of Egypt in Western Monotheism* (Cambridge, Mass.: Harvard University Press, 1997).

14. Eichhorn, *Das Alte Testament*, 2nd ed., 1: 3.

15. Ibid., 1: 5.

16. A passage from the same era, from Goethe's *Farbenlehre*, bears similarities to the *Volksbuch* conception, but places clearer emphasis on *both* biblical canons as the "universal library of the nations" (*allgemeine Bibliothek der Völker*). Still, the passage seems to represent Christianity as an extension or branch of Jewish history—where the "dispersal of Judaism" (*Zerstreuung des Judentums*) is conjoined with the "spread of Christianity" (*Ausbreitung des Christentums*) (FA 1.23.1: 617). That is, Jewish history does not serve in this context as mere historical anticipation or prefiguration, but seems to define the trajectory of Christianity.

17. According to Marvin A. Sweeney, Jewish tradition regards Ezekiel's vision in a messianic context, as a description not of the Second Temple, but of a Third Temple in the time of the Messiah. Sweeney, "Ezekial Introduction and Annotations," in Berlin, Brettler, and Fishbane, *Jewish Study Bible*, 1118n.

18. However, David Frankfurter argues that Revelation—its emphasis on "purity, architecture, and divine presence"—should still be understood in a Jewish context: "Introduction and Annotation to the Book of Revelation," in Levine and Brettler, *The Jewish Annotated New Testament*, 496n.

19. Günter Hartung briefly establishes the connection between the *Volksbuch* and *Journeymen Years*, with a focus on the tour in the Pedagogical Province, in "Goethe und die Juden," 403.

20. For the history of the reception of the work as an "archival novel," see Ehrhard Bahr, *The Novel as Archive: The Genesis, Reception, and Criticism of Goethe's "Wilhelm Meisters Wanderjahre"* (Columbia, S.C.: Camden House, 1998).

21. Sheehan, *Enlightenment Bible*, 214.

22. Gottfried Arnold, *Unpartheyische Kirchen- und Ketzer-Historie vom Anfang des Neuen Testaments biß auf das Jahr Christi 1688*, 2 vols. (Hildesheim: George Olms, 1967), 1: 81.

23. Goethe read about utopian experiments in nineteenth-century America like New Harmony and New Lebanon in this travel account: Heinrich Luden, ed., *Reise Seiner Hoheit des Herzogs Bernhard zu Sachsen-Weimar-Eisenach durch Nord-Amerika in den Jahren 1825 und 1826* (Weimar, 1828), https://archive.org/stream/reisesrhoheitdes00bern#page/n3/mode/2up.

24. Compare Jane Brown, "Im Anfang war das Bild: Wilhelm Meister und die Bibel," in Anderegg and Kunz, *Goethe und die Bibel*, 242.

25. Of course, this metaphor belies the historical dependence of Christianity on those scriptures: in that sense, Judaism fathered Christianity rather than the reverse.

26. For a general history of the myth, see George K. Anderson, *The Legend of the Wandering Jew* (Providence, R.I.: Brown University Press, 1966).

27. See for example, Heinrich August Ottkar Reichard, *Der ewige Jude: Geschicht- oder Volksroman, wie man will* (Riga: Hartknoch, 1785), 10; and *Der ewige Jude: Eine komische Geschichte aus dem achtzehnten Jahrhundert* (Leipzig: Anton Doll, 1800), 86. K. F. Göschel notes this parallel in the *Wanderjahre*: *Uber Göthe's Faust*, 292. While Göschel's book was published between the two versions of Goethe's novel, thus before Goethe had made the comparison between Wilhelm and the Wandering Jew explicit in the 1829 version, he nevertheless picks up on the Wandering Jew motif and seems to anticipate Goethe's later emphasis.

28. Mona Körte's literary history of Ahasverus devotes a chapter to Mignon and the Harpist: *Goethes "Wilhelm Meisters Lehrjahre": Die Uneinholbarkeit des Verfolgten. Der Ewige Jude in der literarischen Phantastik* (Frankfurt: Campus, 2000), 133–62.

29. The play on these terms is evident in the novella "Der Mann von funfzig Jahren" in reference to Flavio's wandering in mental confusion (FA 1.10: 474, 483, 484).

30. A connection between unbridled mobility and the Wandering Jew also appears in the novella "Wer ist der Verräter?" (FA 1.10: 354).

31. Martin Swales, "Goethe's Prose Fiction," in *The Cambridge Companion to Goethe*, ed. Lesley Sharpe (Cambridge, Eng.: Cambridge University Press, 2002), 145. But Swales notes an opposite tendency in *The Journeymen Years* as well. That is, there *are* consistent socioeconomic and pedagogical themes within the novel. He writes, "the *Wanderjahre* exhibits a strange combination of postmodern irony with a kind of hectoring pedagogy in the service of self-discipline and renunciation" (145).

32. Jane Brown, *Goethe's Cyclical Narratives*: "*Die Unterhaltungen deutscher Ausgewanderten" and "Wilhelm Meisters Wanderjahre"* (Chapel Hill: University of North Carolina Press, 1975), 128.

33. Benjamin Bennett, *Beyond Theory: Eighteenth-Century German Literature and the Poetics of Irony* (Ithaca, N.Y.: Cornell University Press, 1993), 61.

34. "Only the Jews—precisely in being unequivocally (and arbitrarily) rejected—can operate as a sign for the actual reading community." Bennett, *Beyond Theory*, 62.

35. Bahr and Dowden, who also emphasize the novel's thoroughgoing irony, still express their strong consternation toward these apparently anti-Semitic instances. Bahr, *Novel as Archive*, 101–2; Steven Dowden, "Irony and Ethical Autonomy in *Wilhelm Meisters Wanderjahre*," *Deutsche Vierteljahrsschrift* 68, no. 1 (1994): 148. Meanwhile Paul E. Kerry, appealing to the ironic interpretations advanced by Brown and Bennett, mounts an astonishing defense of the Society's exclusion of Jews as a "transformation of tolerance through recognizing difference," which ultimately, he suggests, serves the interest of Jewish identity by opposing the anti-religious tendency of Enlightenment tolerance. Kerry, *Enlightenment Thought in the Writings of Goethe: A Contribution to the History of Ideas* (Rochester N.Y.: Camden House, 2001), 183.

36. Tzvetan Todorov, *Theories of the Symbol*, trans. Catherine Porter (Ithaca, N.Y.: Cornell University Press, 1982), 206.

37. Eric A. Blackall, *Goethe and the Novel* (Ithaca, N.Y.: Cornell University Press, 1976), 236–69.

38. Ibid., 237, 239, 242.

39. Hegel's lectures were delivered in 1823, 1826, and 1829 and published posthumously. While the contrastive emphasis on Judaism was strengthened in the 1829 version of *The Journeymen Years*, many of the passages on which I am drawing in my discussion of symbol and allegory, including the discourse on religion in the Pedagogical Province, appear already in the 1821 version of the novel. Hegel's views serve then only as a contemporary point of comparison, with which Goethe may or may not have been familiar.

40. G. W. F. Hegel, *Hegel's Aesthetics: Lectures on Fine Art*, trans. T. M. Knox, 2 vols. (Oxford: Oxford University Press, 1998), 1: 274; G. W. F. Hegel, *Werke*, 20 vols. (Frankfurt: Suhrkamp, 1986), 479.

41. Hegel, *Aesthetics*, 1: 374; Hegel, *Werke*, 13: 482.

42. Hegel, *Aesthetics*, 1: 373; Hegel, *Werke*, 13: 481.

43. Todorov, *Theories of the Symbol*, 201.

44. Ibid., 205–6. See also FA 1.13: 207.

45. Librett, *Rhetoric of Cultural Dialogue*, 33.

46. Marc Redfield, *Phantom Formations: Aesthetic Ideology and the Bildungsroman* (Ithaca, N.Y.: Cornell University Press, 1996), 105. Redfield refers to arguments made by Muenzer. See Clark Muenzer, *Figures of Identity: Goethe's Novels and the Enigmatic Self* (University Park: Pennsylvania State University Press, 1984). See esp. 127–28.

47. While traditional Lutheran theology places primary emphasis on faith over works, Pietist theologians such as Gottfried Arnold, who was influential for Goethe as a young man in Frankfurt, placed greater emphasis on deeds for the Christian life. See F. Ernest Stoeffler, *German Pietism during the Eighteenth Century* (Leiden: Brill, 1973), 179–80. Nevertheless, in Goethe's portrayal of "the Beautiful Soul" in *Apprenticeship*, a character presumably based on his Pietist mentor von Klettenberg, Goethe clearly critiques Pietism as still insufficiently engaged with the external world.

48. Mendelssohn, *Gesammelte Schriften*, 8.2: 166.

49. Ibid., 184.

50. Admittedly, Lessing's play (1779) predates Kant's critical philosophy (1781).

51. Lessing, *Werke und Briefe*, 9: 495.

52. Ibid., 497.

53. Compare Fichte's critique of Christianity in his *Reden an die deutsche Nation*. Johann Gottlieb Fichte, *Sämmtliche Werke*, ed. J. H. Fichte, 8 vols. (Berlin: Veit und Comp, 1846), 7: 378–79.

54. (emphasis in original) Göschel, *Über Göthes "Faust,"* 230–31.

55. See Hess on the drive by Christian thinkers in this period to relegate Judaism to the status of a merely historical religion (*Claims of Modernity*, 12).

56. Compare Muenzer, who also sees in this passage the "infinite deferral of the true self" (*Figures of Identity*, 109).

57. Quoted by Neumann and Dewitz in their textual commentary to the novel (FA 1.10: 1235).

58. Bennett, *Beyond Theory*, 62.

59. Ibid., 62n.

60. Mendelssohn, *Gesammelte Schriften*, 168–69.

61. Ibid., 168.

62. Hess, *Claims of Modernity*, 121–24.

Chapter 4

1. Paul Requadt sees this "morphological principle"—the alternation between contraction and expansion—as the key structure organizing the drama. Paul Requadt, *Goethes "Faust I": Leitmotivik und Architektur* (Munich: Fink, 1972), 25.

2. The Greek word *diatheke* is alternately translated as "covenant" or "testament" in its thirty-three occurrences in the Christian scriptures, and was in turn the translation of the Hebrew word for "covenant," *berith*, in the Septuagint, the Greek translation of the Hebrew Bible in the pre-Christian era. Geerhardus Vos, "Hebrews, the Epistle of the *Diatheke*," *Princeton Theological Review* 13, no. 4 (1915): 587–632, http://www.bible-researcher.com/vos-.

3. Some of the most significant studies of the last half century include O. Durrani, "Biblical Borrowings in Goethe's *Faust*: A Historical Survey of Their Interpretation," *Modern Language Review* 72, no. 4 (1977): 829–44; Gerhard Kaiser, "Goethes *Faust* und die Bibel," *Deutsche Vierteljahrsschrift* 58, no. 3 (1984): 391–413; Hans Hübner, *Goethes "Faust" und das Neue Testament* (Göttingen: Vandenhoeck & Ruprecht, 2003); and several of the essays included in Anderegg and Kunz, eds., *Goethe und die Bibel*. A work that does deal meaningfully with the tension between Hebrew Bible and New Testament or Christian subtexts, and which I will draw on in the next chapter is Johannes Anderegg, *Tranformationen: Über Himmlisches und Teuflisches in Goethes "Faust"* (Bielefeld: Aisthesis, 2010).

4. Jan-Dirk Müller, ed., *Romane des 15. und 16. Jahrhunderts: Nach den Erstdrucken mit sämtlichen Holzschnitten*, 10 vols., Bibliothek der Frühen Neuzeit (Frankfurt am Main: Deutscher Klassiker Verlag, 1990), 1: 932–94.

5. Compare Willi Jasper, *Faust und die Deutschen* (Berlin: Rowohlt, 1998), 48–49; and Ulrich Gaier, ed., *Faust-Dichtungen*, by Johann Wolfgang von Goethe, 3 vols. (Stuttgart: Reclam, 1999), 3: 63.

6. Göschel links the two characters generally over the issue of their *Diesseitigkeit* (worldliness, lit.: this-sidedness).

7. Müller, *Romane des 15. und 16. Jahrhunderts*, 1: 844–45.

8. Habiger-Tuczay, Christa, *Magie und Magier im Mittelalter* (Munich: Diederichs, 1992), 134.

9. See ibid., 135.

10. Listed in the elder Goethe's library holdings: Götting, "Bibliothek von Goethes Vater," 49. Johann Jacob Schudt, *Jüdische Merckwürdigkeiten: Vorstellende was sich curieuses und denckwürdiges in den neuern Zeiten bey einigen Jahrhunderten mit denen in alle IV. Theile der Welt, sonderlich durch Teutschland, zerstreuten Juden zugetragen . . .*, 3 vols. in 1 (Frankfurt: Tobias Hocker, 1715), 2.1: 393. The second volume is divided into two parts, with non-continuous pagination. I will indicate this division by 2.1 and 2.2. Schudt also cites Eisenmenger as one of his sources in this connection. Johann Andreas Eisenmenger, *Entdecktes Judenthum, oder Gründlicher und Wahrhaffter Bericht, Welchergestalt die verstockte Juden die hochheilige Drey-Einigkeit . . . lästern und verunehren . . .*, 2 vols. (Königsberg, 1711), 2: 230.

11. Schudt, *Jüdische Merckwürdigkeiten*, 2.1: 382.

12. See Habiger-Tuczay, *Magie und Magier*, 133–42.

13. Schudt, *Jüdische Merckwürdigkeiten*, 2.2: 190 (an apparent misprint identifies this page as 160 even though it lies between 189 and 191).

14. Schudt, *Jüdische Merckwürdigkeiten*, 2.2, 198–99.

15. A related story also shows up in Hans Wilhelm Kirchhof's collection from 1563–1603, *Wendunmut*. "Wie einer aus einem Faß vielerlei Wein zapfte," in *Scherz und Ernst: Deutsche Schwänke des 16. Jahrhunderts*, ed. Elvira Pradel (Leipzig: Reclam, 1962), 256–58. Friedrich and Scheithauer identify wine-dispensing table as old lore (*altes Sagengut*). Theodor Friedrich and Lothar Scheithauer, *Kommentar zu Goethes "Faust"* (Stuttgart: Reclam, 1978), 188.

16. Schudt, *Jüdische Merckwürdigkeiten*, 2.2: 209.

17. According to Barbara Könneker, legends surrounding Rabbi Adam of Prague, printed in Yiddish in the late seventeenth century, bear surprising similarities to the adventures of Faust in the 1587 chapbook. Rabbi Adam is supposed to have lived in the late sixteenth century and have gained the attention of Emperor Maximilian II. Parallels between the two include the magical summoning of famous dead people to the imperial court—Rabbi Adam summons Joab, Faust summons Alexander the Great—as well as the conjuring of great feasts. Könneker concludes that both works draw on an even earlier store of legends. Barbara Könneker, "Zauberei und Zauberer in der deutschen Literatur des 16. Jahrhunderts," in *Mysticism, Magic and Kabbalah in Ashkenazi Judaism*, ed. Karl Erich Grözinger and Joseph Dan (Berlin: De Gruyter, 1995), 18.

18. Gershom Scholem, *Alchemy und Kabbalah*, trans. Klaus Ottmann (Putnam, Conn.: Spring Publications, 2006), 11.

19. Indeed in an appendix, Schudt includes a text intended to show Jewish dealings in alchemy, "Ein Jüdischer Brief / Mesahab genannt / von der Alchimie und Kunst Gold zu machen." Schudt, *Jüdische Merckwürdigkeiten*, 3: 327–39.

20. See Gaier, *Faust-Dichtungen*, 3: 250–51.

21. Schöne cites kabbalistic numerology as one of a number of approaches commentators have used to try to unlock this rhyme, but follows Goethe's own

lead in concluding that it is nonsense (Schöne, 287). I am not concerned to decipher a meaning, but merely to suggest its kabbalistic ring.

22. The tradition of seeing the Hexen-Einmaleins in relationship to the ten kabbalistic Sephiroth continues in various websites and online forums. See, for example, Sasha Kosta, "J.W. Goethe: Faust, Das Hexeneinmaleins," K. Dautels ZUM-Seiten: Unterrichtsprojekte, Ideen und Materialien, January 2006, http://www.zum.de/Faecher/D/BW/gym/faust/hexen/einmaleins_3.htm.

23. Scholem, *Alchemy und Kabbalah*, 37. Even the sign of the macrocosm that Faust views in the opening scene could have kabbalistic associations, which he might have gleaned from Brucker, *Kurtze Fragen*, 4: 800, 823, 828. Compare also the association of Kabbalah with a macrocosmic view of the human body in a 1797 letter from Friedrich Schiller, *Schillers Werke*, 29: 58.

24. Flavius Josephus, *Translation and Commentary*, ed. Steve Mason (Leiden: Brill, 2000–), 5: 14.

25. Magical wisdom attributed to Solomon circulated in the late antique and medieval periods within both Jewish and Christian communities. Dennis C. Duling, "Solomon, Testament of," *Anchor Bible Dictionary*, ed. David Noel Freedman, 6 vols. (New York: Doubleday, 1992), 6: 119. This work was printed in a Christianized German version in 1686 by a Radical Pietist publisher: *Claviculae Salomonis et Theosophia Pneumatica* (Wesel/Duisburg: Andreas Luppius, 1686). For more on its Pietistic reception, see Hans-Jürgen Schrader, "Salomonis Schlüssel für die 'halbe Höllenbrut,'" in *Goethe und der Pietismus*, ed. Hans-Georg Kemper and Hans Schneider (Tübingen: Niemeyer, 2001), 240.

26. Adelung, *Geschichte der menschlichen Narrheit*, 7: 294.

27. Frank Möbus, "Kein Meister über die Geister: Doctor Fausti 'Höllenzwänge,'" in *Faust*: *Annäherung an einen Mythos*, ed. Frank Möbus, Friederike Schmidt-Möbus, and Gerd Unverfehrt (Göttingen: Wallstein Verlag, 1996), 38. In 1829 Goethe acquired a *grimoire* called *Praxis Cabulae nigrae Doctoris Johannis Faustii*, which appears to be a variation on *Faust's Coercion of Hell*. See FA 2.11: 197–99, 699.

28. Quoted in Agnes Bartscherer, "Faustisches. I. Clavicula Salomonis," *Chronik des Wiener Goethe-Vereins* 27 (1913): 10. Compare Georg von Welling, *Opus Mago-Cabbalisticum et Theosophicum*, trans. Joseph G. McVeigh (San Francisco: Weiser, 2006), 391.

29. Adelung compares seven versions of the *Clavicula* in Latin, French, and German and then prints Luppius's versions of both the *Clavicula* and another magical treatise attributed to Solomon, *Semiphoras und Schemhamphoras Salomonis Regis*. Adelung, *Geschichte der menschlichen Narrheit*, 6: 332–457. Adelung prints *Faust's Coercion of Hell* as an appendix to his final volume, 7: 367–408.

30. Georg Conrad Horst, *Zauber-Bibliothek, oder von Zauberei, Theurgie und Mantik, Zauberern, Hexen und Hexenprocessen, Dämonen, Gespenstern und Geistererscheinungen: Mit einer Einführung von Herbert Kempf*, 6 vols. (Mainz: Florian Kupferberg, 1821; Freiburg im Breisgau: Aurum, 1979), 4: 128.

31. Carl Kiesewetter, *Faust in der Geschichte und Tradition: Mit besonderer Berücksichtigung des okkulten Phänomenalismus und des mittelalterlichen Zauberwesens*, 2 vols., Geheime Wissenschaften, ed. A. v. d. Linden (Berlin: Hermann Barsdorf Verlag, 1921), 2: 66.

32. Agnes Bartscherer poses this question and offers a number of sources that contain warnings about the unholy nature of the *Clavicula* including works by Paracelsus, van Helmont, and Georg von Welling that would have made it seem an appropriate tool for Faust. Bartscherer, "Faustisches," 9–10. Schrader suggests that Bartscherer only knew the *Claviculum Salomonis* secondhand while Goethe could well have known it firsthand ("Salomonis Schlüssel," 238–43). Schrader argues that the more serious Christian pan-sophic content of the *Key* would have made it a better instrument for Faust in his search for knowledge than the hocus-pocus of the *Coercion* (244–45).

33. Solomon and Faust also converge as characters within a second popular genre—the chapbook. Görres's 1807 compendium includes, in addition to a Faustbuch, two chapbooks concerning Solomon (*Die teutschen Volksbücher*, 188, 238).

34. Proven, according to Adelung, by the family's inclusion in a tax on recently converted families in 1512. Johann Christoph Adelung, *Geschichte der menschlichen Narrheit, oder Lebensbeschreibungen berühmter Schwarzkünstler, Goldmacher, Teufelsbanner, Zeichen- und Liniendeuter, Schwärmer, Wahrsager und anderer philosophischer Unholden*, 7 vols. (Leipzig: Weygand, 1785–89), 7: 107.

35. Ibid., 107–8.

36. Ibid., 108.

37. Ibid., 109, 110.

38. Almut Neumann, *Verträge und Pakte mit dem Teufel: Antike und mittelalterliche Vorstellungen im "Malleus maleficarm"* (St. Ingbert: Röhrig Universitätsverlag, 1997), 36.

39. See ibid., 40.

40. See Schöne, 225; Gaier, *Faust-Dichtungen*, 2: 169.

41. Friedrich and Scheithauer, *Kommentar zu Goethes "Faust,"* 177; Schöne, 226; Gaier, *Faust-Dichtungen*, 2: 169; and Cyrus Hamlin, ed., *Faust*, by Johann Wolfgang von Goethe, trans. Walter Arndt, 2nd ed. (New York: Norton, 2001), 20n.

42. Ziony Zevit, "Second Kings, Introduction and Annotation," in Berlin, Brettler, and Fishbane, *Jewish Study Bible*, 727n.

43. On this assumption, shared among both Deists and the Anglican theologian William Warburton, see Assmann, *Moses*, 96.

44. G. E. Lessing, *Werke und Briefe*, 8: 272. In one of his "Tame Xenia," Goethe asserts "Ein Sadduzäer will ich bleiben!" aligning himself with the denial of immortality by members of this ancient Jewish sect (FA 1.2: 737).

45. Lessing, *Werke und Briefe*, 8: 258–59.

46. Ibid., 8: 267. The Jewish philosopher Neil Gillman supports this claim: "the idea that human beings will live again after death cannot be found in Jewish writings much before the second century BCE, and the idea that we possess a soul which never dies is not found until roughly a century later." Neil Gillman, *The Death of Death: Resurrection and Immortality in Jewish Thought* (Woodstock, Vt.: Jewish Lights, 2002), 22.

47. See Daniel Krochmalnik's introduction to Mendelssohn's "Commentary" (LI–LX) as well as Mendelssohn's own preface; Mendelssohn, *Gesammelte Schriften*, 190–93.

48. For Lessing, Judaism thus represents only the childhood stage of a human spiritual development that proceeds through (and beyond) Christianity. Lessing, *Werke und Briefe*, 10: 86.

49. Ibid., 10: 83. Compare *SW* 11: 357–58.

50. Lessing, *Werke und Briefe*, 10: 96.

51. In the left foreground of both images the devout observer (Elisha in the case of Elijah's ascent) is in a partial kneel with countenance raised and mouth agape; in the middle space appears the heavenly vision among fire and cloud; in the background the social realm is signified through a city or fortress. Matthäus Merian the Elder, *Great Scenes from the Bible: 230 Magnificent 17th-Century Engravings* (Mineola, N.Y.: Dover, 2002), 50, 63.

52. Dating back to the period of the Second Temple. Two church fathers, Jerome and Origen, refer to the restricted character of these mysteries. Scholem, *Major Trends*, 42, 356n5.

53. This passage is contradicted earlier in the chapter by the claim, "The LORD would speak to Moses face to face, as one man speaks to another" (Exod. 34:11), which, according to Jeffrey Tigay, is probably from another source. Tigay, "Exodus," 187n. Whether or not an encounter with God is *always* fatal, the danger is clear.

54. Moses Maimonides, *Guide for the Perplexed*, trans. M. Friedländer (London: Kegan Paul, 2006), 251.

55. *Deutsches Wörterbuch von Jacob und Wilhelm Grimm*, s.v. "Sabbatstille," 14: 1588.

56. Kaiser, "Goethes *Faust* und die Bibel," 398–99.

57. Arnd Bohm, "Naming Goethe's Faust: A Matter of Significance," *Deutsche Vierteljahrsschrift* 80, no. 3 (2006): 408–34.

58. While it is standard to refer to the arrangement between Faust and Mephistopheles as a wager (*Wette*) rather than a pact because of its clear competitive terms (in contrast to the period of service established in the legend), the term is too narrow for my purposes. First, a bet *is* a kind of pact or contract (see line 1414); second, I argue that the wager presupposes a more primal contract, like a biblical covenant. See Gerrit Brüning's precise delimitation of the wager, "Die Wette in Goethes *Faust*," *Goethe Yearbook* 17 (2010): 31–54.

59. Eichhorn, *Das Alte Testament*, 2nd ed., 3: 491.

60. Elaine Pagels, *The Origin of Satan* (New York: Vintage, 1996), 39.

61. See ibid., 40–41.

62. Eichhorn, *Das Alte Testament*, 2nd ed., 3: 200.

63. For a nice survey of Mephisto's shifting facets, see Johannes Anderegg, "Wie böse ist der Böse," *Monatshefte* 96, no. 3 (Fall 2004): 343–59.

64. Jasper describes lines 350–51 as a "Loyalitätserklärung." Jasper, *Faust und die Deutschen*, 71.

65. Schöne emphasizes the divinely *chosen* status of these figures (Schöne, 171–72), but one could simultaneously stress their *covenantal* relationship with the Lord, as in the Lord's pronouncement in Psalm 89:4: "I have made a *covenant* with My *chosen one*; / I have sworn to My *servant* David" (my emphasis).

66. Marvin H. Pope, *The Anchor Bible: Job: Introduction, Translation, and Notes* (New York: Doubleday, 1973), 12.

67. Eichhorn concludes that Job, while perhaps raised in Arabia around Edom, was probably a born Hebrew. Eichhorn, *Das Alte Testament*, 2nd ed., 3: 509.

68. David Wolfers notes this broad thematic connection between Job and the Deuteronomic covenant: *Deep Things out of Darkness: The Book of Job: Essays and a New English Translation* (Grand Rapids, Mich.: Eerdmans, 1995), 111–14.

69. Mayer Gruber, "Job: Introduction and Annotations," in Berlin, Brettler, and Fishbane, *Jewish Study Bible*, 1500.

70. Eichhorn, *Das Alte Testament*, 2nd ed., 3: 491. But Eichhorn argues explicitly against any supposition that the prologue and epilogue were added by a different author (3: 522).

71. Ibid., 3: 475, 524.

72. Johann Gottfried Eichhorn, *Einleitung in das Alte Testament*, 4th ed. (Göttingen: Rosenbusch, 1824), 5: 197.

73. Jung-Stilling and his friends eventually arrive at a position echoing Job's final acknowledgment of the unfathomable character of God (FA 1.14: 745).

74. "[The traditional view of the patient Job] ignores the thrust of more than nine tenths of the book and appears to take account only of the beginning and end of the story." Pope, *Job*, xv.

75. Muenzer, "Das Buch Hiob," 161–71.

76. Faust understands servitude as stasis rather than motion, and is unaware of his status as the Lord's servant: "Wie ich beharre bin ich Knecht, / Ob dein, was frag' ich oder wessen" (1710).

77. Mammon appears several times in the New Testament as the personified deity of money or greed.

78. Eichhorn rejects this attribution himself: *Das Alte Testament*, 2nd ed., 3: 519–21.

79. Johann Albert Fabricius, *Codex Pseudoepigraphus Veteris Testamenti . . .* (Hamburg: Theodori Christoph Felginer, 1722), 1059. The entry for Solomon in Zedler's *Universal Lexicon* also addresses the charge, arguing that Solomon is not a skeptic in the Greek sense but that his wisdom was motivated by love and reverence for God. Johann Zedlers, *Großes vollständiges Universallexicon aller Wissenschafften und Künste*, s.v. "Salomon," 64 vols. (Leipzig, 1732–54), 33: 561, http://www.zedler-lexikon.de.

80. Peter Machinist, "Ecclesiastes: Introduction and Annotations," in Berlin, Brettler, and Fishbane, *Jewish Study Bible*, 1603. See for example Eccl. 3:20 and Eccl. 7:15.

81. Eichhorn, *Das Alte Testament*, 2nd ed., 3: 577.

82. Pablo A. Torijano describes the character of Solomon as "problematic" from the start. Pablo A. Torijano, *Solomon the Esoteric King: From King to Magus, Development of a Tradition* (Leiden: Brill, 2002), 2.

83. See Ernst Beutler, ed., *Gedenkausgabe der Werke, Briefe und Gespräche*, by Johann Wolfgang von Goethe (Zurich: Artemis Verlag, 1949), 4: 1021. Also mentioned by Gerhard Sauder, "Kommentar," in *Sämtliche Werke nach Epochen seines Schaffens, Münchner Ausgabe*, by Johann Wolfgang von Goethe, ed. Karl Richter, 21 vols. (Munich: Hanser, 1985–99), 1.2: 854; and FA 1.8: 1096.

84. Flavius Josephus, *Translation and Commentary*, 5: 14. See Götting, "Bibliothek von Goethes Vater," 43. Goethe's knowledge of this source on Solomon is notable because it also contains information about Solomon's magic and dealing

with demons. Goethe may also have become aware of the genre of the plant fable through an indirect source, a 1774 essay by Jacobi (FA 1.8: 1095).

85. Compare Koholeth: "For in respect of the fate of man and the fate of beast, they have one and the same fate" (Eccl. 3:19) with Goethe's Solomonic parable, "A forest stream sent the firs toppling down, over and under each other, into the valley, and bushes and sprouts and grasses and oaks. A prophet, watching from the cliff, called out, 'everything is equal before the lord' " (*Ein Waldstrom stürzte die Tannen drunter und drüber ins Thal herab und Sträucher und Sprößling und Gräser und Eichen. Ein Prophete rief zuschauend vom Fels: Alles ist gleich vor dem Herrn*) (FA 1.8: 571).

86. *Al-Qur'an: A Contemporary Translation*, by Ahmed Ali (Princeton, N.J.: Princeton University Press, 1984), 21: 82; 38: 37–38.

87. See Zedler's *Universallexicon*, s.v. "Eisenmenger, (Jo. Andreas)," 8: 337.

88. Legends of the young and old Solomon appeared in Herder's third collection of "Scattered Leaves," published in 1787 (*SW* 26: 352–54). Suphan suggests Eisenmenger as a source (*SW* 26: 487).

89. While Goethe clearly knew other works by Fabricius, and Burdach sees this collection as a likely source for Goethe, there is no direct evidence of his access to this work. Burdach, "Faust und Moses," 1: 394. See also Zimmermann, *Das Weltbild des jungen Goethes*, 201–2.

90. Zedler, *Universallexicon*, s.v. "Salomon," 33: 560–65.

91. The two sides of Faust—thinker and lover—have a precedent in Solomon, according to Deutschländer, *Goethe und das Alte Testament*, 125–26.

92. See Isaac Rosenberg, "Koheleth und Goethes *Faust*," *Jahrbuch für jüdische Geschichte und Literatur* 11 (1908): 151–75; and William Goodrum, "Ecclesiastes in Goethe's Faust," *McNeese Review* 14 (1963): 74–79. Both Rosenberg (166–67) and Goodrum (75) compare the opening monologue with a slightly later passage from the first chapter of Ecclesiastes. Rosenberg also establishes interesting parallels between Eccl. 1:4–9 and the speeches of the angels in the "Prologue in Heaven" (163–65). See also Deutschländer, *Goethe und das Alte Testament*, 125–28.

93. Compare Herder: *SW* 26: 354.

94. Eichhorn, *Das Alte Testament*, 2nd ed., 3: 575n. See Mendelssohn's preface to his commentary, *Gesammelte Schriften*, 20.1: 184–202.

95. Flavius Josephus, *Translation and Commentary*, 5: 14.

96. Compare Schudt, *Jüdische Merckwürdigkeiten*, 2.2: 193.

97. See ibid., 2.2: 191.

98. Flavius Josephus, *Translation and Commentary*, 5: 13.

99. Otto Pniower, "Goethes Faust und das Hohe Lied," *Goethe Jahrbuch* 13 (1892): 181–98.

100. Pniower, "Faust und das Hohe Lied," 183. The phrase is from Goethe's translation of Song 5:4.

101. Pniower, "Faust und das Hohe Lied," 185–88. Requadt considers other striking parallels in the final scene (*Leitmotivik*, 336).

102. I am using the New English Bible Translation here because it is closer to Luther's version: "Deine Lippen, meine Braut, sind wie trieffender Honigseim" (Song 4:11) and "Denn die lippen der Huren sind süsse wie honigseim" (Prov. 5:3).

103. Other traditions connect Solomon and Lilith through the Queen of Sheba: "Solomon in his great wisdom also possessed might over demons and the Liliths; in later Jewish legends one of the two wives from 1. Kgs 3: 16–28 was identified with Lilith; so was the Queen of Sheba (1 Kgs 10)." Manfred Hutter, "Lilith," *Dictionary of Deities and Demons in the Bible*, ed. Karel van der Toorn, Bob Becking, and Pieter W. van der Horst, 2nd ed. (Leiden and Grand Rapids, Mich.: Eerdmans, Brill, 1999), 521.

104. Eisenmenger recounts how, after a conflict with her husband Adam, Lilith flies off and is pursued by angels. She is to be punished through the death of her own children, but then she declares that she herself has the power to kill children in their first days of life (Eisenmenger, *Entdecktes Judentum*, 2: 417).

105. The casting of Gretchen as at once the Shulamite and a Christian also makes sense within a long tradition of allegorizing the Song of Songs into a love affair between Christ and the church. Eichhorn makes fun of the transformation of this poetry into a "Singspiel" before the grave of Christ. Eichhorn, *Das Alte Testament*, 2nd ed., 3: 540. On Goethe's complex reception of this biblical book and its history of interpretation, see Anne Bohnenkamp, "Goethe und *das Hohe Lied*" in Anderegg and Kunz, eds., *Goethe und die Bibel*, 89–110.

106. In the Lutheran translation, "Jch bin eingesetzt von ewigkeit her, von anfang, vor der Erden."

107. See Maike Orgel, "'The Faustian 'Gretchen': Overlooked Aspects of a Famous Male Fantasy," *German Life and Letters* 64, no. 1 (January 2011): 43–55; and Christa Chilson, "Discovering Meaning in Goethe's *Faust* through Holism," M.A. thesis, University of Oklahoma, 2012, pp. 39–43.

Chapter 5

1. In his 1826 "Second Plan for an Announcement of 'Helena' " ("Zweiter Entwurf zu einer Ankündigung der 'Helena' "), Goethe locates the chasm (*Kluft*) between "the well-known sorrowful end of Part One" (*dem bekannten jammervollen Abschluß des 1. Teiles*) and "the entrance of the Greek heroine" (*dem Eintritt einer griechischen Heldenfrau*) (FA 1.7.1: 63).

2. Gruber, *Job*, 1502.

3. Eichhorn, *Das Alte Testament*, 2nd ed., 3: 472, see also 3: 502–9.

4. On Goethe's broad understanding of "patriarchal," see Hans-Jürgen Schrader, "Von Patriarchensehnsucht zur Passionsemphase: Bibelallusionen und spekulative Theologie in Goethes *Werther*," in Anderegg and Kunz, *Goethe und die Bibel*, 70–72.

5. Schöne, 402–3; Burdach, "Faust und Moses," 2: 643.

6. Brown, *German Tragedy*, 135.

7. As Schöne points out, according to Goethe's optics, light is not broken to form the colors of the rainbow. Rather it is reflected back and in this way becomes a symbol of indirect perception (Schöne, 411).

8. Compare Schöne, 412.

9. Johannes Anderegg, "Wie böse ist der Böse," 355. Anderegg also cites Brown in *The German Tragedy* for his characterization of Mephistopheles as essentially a "reality principle" (359n20).

10. "The rainbow is the synthesis of fire and water literally visible to the spectator. Henceforth in Part II, fire and water will remain the organizing categories"

(Brown, *German Tragedy*, 143). Brown poses as the recurring problem of *Part Two of the Tragedy* how one generates and sustains the synthesis of fire and water in the rainbow.

11. See Brown, *German Tragedy*, 181–82.

12. The passage concerns Helena's connection to Achilles as ghosts of the underworld. Some commentaries suggest that "idol" is used in this passage in an original Greek sense as "phantom or ghost" (Hamlin, *Faust*, 231n; Trunz, *Werke*, 3: 676). The Greek meaning does not preclude the biblical one, if an idol is indeed a frozen or dead image of something dynamic.

13. "As in *Faust*, so too in the Bible, the rainbow signifies that previous crimes are now washed away" (Brown, *German Tragedy*, 139).

14. Levenson, "Genesis," 24.

15. Spinoza, *Complete Works*, 239.

16. In the first iterations (Gen. 15:18 and Gen. 17:7) the Abrahamic covenant obtains with all Abraham's offspring, which would include Ishmael (traditionally father of the Arab peoples); in the second iteration (Gen. 17:21), it is only with the offspring of Isaac his son through Sarah. In any case, it would include the non-Israelite descendants of Esau.

17. Tigay, "Exodus," 145n.

18. In his preface to the Old Testament, Luther describes how God, through Moses, "organizes this people with all kinds of laws and separates it from all other peoples. . . . He appoints princes and officials, and provides his people splendidly with both laws and men, to rule them both in the body before the world and in the spirit before God." Martin Luther, *Works*, ed. Jaroslav Pelikan and Helmut T. Lehmann, 55 vols. (Philadelphia: Muhlenberg, 1955–86), 35: 237. As discussed in chapter 2, in his *Tractatus*, Spinoza understands Moses far more radically as primarily a crafter of a temporal, political commonwealth with specific laws for a specific people.

19. The word appears 16 times in the 4,613 lines of *Part One*, and 51 times in the 7,499 lines of *Part Two*.

20. Burdach, "Faust und Moses," 2: 630.

21. Ibid., 1: 383.

22. FA 2.7: 484, quoted in Seibt, *Goethe und Napoleon*, 246.

23. Seibt, *Goethe und Napoleon*, 247.

24. Compare Burdach, "Faust und Moses," 3: 787. Burdach also sees a link in Goethe's thinking between Moses, Faust, and Frederick the Great, 3: 787, 1: 366–67.

25. "Napoleon appears as the principle of a reality that can be neither voted away, nor even poetically or morally harmonized." Seibt, *Goethe und Napoleon*, 168.

26. Zedler, *Universallexicon*, s.v. "Moses," 21: 947.

27. Burdach, "Faust und Moses," 3: 768.

28. Hans Christoph Binswanger, *Money and Magic: A Critique of the Modern Economy in the Light of Goethe's "Faust,"* trans. J. E. Harrison (Chicago: University of Chicago Press, 1994), 3.

29. Alter, *Five Books of Moses*, 312n. Burdach discusses the role of water imagery, especially as it figures in mystical and theosophical traditions, in Goethe's conception of Faust as Moses. Burdach, "Faust und Moses," 3: 755–66.

30. "Nowhere in the seven-day creation scheme of Genesis 1 does God create the waters; they are likely primordial." Jon D. Levenson, *Creation and the Persistence of Evil: The Jewish Drama of Divine Omnipotence* (Princeton, N.J.: Princeton University Press, 1988), 5.

31. Ibid., 4.

32. Compare ibid., 15.

33. Compare James van der Laan, *Seeking Meaning for Goethe's Faust* (New York: Continuum, 2007), 42.

34. Levenson, *Creation*, 75.

35. Burdach makes this connection as well. Burdach, "Faust and Moses," 3: 778–79.

36. Alter, *Five Books of Moses*, 312n. See also David L. Lieber et al., eds., *Etz Hayim: Torah and Commentary* (New York: Jewish Publication Society, 2001), 322n.

37. Alter, *Five Books of Moses*, 312n.

38. Lieber et al., *Etz Hayim*, 323.

39. Burdach remarks upon this analogy: "Faust und Moses," 2: 643n.

40. Schudt, *Jüdische Merckwürdigkeiten*, 2.2: 209.

41. Multiple historical periods seem to resonate in this, and nearly every scene of *Part Two*. Birk has argued in detail that in *Faust II* Goethe links the transformations of the late Middle Ages to the epochal shifts of the Napoleonic era. Manfred Birk, "Goethes Typologie der Epochenschwelle im vierten Akt des 'Faust II,'" *Jahrbuch der Deutschen Schillergesellschaft* 33 (1989): 264–65. Gaier's description of a "dialectic between omnitemporality and perspectivity" suggests the complex interplay of the specific and paradigmatic aspects of history in this work (Gaier, *Faust-Dichtungen*, 3: 427).

42. Schöne and Schlößler both point to the example of Mordechai Meisel, the Jewish court banker of Emperor Rudolf II. The availability of a historical model does not explain Goethe's choice or emphasis. Schöne, 419; Franziska Schlößler, "Progress and Restorative Utopia in *Faust II* and *Wilhelm Meisters Wanderjahre*," in *A Companion to Goethe's "Faust: Parts I and II,"* ed. Paul Bishop (Rochester, N.Y.: Camden House, 2001), 171.

43. In the *Farbenlehre*, he writes of the modern "haggling and extortion operation of the descendants of Abraham" (*Schacher- und Wucherbetrieb der Nachkommen Abrahams*) (FA 1.23.1: 617).

44. According to the Grimms' dictionary, "murmeln" and "murren" are closely related. *Deutsches Wörterbuch von Jacob und Wilhelm Grimm*, s.v. "murmeln," 12: 2721. Curiously, "verworrene[s] Gemürmel" belongs to an actor's repertoire in imitating a Jewish rabbi in Goethe's unpublished version of what became the *Apprenticeship*, *Wilhelm Meister's Theatrical Calling* (*Wilhelm Meisters Theatralische Sendung*) (FA 1.9: 344).

45. Goethe could well have come across the association of alchemy and paper money in the *Travels of Marco Polo*, which he read in 1813. Marco Polo describes paper money as a sort of alchemy: The Kahn in the city of Kanbalu "may truly be said to possess the secret of the alchemists, as he has the art of producing money." Marco Polo, *The Travels of Marco Polo, the Venetian*, ed. and intro. Manuel Komroff (New York: Liveright, 2003), 159.

46. Binswanger, *Money and Magic*, 3.

47. Ibid., 13.
48. Ibid., 39.
49. Hamlin, *Faust*, 401.
50. Brown, *German Tragedy*, 157.
51. Trunz (*Werke*, 3: 600) and Hamlin (*Faust*, 158n), for example, identify Zoilo-Thersites as Mephistopheles. Schöne eschews the identification (Schöne, 442).
52. Brown, *German Tragedy*, 157. Brown divides the masque into three stages. The third begins with the arrival of Pan (the Emperor).
53. Homer, *The Iliad of Homer*, trans. Richmond Lattimore (Chicago: University of Chicago Press, 1976), 81.
54. Schöne, 442. Compare: "Let every valley be raised, / Every hill and mount made low. / Let the rugged ground become level / And the ridges become a plain" (Isa. 40:4; see also Isa. 45:2).
55. John G. Gager, *Moses in Greco-Roman Paganism* (Nashville, Tenn.: Abingdon, 1972), 137–39.
56. The verse number varies in the Lutheran Bible (Num. 17:13) and the Tanakh translation (Num. 17:28).
57. See FA 1.23.2: 18–19.
58. Hamlin, *Faust*, 398.
59. Schöne, 458.
60. Matthäus Merian the Elder, *Great Scenes from the Bible*, 22; *Martin Luther Bibel: Der komplette Originaltext von 1545 in modernem Schriftbild*, 2 vols. (Bonn: Edition Lempertz, 2008), 1: 184.
61. Don Pedro Calderon de la Barca, *The Great Stage of the World*, trans. George Brandt (Manchester, Eng.: Manchester University Press, 1976), 5.
62. Brown, *German Tragedy*, 158–59.
63. The relevant verses are Gen. 2:22 and Mark 1:11. See Schöne, 446–47.
64. Biblical parallel again noted by Schöne, 447.
65. See Margit Wyder on Goethe's repeated use of this passage from the Gospel of Matthew in order to affirm, rather than reject, worldliness and the realm of nature: Margit Wyder, "'Die Reiche der Welt und ihre Herrlichkeit': Biblische Bezüge in Goethes Gedanken zur Erdgeschichte," in Anderegg and Kunz, *Goethe und die Bibel*, 135–60.
66. Compare Brown, *The German Tragedy*, 221.
67. In a further conflation of disparate biblical figures and contexts, the warrior names, Raufebold, Habebald, and Haltefest, echo Luther's translation of the strange prophetic name of a son of Isaiah. "Raubebald, Eilebeute" (Isa. 8:1), Schöne, 668; Trunz, *Werke*, 3:703.
68. Luther retains the Hebrew word "Belial" to describe the opponents, which takes on a demonizing ring in later contexts. The Tanakh translation labels them simply "the wicked."
69. Schöne, 667; Gaier, *Faust-Dichtungen*, 2: 986.
70. Schöne, 722–23; Gaier, *Faust-Dichtungen*, 2: 1059–60.
71. Trunz, *Werke*, 3: 714.
72. Burdach, "Faust und Moses," 1: 359–60.
73. Burdach acknowledges as an earlier source Karl J. Schröer's edition of *Faust* (1886–88). Burdach, "Faust und Moses," 1: 359.

74. Burdach quotes Herder's "Der Tod Moses" (see *SW* 26: 346–47). Burdach, "Faust und Moses," 1: 385. Among other sources, Burdach mentions *das englische Bibelwerk*, the commentary Goethe read as an adolescent, Fabricius's *Codex pseudoepigraphus Veteris Testamenti*, as well as Eisenmenger's *Entdecktes Judentum*. Burdach, "Faust und Moses," 1: 394.

75. Eisenmenger, *Entdecktes Judentum*, 1: 857–58.

76. Ibid., 861.

77. Ibid.

78. Zedler, *Universallexicon*, s.v. "Moses," 21: 948.

79. Ibid.

80. Examples of interpretations that read the final scene as an exploration of the limits of representation include Stuart Atkins, "Irony and Ambiguity in the Final Scene of Goethe's *Faust*," in *Essays on Goethe* by Stuart Atkins, ed. Jane K. Brown and Thomas P. Saine (Columbia, S.C.: Camden House, 1995); Hannelore Schlaffer, "Paradies und Parodie: Die letzten Szenen in Goethes letztem Werk," in *Interpreting Goethe's Faust Today*, ed. Jane K. Brown, Meredith Lee, and Thomas P. Saine (Columbia, S.C.: Camden House, 1994), 102–11; Jochen Schmidt, "Die 'katholische Mythologie' und ihre mystische Entmythologisierung in der Schluss-Szene des *Faust II*," *Jahrbuch der Deutschen Schillergesellschaft* 34 (1990): 230–56. Examples of recent readings that invert or more radically call into question the religious imagery include Franziska Schlößler, "Progress and Restorative Utopia"; Astrida Orle Tantillo, "Damned to Heaven: The Tragedy of Faust Revisited," *Monatshefte* 99, no. 4 (2007): 454–68; and Heather Sullivan, "Ecocriticism, the Elements, and the Ascent/Descent into Weather in Goethe's *Faust*," *Goethe Yearbook* 17 (2010): 55–72.

81. Brown, *German Tragedy*, 244.

82. Amy-Jill Levine, *The Misunderstood Jew: The Church and the Scandal of the Jewish Jesus* (New York: Harper Collins, 2006), 135.

83. Émile Mâle, *Religious Art in France: The Twelfth Century: A Study of the Origins of Medieval Iconography*, ed. Harry Bober, trans. Marthiel Mathews (Princeton, N.J.: Princeton University Press, 1978), 241–44.

84. Auerbach, "Figura," 61.

85. See the chapter on "Ecclesia versus Synagoga" in Heinz Schreckenberg, *The Jews in Christian Art: An Illustrated History* (New York: Continuum, 1996), 31–74.

86. Hans Hübner, *Goethes Faust und das Neue Testament* (Göttingen: Vandenhoeck & Ruprecht, 2003), 219. Anderegg argues just the opposite, that given the very ambivalent ways in which the word "love" is used in this scene, one really cannot argue for its apotheosis in this scene. Anderegg, *Transformationen*, 178.

87. Jill-Levine, *Misunderstood Jew*, 220

88. Riemer, *Mitteilungen*, 331.

89. These questions echo especially in Job 9. Anderegg, "Wie böse ist der Böse?" 352, 359n11.

90. Eichhorn, *Das Alte Testament*, 4th ed., 5: 197. Although Eichhorn argues for the authenticity of both prologue and epilogue, he refers to doubts about the authenticity and age of the prologue and epilogue. Eichhorn, *Das Alte Testament*, 2nd ed., 3: 524.

91. Jane Brown has called the penultimate scene an "operatic burlesque" (*German Tragedy*, 243) and Johannes Anderegg has identified elements of a "grotesque" in all three final scenes (*Tranformationen*, 138–91).

92. Nicholas Rennie, *Speculating on the Moment: The Poetics of Time and Recurrence in Goethe, Leopardi, and Nietzsche* (Göttingen: Wallstein, 2005), 22–26. Rennie draws the distinction between tragedy and theodicy from Benno von Wiese. Rennie's argument focuses upon a further significant parallel between Job and *Faust* that I will not discuss—between Job's experience of theophany and Faust's experience of the *Augenblick* (Rennie, *Speculating*, 30–38). On these parallels, see also Anderegg, *Transformationen*, 205–24; J. M. van der Laan, *Seeking Meaning*, 48; and Hans-Jürgen Schrader, "'Hiob' in deutscher Dichtung ('Faust'—Joseph Roth—Lyrik nach der Shoah): Muster des Menschen—des jüdischen Leids—der Frage nach Theodizee," *Monathshefte für evangelische Kirchengeschichte des Rheinlandes* 53 (2004): 18.

93. See Anderegg, *Transformationen*, 207–14.

94. Ibid., 210–11.

95. Gruber, "Job," 1529n.

96. See discussion of Jewish versus Christian understandings of this passage in *Das englische Bibelwerk: Die Heilige Schrift, nebst einer vollstaendigen Erklaerung derselben* . . . , ed. Romanus Teller, Johann Augustin Dietelmair, and Johann Jakob Brucker, 19 vols. (Leipzig: Breitkopf, 1749–70), 5: 564–66.

97. Anderegg, *Transformationen*, 222.

98. I have added the quotation marks that were not included in the Atkins translation.

99. Ellis Dye, for example, follows Böhm and Schöne in reading the phrase "Wer immer" as "wer *auch* immer," and follows Trunz in reading "erlösen" as "ablösen." Thus he renders it: "Whoever it may be who unceasingly strives, him (her) we can release." Dye, "Figurations of the Feminine in Goethe's *Faust*," in Bishop, *Companion to Goethe's Faust*, 115. Schößler focuses on the quotation marks around these same lines to suggest it is no more than an earthly (Calvinist) maxim: "To strive in this world is, according to the maxim, sufficient *movens* to reach *this* Heaven." "Progress and Restorative Utopia," 184.

100. Bohm, "Naming Goethe's Faust," 428–34.

101. Anderegg, *Transformationen*, 235.

102. I combined several translations here as well as my own word choice order to stay close to the German.

103. Compare Schöne, who connects the Eternal Feminine to Goethe's conception of polarity and intensification (*Steigerung*) (Schöne, 817).

Conclusion

1. Goethe describes here his negative reaction to performances of plays with subjects drawn from the Hebrew Bible, when he realizes those heroes are in fact Jews.

2. Peter Goßens mentions also Luther, Heine, and Trakl in "Das Frühwerk bis zu *Der Sand aus den Urnen* (1938–1950)," in *Celan Handbuch: Leben—Werk—Wirkung*, ed. Markus May, Peter Goßens, and Jürgen Lehmann (Stuttgart: Metzler, 2008), 47.

3. John Felstiner, *Paul Celan: Poet, Survivor, Jew* (New Haven, Conn.: Yale University Press, 1995), 39. I will use Felstiner's translation of the poem on pages 31–32.

4. Barbara Wiedemann, "Kommentar," in *Todesfuge und andere Gedichte: Text und Kommentar*, by Paul Celan (Frankfurt: Suhrkamp, 2004), 132.

5. Pniower's influential study on the Song of Songs was published in 1892; Burdach's work on Faust and Moses in 1912; and Leo Deutschländer's sweeping *Goethe und das Alte Testament* in 1923.

6. Schöne anchors his comparison in the close parallel between the stage direction in the scene "Palast" where Mephistopheles shrilly whistles for his three violent thugs and the line in Celan's poem describing the camp overseer, "er pfeift seine Rüden herbei" (Schöne, "Vom Betreten des Rasens," 726).

7. I have followed Felstiner in retaining the German in these two lines.

WORKS CITED

Adelung, Johann Christoph. *Geschichte der menschlichen Narrheit, oder Lebensbeschreibungen berühmter Schwarzkünstler, Goldmacher, Teufelsbanner, Zeichen- und Liniendeuter, Schwärmer, Wahrsager und anderer philosophischer Unholden*. 7 vols. Leipzig: Weygand, 1785–89.

Al-Qur'an: A Contemporary Translation. Translated by Ahmed Ali. 2nd rev. ed. Princeton, N.J.: Princeton University Press, 1984.

Alter, Robert. *The Art of Biblical Narrative*. New York: Basic Books, 1981.

———. *The Five Books of Moses: A Translation with Commentary*. New York: Norton, 2004.

———. *The World of Biblical Literature*. New York: Basic Books, 1992.

Alter, Robert, and Frank Kermode. *The Literary Guide to the Bible*. Cambridge, Mass.: Belknap Press of Harvard University Press, 1987.

Anderegg, Johannes. *Transformationen: Über Himmlisches und Teuflisches in Goethes "Faust."* Bielefeld: Aisthesis Verlag, 2011.

———. "Wie böse ist der Böse?" *Monatshefte* 96, no. 3 (2004): 343–59.

Anderegg, Johannes, and Edith Anna Kunz, eds. *Goethe und die Bibel*. Stuttgart: Deutsche Bibelgesellschaft, 2005.

Anderson, George K. *The Legend of the Wandering Jew*. Providence, R.I.: Brown University Press, 1965.

Arnim, Bettina von. *Bettinas Briefwechsel mit Goethe*. Leipzig: Insel, 1922.

Arnold, Gottfried. *Unpartheyische Kirchen- und Ketzer-Historie vom Anfang des Neuen Testaments biß auf das Jahr Christi*. 1688. 2 vols. Frankfurt am Main, 1729. Reprint, Hildesheim: Georg Olms, 1967.

Arnsberg, Paul. *Die Geschichte der Frankfurter Juden seit der Französischen Revolution*. 3 vols. Darmstadt: E. Roether, 1983.

Assmann, Jan. *Moses the Egyptian: The Memory of Egypt in Western Monotheism*. Cambridge, Mass.: Harvard University Press, 1997.

Atkins, Stuart. *Essays on Goethe*. Edited by Jane K. Brown and Thomas P. Saine. Columbia, S.C.: Camden House, 1995.

Auerbach, Erich. *Mimesis: The Representation of Reality in Western Literature*. Translated by Willard R. Trask. Princeton, N.J.: Princeton University Press, 1974.

———. *Scenes from the Drama of European Literature*. Theory and History of Literature. Minneapolis: University of Minnesota Press, 1984.

Augustine. *Confessions*. Translated by R. S. Pine-Coffin. New York: Penguin, 1982.

———. *The Works of St. Augustine*. Edited by Boniface Ramsey. 50 vols. Hyde Park, New York: New City Press, 1990–. http://www.nlx.com/collections/148.

Bahr, Ehrhard. "Goethe and the Concept of *Bildung* in Jewish Emancipation." In Berghahn and Hermand, *Goethe in German-Jewish Culture*, 16–30.

———. *The Novel as Archive: The Genesis, Reception, and Criticism of Goethe's "Wilhelm Meisters Wanderjahre."* Columbia, S.C.: Camden House, 1998.

Barner, Wilfried. "150 Jahre nach seinem Tod: Goethe und die Juden." *Bulletin des Leo Baeck Instituts* 63 (1982): 75–82.

Barrett, C. K. *A Critical and Exegetical Commentary on the Acts of the Apostles*. 2 vols. The International Critical Commentary. Edinburgh: T & T Clark, 1994.

Bartscherer, Agnes. "Faustisches. I. Clavicula Salomonis." *Chronik des Wiener Goethe-Vereins* 27 (1913): 9–11.

Batnitzky, Leora Faye. *Idolatry and Representation: The Philosophy of Franz Rosenzweig Reconsidered*. Princeton, N.J.: Princeton University Press, 2000.

Bell, David. *Spinoza in Germany from 1670 to the Age of Goethe*. Leeds: Institute of Germanic Studies, 1984.

Bennett, Benjamin. *Beyond Theory: Eighteenth-Century German Literature and the Poetics of Irony*. Ithaca, N.Y.: Cornell University Press, 1993.

Berger, Peter L. *The Sacred Canopy: Elements of a Sociological Theory of Religion*. New York: Anchor Books, 1990.

Berghahn, Klaus, and Jost Hermand, eds. *Goethe in German-Jewish Culture*. Rochester, N.Y.: Camden House, 2001.

Berlin, Adele, Marc Zvi Brettler, and Michael Fishbane. *The Jewish Study Bible*. Oxford: Oxford University Press, 2004.

Biblia, das ist: die gantze Schrifft Alten Und Newen Testaments: verteutscht: durch Martin Luther . . . mit . . . Kupfferstuecken Matthaei Merians Gezieret. Strassburg, 1630.

Binswanger, Hans Christoph. *Money and Magic: A Critique of the Modern Economy in the Light of Goethe's "Faust."* Translated by J. E. Harrison. Chicago: University of Chicago Press, 1994.

Birk, Manfred. "Goethes Typologie der Epochenschwelle im vierten Akt des *Faust II*." *Jahrbuch der deutschen Schillergesellschaft* 33 (1989): 261–80.

Bishop, Paul, ed. *A Companion to Goethe's Faust: Parts I and II*. Rochester, N.Y.: Camden House, 2001.

Bloom, Harold. *The Anxiety of Influence*. New York: Oxford University Press, 1973.

———, ed. *Exodus*. Modern Critical Interpretations. New York: Chelsea House, 1987.

Bohm, Arnd. "Naming Goethe's *Faust*: A Matter of Significance." *Deutsche Vierteljahrsschrift für Literaturwissenschaft und Geistesgeschichte* 80, no. 3 (2006): 408–34.

Bollacher, Martin. *Der junge Goethe und Spinoza: Studien zur Geschichte des Spinozismus in der Epoche des Sturms und Drangs*. Studien zur Deutschen Literatur. Tübingen: Niemeyer, 1969.

Börne, Ludwig. *Sämtliche Schriften*. 5 vols. Düsseldorf: Melzer, 1964.

Brettler, Marc Z., and Amy-Jill Levine, eds. *The Jewish Annotated New Testament*. Oxford: Oxford University Press, 2011.

Brown, Jane K. *Goethe's Allegories of Identity*. Philadelphia: University of Pennsylvania Press, 2014.

———. *Goethe's Cyclical Narratives: "Die Unterhaltungen deutscher Ausgewanderten" and "Wilhelm Meisters Wanderjahre."* University of North Carolina Studies in the Germanic Languages and Literatures. Chapel Hill: University of North Carolina Press, 1975.

———. *Goethe's "Faust": The German Tragedy.* Ithaca, N.Y.: Cornell University Press, 1986.

———. "Im Anfang war das Bild: Wilhelm Meister und die Bibel." In Anderegg and Kunz, *Goethe und die Bibel,* 241–60.

Brucker, [Johann] Jacob. *The History of Philosophy, from the Earliest Periods: Drawn up from Brucker's Historia Critica Philosophiæ by William Enfield.* 2 vols. London, 1837. Reprint, Bristol: Thoemmes, 2000.

———. *Kurtze Fragen aus der philosophischen Historie.* 7 vols. Ulm, 1731–37.

Brüning, Gerrit. "Die Wette in Goethes *Faust.*" *The Goethe Yearbook* 17 (2010): 31–54.

Buber, Martin. "The Burning Bush (Exodus 3)." In Bloom, *Exodus,* 29–44.

———. *Moses: The Revelation and the Covenant.* New York: Harper, 1958.

———. *Two Types of Faith.* New York: Harper, 1961.

Buhle, Johann Gottlieb. *Geschichte der neuern Philosophie seit der Epoche der Wiederherstellung der Wissenschaften.* Göttingen, 1800–1805. Reprint, Aetas Kantiana, vol. 52. Brussels: Culture et civilisation, 1969.

Burdach, Konrad. "Faust und Moses." *Sitzungsberichte der Preussischen Akademie der Wissenschaften: Philosophisch-Historische Klasse,* nos. 23, 35, 38 (1912): 358–403, 627–59, 736–89.

"Cabbalisten." In *Deutsche Encyclopädie oder allgemeines Real-Wörterbuch aller Künste und Wissenschaften von einer Gesellschaft Gelehrten.* 23 vols. 4: 707–12. Frankfurt am Main, 1778–1807.

Calderon de la Barca, Don Pedro. *The Great Stage of the World.* Translated by George Brandt. Manchester, Eng.: Manchester University Press, 1976.

Celan, Paul. *"Todesfuge" und andere Gedichte.* Frankfurt am Main: Suhrkamp, 2004.

Chilson, Christa. "Discovering Meaning in Goethe's *Faust* through Holism." M.A. thesis, University of Oklahoma, 2012.

Claviculae Salomonis et Theosophia pneumatica. Wesel/Duisburg: Andreas Luppius, 1686.

Cohen de Herrera, Abraham. *Das Buch Sha'ar Ha-Shamayim, oder, Pforte des Himmels: In welchem die kabbalistischen Lehren philosophisch dargestellt und mit der platonischen Philosophie verglichen werden.* Translated by Friedrich Häussermann. Frankfurt am Main: Suhrkamp, 1974.

Coudert, Allison. *The Impact of the Kabbalah in the Seventeenth Century: The Life and Thought of Francis Mercury Van Helmont (1614–1698).* Brill's Series in Jewish Studies. Leiden: Brill, 1999.

Cusack, Andrew. *The Wanderer in Nineteenth-Century German Literature: Intellectual History and Cultural Criticism.* Rochester, N.Y.: Camden House, 2008.

Dahnke, Hans-Dietrich. "'Das Recht, das Tüchtige aller Zeiten and Völker': Goethe und das Projekt eines 'deutschen Volksbuchs' im Jahre 1808." In *Schönheit, welche nach Wahrheit dürstet: Beiträge zur deutschen Literatur von der Aufklärung bis zur Gegenwart*, edited by Gerhard Kaiser and Heinrich Macher, 85–102. Heidelberg: Universitätsverlag Winter, 2003.

Deetjen, Werner, ed. *Goethe als Benutzer der Weimarer Bibliothek: Ein Verzeichnis der von ihm entliehenen Werke*. Weimar: Böhlaus, 1931.

Der ewige Jude. Eine komische Geschichte aus dem 18. Jahrhundert. Leipzig: Anton Doll, 1800.

Detlef-Müller, Klaus. "Den Krieg Wegschreiben: *Hermann und Dorothea* und *Die Unterhaltungen deutscher Ausgewanderten*." In *Ironische Propheten: Sprachbewußtsein und Humanität in der Literatur von Herder bis Heine*, edited by Birgit Wägenbaur and Markus Heilman, 85–100. Tübingen: Gunter Narr, 2001.

Deutsch, Yaacov. "Johann Jacob Schudt—Der erste Ethnograph der jüdischen Gemeinde in Frankfurt am Main." In *Die Frankfurter Judengasse: Jüdisches Leben in der Frühen Neuzeit*, edited by Fritz Backhaus, 67–76. Frankfurt am Main: Societätsverlag, 2006.

Deutschländer, Leo. *Goethe und das Alte Testament*. Frankfurt: Omonunth, 1923.

Dowden, Steven. "Irony and Ethical Autonomy in *Wilhelm Meisters Wanderjahre*." *Deutsche Vierteljahrsschrift für Literaturwissenschaft und Geistesgeschichte* 68, no. 1 (1994): 134–54.

Duling, Dennis C. "Solomon, Testament of." In *Anchor Bible Dictionary*, edited by David Noel Freedman, 117–19. New York: Doubleday, 1992.

Durrani, O. "Biblical Borrowings in Goethe's *Faust*: A Historical Survey of Their Interpretation." *The Modern Language Review* 72, no. 4 (1977): 829–44.

Dye, Ellis. "Figurations of the Feminine in Goethe's *Faust*." In Bishop, *A Companion to Goethe's Faust*, 95–121.

Eichhorn, Johann Gottfried. *Einleitung in das Alte Testament*. 2nd ed. 3 vols. Leipzig: Weidmann, 1787.

———. *Einleitung in das Alte Testament*. 4th ed. Göttingen: Rosenbusch, 1824.

———. *Einleitung in das Neue Testament*. 3rd ed. Leipzig: Weidmann, 1804–27.

Eisenmenger, Johann Andreas. *Johann Andreä Eisenmengers . . . Entdecktes Judenthum, oder gründlicher und wahrhaffter Bericht, welchergestalt die verstockte Juden die Hochheilige Drey-Einigkeit . . . lästern und verunehren . . . .* 2 vols. Königsberg in Preussen, 1711.

Elior, Rachel. "R. Nathan Adler and the Frankfurt Pietists." In *Jüdische Kultur in Frankfurt am Main von den Anfängen bis zur Gegenwart*, edited by Karl E. Grözinger, 135–78. Wiesbaden: Harrassowitz, 1997.

Elon, Amos. *The Pity of It All: A Portrait of the German-Jewish Epoch, 1743–1933*. New York: Picador, 2002.

Fabricius, Johann Albert. *Codex Pseudoepigraphus Veteris Testamenti*. Hamburg: Theodori Christoph Felginer, 1722.

Felstiner, John. *Paul Celan: Poet, Survivor, Jew*. New Haven, Conn.: Yale University Press, 1995.

Fichte, Johann Gottlieb. *Sämmtliche Werke*. Edited by J. H. Fichte. 8 vols. Berlin: Veit und Comp, 1846.

Flannery, Edward H. *The Anguish of the Jews: Twenty-Three Centuries of Antisemitism*. A Stimulus Book. Rev. ed. New York: Paulist, 1985.

Frankfurter, David. "Introduction and Annotation to the Book of Revelation." In *Jewish Annotated New Testament*, 463–65.

Freud, Sigmund. *Der Mann Moses und die monotheistische Religion*. Frankfurt am Main: Fischer, 1992.

Friedrich, Theodor, and Lothar Scheithauer. *Kommentar zu Goethes "Faust."* Stuttgart: Reclam, 1978.

Gager, John G. *Moses in Graeco-Roman Paganism*. Society of Biblical Literature Monograph Series 16. New York: Abingdon, 1972.

Gaier, Ulrich, ed. *Faust-Dichtungen* by Johann Wolfgang von Goethe. 3 vols. Stuttgart: Reclam, 1999.

Gidion, Jürgen. "Goethe und die Juden." *Neue Sammlung* 40 (2000): 537–54.

Gillman, Neil. *The Death of Death: Resurrection and Immortality in Jewish Thought*. Woodstock, Vt.: Jewish Lights, 2002.

Goethe, Johann Wolfgang von. *Gedenkausgabe der Werke, Briefe und Gespräche*. 24 vols. Zurich: Artemis-Verlag, 1948–71.

———. *Goethes Gespräche*. 10 vols. Leipzig: F. W. v. Biedermann, 1889.

———. *Goethes Werke: Herausgegeben im Auftrage der Großherzogin Sophie von Sachsen*. 133 vols. Weimar: H. Böhlau, Weimar 1887–1919.

———. *Der junge Goethe in seiner Zeit: Texte und Kontexte in zwei Bänden und einer CD-Rom*. Edited by Karl Eibl, Fotis Jannidis, and Marianne Willems. 2 vols. Frankfurt am Main: Insel, 1998.

———. *Sämtliche Werke, Briefe, Tagebücher und Gespräche*, ed. Dieter Borkmeyer et al. 40 vols. Frankfurt am Main: Deutscher Klassiker Verlag, 1985–99.

———. *Sämtliche Werke nach Epochen seines Schaffens, Münchner Ausgabe*. 21 vols. Munich: Hanser, 1985–99.

———. *Werke: Hamburger Ausgabe*. Edited by Erich Trunz. 14 vols. Munich: Beck, 1981.

Goldschmidt, Hermann Levin. *Werkausgabe in neun Bänden*. Edited by Willi Goetschel. 9 vols. Vienna: Passagen, 1997.

Goldstein, Rebecca. *Betraying Spinoza: The Renegade Jew Who Gave Us Modernity*. Jewish Encounters. New York: Schocken, 2006.

Goodrum, William. "Ecclesiastes in Goethe's *Faust*." *The McNeese Review* 14 (1963): 74–79.

Görres, Joseph. *Die Teutschen Volksbücher*. Heidelberg: Mohr and Zimmer, 1807. Reprint, Hildesheim: Georg Olms, 1982.

Göschel, K. F. *Über Göthes "Faust" und dessen Fortsetzung: Nebst einem Anhange von dem Ewigen Juden*. Leipzig: Hartmann, 1824.

Goßens, Peter. "Das Frühwerk bis zu *Der Sand aus den Urnen* (1938–1950)." In *Celan-Handbuch: Leben, Werk, Wirkung*, edited by Markus May, Peter Goßens, and Jürgen Lehmann, 39–53. Stuttgart: Verlag J.B. Metzler, 2008.

Gottfried, Johann Ludwig. *Johann Ludwig Gottfrieds Historische Chronick oder Beschreibung der Merckwürdigsten Geschichte, so sich von Anfang der Welt bis auf den heutigen Tag zugetragen*. 3 vols. Frankfurt am Main: Hutter, 1743–59.

Götting, Franz. "Die Bibliothek von Goethes Vater." *Nassauische Annalen* 24 (1953): 23–69.

Grafton, Anthony, Glenn W. Most, and James E. G. Zetzel. Introduction to *Prolegomena to Homer*, by F. A. Wolf, 3–36. Princeton, N.J.: Princeton University Press, 1985.

Grimm, Jacob, and Wilhelm Grimm. *Deutsches Wörterbuch*. 16 vols. Leipzig: Hirzel, 1854–1961. dwb.uni-trier.de.

Gruber, Mayer. "Job: Introduction and Annotations." In Berlin, Brettler, and Fishbane, eds., *The Jewish Study Bible*.

Guenée, Antoine. *Letters of Certain Jews to Monsieur Voltaire Containing an Apology for Their Own People and for the Old Testament*. Philadelphia, 1795. https://archive.org/stream/lettersofcertain00gu#page/n3/mode/2up.

Gusdorf, Georges. "Conditions and Limits of Autobiography." Translated by James Olney. In *Autobiography: Essays Theoretical and Critical*, edited by James Olney, 28–48. Princeton, N.J.: Princeton University Press, 1980.

Habiger-Tuckzay, Christa. *Magie und Magier im Mittelalter*. Munich: Diederichs, 1992.

Hahn, Barbara. "Demarcations and Projections: Goethe in the Berlin Salons." In *Goethe in German-Jewish Culture*, edited by Berghahn and Hermand, 31–43.

Hamlin, Cyrus, ed. *Faust* by Johann Wolfgang Von Goethe. 2nd ed. New York: Norton, 2001.

Hanson, James. "The Endangered and Reaffirmed Promises of God: A Fruitful Framework for Biblical Theology." *Biblical Theology Bulletin* 30, no. 3 (2000): 90–101.

Hardt, Michael, and Antonio Negri. *Empire*. Cambridge, Mass.: Harvard University Press, 2000.

Hartung, Gunter. "Goethe und die Juden." *Weimarer Beiträge* 40, no. 3 (1994): 398–416.

Hartwich, Wolf-Daniel. *Die Sendung Moses: Von der Aufklärung bis Thomas Mann*. Munich: Fink, 1997.

Hegel, Georg Wilhelm Friedrich. *Hegel's Aesthetics: Lectures on Fine Art*. Translated by T. M. Knox. 2 vols. Oxford: Oxford University Press, 1998.

———. *Werke*. 20 vols. Frankfurt: Suhrkamp, 1986.

Heine, Heinrich. *The Romantic School and Other Essays*. Edited by Jost Hermand and Robert C. Holub. The German Library, vol. 33. New York: Continuum, 1985.

Helfer, Martha B. *The Word Unheard: Legacies of Anti-Semitism in German Literature and Culture*. Evanston, Ill.: Northwestern University Press, 2011.

Henkel, Hermann. *Goethe und die Bibel*. Leipzig: Biedermann, 1890.

Henning, Hans, ed. *D. Fausts Original Geister Command der Höllen und aller ander Geister Zwang*. Leipzig: Zentralantiquariat der DDR, 1979.

Herder, Johann Gottfried. *Sämtliche Werke*. Ed. Bernhard Suphan et al. 33 vols. Berlin: Weidmann, 1877–1913.

———. *Werke in zehn Bänden*. Ed. Günter Arnold et al. 10 vols. Frankfurt: Deutscher Klassiker Verlag, 1993.

Hess, Jonathan. *Germans, Jews and the Claims of Modernity*. New Haven, Conn.: Yale University Press, 2002.

Hezel, Wilhelm Friedrich. *Biblisches Real-Lexicon über Biblische und die Bibel Erläuternde alte Geschichte*. . . . Leipzig: Weygand, 1783.

Hoecherl-Alden, Gisela. "German-Jewish Scholars in U.S. Exile." In Berghahn and Hermand, *German-Jewish Culture*, 123–45.

Holmes, T. M. "Goethe's Hermann und Dorothea: The Dissolution of the Embattled Idyll." *Modern Language Review* 82, no. 1 (January 1987): 109–18.

Homer. *The Iliad of Homer*. Translated by Richmond Lattimore. Chicago: University of Chicago Press, 1976.

Horch, Hans Otto. "Die Juden und Goethe." In Weber, *Goethes Begegnung mit Juden*, 117–31.

Horst, Georg Conrad. *Zauber-Bibliothek, oder, von Zauberei, Theurgie und Mantik, Zauberern, Hexen, und Hexenprocessen, Dämonen, Gespenstern, und Geistererscheinungen. . . .* 6 vols. Mainz: F. Kupferberg, 1821. Reprint, Freiburg in Breisgau: Aurum, 1979, with an introduction by Herbert Kempf.

Hübner, Hans. *Goethes "Faust" und das Neue Testament*. Göttingen: Vandenhoeck & Ruprecht, 2003.

Hume, David, and Dorothy Coleman. *Dialogues concerning Natural Religion and Other Writings*. Cambridge Texts in the History of Philosophy. Cambridge: Cambridge University Press, 2007.

Hutter, Manfred. "Lilith." In *Dictionary of Deities and Demons in the Bible*, edited by Karel van der Toorn, Bob Becking, and Pieter W. van der Horst, 520–21. Leiden and Grand Rapids, Mich.: Eerdmans, Brill, 1999.

Jacobi, Friedrich Heinrich. *Über die Lehre des Spinoza in Briefen an den Herrn Moses Mendelssohn*. Breslau: 1789. Reprint, Aetas Kantiana, vol. 116. Brussels: Culture et civilisation, 1968.

Jasper, Willi. "Die Entstehung eines nationalen Goethe-Bildes im 19. Jahrhundert." In Weber, *Goethes Begegnung mit Juden*, 133–44.

———. *Faust und die Deutschen*. Berlin: Rowohlt, 1998.

Josephus, Flavius. *Flavius Josephus, Translation and Commentary*. Edited by Steve Mason. 10 vols. Leiden: Brill, 2000–2007.

Josipovici, Gabriel. "An Open Book: How the Bible Places Realism above Consolation." *Times Literary Supplement*, February 24, 2006, 12–13.

Kafka, Franz. *Tagebücher 1910–1923*. Frankfurt am Main: Fischer, 1951.

Kaiser, Gerhard. *Goethe—Nähe durch Abstand: Vorträge und Studien*. Jena: Verlag und Datenbank für Geisteswissenschaften, 2000.

———. "Goethes *Faust* und die Bibel." *Deutsche Vierteljahrsschrift für Literaturwissenschaft und Geistesgeschichte* 58, no. 3 (1983): 391–413.

Kant, Immanuel. *Critique of Judgement*. Oxford World's Classics. Oxford: Oxford University Press, 2007.

Kemper, Hans-Georg, and Hans Schneider, eds. *Goethe und der Pietismus*. Tübingen: Verlag der Franckeschen Stiftungen Halle im Max Niemeyer Verlag, 2001.

Kerry, Paul E. *Enlightenment Thought in the Writings of Goethe: A Contribution to the History of Ideas*. Rochester, N.Y.: Camden House, 2001.

Knorr von Rosenroth, Christian, ed. *Kabbala Denudata*. 2 vols. Sulzbach, 1677. Reprint, Hildesheim: G. Olms, 1974.

Könnecker, Barbara. "Zauberei und Zauberer in der deutschen Literatur des 16. Jahrhunderts." In *Mysticism, Magic and Kabbalah in Ashkenazi Judaism*, edited by Karl Erich Grözinger and Joseph Dan, 181–94. Berlin: De Gruyter, 1995.

Körte, Mona. *Die Uneinholbarkeit des Verfolgten : Der Ewige Jude in der literarischen Phantastik*. Frankfurt: Campus, 2000.

Kosta, Sasha. "J.W. Goethe: *Faust*, Das Hexeneinmaleins." K. Dautels ZUM-Seiten: Unterrichtsprojekte, Ideen und Materialien. Last modified January 2006. http://www.zum.de/Faecher/D/BW/gym/faust/hexen/einmaleins_3.htm.

Kracauer, Isador. *Geschichte der Juden in Frankfurt am Main (1150–1824)*. 2 vols. Frankfurt am Main: I. Kauffmann, 1927.

Kremer, Detlef. "Kabbalistische Signaturen: Sprachmagie als Brennpunkt Romantischer Imagination bei E.T.A. Hoffmann und Achim von Arnim." In *Kabbala und die Literatur der Romantik: Zwischen Magie und Trope*, edited by Eveline Goodman-Thau, Gert Mattenklott, and Christoph Schulte, 197–222. Tübingen: Niemeyer, 1999.

Kreutzer, Hans Joachim. *Der Mythos vom Volksbuch: Studien zur Wirkungsgeschichte des frühen deutschen Romans seit der Romantik*. Stuttgart: Metzler, 1977.

Laan, James van der. *Seeking Meaning for Goethe's "Faust."* New York: Continuum, 2007.

Lang, Bernhard. *Joseph in Egypt: A Cultural Icon from Grotius to Goethe*. New Haven, Conn.: Yale University Press, 2009.

Lange, Horst. "Goethe and Spinoza: A Reconsideration." *Goethe Yearbook* 18 (2011): 11–33.

———. "Issac, Iphigeneia, Christ: Human Sacrifice and the Semiotics of Divine Intentions in Goethe." *Publications of the English Goethe Society* 78, no. 3 (2009): 166–88.

———. "Reconstructing a Nation's Birth: Monotheism, Nationalism, and Violence in Goethe's Reading of the Pentateuch." *Colloquia Germanica* 33, no. 2 (2000): 103–21.

Lessing, Gotthold Ephraim. *Werke und Briefe: In zwölf Bänden*. Bibliothek Deutscher Klassiker. Edited by Wilfried Barner. 12 vols. Frankfurt am Main: Deutscher Klassiker Verlag, 1985–2003.

Levenson, Alan T. *Between Philosemitism and Antisemitism: Defenses of Jews and Judaism in Germany, 1871–1932*. Lincoln: University of Nebraska Press, 2004.

Levenson, Jon D. *Creation and the Persistence of Evil: The Jewish Drama of Divine Omnipotence*. Princeton, N.J.: Princeton University Press, 1988.

Levine, Amy-Jill. *The Misunderstood Jew: The Church and the Scandal of the Jewish Jesus*. New York: Harper Collins, 2006.

Levine, Amy-Jill, and Marc Zvi Brettler, eds. *The Jewish Annotated New Testament*. Oxford: Oxford University Press, 2011.

Levinson, Bernard. "Goethe's Analysis of Exodus 34 and Its Influence on Wellhausen: The *Pfropfung* of the Documentary Hypothesis." *Zeitschrift für die alttestamentliche Wissenschaft* 114 (2002): 212–23.

Librett, Jeffrey. *The Rhetoric of Cultural Dialogue: Jews and Germans from Moses Mendelssohn to Richard Wagner and Beyond*. Stanford, Calif.: Stanford University Press, 2000.

Lieber, David L. et al. *Etz Hayim: Torah and Commentary*. New York: Jewish Publication Society, 2001.

Linder, Luz-María. *Goethes Bibelrezeption: Hermeneutische Reflexion, fiktionale Darstellung, historisch-kritische Bearbeitung*. Europäische Hochschulschriften Reihe I, Deutsche Sprache und Literatur. Frankfurt am Main: Peter Lang, 1998.

Luden, Heinrich. *Reise Seiner Hoheit des Herzogs Bernhard zu Sachsen-Weimar-Eisenach durch Nord-Amerika in den Jahren 1825 und 1826*. Weimar: Hoffmann, 1828. https://archive.org/stream/reisesrhoheitdes00bern#page/n3/mode/2up.

Luther, Martin. *Luther's Works*. Edited by Jaroslav Pelikan and Helmut T. Lehmann. 55 vols. Philadelphia: Muhlenberg, 1955–86.

———, trans. *Martin Luther Bibel: Der komplette Originaltext von 1545 in modernem Schriftbild*. 2 vols. Bonn: Edition Lempertz, 2008.

Lützeler, Paul Michael. *Geschichte in der Literatur: Studien zu Werken von Lessing bis Hebbel*. Munich: Piper, 1987.

Machinist, Peter. "Ecclesiastes: Introduction and Annotations." In Berlin, Brettler, and Fishbane, *The Jewish Study Bible*, 1603–22.

Maimon, Salomon. *Salomon Maimons Lebensgeschichte: Von ihm selbst geschrieben und herausgegeben von Karl Philipp Moritz*. Frankfurt am Main: Insel, 1984.

Maimonides, Moses. *Guide for the Perplexed*. Translated by M. Friedländer. London: Kegan Paul, 2006.

Mâle, Émile. *Religious Art in France: The Twelfth Century: A Study of the Origins of Medieval Iconography*. Translated by Marthiel Mathews. Princeton, N.J.: Princeton University Press, 1978.

Mendelssohn, Moses. *Gesammelte Schriften: Jubiläumsausgabe*. Edited by Fritz Bamberger and Alexander Altmann. 25 vols. Stuttgart-Bad Cannstatt: F. Frommann, 1971– .

Merian, Matthäus (the Elder). *Great Scenes from the Bible: 230 Magnificent 17th-Century Engravings*. Mineola, N.Y.: Dover, 2002.

———. *Iconum Biblicarum*. Wenatchee, Wash.: AVB, 1981.

Möbus, Frank. "Kein Meister über die Geister: Doctor Fausti "Höllenzwänge." In *Faust—Annäherung an einen Mythos*, edited by Frank Möbus, Friederike Schmidt-Möbus, and Gerd Unverfehrt Frank, 36–50. Göttingen: Wallstein, 1995.

Morgan, Peter. *The Critical Idyll: Traditional Values and the French Revolution in Goethe's "Hermann und Dorothea."* Columbia, S.C.: Camden House, 1991.

Muenzer, Clark. "Das Buch Hiob und Goethes Naturbegriff." In Anderegg and Kunz, *Goethe und die Bibel*, 161–71.

Müller, Jan-Dirk. *Romane des 15. und 16. Jahrhunderts: Nach den Erstdrucken mit sämtlichen Holzschnitten*. Bibliothek der Frühen Neuzeit. Frankfurt am Main: Deutscher Klassiker Verlag, 1990.

Muschg, Adolf. "War Goethe Antisemit?" In *Innenaussichten aus Europa*, edited by Richard von Weizsäcker and Helmut Schmidt, 46–88. Die Neue Mittwochgesellschaft. Munich: Beck, 2007.

Neiman, Susan. *Evil in Modern Thought: An Alternative History of Philosophy*. Princeton, N.J.: Princeton University Press, 2002.

Neumann, Almut. *Verträge und Pakte mit dem Teufel: Antike und Mittelälterliche Vorstellungen im "Malleus Maleficarum."* St. Ingbert: Röhrig, 1997.

Nicolai, Heinz. *Zeittafel zu Goethes Leben und Werk*. Munich: Beck, 1977.

Niggl, Günther. *Studien zur Literatur der Goethezeit*. Berlin: Duncker & Humblot, 2001.

Obenauer, Karl Justus. "Goethe Als Naturforscher." *Das deutsche Wort* 11, no. 34 (1935): 8–10.

Och, Gunnar. *Imago Judaica: Juden und Judentum im Spiegel der deutschen Literatur 1750–1812*. Würzburg: Königshausen & Neumann, 1995.

Oellers, Norbert. "Goethe und Schiller in ihrem Verhältnis zum Judentum." In *Conditio Judaica: Judentum, Antisemitismus und deutschsprachige Literatur vom 18. Jahrhundert bis zum Ersten Weltkrieg*, edited by Hans Otto Horch and Horst Denkler, 108–30. Tübingen: Niemeyer, 1988–93.

Oetinger, Friedrich Christoph. *Friedrich Christoph Oetinger*. Edited by Gerhard Karl Schäfer and Martin Schmidt. 3 vols. *Texte zur Geschichte des Pietismus, Abt. 7*. Berlin: Walter de Gruyter, 1999.

Orgel, Maike. "The Faustian 'Gretchen': Overlooked Aspects of a Famous Male Fantasy." *German Life and Letters* 64, no. 1 (January 2011): 43–55.

Pagels, Elaine. *The Origin of Satan*. New York: Vintage, 1996.

Pniower, Otto. "Goethes *Faust* und das Hohe Lied." *Goethe-Jahrbuch* 13 (1892): 181–98.

Polo, Marco. *The Travels of Marco Polo, the Venetian*. New York: Liveright, 2003.

Pope, Marvin H. Introduction, translation, and notes to "Job," in *The Anchor Bible*. New York: Doubleday, 1973.

Popkin, Richard. "Spinoza, Neoplatonic Kabbalist?" In *Neoplatonism and Jewish Thought*, edited by Lenn E. Goodman, 387–409. Albany, N.Y.: SUNY Press, 1992.

Pradel, Elvira, ed. *Scherz und Ernst: Deutsche Schwänke des 16. Jahrhunderts*. Leipzig: Reclam, 1962.

Redfield, Marc. *Phantom Formations: Aesthetic Ideology and the Bildungsroman*. Ithaca, N.Y.: Cornell University Press, 1996.

Reichard, Heinrich August Ottkar. *Der ewige Jude: Geschicht- oder Volksroman, wie man will*. Riga: Hartknoch, 1785.

Reinhold, Carl Leonhard, Jan Assmann, and Friedrich Schiller. *Die Hebräischen Mysterien, oder, die älteste religiöse Freymaurerey*. Neckargemünd: Mnemosyne Edition, 2001.

Rennie, Nicholas. *Speculating on the Moment: The Poetics of Time and Recurrence in Goethe, Leopardi, and Nietzsche*. Göttingen: Wallstein, 2005.

Requadt, Paul. *Goethes "Faust I": Leitmotivik und Architektur*. Munich: Fink, 1972.

Ricoeur, Paul. "Evil." In *The Encyclopedia of Religion*, edited by Mircea Eliade. 16 vols. in 8. New York: Macmillan Library Reference, 1995.

Riemer, Friedrich Wilhelm. *Mitteilungen Über Goethe*. Leipzig: Insel-Verlag, 1921.

Rosenberg, Isaac. "Koheleth und Goethes *Faust*." *Jahrbuch für jüdische Geschichte und Literatur* 11 (1908): 151–75.

Rousseau, Jean-Jacques. *Confessions*. Translated by Angela Scholar. Oxford: Oxford University Press, 2000.

Rudavsky, T. M. "Galileo and Spinoza: Heroes, Heretics, and Hermeneutics." *Journal of the History of Ideas* 62, no. 4 (2001): 611–31.

Sauder, Gerhard. "Aufklärerische Bibelkritik und Bibelrezeption in Goethes Werk." *Goethe-Jahrbuch* 118 (2001): 108–25.

Schapkow, Carsten. *"Die Freiheit zu philosophieren": Jüdische Identität in der Moderne im Spiegel der Rezeption Baruch de Spinozas in der deutschsprachigen Literatur*. Bielefeld: Aisthesis, 2001.

Schiller, Friedrich. *Werke: Nationalausgabe*. Edited by Julius Petersen et al. 42 vols. Weimar: H. Böhlaus Nachfolger, 1943– .

Schings, Hans-Jürgen. *Melancholie und Aufklärung: Melancholiker und ihre Kritiker in Erfahrungsseelenkunde und Literatur des 18. Jahrhunderts*. Stuttgart: Metzler, 1977.

Schirach, Baldur von. "Goethe-Rede." Reprinted in *Diskussionen Deutsch* 19 (1988): 153–56.

Schlaffer, Hannelore. "Paradies und Parodie: Die letzten Szenen in Goethes letzten Werken." In *Interpreting Goethe's "Faust" Today*, edited by Meredith Lee, Jane K. Brown, and Thomas P. Saine in collaboration with Paul Hernadi and Cyrus Hamlin, 102–11. Columbia, S.C.: Camden House, 1994.

Schlick, Gabriela. "Was Johann Wolfgang Goethe hätte sehen können . . . Die Judengasse in Frankfurt am Main." In Weber, *Goethes Begegnung mit Juden*, 47–66.

Schlößler, Franziska. "Progress and Restorative Utopia in *Faust II* and *Wilhelm Meisters Wanderjahre*." In Bishop, *A Companion to Goethe's Faust*, 169–93.

Schmidt, Jochen. "Die 'Katholische Mythologie' und ihre mystische Entmythologisierung in der Schluss-Szene des *Faust II*." *Jahrbuch der deutschen Schillergesellschaft* 34 (1990): 230–56.

———. *Goethes "Faust, Erster und Zweiter Teil": Grundlagen—Werk—Wirkung*. Arbeitsbücher zur Literaturgeschichte. Munich: Beck, 1999.

Schmidt, Josef, ed. *Erläuterungen und Dokumente: Johann Wolfgang Goethe, "Hermann und Dorothea."* Stuttgart: Reclam, 1970.

Schneider, Helmut J. "Satan and the Adamitic Gaze: Enlightenment Autonomy and the Gift of Creation: Versions of the Genesis from Milton to Goethe." *Colloquium Helveticum* 34 (2003): 143–56.

Scholem, Gershom. "Alchemie und Kabbala." *Eranos* 46 (1977): 1–96.

———. "Die Wachtersche Kontroverse über den Spinozismus und ihre Folgen." In *Spinoza in der Frühzeit seiner religiösen Wirkung*, edited by Karlfield Gründer and Wilhelm Schmidt-Biggemann, 15–25. Heidelberg: Lambert Schneider, 1984.

———. *Major Trends in Jewish Mysticism*. New York: Schocken, 1995.

Schöne, Albrecht. *Goethe: "Faust," Kommentare*. Frankfurt: Deutscher Klassiker Verlag, 2005.

———. *Vom Betreten des Rasens: Siebzehn Reden über Literatur*. Edited by Jürgen Stenzel, Ulrich Joost, and Ernst Peter Wieckenberg. Munich: Beck, 2005.

Schottroff, Willy. "Goethe als Bibelwissenschaftler." In *Allerhand Goethe: Seine wissenschaftliche Sendung aus Anlaß des 150. Todestages und des 50.*

Namentages der Johann Wolfgang Goethe-Universität in Frankfurt am Main, edited by Dieter Kimpel and Jörg Pompetzki, 111–37. Frankfurt am Main: Peter Lang, 1985.

Schrader, Hans-Jürgen. "Hiob in Deutscher Dichting (*Faust*—Joseph Roth—Lyrik nach der Shoah): Muster des Menschen—des Jüdischen Leids—die Frage nach Theodizee." *Monatshefte für evangelische Kirchengeschichte des Rheinlands* 53 (2004): 1–32.

———. "Von Patriarchensehnsucht zur Passionsemphase: Bibelallusionen und spekulative Theologie in Goethes *Werther*." In Anderegg and Kunz, *Goethe und die Bibel*, 57–88.

Schreckenberg, Heinz. *The Jews in Christian Art: An Illustrated History*. New York: Continuum, 1996.

Schudt, Johann Jacob. *Jüdische Merckwürdigkeiten, vorstellende was sich curieuses und denckwürdiges in den neuern Zeiten bey einigen Jahrhunderten mit denen in alle IV. Theile der Welt, sonderlich durch Teutschland, zerstreuten Juden zugetragen* . . . 3 vols. in 1. Frankfurt: Tobias Hocker, 1715.

Schulte, Christoph. "Zimzum bei Schelling." In *Kabbala und Romantik*, edited by Eveline Goodman-Thau, Gert Mattenklott, and Christoph Schulte, 97–118. Tübingen: Niemeyer, 1994.

Schulz, Guenther. "Goethe und die bäuerliche Welt." Special printing. *Odal: Monatschrift für Blut und Boden* 9 (1940).

Seibt, Gustav. *Goethe und Napoleon: Eine historische Begegnung*. Munich: C.H. Beck, 2008.

Sheehan, Jonathan. *The Enlightenment Bible: Translation, Scholarship, Culture*. Princeton, N.J.: Princeton University Press, 2005.

Solms, Wilhelm. *Goethes Vorarbeiten zum Divan*. Münchner Germanistische Beiträge 12. Munich: Fink, 1977.

Spinoza, Benedictus de. *Complete Works*. Translated by Samuel Shirley. Indianapolis, Ind.: Hackett, 2002.

Stenzel, Jürgen, and Oliver Höher. "'Die Verschrobenheit eines veralteten Unsinns': Goethe's 'Judenpredigt.'" *Jahrbuch des Freien Deutschen Hochstifts* special printing (2000): 1–26.

Stoeffler, F. Ernest. *German Pietism during the Eighteenth Century*. Leiden: Brill, 1973.

Sullivan, Heather I. "Ecocriticism, the Elements, and the Ascent/Descent into Weather in Goethe's *Faust*." *Goethe Yearbook* 17 (2010): 55–72.

Swales, Martin. "Goethe's Prose Fiction." In *The Cambridge Companion to Goethe*, edited by Lesley Sharpe, 129–46. Cambridge, Eng.: Cambridge University Press, 2002.

Sweeney, Marvin A. "Ezekial: Introduction and Annotations." In Berlin, Brettler, and Fishbane, *The Jewish Study Bible*, 1042–1138.

Tantillo, Astrida. "Damned to Heaven: The Tragedy of Faust Revisited." *Monatshefte* 99, no. 4 (2007): 454–68.

———. *The Will to Create: Goethe's Philosophy of Nature*. Pittsburgh, Pa.: University of Pittsburgh Press, 2002.

Teller, Romanus, Johann Augustin Dietelmair, and Johann Jakob Brucker, eds. *Die Heilige Schrift, nebst einer vollstaendigen Erklaerung derselben* . . . 19 vols. Leipzig: Breitkopf, 1749–70.

Thielicke, Helmut. *Goethe und das Christentum*. Munich: Piper, 1982.

Tiedemann, Dietrich. *Geist der spekulativen Philosophie*. Marburg, 1791–97. Reprint, Aetas Kantiana, vol. 274. Brussels: Culture et civilisation, 1969.

Tigay, Jeffrey H. "Exodus: Introduction and Annotations." In Berlin, Brettler, and Fishbane, *The Jewish Study Bible*, 102–202.

Tillmann, Thomas. "Vom Sprechen zum Lallen: Glossolalie und Prophetie in Goethes 'Zwo wichtige bisher unerörterte biblische Fragen.' " In Anderegg and Kunz, *Goethe und die Bibel*, 17–34.

Todorov, Tzvetan. *Theories of the Symbol*. Translated by Catherine Porter. Ithaca, N.Y.: Cornell University Press, 1982.

Torijano, Pablo A. *Solomon, the Esoteric King: From King to Magus, Development of a Tradition*. Supplements to the *Journal for the Study of Judaism*. Leiden: Brill, 2002.

Updike, John. "The Great I Am: Robert Alter's New Translation of the Pentateuch." Review of Robert Alter, *Five Books of Moses*. *The New Yorker*, November 1, 2004, 100–104.

Vaget, Hans. "The GDR Faust: A Literary Autopsy." *Oxford German Studies* 24, no. 1 (1995): 145–74.

Veltri, Giuseppe. "Jews and Judaism in Goethe's Esthetical and Reactionary World: A Typological Study." *Revue des Études Juives* 162, no. 1–2 (January–June 2003): 123–44.

Vos, Geerhardus. "Hebrews, the Epistle of the Diatheke." *Princeton Theological Review* 13, no. 4 (1915): 587–632. http://www.bible-researcher.com/vos-diatheke.html.

Waldman, Mark. *Goethe and the Jews: A Challenge to Hitlerism*. New York: G. P. Putnam's Sons, 1934.

Wall, Robert W. "The Acts of the Apostles: Introduction, Commentary, and Reflections." In *The New Interpreter's Bible*. 12 vols. 10: 1–368. Nashville, Tenn.: Abingdon, 2002.

Weber, Annette, ed. *"Außerdem waren sie ja auch Menschen": Goethes Begegnung mit Juden und Judentum*. Berlin: Philo, 2000.

Weiser, Benedikt, ed. *Goethe als Kämpfer: Zitate*. Field post edition. Berlin: Mittler, 1942.

Welling, Georg von. *Opus Mago-Cabbalisticum et Theosophicum*. Translated by Joseph G. McVeigh. San Francisco: Weiser, 2006.

Wilson, W. Daniel. "Goethes Haltung zur Judenemanzipation und jüdische Haltungen zu Goethe." In Weber, *Goethes Begegnung mit Juden*, 19–46.

———. " 'Humanitätsalbader': Goethe's Distaste for Jewish Emancipation and Jewish Responses." In Berghahn and Hermand, *German-Jewish Culture*, 146–64.

Wolfers, David. *Deep Things out of Darkness: The Book of Job: Essays and a New English Translation*. Kampen, Neth., and Grand Rapids, Mich.: Pharos and Wm. B. Eerdmans, 1995.

Wüthrich, Lucas Heinrich. *Matthaeus Merian d. Ä.: Eine Biographie*. Hamburg: Hoffmann und Campe, 2007.

Wyder, Margit. " 'Die Reiche der Welt und ihre Herrlichkeit': Biblische Bezüge in Goethes Gedanken zur Erdgeschichte." In Anderegg and Kunz, *Goethe und die Bibel*, 135–60.

Zedler, Johann Heinrich. *Großes Vollständiges Universallexicon aller Wissenschaften und Künste.* 64 vols. Leipzig, 1732–54.

Zevit, Ziony. "Kings: Introduction and Annotations." In Berlin, Brettler, and Fishbane, *The Jewish Study Bible*, 668–725.

Zimmermann, Rolf Christian. *Das Weltbild des jungen Goethe: Studien zur hermetischen Tradition des deutschen 18. Jahrhunderts.* 2 vols. Munich: W. Fink, 1969, 1979.

Zipfel, Frank. "'Ich hätte euch einen ganz anderen Moses machen wollen': Überlegungen zu Goethes Moses-Bild in 'Israel in der Wüste.'" In Anderegg and Kunz, *Goethe und die Bibel*, 185–216.

INDEX

Adam of Prague, 211n17
Adelung, Johann Christoph, 129–30
Adler, Nathan, 54
afterlife, conceptions of, 131–34, 177
Ahasverus. *See* Wandering Jew legend
Albrecht, Johann Georg, 20, 42–43
alchemy, 52, 127, 128–29, 144, 164–65; money-making and, 219n45; Moses and, 159–60, 165
allegory, 36, 114–16, 166
Alter, Robert, 20, 22, 100, 160, 161–62, 196n61
Anaxagoras, 159
Anderegg, Johannes, 154, 183, 221n86, 222n91
anti-Semitism, 5–7, 17–19, 34, 71–74, 127–28, 143, 193nn17–19, 196n57; in *Faust*, 163–64; in *Wilhelm Meister's Journeyman Years*, 109–10, 120–24
apocrypha and pseudepigrapha, 142–43, 145–46, 148
Arnim, Bettina von, 7, 202n79
Arnold, Gottfried, 105, 181, 209n47
Astruc, Jean, 21
Auerbach, Erich, 12–13, 20, 180
Augustine, 10, 25, 29–31, 36, 41, 59, 64, 74; on original sin, 29, 56, 57
autobiography genre, 30–31

Bahr, Ehrhard, 191
Bartscherer, Agnes, 213n32
Benjamin, Walter, 4, 114
Bennett, Benjamin, 110, 122
Berger, Peter, 31, 32
Bible. *See* Hebrew Bible; New Testament
Binswanger, Hans Christoph, 160, 164–65
Birk, Manfred, 219n41
Blackall, Eric A., 112
"blood libel," 128
blood pacts, 130–31, 134
Bloom, Harold, 12, 192n14
Bodmer, Johann Jacob, 84
Böhm, Arnd, 137, 184
Boiserée, Sulpiz, 7, 158
Börne, Ludwig, 4
Brettler, Marc Zvi, 22
Brown, Jane, 110, 153, 166, 170, 178, 222n91
Brucker, Johannes Jacob, 53–59 passim
Buber, Martin, 23, 46, 197n74
Buddeus, Johann Franciscus, 52
Buhle, Johann Gottlieb, 53, 55–56, 201n54
Burdach, Konrad, 157–58, 159–60, 175–76

Calderón de la Barca, Pedro, 169
cameralism, 80
Celan, Paul, 188–90
Charles V, 163
Christianity, 7–9, 25, 35, 37, 46, 71, 80–81, 102–3, 105, 108, 110–18, 121–24, 194n32; in *Faust*, 125–26, 131, 133–37, 147–48, 177–86; supersession of Judaism, 12–13, 26, 34, 42, 60, 74–78, 80, 105–7, 116, 122, 124, 134, 156, 178–81, 184, 189, 195n47, 207n16, 208n25; Wandering Jew and, 59–60, 126

contraction and expansion principle, 24, 51, 55, 57–58, 61, 64, 113, 125, 131, 136, 142, 155, 158, 171, 185, 210n1
Coudert, Alison, 53
covenant concept, 13, 26, 46, 62, 74, 76–77, 89, 203n12, 218n16; in *Faust*, 125–26, 130–31, 134, 138–39, 141, 147–48, 154–58, 171, 173, 179–80, 186, 210n2, 214n58, 214n65
Cusack, Andrew, 10, 32

Dahnke, Hans Dietrich, 98

Eckermann, Johann, 5, 111
Eichhorn, Johann Gottfried, 21, 22, 44, 84, 100, 101–2, 104, 138, 139, 142, 144, 152, 182
Eisenmenger, Johann Andreas, 127, 143, 145, 147, 177
Elon, Amos, 191n9
Enlightenment, 4–5, 72–73, 76; religion and the, 20, 37, 117, 131, 209n35
epic genre, 82–85, 91, 96, 204n29
Epicurus, 30
Erwin von Steinbach, 69–71, 81
Eternal Feminine, 136, 148, 162, 181, 185, 222n103
evil, problem of, 30–31, 51, 55–56, 155–56

fables: Goethe on, 91
Fabricius, Johann Alberta, 143, 216n89
Faust (character): death of, 3, 177–78, 181, 183, 189; heroism, 8, 125; Jewish characterization, 26, 125, 127–31; Job and, 26, 126, 137–42, 182–84, 189; Moses and, 26, 96, 156–63, 167–72, 175–77, 190; near-suicide, 131–34; religious conflicts, 131–37; as servant of God, 137, 138, 141, 142, 149, 177, 215n76; Solomon and, 26, 62, 126, 129–30, 142, 144–49, 155, 189, 213n33, 216n91; as wanderer (and Wandering Jew), 11, 119, 125, 126–27, 141
Faust's Coercion of Hell, 129–30
Faustus legend, 126–30, 163
Felstiner, John, 188
First Coalition War, 81
Flaubert, Gustave, 20
Freemasonry, 143–44
French Revolution, 81, 87, 91, 94, 96, 97
Freud, Sigmund, 206n48
Fugger, Jakob, 163

Gaier, Ulrich, 219n41
Galilei, Galileo, 43
Geiger, Ludwig, 3–4
Gidion, Jürgen, 193n17
Gillman, Neil, 213n46
Goethe, August von, 97
Goethe, Johan Caspar, 36, 38–40, 53, 127, 143
Goethe, Johann Wolfgang von: anxiety of Jewish influence, 4, 66, 192n14; on authentic art, 69, 73; childhood, 36–43, 64–66, 133, 160; conservatism, 4, 7, 23, 163; contradictory spirit, 24, 27, 32, 35, 58; on the daemonic, 202n72; editor concept, 68; elitism, 4, 23, 81, 83; on the French, 70–71, 72, 81, 82–83, 91; on the German public, 83; Hebrew language studies, 41–42; Jewish views of, 3–4, 191n8; Joseph story appeal, 14–15, 49, 92–93, 164, 195n53; Kabbalah studies, 51–58, 66; legacy, 3–4, 188–90; nationalist concerns, 9, 25, 67–99, 101, 102–3; religious studies and views, 7, 8–9, 13–15, 19, 20–25, 36–52, 57, 61–63, 106, 111, 117–18, 133, 140–41, 183, 198nn18–20; scientific views, 24, 58, 160; symbolism techniques, 111–12, 114–16
WORKS:
De Legislatoribus, 78
Egmont, 29

Faust, Part One, 11–12, 25–26, 30, 125–49, 151–52, 154, 157, 184
Faust, Part Two, 26, 120, 128, 151–86, 188–89
"The Golden Words of Solomon," 143
Götz von Berlichingen, 163
Hermann and Dorothea, 25, 82–89, 91, 95–96, 163, 166, 204nn23–24, 205n41
"Israel in the Desert," 21, 23, 25, 82, 85, 90–96, 157, 164, 204n22, 204n24
"Jewish Sermon," 27
"Letter of the Pastor at *** to the New Pastor at ***," 67, 71–73, 76, 181
"On Epic and Dramatic Poetry" (with Schiller), 85, 205n33
"On German Architecture," 67, 69–71, 81
The Plundersweil Fair, 27
"Poems by a Polish Jew," 27, 197n77
poetry, 9, 45, 79, 147–48, 152, 158, 185
Poetry and Truth, 7, 10, 11, 13, 18, 19, 21, 22, 24–25, 29, 31–66, 68, 77, 84, 100, 106, 113, 125, 140–41, 142, 155, 157, 185, 199n32
"Response to a Literary Rabble-Rouser," 83
scientific writings, 58
The Sorrows of Young Werther, 9, 111, 167
Theory of Colors, 58, 193n18, 207n16, 219n43
"Two Important, Hitherto Undiscussed Biblical Questions," 21, 67, 71, 73–81, 90
Volksbuch project, 25, 98–106, 124, 151, 187, 207n5
Wilhelm Meister's Apprenticeship, 8, 104, 105–7, 111, 121, 151, 209n47, 219n44
Wilhelm Meister's Journeyman Years, 11, 25, 60, 103–25, 151, 187–88, 208n31, 209n35, 209n39
Xenia (with Schiller), 9, 83, 158, 176
Goethe, Katharina Elisabeth, 46, 50, 202n79
Goldschmidt, Hermann Levin, 96
Görres, Josef, 99
Göschel, Karl Friedrich, 119, 127, 195n43, 208n27
Gottfried, Johann Ludwig, 17–18
Gretchen (character), 131, 136–37, 146–48, 171, 178, 180, 184–85, 189, 217n105
Gruber, Mayer, 139, 183
Gusdorf, Georges, 24–25, 31

Hahn, Barbara, 191n4
Hamann, Johann, Georg, 69
Hamlin, Cyrus, 168
Hardt, Michael, and Antonio Negri, 5
Hartung, Gunter, 193n17
Hebrew Bible, 9, 12–27, 30, 37, 40–42, 68, 99–101, 116, 124, 125–26, 130, 167, 171, 185–88, 194n36, 196n58; relationship to New Testament, 19–20, 37, 103, 105, 126, 131, 135–36, 138, 139–40, 151, 156, 181
BOOKS:
Genesis, 5, 11, 12, 14–16, 19, 20, 21–24, 30, 37–38, 40–51, 55, 61–62, 64, 68, 70, 89, 92–95, 106, 113, 125, 151–56, 160–62, 164, 167, 170, 174, 175, 179, 205n41
Exodus, 9, 12–13, 16–18, 22–24, 25, 26, 73–74, 76–78, 81–82, 84, 86–90, 92–94, 130, 133, 135, 151, 156, 159–69 passim, 203n12, 204n24
Leviticus, 90
Numbers, 30, 88, 90, 157, 160, 164, 175
Deuteronomy, 77, 88, 90, 139, 140

Hebrew Bible, BOOKS, *continued*
Joshua, 12–13, 43, 86–88, 95, 152, 172
Judges, 95, 152, 172, 205n37
1 Samuel, 106
2 Samuel, 172–73
1 Kings, 142, 143, 145, 147, 173, 174
2 Kings, 131, 160
Isaiah, 38, 74, 167, 181, 202n70
Jeremiah, 74
Ezekiel, 103, 133, 207n17
Psalms, 12, 38, 70, 173–74, 206n49
Proverbs, 142, 147, 148; Job, 21, 26, 137–41, 151–52, 156, 161, 182–84, 215nn73–74, 221n90
Song of Songs, 21, 142–43, 146–48, 152, 189, 217n105
Ruth, 100, 207n11
Ecclesiastes, 21, 62, 122, 142, 143, 144, 146, 216n85, 216n92
Esther, 100, 207n11
2 Chronicles, 142
Hegel, Georg Wilhelm Friedrich, 31, 113–14, 115, 123, 209n39
Heine, Heinrich, 4, 31, 189
Herder, Johann Gottfried, 24, 31, 67–74 passim; on Hebrew Bible, 19, 21, 25, 45, 46, 68, 84, 138, 152, 156, 175, 202n1; on Jewish legends ("Scattered Leaves"), 133, 143, 176, 216n88; on Kabbalah, 53, 129; tree imagery, 68, 73, 74, 203n9
Herrera, Abraham Cohen, 52–53, 54–55, 64, 202nn74–75
Hess, Jonathan, 4–5, 124
Hezel, Wilhelm Friedrich, 46
Hillel, 124
Homer (and Homeridae), 70, 83, 84–85, 99, 152, 166–67, 204n28
Horch, Hans Otto, 191n8
Hübner, Hans, 180
Humboldt, Wilhelm von, 86
Hume, David, 30

idolatry: in Goethe's work, 111, 142, 147, 155, 163, 164, 170–71, 174, 181–82, 185–86; in Judaism, 9, 26, 113–16, 117, 123, 142, 159–60, 166, 168; Solomon and, 143, 145–48, 155, 174, 185

Jacobi, Friedrich Heinrich, 54, 55
Jewish emancipation, 7–8, 81, 82, 91–92, 94–96, 110
Jewish stereotypes, 5–6, 8, 119–20, 127–28, 130, 163–64, 193n18, 219n43
Josephus, Flavius, 129, 143, 145, 215n84
Josipovici, Gabriel, 20, 44
Judaism: afterlife disbelief, 131–32, 142, 213n46; ban on images, 9, 26, 113–16, 117, 123, 124, 133, 159–60, 166, 168; divine visions in, 133; faith and, 45–49, 93, 126; in Goethe's autobiography, 29–66, 77; "heroic obedience," 132; Mendelssohn on, 117–18, 123–24; in the New Testament, 178–79, 181; originality of, 101–2; Ten Commandments, 76–78, 168; wandering and, 10–11, 29–30, 42, 49, 88, 101, 105, 109, 116, 118, 125, 187; in *Wilhelm Meister's Journeyman Years*, 109–10, 113–16, 119, 121–23. *See also* anti-Semitism; Hebrew Bible; Kabbalah
Jung-Stilling, Johann Heinrich, 33–34, 140, 215n73

Kabbalah, 25, 51–58, 63–64, 66, 113, 125, 128–29, 155, 163, 181, 199nn34–35, 211–12nn21–23; Christian vs. Jewish, 56, 128, 199n35
Kafka, Franz, 20
Kaiser, Gerhard, 136, 205n39
Kant, Immanuel, 9, 111, 113–14, 115, 132–33, 181
Kerry, Paul E., 209n35
Key of Solomon, 129–30, 144, 145, 213n32
Kiesewetter, Carl, 130

Klettenberg, Susanne von, 53, 59, 209n47
Klopstock, Friedrich Gottlieb, 84, 144
Knorr von Rosenroth, Christian, 53, 55
Koholeth. *See* Solomon
Koran, 100, 143
Kulturnation, 9–10, 24, 25, 91, 96, 194n35

Laan, James van der, 161
Landauer, Gustav, 4
Lange, Horst, 9, 91, 197n75, 201n68
Lavater, Johann Kaspar, 8, 104, 111, 117–18, 124
Leibniz, Gottfried Wilhelm, 53
Lersé, Franz Christian, 78
Lessing, Gotthold Ephraim, 55, 118, 123, 131–32, 214n48
Levenson, Alan, 6–7
Levenson, Jon D., 160, 198n24
Levine, Amy-Jill, 179
Levinson, Bernard, 75
Librett, Jeffrey, 115
Linder, Luz-María, 41, 204n24
Lisbon earthquake, 39, 46–47, 66, 156, 181
Lucian, 43
Lucifer, 51, 56–58
Luria, Isaac, 52–53, 55, 57. *See also* Kabbalah
Luther, Martin, 13, 46, 74, 127, 157, 218n18; translation of the Bible, 13, 87, 99, 100, 131, 137, 145–46, 161, 162, 164, 168–69, 173, 183–84, 220nn67–68

Maimon, Solomon, 54
Maimonides, Moses, 133
Martius, Carl Friedrich Philipp von, 5
Mary of Egypt, 180
Maximilian I, 163
Meisel, Mordechai, 219n42
Mendelssohn, Moses, 46, 54, 117–18, 123–24, 132, 194n33
Mephistopheles (character), 30, 128, 130–32 passim, 137–38, 142, 154, 164–66, 168–69, 171–72, 174, 182, 188
Merian, Matthäus, 13–19, 23, 133, 160, 169, 196nn54–55
Merkabah mysticism, 133
Michelangelo, 14–15
Milton, John, 84
modernity, 4–5, 10, 23, 119–20, 151, 157, 166, 171, 187
Montanus, 105
Morgan, Peter, 205n36
Moses, 12–13, 20, 23, 31, 68–70, 76–78, 80–81, 82, 86–96, 130, 156–63, 167–72, 206n43, 218n18; death of, 175–77, 206n48; and epic tradition, 84, 85, 92
Muenzer, Clark, 21, 117, 140
Müller, Friedrich von, 7, 98, 176
Muschg, Adolf, 5, 192n13

Napoleon Bonaparte, 97, 98, 158, 170, 218n25
Nazis and Goethe, 3, 4, 6–7, 86, 189
Neiman, Susan, 31
Neoplatonism, 51, 55, 56, 158
Neumann, Almut, 130
New Jerusalem, 103, 105, 124, 151
New Testament, 11, 12–13, 15–20, 22, 24, 27, 30, 46, 59–60, 61–62, 70–71, 74–75, 78–79, 103, 124, 126, 130, 176, 178–81, 203n19; *Faust* and, 133–36, 170, 171–72, 178–79; Goethe on, 19, 37, 40–41, 43; relationship to Hebrew Bible, 19–20, 37, 103, 105, 126, 131, 135–36, 138, 139–40, 151, 156, 181, 183–84; *Wilhelm Meister's Journeyman Years* and, 105–6
Nibelungenlied, 83–84
Niethammer, Immanuel, 98–100, 103
Nietzsche, Friedrich, 12, 190
Nostradamus, 130
Novalis, 31

Oellers, Norbert, 193n17
Oetinger, Friedrich Christoph, 53, 54
Old Testament. *See* Hebrew Bible
Origen, 181
original sin, 30, 38, 56–57, 66
Ovid, 175

Pagels, Elaine, 137
paper money, 119–20, 163, 164–65, 168, 219n45
Paracelsus, 52
Paul, 13, 74–75, 79, 140
Pelagianism, 57–58, 59, 201n59
philo-Semitism, 6–7, 9–10
Pietism, 8, 40, 53, 59, 71, 73, 209n47
Pinto, Isaac de, 72
Pniower, Otto, 146–47
Polo, Marco, 219n45
polygenesis, 5–6

rainbow symbolism, 154–56, 159, 182, 217n7, 217n10, 218n13
Redfield, Marc, 117
Reimarus, Hermann Samuel, 131–32, 206n43
Reinhold, Carl Leonhard, 101
Rennie, Nicholas, 183, 222n92
resignation and renunciation, 61–62; in *Wilhelm Meister's Journeyman Years*, 104, 105, 112, 117, 123, 124
Ricoeur, Paul, 31, 38
Riemer, Friedrich Wilhelm, 3, 181
Rochlitz, Johann Friedrich, 29
Rosenzweig, Franz, 4, 191n9
Rousseau, Jean-Jacques, 36, 64

Sabbath, 135
Satan, 137–38, 139, 158, 176–77
Schiller, Friedrich von, 4, 9, 31, 32, 83, 84–86, 90–91, 94, 101, 206n43
Schings, Hans-Jürgen, 206n45
Schlaffer, Hannelore, 185
Schlegel, August Wilhelm von, 86
Scholem, Gershom, 55, 56, 57, 64, 128–29
Schöne, Albrecht, 132, 138, 140, 147, 157, 181, 185, 188, 223n6
Schudt, Johann Jacob, 127–29, 163, 197n77
Schulte, Christoph, 199n37
Seibt, Gustav, 158
Sheehan, Jonathan, 20, 24, 37, 104
Solomon, 26, 62, 126, 129–30, 142–49, 152, 173, 212n25, 215n82, 215n84, 217n103
Spiess, Johann, 126–27
Spinoza, Baruch, 11–12, 21, 25, 35, 43, 58, 60–64, 108, 140–41, 156, 157, 193n15, 201nn67–68; Kabbalah and, 54, 64; on Moses, 206n43, 218n18; on providence, 61, 202n71; on the Ten Commandments, 77–78
Stephen, 15–16
striving ideal, 8, 37, 49, 57, 61, 92; in *Faust*, 125–26, 131, 133, 137, 142, 146, 148, 153–56, 158, 162, 173, 183–85, 222n99; Spinoza on, 202n71; Wilhelm Meister and, 25, 124
sublime, the, 9, 99, 113, 115, 123
Swales, Martin, 110, 208n31

Thales, 159, 162
Thielicke, Helmut, 194n32
Tiedemann, Dietrich, 54
Tigray, Jeffrey, 77
Tillmann, Thomas, 203n17
Todorov, Tzvetan, 112, 114
Trautmann, Johann Georg, 15–16
Trunz, Erich, 175, 199n35
typology, 13, 26, 59–60, 103, 105, 108, 126, 131, 135, 170, 188–90

Updike, John, 20
utopian communities, 104–5, 208n23

Valentinus, Basilius, 52
Varnhagen, Rahel von, 3
Veltri, Giuseppe, 4, 192n12
Virgil, 83
Vital, Hayyim, 52
Voltaire, 72

Wachter, Johann Georg, 54, 64, 202n74
Waldman, Mark, 6
Wandering Jew legend, 11–12, 25, 34–35, 58–60, 119, 126–27, 180;

Faust and, 11, 119, 125, 126–27; Goethe's epic on, 11–12, 35, 58–60, 63–64, 107, 108, 201n65; in *Wilhelm Meister* novels, 11, 25, 60, 107–9, 116, 118–19, 124, 208n27
wandering topos, 4, 10–12, 19, 24, 25, 29, 32–33, 47–50, 96, 104, 108–10, 114. *See also under* Judaism
Wellhausen, Julius, 21
Welling, Georg, 52, 129
Wilson, W. Daniel, 7, 194nn26–27
Wolf, Friedrich August, 84, 99–100, 205n32

Zedler, Johann Heinrich, 144, 159, 177
Zelter, Carl Friedrich, 46
Zimmermann, Rolf Christian, 199n35
Zimzum, 55, 56–58, 64, 199n37
Zohar, 52, 129